# THE CONSERVATIVE PARTY AND SOCIAL POLICY

Edited by Hugh Bochel

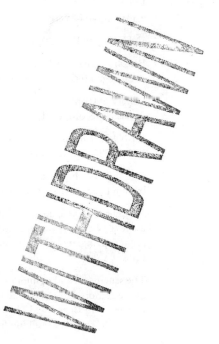

First published in Great Britain in 2011 by

The Policy Press
University of Bristol
Fourth Floor
Beacon House
Queen's Road
Bristol BS8 1QU
UK

Tel +44 (0)117 331 4054
Fax +44 (0)117 331 4093
e-mail tpp-info@bristol.ac.uk
www.policypress.co.uk

North American office:
The Policy Press
c/o International Specialized Books Services (ISBS)
920 NE 58th Avenue, Suite 300
Portland, OR 97213-3786, USA
Tel +1 503 287 3093
Fax +1 503 280 8832
e-mail info@isbs.com

British Library Cataloguing in Publication Data
A catalogue record for this book is available from the British Library.

Library of Congress Cataloging-in-Publication Data
A catalog record for this book has been requested.

ISBN 978 1 84742 432 7  paperback
ISBN 978 1 84742 433 4  hardcover

The right of Hugh Bochel to be identified as editor of this work has been asserted
by him in accordance with the 1988 Copyright, Designs and Patents Act.

The Policy Press works to counter discrimination on grounds
of gender, race, disability, age and sexuality.

Cover design by Qube Design Associates, Bristol
Front cover: image kindly supplied by www.istock.com
Printed and bound in Great Britain by Hobbs, Southampton
The Policy Press uses environmentally responsible print partners

FSC
www.fsc.org
MIX
Paper from
responsible sources
FSC® C020438

# Contents

# List of tables and figures

## Tables

## Figures

# Notes on contributors

**Rob Baggott** is Professor of Public Policy and Director of the Health Policy Research Unit at De Montfort University, Leicester. His publications include *Health and Health Care in Britain* and *Public Health: Policy and Politics*, and his research interests include health policy, public health, and patient and public involvement in the NHS.

**Stephen J. Ball** is the Karl Mannheim Professor of Sociology of Education at the Institute of Education, University of London. He has written and published extensively in the areas of education policy, choice and markets and social class. His most recent book is *The Education Debate*, published by The Policy Press in 2008. He is a Fellow of the British Academy.

**Catherine Bochel** is Principal Lecturer in Policy Studies at the University of Lincoln. She has published widely on the policy process. Her publications include *Social Policy: Themes, Issues and Debates* (co-edited with Hugh Bochel, Robert Page and Rob Sykes) and *The UK Social Process* (with Hugh Bochel).

**Hugh Bochel** is Professor of Public Policy at the University of Lincoln. He has published widely on public and social policy including *Making Policy in Theory and Practice* (with Sue Duncan) and *Welfare Policy under New Labour: Views from inside Westminster* (with Andrew Defty).

**Paul Daniel** is a Senior Lecturer in Social Policy at Roehampton University. His principal teaching and research interests are in the field of children's rights and the politics of childhood. Among his publications is *Children and Social Policy* (with John Watts).

**Alan Deacon** is Emeritus Professor of Social Policy at the University of Leeds. He has published widely on welfare reform and from 1999 to 2004 was a member of the ESRC Research Group on Care, Values and the Future of Welfare, also at Leeds. He was Chair of the Social Policy Association from 2001 to 2004, and is an Academician of the Academy of Social Sciences.

**Andrew Defty** is a Research Fellow in the School of Social Sciences at the University of Lincoln. His previous research has included a study of MPs' attitudes to welfare, *Welfare Policy under New Labour: Views from* *inside Westminster* (with Hugh Bochel), published by The Policy Press, and work on the scrutiny role of the House of Lords.

**Nick Ellison** is Professor of Sociology and Social Policy at the University of Leeds. His research interests are wide-ranging and include the politics of social policy in the UK, the UK policy process, the comparative politics of welfare and theories of social policy with particular reference to citizenship, democracy and social equality. Recent publications include *The Transformation of Welfare States?*, and 'We Nicked Stuff from All Over the Place: Policy Transfer or Muddling Through?', *Policy & Politics*, 2009 (with Peter Dwyer).

**Sonia Exley** is a British Academy Postdoctoral Fellow at the Institute of Education, University of London. Her research focuses on school choice and its regulation, normative discursive assumptions underpinning choice and school choice policy infrastructure in the UK and abroad. She has an interest more broadly in the politics of educational policy-making and the history of British education.

**Jon Glasby** is Professor of Health and Social Care and Director of the Health Services Management Centre at the University of Birmingham. A qualified social worker by background, he is involved in regular policy advice, consultancy, research and teaching around inter-agency working, community care and personalisation. He is also a Non-Executive Director of the Birmingham Children's Hospital and a former trustee of the Social Care Institute for Excellence.

**Mike Hough** is Director of the Institute for Criminal Policy Research and a Professor at the School of Law, Birkbeck College, University of London. His research interests include procedural justice theory, public attitudes to crime and justice, sentencing, and work with offenders.

**Stephen McKay** is Professor of Social Research in the School of Social Policy at the University of Birmingham. He conducts research on the social security system and has particular expertise in the secondary analysis of complex datasets.

**Robert M. Page** is a Reader in Democratic Socialism and Social Policy at the University of Birmingham. He is the author/editor of a number of books on social policy including *Revisiting the Welfare State*, and *Social Policy: Themes, Issues and Debates* (co-edited with Hugh Bochel, Catherine Bochel and Rob Sykes).

—

**Richard Parry** is Reader in Social Policy in the School of Social and Political Science at the University of Edinburgh, where he teaches on Scottish, UK and European social policy and on public policy and management. His major research projects have been on the role of the Treasury in social policy, the impact of devolution on the civil service throughout the United Kingdom, and a cross-national comparison of public sector employment.

**Ruth Patrick** is a postgraduate researcher in the School of Sociology and Social Policy at the University of Leeds. Her research interests include welfare reform, conditionality in welfare and disability. She is a columnist for the monthly magazine, *Disability Now*, and has previously authored pamphlets on Inheritance Tax reform (*Wealth's Fair Measure*, 2003) and housing affordability (*Squeezed Out*, 2001) for the Fabian Society and the Institute for Public Policy Research respectively.

**Karen Rowlingson** is Professor of Social Policy and Director of the Centre on Household Assets and Savings Management (CHASM) at the University of Birmingham. Her research interests include personal finance, inequality and social security policy.

**Peter Somerville** is Professor of Social Policy and Head of the Policy Studies Research Centre at the University of Lincoln. His latest book, *Understanding Community: Politics, Policy and Practice* was published by The Policy Press in February 2011. He is currently researching on multiple exclusion homelessness, funded by the Economic and Social Research Council.

# ONE

# Conservative approaches to social policy since 1997

*Hugh Bochel*

This book considers the development of the Conservative Party's social policies from 1997 to the period following the 2010 general election. That election brought a number of major surprises. One was that despite large opinion poll leads throughout most of 2008 and 2009, the Conservatives failed to gain an overall majority in the House of Commons; another was the coalition subsequently formed with the Liberal Democrats and the policy agreements that emerged from it. This chapter considers the genesis of the Conservatives' positions on social policy up to the general election and its immediate aftermath, and thus provides a broad framework for the remainder of the book. It outlines a number of issues that are considered in greater depth in the chapters that follow.

Following the 1997 general election considerable attention was paid to the extent to which the policies, and particularly the social policies, of 'New Labour' differed from those of 'Old Labour', and, at the same time, the extent to which they were similar to or different from the New Right-influenced Thatcher and Major governments that preceded them. After 18 years of Conservative government and the changes in Labour policies, those questions were entirely understandable. When the Conservatives returned to office in 2010, after 13 years of Labour in power, and with some having argued that the intervening years had seen the emergence of something of a new political consensus on welfare, there were a number of issues worthy of consideration, even before the coalition with the Liberal Democrats:

- the extent to which the Conservatives' policies were similar to or different from those of previous Conservative governments and oppositions, including from both the Thatcher era and earlier;
- the extent to which Conservative policies differed from those of the Labour governments led by Tony Blair and Gordon Brown;
- how the Conservatives reached the policy positions that they held by the time of the 2010 general election;

- the ideas and beliefs that underpinned the Conservatives' approach to social policies;
- the implications of these policies for the future of social policy and the welfare state in the United Kingdom;
- and (following the election and the formation of the Coalition government) the extent of the influence of the Liberal Democrats on the new government's policies.

This chapter is primarily concerned with the first three of these, although the book as a whole deals in varying depth with all six.

## Social policy under Labour, 1997–2010

In the second edition of *New Labour*, one of the many books examining the Labour Party and governments since the mid-1990s, Driver and Martell (2006, pp 4–5) argued that, looking back, New Labour had:

> not simply acceded to some new neo-liberal consensus on how to run the country.... The balance between state and market in public policy-making has tilted towards the private sector. But it is clear that many of the debates at the heart of the 'modernization' of Labour in the 1980s and 1990s were about how new means could be found to further old ends

and that 'New Labour is ... a far messier affair than is often suggested', with the causes of Labour Party reform in the late 20th century including electoral pressures, the perceived failures of Labour governments in the 1960s and 1970s, the impact of Thatcherism in the 1980s, and wider economic and political changes associated with 'globalisation'. In addition, like all governments, the Blair and Brown governments were affected by events, including the 11 September 2001 attacks on New York and Washington and the subsequent 'war on terror', the BSE crisis, and the financial crisis of late 2008 and early 2009.

Given that, to reduce the danger of being labelled a 'tax and spend' party, prior to the 1997 general election Labour had committed itself to abiding by the preceding Conservative administration's public expenditure plans for the first two years of government, it was perhaps unsurprising that the first Blair government was generally cautious in its approach to social policy, in contrast to its early enthusiasm for significant constitutional change. The one area where there was fairly rapid radical change was employment and welfare-to-work, with, for example, the introduction of the New Deal programme and the National Minimum Wage. However, from 2000 there began to be a significant increase in public expenditure on collective public services, particularly the NHS and education, and there was some degree of redistribution, particularly to poorer families with children through tax credits. These increases in expenditure continued through the second Blair government and into the Brown period, up to the financial crisis of 2008–09, following which plans for future public expenditure became much more uncertain because of the rapid increase in government borrowing. Throughout the period from 1997 to 2010 there was a whole series of attempts to 'modernise' public services including the welfare state (Powell, 2008), but from 2001 the 'modernisation' of public services became a major part of the mantra of the government, with increased public spending being accompanied by promises of reform in the delivery of services (Driver and Martell, 2006).

Other factors also impacted, directly and indirectly, upon politics and thus upon social policy under Labour. The war in Iraq, particularly in combination with Blair's announcement in September 2006 that he would stand down as Prime Minister within a year, undoubtedly weakened his position and thus the government's ability to get its legislation through parliament. This was arguably exacerbated by a greater willingness on the part of the partially reformed House of Lords to challenge the government (Bochel and Defty, 2007b), which was in turn reinforced by opponents of particular legislation from all parties working together across both Houses of Parliament. In addition the financial crisis, 'credit crunch' and the economic recession that affected the United Kingdom and much of the world in late 2008 and through much of 2009 also significantly affected the world of politics. The Brown government's decision to borrow in order to spend large amounts of public funds not only on supporting the banks, but also expenditure designed to reduce the effects of the recession on the economy and on employment, although arguably at odds with New Labour's previous emphasis on 'prudence', appeared to differentiate the government's position from that of the Conservatives. From a position where some had suggested that there was relatively little difference between the parties on a number of major policy areas, over a very short period of time the gap widened considerably, particularly over how and when to deal with the budget deficit. However, the Conservative Party's lead in voting in European and local elections in 2009 and in the opinion polls throughout 2009 and early 2010 remained significant, if not perhaps great enough to ensure victory in a general election.

## Transition and change: Conservative social policy, 1997–2010

In the same way as Labour arguably took many years to come to terms with and recover from the election defeat of 1979 and the subsequent dominance of Margaret Thatcher, the Conservative Party too seemed for some time unable to learn the lessons of defeat in 1997 and to move away from its Thatcherite position and its influences on the development of social policy within the Conservative Party.

### The Thatcher legacy

Having been a member of Ted Heath's government from 1970 to 1974, Margaret Thatcher won the 1979 general election on the back of the 'winter of discontent', which had seen high levels of trade union action, including strikes, and set out to reduce and restructure government in the United Kingdom. She had become converted to free-market views and believed that the state had grown excessively, with levels of taxation too high and the subversion of individuals' responsibility. Her governments sought, albeit with mixed success, to cut taxation and expenditure on public services, to reduce government involvement and regulation, and to privatise state enterprises, and these policies, together with three successive general election victories in 1979, 1983 and 1987, reinforced her popularity with Conservative Party members, although not necessarily with the electorate. While the Heath government of 1970–74 has often been viewed, in hindsight, as something of a transition from the One Nation Conservatism that had been seen as dominating the leadership of the Conservative Party since the 1950s, the Thatcher governments brought the New Right-influenced wing of the Conservatives to the fore.

Indeed, the extent of Thatcher's dominance, and the support for her and her policies among party members, was to have a major impact upon the Conservative Party for more than a decade. Although her successor, John Major, won the 1992 general election despite virtually a decade of poor economic performance and high unemployment, his government immediately ran into difficulty when the pound was forced out of the Exchange Rate Mechanism. This was compounded by internal divisions, particularly over Europe, and a growing concern over 'sleaze' within the government, and the Conservatives were heavily defeated by Blair's New Labour at the 1997 general election.

## The New Labour challenge

The general election results of 1997, 2001 and 2005 serve to highlight the difficulties that the Conservative Party experienced in responding to New Labour. From the mid-1990s, Labour's shift towards the centre and apparent control of the political agenda, together with the Conservatives' attachment to Thatcherism, meant that the Conservatives found it hard to develop an alternative identity and policies, so that they found it difficult, for example, to reconcile the public's apparent desire for increased expenditure on public services with their party's attachment to tax cuts. New Labour may have failed to make the decisive break with Thatcherism that many of its supporters might have wished, but in the same way the Conservatives found it hard to develop an approach that was distinctive from New Labour and appealing to the public.

## Changing leadership

Part of Margaret Thatcher's legacy to the Conservative Party was arguably to leave it more ideologically driven than it had ever been. The party that had frequently been described as flexible and pragmatic in its pursuit of government, was now divided, including over Europe, the role of the public sector and moral issues, with the right of the party generally dominant, inside and outside parliament. This was to be reflected in the party's struggle to come to terms with New Labour and its own position in opposition.

Following John Major's resignation in 1997, his successor, William Hague, arguably tried to follow Blair in 'modernising' his party. Like Blair he took up the principle of 'one member, one vote', increasing the power of party members in electing the leader at the expense of the MPs by giving them a ballot on the final two candidates, and creating a position where all members of constituency associations were able to participate in selecting candidates; he also created a new policy forum to discuss and debate party policy.

Hague also initially attempted to reach out to a broader group of potential supporters by apologising for the Conservatives' failure to listen to voters in the final years of the Major government and adopting a more liberal line on some social issues, such as gender, race and sexuality. However, he struggled to persuade many within the party of the need to convince the electorate that the public services were safe in Conservative hands, and in practice the party continued to argue for privatisation, low income tax and a flexible labour force. Ultimately

5

his period as leader was characterised by an attempt to consolidate the Conservatives' core support, and in terms of policy, Hague's most distinctive shift was to harden the party's line on the euro, saying that the UK would not join the single currency for at least two parliaments.

One notable example under Hague illustrates the problems facing the Conservatives in seeking to move towards the political centre ground. In April 1999, Peter Lilley, who had been appointed Deputy Leader by Hague and charged with undertaking a major policy review, delivered the R.A. Butler memorial lecture, in which he stated that there was a need to renew public confidence in the Conservatives' commitment to the welfare state, but argued that 'we will only do so if we openly and emphatically accept that the free market has only a limited role in improving public services like health, education and welfare' (Lilley, 1999). In a significant break with Thatcherism, Lilley argued that most Conservatives did not believe that the market could effectively deliver universal services like health and education, and that the party had no plans to extend privatisation in those areas. Lilley's speech caused consternation in the party and within the shadow cabinet, compounded by the fact that it was delivered on the 20th anniversary of Thatcher's election. This is reputed to have resulted in criticism in the shadow cabinet from former Thatcherite ministers such as Michael Howard (White, 1999), and some veiled criticism from Thatcher herself (Pierce, 1999). Hague was forced to clarify Lilley's points in an article in *The Times*, in which he argued that Lilley's speech did not mark a radical departure from the Conservative past, but that what he had meant to say was that the private sector had a role in making additional provision, and that there should be greater partnership between the state, private and voluntary sectors (Hague, 1999).

By the time of the 2001 general election, with press speculation rife about who was likely to succeed Hague, the Conservatives had failed to regain a reputation for economic competence and had produced few new significant policy initiatives, in part because they found it difficult to deal with New Labour's shift to the centre ground, in part because those issues on which they were potentially electorally strongest were those of least salience to voters, and in part because the primary emphasis was on maintaining the party's 'core vote', rather than reaching out to potential new supporters. The 2001 general election manifesto, therefore, again called for a smaller state and 'welfare without the state', and emphasised the party's support for the family, including tax cuts, 'freeing' schools from local authority control, increasing police numbers, tougher sentencing for criminals and increased expenditure on the health service. Within hours of the election result being announced

Hague resigned, with the Conservatives effectively having failed to regain any of the ground that they had lost in 1997.

In the ensuing leadership contest perhaps the biggest surprise was the defeat of Michael Portillo. However, while he had previously been associated with the right, following the 1997 general election he had generally moved towards a more liberal and socially inclusive approach, and he clearly wished to take the Conservative Party in such a direction. One of the other contenders, Kenneth Clarke, was pro-European, while the party as a whole had become more Eurosceptic. The final three candidates were David Davis, Michael Ancram and Iain Duncan Smith. After the ballots of MPs left members a choice between Clarke and Duncan Smith, it was not surprising that Duncan Smith received 61% of the vote in the membership ballot.

To some extent Duncan Smith's leadership followed a similar line to that of Hague, with attempts to be more positive about public services, more socially inclusive and to recognise the 'sins of the past', perhaps best summed up in the speech by the then Party Chairman, Theresa May, to the Conservative conference in October 2002, when she said that the public viewed the Conservatives as the 'nasty party' (BBC News, 2002). Duncan Smith himself set out his vision of 'compassionate Conservatism' in a speech delivered on a Glasgow housing estate in February 2002, in which he pledged his commitment to public service reform and helping 'the vulnerable' (Seldon and Snowdon, 2005). However, like Hague, he struggled to generate widespread support for a more inclusive approach to social policy within the Conservative Party, and particularly within the shadow cabinet. However, unlike Hague, Duncan Smith's advocacy of 'compassionate Conservatism' did find an audience, particularly among a group of newer Conservative MPs who would eventually come to prominence when David Cameron became leader in 2005. Duncan Smith also had strong support from David Willetts, who held the Conservatives' social security portfolio from 1997 to 2006 (a period in which six Labour Secretaries of State held the same brief), and who was a strong advocate of 'compassionate Conservatism' (Willetts, 2005a). In the run-up to the Conservative leadership contest in 2005, while older figures such as Malcolm Rifkind called for a return to One Nation Conservatism, Willetts argued that it was not sufficient for the Conservatives to be 'a bunch of backward looking people who want to recreate British society as it was in the 1950s', and instead advocated a 'new Conservatism', which combined a commitment to a strong economy with social justice (Willetts, 2005b). Interestingly, following Cameron's election as party leader, it was Duncan Smith who was rewarded with the chair of the policy review group on social justice.

Under Duncan Smith there continued to be no improvement in the Conservatives' performance in opinion polls, although they did do somewhat better in European and local elections. Perhaps as a result there continued to be whisperings, conspiracies and divisions about Duncan Smith's leadership; there was also some concern about payments to his wife for work done as part of his office, which did not help his position. In autumn 2003 he was challenged by a request for a no-confidence vote by the backbench MP Derek Conway, which received support from at least 25 Conservative MPs. Upon losing the confidence vote he resigned.

The next Conservative Party leader was Michael Howard, a former Home Secretary. While some saw this as something of a return to the Thatcher/Major era, Howard did make the Conservative Party in parliament something more of a political force. However, having backed the war in Iraq, he was unable to exploit one of the government's biggest weaknesses and at the 2005 general election, while the party did gain 33 seats, in part aided by Blair's and Labour's increasing unpopularity, its share of the vote increased by only 0.5%, undermining any claims of a significant advance, and Howard stood down as leader.

Each of Cameron's three predecessors did appear to embrace more socially liberal and inclusive policies early in their leaderships, but none appeared particularly comfortable in this position, and it was perhaps unsurprising that each moved back to the right after failures to increase the Conservatives' standing in the opinion polls (Dorey, 2007). Indeed, the continued support for Thatcherism within the party led Bale (2008, p 282) to point out that the Conservatives failed 'to separate the impressive election victories (and huge personal following among party activists) by Mrs Thatcher and her far more ambivalent record when it came to public policy and indeed public support', and that the failure to admit that things went wrong made it difficult for the party to produce credible policy responses to New Labour.

## David Cameron's leadership

Following Michael Howard's resignation, in December 2005 David Cameron defeated David Davis for the leadership of the Conservative Party, following a contest that was seen by some as a 'moderniser' versus a Thatcherite traditionalist, with the former gaining 68% of votes cast by party members. His view of 'modernisation' appeared to suggest a break with Thatcherism, with more socially liberal and inclusive policies, and an emphasis upon the party being more socially representative in its membership and particularly within parliament (Denham and O'Hara, 2007).

Almost immediately Cameron sought to move his party towards the centre ground of British politics, arguing, for example, for the Conservatives to support social action to promote social justice and combat poverty, stating that economic stability would take precedence over tax cuts, and suggesting that the party should reach out beyond its core support. Cameron's stance on such issues was widely perceived as genuine, and as harking back to 'Tory paternalism' and One Nation Conservatism (Dorey, 2007), as well as reflecting his experiences of the NHS with his disabled son, Ivan, who died in February 2009 aged only six. Critics noted, however, that he had been one of the architects of the party's 2005 general election manifesto, which had been relatively hard-line in its policies.

In the same way as Blair had sought to 'modernise' the Labour Party, Cameron sought to make significant change to the Conservatives. Denham and O'Hara (2007) have suggested that Conservative 'modernisation' has enshrined three key dimensions: leadership, organisation and, of greatest relevance here, policies.

Where policy development was concerned, the early years of Cameron's leadership were, arguably deliberately, 'policy-lite', with frequent general statements of principle from the leader together with assertions that policies take time to develop. Kenny (2009, p 152) has pointed out that:

> The first two years of his leadership witnessed a concerted attempt to shift public perceptions of the Tories and to develop Cameron's own political persona in ways that symbolised this transformation. This involved a set of often symbolic rhetorical and policy shifts, designed to ram home the message that the party was willing to move away from Thatcherism and the rightward lurches on crime, migration and morality attempted by his predecessors William Hague and Michael Howard.

With echoes of New Labour's Policy Forum, the Conservatives established six policy review groups including those on 'Public services improvement' (to look at issues including health, education, social care and social housing), chaired by Stephen Dorrell and Baroness Perry; 'Social justice' (examining topics such as family breakdown, educational failure, economic dependency, addictions and the voluntary sector), chaired by Iain Duncan Smith; and 'Globalisation and global poverty' (looking at areas such as overseas aid, international development and international conflict), chaired by Peter Lilley. These groups included people drawn from outside the world of mainstream party politics, such as academics or practitioners, generally establishing subgroups to look at particular issues, again often drawing upon additional outside experts. The groups produced a series of 'Policy Green Papers', but in many cases these were without clear policy proposals or commitment from the leadership to follow policy recommendations that were sometimes contradictory across the groups.

While specific policy proposals were often lacking, and indeed the party leadership generally failed to endorse particular policies or recommendations, it is nevertheless possible to identify a number of trends or common features across the Policy Green Papers. These included: a continued use of assessment and increased sanctions for benefit claimants; a commitment to a strong voluntary and social enterprise element in society and the provision of public services together with significant private-sector input; promises of reductions in bureaucracy, but retaining inspections and audits; and choice for consumers of services.

Cameron's attempts to realign the Conservative Party were arguably helped by the Labour government's difficulties in persuading the electorate that its public services reforms were working, with problems with NHS Trusts' deficits in 2006–07, and crises around the work of the Home Office over crime, particularly knife crime, and immigration, as well as the loss of confidential data. Indeed, the Home Secretary, John Reid, was led to acknowledge to the House of Commons Home Affairs Committee, in May 2006, that the Home Office was 'not fit for purpose'. More generally Labour's grip on the political agenda was loosening, so that it was increasingly in the position of having to respond to rather than shaping issues and debates. At the same time, the attention of the media was increasingly focusing upon the travails of the government, leaving the Conservatives and their policies relatively free from detailed scrutiny.

In terms of key personnel, prior to the general election in 2010 the shadow cabinet contained a mix of those who might be described as 'modernisers' and those who certainly might not. In terms of the posts of direct relevance to social policy, in addition to Cameron and the Shadow Chancellor, George Osborne, there were Dominic Grieve (Justice), Michael Gove (Children, Schools and Families), David Willetts (Universities and Skills), Sayeeda Warsi (Community Cohesion), Andrew Lansley (Health), Chris Grayling (Home Secretary), Caroline

Spelman (Community Cohesion and Social Action), Philip Hammond (Chief Secretary to the Treasury), and Theresa May (Work and Pensions, and also Women), while Oliver Letwin was responsible for the policy reviews and the Conservative Research Department. However, some were arguing (for example, Rawnsley, 2009) that there was a small clique at the centre of power in the Conservative Party, with at least some shadow ministers excluded. All of these listed above were given cabinet or senior ministerial positions followiing the 2010 general election.

## From 'nasty party' to 'compassionate Conservatism'?

Having been the dominant political party in Britain for the bulk of the 20th century, from 1997 the Conservative Party suffered an unprecedented three general election defeats and three consecutive Labour governments. These, and other developments, meant that the party faced a series of major challenges including: the political challenge of having to respond to New Labour and to socio-economic change, so that simple appeals to 'core voters' were insufficient to win elections; the ideological challenge of overcoming the dominance of Thatcherism within the Conservative Party; the challenge of having to adapt to a world of globalisation but also, towards the end of the period, financial crisis and economic downturn; and the need to respond to new themes and issues, such as global warming and terrorism.

Following the 2001 general election the Conservative Party had made almost no electoral progress, and even after 2005 the gains that they had made were at least in part down to the growing unpopularity of Tony Blair and the Labour government, particularly over the war in Iraq, but also with the loss of middle-class voters in seats in the Midlands and the South of England. The harsh reality was that the Conservatives' share of the vote was 30.7% in 1997, 31.7% in 2001 and 32.4% in 2005. Even allowing for parties needing a smaller share of the vote to win a parliamentary majority than in the past, the lack of progress over eight years and the distance required to win office, meant that the party continued to face a major electoral challenge.

After three successive leaders had failed to make any significant inroads into Labour's majority, and in particular had failed to increase support for the Conservatives at the ballot box, when Cameron became leader he made clear that the Conservatives needed to broaden their electoral appeal beyond the core vote, which was then insufficient to deliver victory. In particular he quickly sought to make Conservative candidates more diverse, including attempting to get more women and black candidates selected for winnable seats through the development of an 'A-list', albeit with only limited success. He also argued that the Conservatives had to accept that Blair and New Labour had been right in their analysis of the mood of the United Kingdom in the 1990s, with economic success and social justice going hand-in-hand.

The Conservatives were also weak on what had traditionally been one of their strongest cards – economic competence. The recessions of the 1980s and early 1990s, and the debacle over Black Wednesday, 16 September 1992, when the United Kingdom was forced to pull Sterling out of the European Exchange Rate Mechanism, had damaged them. In contrast, the first two Blair governments saw the United Kingdom economy grow steadily, and even when, in late 2008, recession loomed and financial crisis struck, Gordon Brown's response meant that the Conservatives found it hard to respond. In addition, the initial responses in the UK and several other countries tended to favour the idea of active action by governments and large-scale public expenditure, which lay much closer to traditional Labour territory than to that of the Conservatives, including Cameron and the Shadow Chancellor, George Osborne. While the rapid increase in the budget deficit in 2009 and 2010 raised hard questions for the Labour government on how and when they would seek to reduce the deficit and which areas of public expenditure would be most affected, the Conservatives too found it difficult to respond with any degree of clarity, so that prior to the economic crisis they were talking about matching Labour's spending plans, but following the growth of a large deficit they talked about a need for rapid and deep spending cuts, before appearing to talk about cuts slightly further into the future.

Like Blair and the other architects of New Labour, Cameron also had to respond to what he saw as new political realities, including, for example, that issues such as inflation and trade union power were no longer key concerns, and that opinion among the electorate had changed (Norton, 2008). This led to a view that the Conservative Party had to 'modernise', so that, for example, in responding to issues such as poverty and social 'breakdown', they should recognise a role for the state and for public services, including in creating the conditions for a flourishing voluntary sector. This would therefore seek to draw upon both One Nation and neo-liberal approaches, as well as aspects of New Labour discourses (Kerr, 2007).

In addition to areas such as environmental issues, Cameron's early years as leader saw a considerable emphasis, and arguably a significant break with the Thatcherite past, on social inclusion. In the 2006 Scarman Lecture, he said:

> Let me summarise my argument briefly. I believe that poverty is an economic waste and a moral disgrace. In the past, we used to think of poverty only in absolute terms – meaning straightforward material deprivation. That's not enough. We need to think of poverty in relative terms – the fact that some people lack those things which others in society take for granted. So I want this message to go out loud and clear: the Conservative Party recognises, will measure and will act on relative poverty. (Cameron, 2006c)

He also argued, however, that such a response 'involves a dramatic decentralisation, a big shift in emphasis … from the state to society', and emphasised the role of the voluntary sector in tackling poverty (Cameron, 2006c). He later suggested that 'Communities, rather than the state, are best equipped to effectively tackle social deprivation', that 'The answer lies in communities themselves, not in well-meaning schemes directed from Whitehall' and that 'Social enterprises in particular represent a huge potential resource for our most hard-pressed communities…. The social enterprise is the great institutional innovation of our times. At the moment, however, we are not making nearly enough use of the potential of the voluntary sector' (Cameron, 2007a).

Ideologically, Thatcherism posed as much of a challenge for the Conservatives as it had done for Labour. While Blair and some others within the Labour Party had sought to respond to Thatcherism and the changing world economic system through the development of the 'Third Way', many Conservatives found it hard to accept that there was anything problematic about it, that social and economic realities were changing, and that the public were increasingly willing to see increased public expenditure and improved public services rather than tax cuts. Nevertheless, there were some signs of change, so that when undertaking interviews with MPs on their attitudes to welfare in 2004 and 2005, Bochel and Defty (2007a, 2007b) identified a significant number of Conservative MPs, including frontbenchers, who held views at variance from those that had dominated the party's recent thinking and policies. Some of those MPs were keen to emphasise, in confidential interviews, that they had very different beliefs. While, for the most part, these individuals were clearly unaware that there were a significant number of their parliamentary colleagues who held similar views, these might arguably have been early signs of support for some form of 'compassionate' Conservatism.

Soon after his election to the party leadership, David Cameron sought to distance himself from his predecessors, and arguably to shrug off the 'nasty party' reputation and decontaminate the Conservative brand (Bale, 2008). While considerable attention was focused upon his early expressions of concern about the environment, at the 2006 party conference he promised to make the preservation of the NHS a priority and at the same time rejected 'pie-in-the-sky tax cuts' (Cameron, 2006b). However, in the following weeks he also promoted traditional Conservative concerns such as crime and support for traditional family structures.

Writing in *The Daily Telegraph* in September 2007, Cameron (2007b) sought to explain how his 'new' approach fitted with more traditional Conservative positions, arguing:

> I am a Conservative because of the values that I have believed in all my life: family, responsibility and opportunity. I am a Conservative because I believe that those values lead inexorably to a political agenda whose central mission is to give people more power and control over their lives ... because we want people to rely on their family, not the state; because you can't take responsibility for something unless you have control over it; and because true opportunity means having the freedom to achieve all you can in life.

Cameron also placed considerable emphasis upon 'quality-of-life' issues, such as climate change, the environment and work–life balance, thus linking the Conservative Party's traditional emphasis upon the family as a desirable social institution, with ideas such as 'flexible' patterns of work, arguably in a more sympathetic way than either Thatcherite Conservatism or New Labour (Dorey, 2007). Having previously supported the 2004 Civil Partnerships Act, as leader he took a more tolerant line than many of his predecessors on sexual orientation and lifestyles.

In relation to crime and anti-social behaviour, Cameron famously departed from the Conservative Party's traditionally punitive stance, when he argued, in July 2006, in a speech to the Centre for Social Justice that the recent media furore over young people wearing 'hoodies' was misplaced and that:

> The long-term answer to anti-social behaviour is a pro-social society where we really do get to grips with the causes of crime.... Family breakdown, drugs, children in

> care, educational underachievement – these provide the
> backdrop to too many lives and can become the seed bed
> of crime.... Of course, not everyone who grows up in
> a deprived neighbourhood turns to crime – just as not
> everyone who grows up in a rich neighbourhood stays on
> the straight and narrow. Individuals are responsible for their
> actions – and every individual has the choice between doing
> right and doing wrong. But there are connections between
> circumstances and behaviour. (Cameron, 2006a)

He went on to argue that to understand what causes such behaviour requires an understanding of the reasons for it, that law enforcement is not sufficient as an answer, and that the role of the voluntary sector is crucial in contributing to an understanding of the challenges that young people face and in offering the care and emotional support that they need (Cameron, 2006a). However, Bennett (2008, p 464) argues that within a year Cameron was reiterating the view 'that punishment is legitimate, that we are faced with dystopian moral decay and that the long-term solution lies in a reassertion of a traditional family structure'.

A significant element of Cameron's message, particularly around social policy, was the idea that society is 'broken', whether applied to family breakdown, welfare dependency or poverty, or to problems with public services, such as schools, hospitals, policing and housing. In this respect Cameron's Conservatism owes something to his predecessor as Conservative leader, Iain Duncan Smith, who, after standing down, established the Centre for Social Justice, which produced a report entitled *Breakdown Britain* (Social Justice Policy Group, 2006) and a subsequent report *Breakthrough Britain* (Social Justice Policy Group, 2007). While the reports contained a mix of fairly traditional Conservative thinking, such as support for the traditional family and tax incentives for married couples, they also provided some new ideas such as a childcare tax credit and the tapering of financial support for parents. The reports also highlighted the way in which state provision could be seen as having replaced the role of charities and community organisations, to the detriment of the role and ideas of those groups. As a response to this there is a perceived need for a smaller central state, with more significant roles being played by many of the organisations of civil society. Cameron took on many of these ideas, and in a speech entitled 'The Big Society' argued that 'Our alternative to big government is the big society', that the new role for the state is in 'Galvanising, catalysing, prompting, encouraging and agitating for community engagement and renewal. It must help families, individuals, charities and communities come together to solve problems' and that social entrepreneurs, community activists and mass engagement (a 'broad culture of responsibility, mutuality and obligation') are necessary (Cameron, 2009a).

## The 2010 general election

Despite the Conservatives having held large leads over Labour in the opinion polls for much of 2008 and 2009, in the six months before the general election the gap narrowed somewhat, and at the start of the election campaign it appeared uncertain whether the Conservatives would be able to win a majority in the House of Commons.

Given the impact of the financial crisis, the recession and the Labour government's decision to borrow to maintain public expenditure and to stimulate the economy, it was inevitable that the Conservatives' manifesto for the 2010 election (Conservative Party, 2010e) emphasised the need to substantially reduce the size of the country's deficit over a five-year period, beginning with £6 billion of cuts in 2010. While there were clearly likely to be significant implications for social policy of public expenditure cuts in all areas other than health and foreign aid, which it promised to protect, the manifesto continued to argue that British society was 'broken' and that to repair it, rather than 'big government', it was necessary to build a 'Big Society', enabling charities, social enterprises and voluntary groups to play a greater role in tackling social problems, and to empower communities. This was to include enabling trusts, charities and other organisations to establish new Academy schools, independent of local authority control. Among other promises the manifesto committed the Conservatives to supporting marriage through the tax system, giving families more control over their own lives, and linking increases in the basic state pension to inflation in the higher of either earnings or prices.

During the course of the campaign the introduction of three televised prime ministerial debates appeared to make the outcome even less certain, with an apparent surge in support for the Liberal Democrats after their leader, Nick Clegg, appeared on equal terms with Gordon Brown and David Cameron, and was seen by many as having 'won' the first debate. Nevertheless, the final result saw the Conservatives winning 36% of the vote (to Labour's 29% and the Liberal Democrats' 23%) and 306 seats, 20 short of a majority, and after four days of discussions between the political parties, a coalition between the Conservatives and the Liberal Democrats was announced and David Cameron became Prime Minister. The agreement between the two parties, released on

11 May with a somewhat more detailed version following on 20 May (Cabinet Office, 2010), provided for tax cuts amounting to £10 billion, meaning that in other areas reductions in public expenditure would need to be even greater than those initially envisaged, while the commitment to real increases in NHS spending for each year of the parliament was to be partly funded by savings from within the health service. It also allowed for a premium for disadvantaged pupils in schools, the entry into the state school system of new providers responding to parental demand, the restoration of the link between pensions and earnings, the raising of the personal tax allowance to £10,000 over a period of years, an annual limit on immigration from outside the EU, a faster raising of the state pension age than that introduced by Labour, and the creation of a single welfare-to-work programme. In reality, the short document left many questions unanswered, as much would inevitably depend on the detail and timing of both public expenditure cuts and policy change, while decisions about other difficult areas, such as higher education tuition fees and long-term care, were simply delayed. Nevertheless, it did suggest that Cameron and other senior Conservatives were willing to make compromises, and in some areas, such as the increase in the personal tax allowance, it was possible to identify significant Liberal Democrat influence, while in others, where there were major policy differences between the parties, such as tuition fees, they effectively gained the right to opt out of voting with the government in divisions in the House of Commons.

The formation of the Coalition had significant implications for the personnel of government, with the new cabinet containing five Liberal Democrats, although one, David Laws, resigned as Chief Secretary to the Treasury within weeks following newspaper revelations about his expenses claims as an MP. Where social policy was concerned the Conservatives held most of the major posts, so that in addition to George Osborne as Chancellor, Theresa May became Home Secretary, Eric Pickles Community Secretary, Michael Gove Education Secretary, Andrew Lansley Health Secretary and Iain Duncan Smith Work and Pensions Secretary, while following David Laws' resignation, another Liberal Democrat, Danny Alexander, became Chief Secretary to the Treasury.

## Conclusions

Following a long period of opposition, and considerable turmoil within the Conservative Party, it is worth asking to what extent it is appropriate to portray the brand of Conservatism that had developed under David Cameron as similar to or different from what had come before it. This is not an easy task, in part because, for all of the rhetoric in speeches, and the attempts to make the Conservatives appear a more open and friendly party, Cameron's approach in opposition was as notable for what was not said or emphasised as for changes in policies (Dorey, 2007), and despite the policy reviews there were relatively few specific policies adopted, with the emphasis instead having been on emphasising the shift away from Thatcherism and a broader approach to policy. In addition, as noted earlier and elsewhere in this book, some, although by no means all, of the Conservatives' manifesto commitments appeared to be rapidly watered down in the Coalition agreement with the Liberal Democrats. At the same time, the depth and speed of public expenditure cuts proposed by the incoming government were such that they implied a massive retrenchment of the state, including in many areas of social policy.

After the first five years of his leadership it was perhaps possible to put forward a number of different, but not necessarily contradictory, views of the Conservatives under Cameron:

1. *Cameron's Conservatism is a variety of Thatcherism.* While Cameron made a number of determined attempts to distance the Conservatives from the policies of the Thatcher period, the ideas of those such as Thatcher and Hayek have continued to be cited approvingly by frontbenchers and MPs and to receive support from party members, so that Katwala (2009, p 10) has argued that '"Progressive Conservatism" will remain primarily an exercise in political positioning until it does find something coherent to say about Thatcherism'. While this may be because of the importance of the Thatcher era to many Conservative members and supporters, it may also be because the anti-statist approach of today's party is something of a natural progression from the approaches of the Thatcher governments. Indeed, some elements of the Conservatives' approach, including the work of some of the policy groups, such as that on economic policy, chaired by John Redwood, continued to reflect the economic policy of the Thatcher governments, with the emphasis on the free market and light-touch regulation, at least until the financial crisis of 2008, and service provision by the private and third sectors. Indeed, it is difficult to see the Conservatives having been able to undertake the degree of intervention that Labour did with the banks in late 2008. Taken together, the Conservatives' economic and social policies, including the enthusiasm for public expenditure cuts, and the idea of the 'Big Society', emphasise and

are likely to produce a small state, with services provided by the private and not-for-profit sectors. In addition, Cameron was a key author of the Conservatives' 2005 general election manifesto, which had emphasised asylum, immigration and Euro-scepticism. However, despite the anti-statism of some speeches and policy proposals, the Conservatives' commitment to state health care, and to some extent state education, or at least education funded by the state, contrasts with Thatcher's views, while Cameron's willingness to make concessions in the creation of the Coalition government also suggests in some respects a less ideologically driven approach.

2. *Cameron's Conservatism is related to One Nation Conservatism.* While the idea of 'compassionate' or 'progressive' Conservatism was arguably overrated, even in the first two years of Cameron's leadership, the party has moved towards a more centrist position on many aspects of social policy. Indeed, David Marquand (2008) has argued that rather than being a closet Thatcherite, Cameron's thinking owes more to the Whig-imperialist tradition associated with moderate reform, including the mixed economy in the 1960s. Cameron, particularly in the first two years of his leadership, sought to emphasise socially tolerant and compassionate Conservatism, which recognises and represents the social and cultural diversity of the United Kingdom. At times this involved public disavowal of some of the policy positions of the Thatcher years, Cameron's statement, in *Built to Last: The Aims and Values of the Conservative Party* (Conservative Party, 2006), that 'there is such a thing as society, it's just not the same thing as the state', and repeated by him on a number of occasions (for example, Cameron, 2008b). This was deliberately designed to set Cameron apart from Thatcher's claim that 'there is no such thing as society', although she did go on to say that 'There are individual men and women, and there are families' (Thatcher, 1987). Cameron also argued that 'John Moore was wrong to declare the end of poverty' (Cameron, 2006b). Yet when the Conservatives' policy reviews contained a number of proposals that might have been taken up to reinforce Cameron's apparent attempt to move the Conservatives into the centre ground and to promote new issues, such as proposals for a carer's allowance, changes to Child Benefit, establishing a consumer body for NHS patients and establishing a national fund to target public money into local schemes for affordable rented housing, rather than accepting these proposals the leadership merely accepted them as input into the party's development of policies. Similarly, the Conservatives' 2010 election manifesto and the Coalition's 'programme for government' both emphasised a smaller role for the public sector and the much

greater use of private, social enterprise and voluntary organisations in the provision of services.

3. *Cameron's Conservatism draws heavily on Blair's New Labour/Third Way ideas.* Certainly, while Blair was still Prime Minister the Conservatives adopted a number of policy stances that were very close to those of the Labour Party, such as the need for an active welfare state to move people from benefits and into work, and the commitment to end child poverty. Even from late 2007, when the Conservatives became more openly critical of the government, including Brown's economic policies, they were claiming to be able to deliver public services and progressive ends, albeit through the use of more traditional Conservative means, including greater use of the voluntary sector, and for a period they agreed to abide by Labour's plans for public expenditure, although they later dropped this commitment. However, while in some key areas, such as education and welfare-to-work, the proposals in the Conservatives' general election manifesto might be seen as broadly similar to New Labour's approaches, at the same time, other proposals, including the idea of the 'Big Society', and the speed and depth of public expenditure cuts, were likely to mean that in many areas the role of the state would be largely restricted to allocation of resources and contracting with the private and not-for-profit sectors for their delivery. Even if some of the mechanisms of policy may be similar to those of New Labour, arguably the implications for the size of the state and for the allocation of responsibility between individuals and the state would be quite different

4. *Conservative social policy under Cameron is complicated and dynamic.* In the same way as it is possible to argue that New Labour was effectively a response to Thatcherism and neo-liberalism that melded some ideas drawn from those perspectives with traditional Labour policies and approaches, so that many analysts found it difficult to comfortably fit aspects of New Labour's policies and achievements into a neo-liberal paradigm, so it may be that Cameron's Conservatism has been created and influenced by political and ideological pragmatism, a variety of political traditions, and involves a combination of ideas and policies that derive from this complex mix, and in some respects represents a return to earlier forms of Conservatism that were less ideologically driven and less policy based. Certainly, the development of Conservative policies from 2006, the 2010 general election manifesto and the formation of the Coalition government with the Liberal Democrats with the willingness to compromise

on a range of policies, suggests a significant degree of pragmatism on the part of Cameron and his allies.

The remainder of this book examines Conservative social policies in greater depth, with many of the chapters suggesting different possible interpretations of the ideas outlined above. Chapters 2, 3 and 4 develop the context, with Robert Page considering the longer-term development of Conservative Party thinking, Nick Ellison focusing upon the party's attitudes to public expenditure, and Andrew Defty providing an assessment of public attitudes to the Conservatives' policies and public opinion.

In Chapter 5, Rob Baggott focuses upon health, while Sonia Exley and Stephen Ball consider education in Chapter 6. Both chapters suggest that it is possible to identify continuities with Labour's approach, but also new policy departures. In Chapters 8 and 9 Stephen McKay and Karen Rowlingson and Alan Deacon and Ruth Patrick deal with the closely related areas of social security and welfare reform and welfare-to-work, and it is clear that decisions made in each of these policy realms are likely to affect the other. Writing on family policy in Chapter 11, Paul Daniel suggests that this is one part of social policy where the coalition with the Liberal Democrats may push the Conservatives in a more socially liberal direction. Of course, in some areas, such as housing, community care and crime and criminal justice, Conservative policy has been less clear and/or has emerged later than others, as discussed by Peter Somerville, Jon Glasby and Mike Hough in Chapters 7, 10 and 12, respectively, making it much less certain what path the Conservatives and the Coalition government are likely to pursue, although the chapters also outline some of the challenges they face.

The book moves on to consider what might broadly be described as 'governance' issues. During the Thatcher era the Conservatives were often argued to be in favour of minimal government and a strong state, and the commitment to free-market delivery mechanisms was seen as central to Conservative policies, although in many areas of social policy the rhetoric was not always matched by reality. However, after three consecutive Labour governments the position in 2010 was very different. In Chapter 13, Richard Parry analyses the impact of devolution on the Conservatives and the devolved administrations in Northern Ireland, Scotland and Wales, while Catherine Bochel, in Chapter 14, considers the implications of the Conservatives' proposals for the reform of government and public services on the formulation and implementation of social policies. Finally, Chapter 15 seeks to bring together the main themes from the book and to reflect further upon the issues raised in this chapter.

# TWO

# The Conservative Party and the welfare state since 1945

*Robert M. Page*

'Vote for change', the Conservatives' (ultimately highly prescient) campaign slogan for the 2010 general election, appears at first sight to be an unlikely catchphrase for a party that has historically been associated with order, tradition, hierarchy and institutional arrangements that have stood the test of time. However, this embrace of change becomes more understandable when one recognises that the party's longevity and unparalleled electoral success has resulted from its willingness to modify both its principles and policies in the light of new circumstances. As Rodney Lowe (2005, p 25) remarks, echoing the influential 18th-century philosopher Edmund Burke, traditional Conservative philosophy is based on 'conserving what is best in the old while adapting constantly to the new'. One of the consequences of this 'adaptive' mindset is that it can lead to the charge that the party has no settled convictions or principled policy prescriptions (Green, 2002). During the course of their history the Conservatives have, as Marquand (2010, p 24) observes,

> changed sides – sometimes more than once – on virtually all the great questions dividing the political nation. They have been for protection and for free trade, for fiscal orthodoxy and for Keynesian economics, for local democracy and for relentless centralisation, for appeasing Hitler and for resisting him, for entry into the European Community and for keeping Europe at arm's length.

The thorny question of what the Conservative Party stands for will be explored briefly in the opening section of this chapter. This discussion will form the backdrop to a three-part examination of the Conservative approach to the welfare state. Attention will be focused first on the emergence and development of modern One Nation Conservatism from the end of the war until the demise of the Douglas-Home government in 1964. Second, the neo-liberal turn in the Conservative approach to the welfare state, which surfaced briefly in the early years of the Heath government and came to fruition during the Thatcher (1979–90) and Major (1990–97) eras, will be considered. Third, David Cameron's 'progressive' Conservative approach to social welfare will be explored. The concluding section of the chapter will consider whether a common thread can be detected in the Conservative approach to the welfare state since the Second World War.

## Conservatism and the Conservative Party

Although all political parties are likely to change and adapt over time, it is arguably more difficult to provide a clear-cut summary of core Conservative convictions and approaches than. say, for example, those of the Labour Party (although see McKibbin, 2010; Pugh, 2010). This is linked to the fact that the Conservatives have at different times sought to 'represent' the diverse interests of the aristocracy, industrialists and growing numbers of middle- and working-class voters. Moreover, the party has always been reluctant to provide a distinctive vision of what it regards as the 'good' society (Charmley, 2008). Indeed, those who attempt to devise 'ideological' blueprints of this kind are regarded as misguided, on the grounds that they will often overlook their own fallibilities and shortcomings and underestimate the negative consequences of rapid social change. Conservatives prefer to work with what they perceive as the grain of a slowly evolving society.

It is possible, however, to identify what might be termed as underlying Conservative 'dispositions' (Oakeshott, 1975; Norton, 1996; Letwin, 2002, 2008; Norman, 2010). These would include, for example, a commitment to personal freedom and responsibility, support for the family, paternalism, patriotism, order, voluntary action, property rights, inequality as opposed to equality, and the free market. However, the relative importance that Conservatives attach to these dispositions is quite fluid. Some have, for example, been much more committed to the paternalist strand in Conservative thinking, while others have been more supportive of its libertarian 'tradition' (Greenleaf, 1983). Moreover, as Green (2002, p 260) reminds us, it is not unusual for Conservatives to 'hold both libertarian and paternalist views at the same time, with the outlook depending less on clearly stated principles than on the particular issue or realm of activity that was being addressed'.

Pragmatic adaptation, rather than deep-rooted 'ideology', has also been the hallmark of Conservative policymaking when in government (Blake, 1998). Although philosophical differences between those Conservatives who adhere to a minimal view of the state and those who are more willing to countenance greater degrees of government action (see McGowan, 2007) should not be underestimated, interventionism has tended to be justified on practical grounds rather than doctrine. For example in the pre-war era (1918–39), Conservative support for increased government intervention was driven by the perceived need to adjust to prevailing economic and social conditions (not least the challenge posed by organised labour; see Gilbert, 1970; Macnicol, 1998), rather than a deep-rooted ideological conversion to the merits of collective action. As Francis (1996, p 60) points out, during the 1930s 'the National government was remarkably interventionist in the economic sphere, pursuing cheap money policies to encourage investment, creating public corporations and marketing boards to aid industrial efficiency'. There were also significant developments in the area of social policy. During Neville Chamberlain's tenure at the Ministry of Health (1924–29), for instance, there was a plethora of initiatives and reforms in areas such as old-age pensions, unemployment insurance, housing and public health (see Harris, 2004; Fraser, 2009).

## Modern One Nation Conservatism, 1945–64

In turning to developments in the Conservative Party's approach towards the welfare state in the post-1945 era, there has been a lively debate over the question of whether the party could be said to have continued with a strategy of pragmatic adaptation, or whether a more fundamental ideological shift occurred (Raison, 1990; Hickson, 2005).

Although the Conservative Party promised to maintain 'a high and stable level of employment' and introduce 'a comprehensive health service covering the whole range of medical treatment from the general practitioner to the specialist' (Dale, 2000, p 63) in their general election manifesto of 1945, they failed to persuade a majority of the electorate that they were no longer the party of privilege or that they were now fully committed to the welfare state and the creation of a fairer society. Labour's electoral victory prompted those on the 'progressive' wing of the Conservative Party to press for a more enlightened policy agenda that would strike a better balance between individualism and collectivism as well as the market and the state. Churchill, who continued to lead the party, responded to the call for a clearer statement of modern Conservative aims and principles by appointing a committee under the chairmanship of R.A. Butler to examine industrial policy. This gave rise to *The Industrial Charter* (Conservative and Unionist Central Office, 1947), which many commentators have come to regard as 'one of the most pivotal statements' of post-war Conservatism (Taylor,

2002, p 85). Although the Charter reaffirmed the party's commitment to free enterprise and the limited regulation of industry, it also sought to reassure a sceptical public that the Conservatives were committed to full employment and the fostering of harmonious relationships with the trade unions. These themes were reiterated in *The Right Road for Britain* (Conservative and Unionist Central Office, 1949), which was drafted by Quintin Hogg, whose influential book, *The Case for Conservatism* (1947), had appeared two years earlier. *The Right Road* also confirmed that the modern Conservatives were supportive of the 'new social services' and would endeavour 'to maintain the range and scope' of such provision and the prevailing 'rates of benefit' (1949, p 42). Significantly, however, there were strong signals that the Conservative approach to social policy would differ from Labour's. Concern was expressed about the escalating cost of the NHS, the creation of 'enormous and unwieldy multilateral schools' and the 'shameful' levels of waste and extravagance to be found in the public sector (1949, p 42).

Following the Conservatives' narrow defeat in the 1950 general election, a further attempt to develop the party's welfare policy was undertaken by the newly formed One Nation Group (Walsha, 2000, 2003; Seawright, 2005). In their influential booklet, *One Nation: A Tory Approach to Social Problems* (Macleod and Maude, 1950), the One Nation Group attempted to formulate a distinctive Conservative welfare agenda, which would prioritise economic stability above costly egalitarian social spending, selectivity over universality and minimal rather than optimal levels of state provision. This embrace of a more modest form of welfare collectivism was seen as perfectly compatible with traditional Conservative concerns such as sound finance, efficiency, lower taxation, thrift, self-reliance, voluntarism and charitable endeavour.

Although the contributors to *One Nation* were concerned primarily with formulating the broad parameters of the modern Conservative approach to the welfare state, illustrations of specific policy initiatives were also sketched out. In the case of housing, for example, a large and expanded private sector was to play a major role in the construction of competitively priced homes for sale or rent, while local authorities would be expected to focus on slum clearance and 'the abatement of overcrowding' (1950, p 36). The need to curb the growing level of 'unnecessary' demand for health care was to be resolved by better systems of prioritising need and the imposition of user charges.

These concerted efforts to counter the idea that the Conservatives were 'ideologically' opposed to the welfare state did not, however, lead to a strategic focus on welfare issues in the Conservative electoral campaign of 1951. Although the party's commitment to the welfare state was reaffirmed, it was the theme of 'setting the people free' that the Conservatives chose to highlight (Francis, 1996; Jefferys, 1997). In his electoral address, Churchill maintained that it was only a stable Conservative government 'not biased by privilege or interest or cramped by doctrinal prejudices or inflamed by the passions of class warfare' that would be able to foster enterprise, increase the availability of consumer goods, 'halt the rising cost of living', and 'prune [government] waste and extravagance' (quoted in Dale, 2000, pp 95–9). One of the reasons why the Conservatives attached such importance to improving the supply of consumer goods was to persuade women voters that they were the party that best understood the particular difficulties they were having to endure (such as endless queuing in shops) and would act decisively to bring an end to the age of austerity (see Zweiniger-Bargielowska, 1996, 2000; Francis, 1997).

The Conservatives' ambitious proposals for a rapid expansion in house-building were intended to draw attention to the inadequacies of Labour's 'partisan' forms of social policy and the corresponding need for an enhanced role for the private sector. As Jones (2000, p 117) points out:

> The perception of Labour failures in housing gave Conservative policy-makers the opportunity to showcase free enterprise, which they argued would provide more houses more quickly and more efficiently. The promise to build 300,000 houses a year was therefore seen within the party as central to the revival of popular support for market values in post-war Britain.

The depth of Conservative support for the welfare state was put to the test in the immediate aftermath of their narrow general election victory in 1951. In the face of international pressure on Sterling occasioned by a balance of payments 'crisis', the newly appointed Chancellor, R.A. Butler, sought to cut imports, tighten monetary policy and review public spending (Boxer, 1996). In terms of social policy, this resulted in the introduction of selective NHS charges and the paring back of the school-building programme. Significantly, however, there was no appetite for the major forms of retrenchment that had occurred at the end of the First World War – the infamous 'Geddes axe' (see Bridgen and Lowe, 1998; Harris, 2004).

During what proved to be Churchill's final term in office (1951–55), the Conservatives sought to make an 'accommodation' with

Labour's post–war welfare reforms. This involved an acceptance of the institutional framework that Labour had created, but a change in its role and purpose to ensure that it dovetailed with broader Conservative ideals. This accommodative strategy was based on recognition that key parts of the welfare state, such as the NHS, had proved popular with Conservative supporters and voters. Moreover, a number of influential ministers such as Butler, Macmillan, Macleod and Eccles were convinced that an explicitly Conservative vision for welfare reform could be developed (Dutton, 1991; Garnett and Hickson, 2009). Conservative support for the welfare state and the mixed economy also formed part of a wider political imperative, namely, the engendering of 'a broad popular consensus around a new "humanized capitalism" in order to fight the Cold War with as unified and solid a front as possible' (Jones, 1996, p 252).

In developing a distinctive Conservative approach to the welfare state, emphasis was placed on increased targeting, a greater reliance on user charges and tighter expenditure controls (Raison, 1990). It was recognised that the pace of change should be measured and gradual in order to retain public support. For example, Butler's decision to authorise a review of NHS spending (Guillebaud Committee, 1956), rather than the totality of social service expenditure, reflected his fear that a more comprehensive undertaking would revive public unease about the shallowness of Conservative support for the welfare state (Glennerster, 2007a).

At the 1955 general election the new Conservative leader, Anthony Eden, emphasised that the party's 'modern' approach to the welfare state was categorically different from the 'egalitarian uniformity' promoted by the Labour opposition. Under the Conservatives, citizens would be provided with greater opportunities and enhanced choice:

> We denounce the Labour Party's desire to use the social services, which we all helped to create, as an instrument for levelling down. We regard social security not as a substitute for family thrift, but as a necessary basis or supplement to it. We think of the national health service as a means, not of preventing anyone from paying anything for a service, but of ensuring that proper attention and treatment are denied to no one. We believe that equality of opportunity is to be achieved, not by sending every boy and girl to exactly the same kind of school, but by seeing that every child gets the schooling most suited to his or her aptitudes. We see a sensible housing policy in terms, not of one hopeless

Council waiting list, but of adequate and appropriate provision both for letting and for sale. (*United for Peace and Progress: The Conservative and Unionist Party's General Election Manifesto 1955*, reprinted in Dale, 2000, p 119)

Eden's embrace of a modern One Nation Conservatism – which involved striking a delicate balance between the party's long-standing commitment to low taxation and price stability and 'new' social imperatives, such as the maintenance of full employment and support for the welfare state; see Carlton, 2010 – was even more deeply held by his successor Harold Macmillan (1957–63). In practice, however, it was always going to be difficult for the Conservatives to maintain economic stability without recourse to price or wage controls, tax increases or reductions in social expenditure (Rollings, 1996; Whiteside, 1996). Indeed, a special Cabinet Committee on the Social Services was appointed in 1956 in response to heightened Treasury concerns about the growing cost of the welfare state. Despite the best efforts of Treasury officials to secure support for a range of policy options designed to restrain the growth of such expenditure, including increased NHS charges, raising the school entry age to six and increasing the price of school meals, the Committee was able to rebuff these suggestions by stressing the importance of viewing welfare expenditure as a form of long-term investment rather than consumption (Lowe, 1989). The growing willingness of the modern Conservatives to protect social spending even in the face of Treasury demands for greater economies did, however, give rise to intra-party tensions as evidenced by the resignation of the Chancellor of the Exchequer, Peter Thorneycroft, in 1958 after he failed to secure cabinet agreement for a raft of expenditure cuts (see Rollings, 1996). Macmillan's general election victory in 1959 seemed to signify that the public had been persuaded that the Conservatives' modern One Nation strategy could deliver both higher living standards and enhanced social security. However, this electoral popularity proved short-lived as Macmillan was confronted with economic difficulties on the home front, a French veto on Britain's application to join the Common Market and the highly damaging Profumo affair in 1963 (Jefferys, 1997). The party's narrow election defeat in 1964 under Macmillan's successor Douglas-Home signalled that the high point of modern Conservatism had passed.

## The 'neo-liberal' turn in Conservative social policy

Concerns about the efficacy of the modern Conservative approach in relation to both economic and social policy intensified during the party's time in opposition from 1964 to 1970. This period was marked by continued economic turbulence and growing fears about the adverse social impact of alternative 'lifestyles' and values. Such conditions proved fertile ground for 'instinctive' anti-collectivists within the party and beyond. Enoch Powell (1969) had begun to map out a more limited role for government in economic and social policy while the 'neo-liberal' ideas of Hayek and Friedman were having increasing influence in policy circles both in Britain and the United States (Critchlow, 2007; Regnery, 2008). The Institute of Economic Affairs, which had been established in 1955 (Cockett, 1995), played a major role in bringing these ideas to public attention through the publication of a series of pamphlets on topics such as state pensions (Seldon, 1957) and choice in health care (Lees, 1961).

The party's general election manifesto of 1970, *A Better Tomorrow* (Conservative Party, 1970), reflected this growing neo-liberal influence with calls for lower direct taxes, a reduction in trade union power and a tougher approach to issues of law and order. Following Edward Heath's rather unexpected electoral victory, efforts were made to put some of these ideas into practice. On the economic front, attempts were made to curb trade union influence and reduce government subsidies to 'lame duck' industries, while judicious forms of selectivity were introduced in the areas of housing and social security. However, the fact that the government proved willing to return to a more interventionist strategy when faced with inflationary pressures and rising levels of unemployment suggests that the neo-liberal turn was not as deep-rooted as some might have assumed. Indeed, in certain areas of social policy, such as education, plans were put in place to increase, rather than reduce, government spending (Timmins, 2001; Lowe, 2005).

It was not until after the fall of the Heath government in 1974 that neo-liberal ideas really took hold within party circles. The key playmaker in this process was Keith Joseph. Converted to the merits of monetarism by influential neo-liberals such as Alfred Sherman, Peter Bauer, Ralph Harris and Alan Walters, Joseph argued that the pursuit of 'true' Conservatism necessitated the outright rejection of the interventionist strategy that both Labour and Conservative governments had followed since 1945. Significantly, he now judged that his earlier support for the welfare state had been misplaced. Instead of providing people with security and opportunity, the welfare state had created an undesirable dependency culture. Joseph established the Centre for Policy Studies in 1974 as an institutional base for the dissemination of his revisionist agenda. Adverse publicity following a controversial speech delivered by Joseph to the local Edgbaston constituency party in 1974 (see Sherman, 2005), in which he had criticised young single mothers for undermining the human stock of the nation, led him to pass up the opportunity to stand as the 'anti-collectivist' candidate in the party's leadership contest in 1975. This paved the way for the vice-chair of the Centre for Policy Studies, Margaret Thatcher, to take on the role. After defeating Heath in the first ballot, and four new challengers in a second contest, Thatcher became leader of the Conservative Party, and subsequently Prime Minister after the party secured victory in the general election of 1979.

While some have questioned whether the Heath government actually deviated from the modern Conservative approach forged by Eden and Macmillan (see Lowe, 1996), few would question Margaret Thatcher's desire to abandon this strategy. Thatcher believed that modern Conservatism was barely distinguishable from the social-democratic path forged by successive post-war Labour governments. In her view Britain had lost its economic dynamism and, as a consequence, a culture of decline and dependency had been allowed to take hold. If Britain was to regain its global influence a change in direction was required. A more confrontational stance was, for example, deemed necessary in relation to the 'politicised' trade unions; an approach that culminated in a bitter confrontation with the miners in 1984–85 (Milne, 2004). The control of inflation was now to take precedence over full employment and state support for ailing industries was to be abandoned. The welfare state was deemed to have become both dysfunctional and costly. Instead of providing basic security for those in need it was now deemed to be undermining the economic and social fabric of the nation.

This dramatic change of direction led some paternalist One Nation Conservatives, such as Pym (1984) and Gilmour (1992), to argue that Thatcher had abandoned the central 'tenets' of Conservatism in pursuit of an avowedly neo-liberal agenda. Certainly, the emergence and growing use of the term 'Thatcherism' supports this viewpoint. But Thatcher's desire to reverse Britain's decline by radical means was not indicative of a non-Conservative disposition. On the contrary, she proved to be a firm supporter of the nation-state, the family, voluntarism and free enterprise. Thatcher's Conservative dispositions were particularly to the fore in relation to social issues. She supported capital punishment, tighter controls on immigration and 'disapproved of those so lazy, feckless or lacking in self-respect that they were content to live in subsidised housing or on benefits' (Campbell, 2003, p 248; see also, Vinen, 2009).

However, although Thatcher had strong convictions, she was a pragmatist who recognised that many of the changes she sought to bring about would take time to achieve. This 'pragmatic' mindset led Thatcher to pursue incremental, rather than radical, welfare reforms during her first term in office. This reflected the priority that was to be accorded to economic concerns, the lack of viable blueprints for welfare reform and the fact that a number of her ministers, such as Gilmour, Pym, Prior and Walker, were resistant to any idea of root-and-branch reform. Indeed, it was not until preferment was given to 'true believers', such as Cecil Parkinson, Norman Tebbit and Nigel Lawson, that more far-reaching reforms were given detailed consideration.

It would be misleading, though, to underplay the change of direction that occurred in social policy in the first term of the Thatcher government from 1979 to 1983. There were significant expenditure cuts in the fields of education, social security and housing. Although Thatcher exempted the NHS from these cost-cutting measures because of what American policy analysts would term its 'third-rail' (untouchable) status, little was done to redress the historic underfunding of the service (Webster, 2002).

Although only a limited number of 'structural' reforms of the welfare state were contemplated at this time, they were all in accord with the neo-liberal ideals of the new government. The sale of council houses is particularly noteworthy in this regard. By persuading aspirational working-class Labour voters to join the ranks of the property-owning middle classes there was the concomitant possibility that their political allegiance might shift 'rightwards' (Campbell, 2003). Although this measure proved popular (around half a million tenants had bought their own homes by 1983), other prospective reforms, such as the introduction of education vouchers and private health insurance, remained on the drawing board as a result of reservations about their viability within the cabinet and beyond (Lawson, 1992). Indeed, it seemed at one stage that the steep rise in unemployment, coupled with serious inner-city disturbances in areas such as Brixton, Toxteth and Moss Side, would scupper any possibility of a second Thatcher government. As it transpired, however, the Conservatives, bolstered by a recovery in the world economy, military success in the Falkland Islands and a divided opposition, succeeded in increasing their Commons majority from 43 seats in 1979 to 144 seats in 1983, albeit with a slightly reduced share of the popular vote.

Given that economic reform remained the central focus of the second Thatcher government (1983–87), a major overhaul of the welfare state was put on hold. However, the ideological attack on the welfare state was maintained, thereby softening up the public for the subsequent and more far-reaching third-term reforms. The main focus during this second phase of Thatcherism was on controlling social spending and increasing efficiency including the importation of managerial methods from the private sector, which it was hoped would 'persuade' service providers to focus more sharply on the quality and cost of the services they were providing to welfare 'consumers' (Timmins, 2001; Glennerster, 2007a).

It was only after further electoral success in 1987 that the Conservative government finally pressed ahead with more significant welfare reforms. Interestingly, the party's general election manifesto (Conservative Party, 1987) only hinted at the major restructuring that was to come. While this might have reflected a desire to avoid arousing any unnecessary voter unease prior to the election, it is entirely plausible to suggest that it was subsequent events that proved to be the catalyst for change. For example, further criticism of the government's stewardship of the NHS by senior members of the medical profession in the immediate post-election period led Thatcher to announce, quite unexpectedly, a wide-ranging review of the service.

The pattern of change favoured by the third-term Thatcher government with regard to the welfare state was not outright abolition or privatisation. Instead, publicly funded services were to be retained, but delivered in radically different ways by diverse providers in an effort to increase efficiency and constrain costs. In the NHS this led, for example, to hospitals (operating as self-governing Trusts) entering into service agreements with budget-holding District Health Authorities. A number of GP fund-holders were also provided with the financial autonomy to commission services from a broader range of providers. The Conservatives also introduced significant reforms in the area of education. Under the 1988 Education Act a 10-subject National Curriculum was introduced, as well as a system of national testing at the ages of 7, 11, 14 and 16 to ensure that all pupils reached a satisfactory standard in relation to knowledge, skills and understanding. This legislation also allowed schools to opt out of local authority control and become part of a new grant-maintained sector. Those schools that remained under the auspices of the local authority were given greater autonomy over the use of their budgets and in the appointment of staff. Privately sponsored (but predominantly state-funded) City Technology Colleges were also established in educationally disadvantaged neighbourhoods where the comprehensive system was deemed to have failed.

At the end of the Thatcher era, which came about suddenly following a leadership challenge from Michael Heseltine in 1990, the key institutions of the welfare state remained intact, if somewhat battered. However, the broader 'transformative' role of the welfare state, which had formed part of Labour's post-war strategy, had been significantly undermined. The public were now being encouraged to regard the welfare state as a multifaceted deliverer of consumer services, rather than as an integral part of the social fabric of the nation designed to promote equality and solidarity and provide security for all.

Although Thatcher's successor, John Major (who went on to win the 1992 general election with more votes than any party in British political history), proved adept at abandoning some of the most unpopular policies of his predecessor, such as the Community Charge or Poll Tax, he showed no desire to reset the prevailing political compass. Unlike Thatcher, who gave 'the impression that the public services were inherently second-class, and that most people should aspire to opt out of them, by sending their children to private schools, and using private doctors in preference to the National Health Service' (Bogdanor, 2010, p 176), Major (1999) displayed a greater degree of personal affection for the welfare state. Nevertheless, he remained committed to the idea that private-sector mechanisms such as performance-related pay, competition, audit and inspection could enhance the performance of service providers. Citizen's Charters (first introduced in 1991), which required service providers to devise independently monitored performance targets, respond promptly to user complaints and provide redress where necessary, formed an integral part of this process.

Major's attempt to consolidate Thatcher's third-term reforms proved far from straightforward. Shortly after his general election victory he was forced to preside over a humiliating withdrawal from the Exchange Rate Mechanism (see Jefferys, 2002). He also faced growing professional opposition to some of the other Thatcher reforms, so that in education, for example, teachers refused to participate in the national testing of pupils.

Major's commitment to the Thatcher 'revolution' was confirmed in the party's general election manifesto of 1997 (Conservative Party, 1997). The virtues of the free market, a smaller state, low taxes, privatisation, deregulation, shareholding, restrained public spending, trade union reform and a tough law-and-order policy were once again extolled. Unfortunately, from Major's perspective, the British public appeared to have lost faith in this Conservative vision of the 'good society'. The Conservatives lost 182 seats and secured just under 31% of the popular vote as 'New' Labour swept to power.

## David Cameron's 'progressive' Conservatism

On what proved to be a long and difficult path back into government (see Bale, 2010; Snowden, 2010; and Chapter 1, this volume), it was following the election of David Cameron as party leader in 2005 that the Conservatives were finally to return to power. Cameron recognised that although Margaret Thatcher had been out of office for some 15 years, there was still a strong public sense that the Conservatives were indifferent to the plight of those in poverty and hostile to those groups, such as lone parents, who were seen as posing a threat to the family and traditional social values (see Fielding, 2009; Willetts, 2009). Drawing on the doctrine of compassionate Conservatism, which had underpinned the early years of the Republican Presidency of George W. Bush (see Olasky, 2000; Ashbee, 2003; Montgomerie, 2004), Cameron sought, as New Labour had done so successfully in the 1990s (see Page, 2009), to rebrand his party in order to broaden its electoral appeal. As Norton (2009, pp 39–40) notes, 'the party was seen as being against things, be it European integration, immigrants or gay sex'; for Cameron, it was important to be *for* things, such as 'the National Health Service – keeping and improving it was identified as a top priority; to be *for* the family (rather than being against, or appearing to be against, certain family units); and to be *for* equality on issues such as gay rights'. Refocusing of this kind was intended to demonstrate that the Conservatives were now part of what Lilla (2010, p 53) has termed the 'budding liberal consensus on social issues'.

Given New Labour's apparent lack of idealism (see Page, 2007), Cameron also seized the opportunity to portray his party as being both modern and progressive. In contrast to New Labour's supposedly backward-looking statism, the 'progressive' Conservatives would, he argued, endeavour to create a cohesive and tolerant society in which individuals would take greater responsibility for their own well-being, philanthropy would flourish, civic society would be reinvigorated, and poverty and inequality would become less entrenched (see Hickson, 2008; Garnett, 2010).

Cameron's emphasis on social issues was intended to demonstrate that, notwithstanding his continued support for the neo-liberal economic agenda that previous Conservative governments had pursued, he accepted that the party had ignored the adverse social consequences that accompanied such rapid change. Indeed, as discussed in Chapter 1, one of the first steps he took after becoming leader was to refashion the party's approach to poverty and social justice. The former party leader, Iain Duncan Smith, was given responsibility for this task as head of the newly established Social Justice Policy Group (SJPG). Working under the umbrella of the Centre for Social Justice (which Duncan Smith had established in 2004), the SJPG produced three influential reports. The first report, *Breakdown Britain*, identified five interconnected 'pathways' into poverty (worklessness and economic dependency, family breakdown, addictions, education failure, and indebtedness; see Social Justice Policy Group, 2006). The second, *Breakthrough Britain*, focused on the 'integrated and long-term' policy initiatives that could be used to tackle the 'costs' of social disadvantage (Social Justice Policy Group, 2007). The third report, *Dynamic Benefits: Towards Welfare That Works*, examined some specific policy measures designed to repair Britain's 'broken' benefits system, which was said to have disincentivised work, penalised pro-social behaviour such as marriage and stable cohabitation, and deterred personal saving and home ownership (Centre for Social Justice, 2009; see also Chapters 8 and 9, this volume). At the heart of Duncan Smith's approach was a desire to combat poverty in a holistic way that could be distinguished from what he regarded as Labour's narrow one-dimensional approach to this phenomenon (a reliance on the benefits system, rather than more wide-ranging measures to reduce the level of state dependency). As one of the converts to progressive Conservatism, David Willetts (1992, p 6), had previously pointed out, a successful anti-poverty strategy should recognise the multiple dimensions of this phenomenon:

> What if a family that does receive extra money is unable to let their children out to play because there are drug users' syringes on the stairwell outside the flat? And what if their children are unable to learn because of an endlessly changing cast of supply teachers at the local school? And what if they come from a broken home without stability and love? Conservatives understand that that is poverty, too.

The willingness to embrace the concept of social justice also distinguishes the 'progressive' Conservatives from anti-collectivist thinkers such as Hayek (see Hickson, 2010) and Powell (see Garnett and Hickson, 2009), who were fundamentally opposed to this idea. For Willetts (1992, p 112), who had formerly regarded the concept as 'slippery', 'social justice can be a good word which captures the idea that the distribution of opportunities in life are not simply determined by the market' (see

Seawright, 2005, p 85). Accordingly, Willetts now accepts, like other progressive Conservatives, that the government has an important strategic role to play in combating poverty and creating opportunities to combat disadvantage. Crucially, however, the key to tackling poverty and to repairing what has been termed as Britain's 'broken' society (see Driver, 2009a; Kirby, 2009) is to harness the insights and resources of the whole community rather than relying solely, or even mainly, on state action (see Letwin, 2002). As the party's 2010 general election manifesto, *Invitation to Join the Government of Britain* (Conservative Party, 2010e, p 35), makes clear, the regeneration of British society is to be achieved by 'a new approach: social responsibility not state control; the Big Society, not big government'. Power is to be redistributed 'from the state to society' and from the 'centre to local communities', thereby enabling citizens 'to take more control over their lives' (2010e, p 37; see also Chapter 14, this volume). All adults are to be encouraged to become members of an active neighbourhood group that, along with charities and social enterprises, will be able to apply for funding from a newly established Big Society Bank. Other concrete examples of 'progressive non-state' policy initiatives include the establishment of autonomous, state-funded free schools along the lines developed in Sweden (see Hultin, 2009; and Chapter 6, this volume) and the United States (Charter schools) and giving social workers and nurses the opportunity to set themselves up as publicly funded social enterprises so that they will be better able to use their professional expertise to improve the quality of the services they provide.

In their 2010 general election manifesto, the progressive Conservatives also reiterated their belief that the welfare state, for all its inefficiencies, needs to be reformed rather than abolished. In particular, they made it clear that despite the adverse economic climate they would continue to increase NHS spending in real terms.

Although the Conservatives failed to secure an outright majority in the inconclusive general election of 2010, which resulted in the eventual formation of a Coalition government with the Liberal Democrats, this did not appear to result in any significant dilution of the progressive Conservative agenda. This is not surprising, given that the Liberal Democrats shared many of the progressive Conservatives' ideas on issues such as localism and welfare reform (see Marshall and Laws, 2004; Liberal Democrats, 2010). Importantly, both parties were keen to stress their desire to protect the poorest groups in society, while still bearing down on the substantial public deficit. In their foreword to the post-election Coalition programme, both party leaders promised to 'protect those on low incomes from the effects of public sector pay constraints and other spending constraints', 'restore the earnings link for the basic pension from April 2011' and 'protect key benefits for older people such as the winter fuel allowance, free TV licences, free bus travel, and free eye tests and prescriptions' (Cabinet Office, 2010, pp 15, 26). Of course, the key question remained as to whether this would be implemented in practice. It is certainly possible that the impact of both spending cuts (see Browne and Levell, 2010) and wide-ranging reforms such as those planned for social security (Department for Work and Pensions, 2010a) and the health service (Department of Health, 2010) may have a regressive, rather than progressive, impact on the least well-off groups in society. Moreover, the Coalition's expressed determination to shrink the size of the state (see Maude, 2010) may signal a covert desire to complete a major overhaul of the welfare state, which both the Thatcher and Major governments had shied away.

## Conclusion: Clear blue water? Conservative social policy and the welfare state since 1945

There have been significant changes in Conservative approaches to the welfare state over the post-war period. Following electoral defeat in 1945, the Conservatives came to a somewhat uneasy accommodation with the welfare state. Given the breadth of public support for Labour's reforms in areas such as health and social security, Conservative modernisers (such as the One Nation Group) were able to persuade the party that the adoption of what might be termed a 'reluctant collectivist' welfare strategy (George and Wilding, 1976) posed little threat to traditional Conservative ideals.

By the 1970s, however, this new accord was beginning to unravel in the face of recurrent economic difficulties and the burgeoning cost of the welfare state. Although the Heath government initially appeared to be willing to adopt a more adversarial position with regard to the welfare state, it was not until the premiership of Margaret Thatcher that concerted attempts were made to refashion the welfare state so that it would complement rather than challenge 'traditional' Conservative dispositions. Although Thatcher presided over a marked growth in poverty and inequality, she did not dismantle the welfare state. However, her 'cultural' onslaught on what were perceived as the 'socialist' elements of the welfare state as well as the notion of public service was arguably more successful. The fact that the public had come to accept that it is 'natural' or inevitable to engage with the welfare state as discerning consumers, rather than solidaristic citizens, can be linked directly to the influence of the Thatcher era (although see also Chapter 4).

Under David Cameron's 'progressive' form of Conservatism, the party has adopted a more sympathetic attitude towards those in poverty and those pursuing 'non-traditional' lifestyles. While recognising that the state still has an important role to play in *funding* welfare services, greater emphasis is now being placed on non-state provision, and the need for both individuals and communities to take on a more extensive 'welfare' role. This latest adaptation in Conservative thinking mirrors the party's continued willingness to modify its stance in the light of new circumstances.

In conclusion, Conservative 'support' for the welfare state has waxed and waned since the Second World War, depending to some extent on the relative strength of underlying paternalist or libertarian 'dispositions'. However, the degree of hostility or acceptance displayed towards the welfare state at any particular point in time has tended to be linked to fine calculations as to whether it was operating in ways that bolstered or threatened deeply held Conservative beliefs, such as freedom, responsibility, inequality, voluntarism and the family.

# THREE

# The Conservative Party and public expenditure

*Nick Ellison*

This chapter examines the Conservative Party's attitudes to public spending since 1945, concentrating on two key periods of sustained Conservative rule, 1951–64 and 1979–97. The argument, put briefly, is that Conservative attitudes to public spending have been rather more 'ambivalent' over the years than the party's embedded scepticism about the benefits of public expenditure would suggest. Bulpitt's (1986) important observation about Conservative 'statecraft' – that Tory governing elites have always attempted to insulate themselves from too close an engagement with immediate political pressures by attending to matters of 'high politics', particularly the competent management of prevailing macro economic conditions – provides a possible explanation for this ambivalence. It is certainly the case, for example, that Conservative governments have presided over very different macro-economic conditions at different times, and have tried to adjust their approach to public spending accordingly. However, as Stevens has pointed out, Bulpitt's account is essentially 'agency-driven'. He argues instead that other factors such as 'political contingency and underlying political and economic circumstances' (2002, p 122) are likely to play a significant role in attitudes to, and the management of, public expenditure. This broader perspective seeks to blend 'agency' and 'structure', and in so doing provides a richer account of 'ambivalence' and Tory vicissitudes in relation to public spending, both within and between the two periods under review.

## Patterns of public spending, 1945–2010

The key 'facts and figures' about UK public spending provided in the tables in this section give some basic information about spending levels as a percentage of Gross Domestic Product (GDP) since the Second World War. But what is 'public expenditure'? For the purposes of this chapter, 'Total Managed Expenditure' (TME) is used to depict *overall* spending levels since 1945. The key elements of TME have not changed markedly over time and comprise public sector current expenditure and public sector net investment and depreciation (Crawford et al, 2009, p 14). Table 3.1 shows TME as a percentage of GDP in selected years since 1950/51. It shows that TME rose gradually throughout the 1950s and then more rapidly through the 1960s until it peaked in 1976. Thereafter, TME has continued to rise in real terms but has fluctuated with the economic cycle, increasing in the recessions of the early 1980s and early 1990s, but in both instances falling back as growth resumed.

**Table 3.1: Total Managed Expenditure (TME), selected years (percentage of GDP)**

| | TME | Current spending | Public sector net investment | Depreciation |
|---|---|---|---|---|
| 1950–51 | 37.3 | 31.2 | 2.7 | 3.4 |
| 1955–56 | 36.0 | 29.0 | 3.5 | 3.5 |
| 1959–60 | 36.7 | 29.8 | 3.5 | 3.4 |
| 1965–66 | 39.8 | 31.0 | 5.2 | 3.3 |
| 1971–72 | 42.5 | 33.4 | 5.2 | 3.9 |
| 1975–76 | 49.7 | 39.7 | 5.5 | 4.4 |
| 1979–80 | 44.6 | 38.1 | 2.3 | 4.2 |
| 1982–83 | 48.1 | 42.3 | 1.6 | 4.2 |
| 1985–86 | 45.0 | 40.5 | 1.2 | 3.3 |
| 1989–90 | 39.2 | 35.3 | 1.2 | 2.7 |
| 1992–93 | 43.7 | 39.8 | 1.8 | 2.0 |
| 1995–96 | 41.8 | 38.7 | 1.4 | 1.7 |
| 1996–97 | 39.9 | 37.6 | 0.7 | 1.6 |
| 2002–03 | 38.6 | 36.0 | 1.3 | 1.3 |
| 2007–08 | 41.1 | 37.8 | 2.1 | 1.3 |

*Source:* Institute for Fiscal Studies (2010a).

Table 3.2 provides information about real increases over time in key policy areas. The second column illustrates how Conservative governments between 1979 and 1997 managed spending in these areas. With the exception of defence, which was cut back markedly in the wake of the ending of the Cold War, and, importantly, capital investment, each area saw real spending increases, albeit at rates below those achieved by previous governments or those attained by New Labour governments between 1997 and 2008. It is worth pointing out that the bulk of Conservative retrenchment during these years was focused on TME net investment (capital spending), reflecting the sales of public housing and nationalised industries that took place throughout the 1980s and into the 1990s. Table 3.3 portrays spending in the main areas as a percentage of national income. Of note here is the rising proportion of spending taken by social security and the NHS. Education also increases over the period but at a slower and less consistent rate.

**Table 3.2: Real increases in spending in the main areas (percentages)**

|  | Long-term trend | April 1979–March 1997 |
|---|---|---|
| TME | 3.4 (1949/50–2008/09) | 1.5 |
| TME net investment | 3.7 | −5.0 |
| TME current spending | 3.5 | 2.1 |
| Social security | 4.5 (1950/51–2008/09) | 3.8 |
| NHS | 4.6 (1950/51–2008/09) | 3.2 |
| Education | 4.4 (1954/55–2008/09) | 1.5 |
| Defence | 0.2 (1954/55–1997/98) | −0.5 |

*Source:* Adapted from Crawford et al (2009, p 16).

**Table 3.3: Spending as a percentage of national income in the main areas**

|  | 1958/59 | 1978/79 | 1996/97 | 2008/09 |
|---|---|---|---|---|
| Social security | 6.0 | 9.8 | 13.1 | 11.9 |
| NHS | 3.2 | 4.4 | 5.1 | 7.8 |
| Education | 3.3 | 5.2 | 4.6 | 5.7 |
| Defence | 6.4 | 4.5 | 2.8 | 2.6 |
| Public order/safety | – | 1.5 | 2.0 | 2.4 |
| TME | 36.9 | 45.1 | 39.9 | 43.2 |
| TME net investment | 3.4 | 2.5 | 0.7 | 2.5 |
| TME current spending | 33.5 | 42.6 | 39.2 | 39.4 |

*Source:* Adapted from Crawford et al (2009, p 17).

These illustrations of public spending patterns over time, although they suggest that Conservative governments have not been wholly successful in controlling expenditure, convey little either about Conservative Party attitudes to public spending or about the reasons why Conservative administrations have found it difficult to restrict the growth of the state. What follows will attempt to make sense of Tory attitudes to public expenditure and, beyond that, to the role of the modern state itself. At least three 'explanations' are important, each representing different configurations of 'structural' and agency-driven factors. Macro-economic explanations suggest that governments of all colours have to deal with both the 'real-world' economy and the political and electoral constraints that global economic conditions help to produce. How public spending is perceived is partly dependent on these macro-economic issues, as the following section will make clear. A second level of explanation relates to the state of internal Conservative Party politics and the role of ideas over time. This 'agency-driven' dimension is important because 'structure' is never entirely determining, and the cut and thrust of ideological debate can influence the shape of policy and governmental decisions. Alongside these accounts lies a third explanation that focuses on the difficulties governments can face in achieving spending cuts even when economic conditions and the state of internal party politics are broadly in their favour. 'Institutionalist' theory offers a powerful account of how 'positive feedback' mechanisms can, over time, make changes in policy hard to realise (Pierson, 2004). For present purposes, however, it is enough to point out that demographic changes, or rising expectations about, say, the availability and effectiveness of health care, make it difficult for governments to reduce resources irrespective of ideology or the state of the macro-economy.

## The Conservatives, public expenditure and the UK macro-economy since 1945

One set of factors that throws light upon why Conservative governments – indeed, governments in general – have struggled to control public expenditure relates to exogenous economic conditions that have, at different times, conspired to encourage or thwart ideologically driven ambitions. As the following discussion will demonstrate, the Conservative Party, at least in its election manifestos, has consistently adopted a sceptical attitude to public spending, preferring to believe that the traditional Tory goals of personal responsibility and individual freedom are best fostered by an extensive private sector operating in the context of 'sound money' and a free market. However, differing macro-economic conditions have 'mediated' this apparently simple outlook on the role of the state and public expenditure in different ways at different times. In the 1950s, for instance, a relatively benign global economy created an environment favourable to public spending in the interests of maintaining full male employment and new forms of social protection, each of which entailed an increased role for the public sector. Conversely, in the 1980s and 1990s, a different macro-economic environment in which the control of inflation came to be regarded as the key goal of economic policy meant that Tory governments found it easier to sustain an ideological position organised around public spending cuts, higher unemployment and welfare retrenchment.

## Public spending in the 'Keynesian' era

Turning to the period between 1951 and 1964, much has been said about the life and death (or not) of 'Keynesian' economic policies in the UK (Tomlinson, 1990, 2007; Glynn and Booth, 1996; Skidelsky, 1996). For Skidelsky (1996, p 48), 'Keynesianism was a collection of ideas, policies and institutions designed to maintain full employment'. The publication of the *Employment Policy* White Paper in 1944 is an obvious 'foundational' moment for this eclectic and pragmatic understanding of Keynesianism. This document, drafted under the auspices of the wartime coalition government, committed post-war governments to maintaining 'high and stable' employment, through the management of aggregate demand using fiscal and monetary policies to stimulate consumption. Although, as Glynn and Booth (1996) point out, there was nothing explicit in the White Paper to commit governments to running fiscal deficits, and indeed governments in the 1950s did not do so, the agreement that full employment was a key goal of economic policy, together with the acceptance of the Beveridgean welfare state, created a 'frame' for economic and social policy – and therefore for public spending – for a generation. Certainly, in the later 1940s and early 1950s, 'Keynesian' budgetary techniques came to be widely accepted as a method of managing employment levels and underpinning welfare state spending, these practices stemming from the gradual, but persistent, advance of Keynesian thinking within Labour government circles, led by key figures such as James Meade and Robert Hall in the Economic Section of the Treasury. Labour's last budgets under Hugh Gaitskell's Chancellorship were a measure of this advance, taking a decidedly Keynesian turn in their attention to fiscal and monetary adjustments, rather than physical planning, and setting the broad scene for economic management under the Conservatives.

'Conservative Keynesianism' in the 1950s was nevertheless a different beast from Labour's early prototype, no doubt because the Conservative Party was simply not so fundamentally disposed as Labour to state expansion and rising spending levels (see later). Even so, TME averaged 37.6% of GDP between 1952/53 and 1963/64, these levels being much the same as those under the previous Labour administration. At the macro-economic level, full male employment was supported, if not guaranteed, for the greater part of the 1950s by a high growth rate that resulted from favourable terms of trade, itself an outcome of excess world demand fuelled by a global private investment boom (Skidelsky, 1996). Certainly until the mid-1950s, with growth at 2.9% per year between 1950 and 1955, Conservative governments needed to do little actively to sustain full employment. This picture had changed by the latter part of the decade as a range of factors – declining demand for UK exports, greater competition from abroad, comparatively low productivity and rising import penetration – exposed the UK's incipient economic weakness. However, the commitment to full employment and the welfare state had by this time become embedded components of the policy landscape, making any serious attempt to renegotiate the broad outlines of the settlement electorally risky.

Whether counter-cyclical demand management policies were actively attempted in this environment of 'Keynes-plus-capitalism-plus-welfare-state', as Labour's Tony Crosland (1956, p 115) characterised it, is open to question. Less contentious is the fact that a combination of the Conservatives' commitment to maintaining the value of Sterling, full male employment and the welfare state led to a sort of Keynesian-inspired 'fine-tuning' that saw governments alternating between deflationary measures to maintain Sterling's value and reflationary policies to maintain employment levels (Tomlinson, 1990). As Skidelsky (1996, p 51) notes, this '"stop–go" or "fine-tuning" the economy may be seen as a specific British contribution to Keynesianism arising from the economic characteristics of a declining economy, the tightness of the political battle between Conservative and Labour and the ability of a British Prime Minister to fix … the date of the next general election'.

Symbolically for the period, when the Conservatives stepped beyond fine-tuning in the early 1960s, they did so not in the direction of a greater reliance on monetarist orthodoxy and the free market, but in the form of an increased reliance on state-led planning. Faced with the disruptive consequences of the stop–go approach, concerned by the UK's declining growth levels and influenced by the apparently successful 'indicative planning' regime in France, the Macmillan government embraced a version of 'planning' in the form of the National Economic Development Council (NEDC), created in 1961. Complete with growth and export targets, and a nascent incomes policy, the NEDC was the apogee of Conservative 'statism', representing, however fleetingly, an optimism in Conservative circles about the state's capacity to manage the economy. Although this turn to planning did not prove conducive to electoral success for the Conservatives, partly no doubt because the Labour Party, with its history of post-war planning, was in a better position to capitalise on the perceived need for a modern 'organised' economy, the creation of the NEDC nevertheless illustrates how deeply embedded assumptions had become about the role of the state as the guarantor of full employment and social welfare.

## The Conservative Party and the UK macro-economy in the 1980s and 1990s

A great deal changed over the course of the period between the early 1960s and late 1970s, not least the entire financial and economic architecture of the post-war developed world. The collapse of the Bretton Woods system of fixed exchange rates in 1971 removed traditional worries about the need to preserve the value of Sterling at specified (usually too high) levels, but introduced new difficulties associated with the maintenance of a competitive balance of payments in a considerably more volatile economic environment. Furthermore, increasing primary product prices, most obviously oil, combined with rising overseas competition to produce higher unemployment as the UK's manufacturing base entered a period of sustained decline. To make matters worse, economic stagnation, instead of being accompanied by lower inflation in line with expectations, saw inflation rising as trade unions pursued pay claims designed to protect their members from rising prices. These factors, combined with the apparent inability of both the 1970–74 Heath government and subsequent Labour administrations in the 1970s, to control 'stagflation', contributed to the growing conviction within Conservative ranks that 'Keynesianism' no longer had any solutions to offer. This paradigmatic shift within the party was symbolised by Margaret Thatcher's election as leader in 1975, but the relevant point for the present discussion is that changes in the macro-economy helped to pave the way for the emergence of a Conservative leadership that felt able to draw upon monetarist economic strategies that privileged the control of inflation, reductions in public spending and the stimulation of private-sector activity over the concern with full employment. Significant, too, was the fact that an emerging post-Keynesian generation of Conservative intellectuals was influenced by economists and political scientists who believed that governments, far from being able to provide solutions to contemporary economic challenges, were in fact part of the problem (Niskanen, 1971; Bacon and Eltis, 1976). In this sense, as Keith Joseph (1976) argued, 'monetarism' per se was not enough. The size of the state had to be reduced, taxes lowered and so on, irrespective of macro-economic policy.

In sum, by the early 1980s, the international economy had become a far less stable entity than it had been 20 years earlier. Exchange rates fluctuated, overseas competition had increased and was continuing to do so, full employment was seemingly a thing of the past, and inflation had come to be regarded as the biggest single threat to economic and social stability. This backdrop clearly facilitated the neo-liberal ideological assault on the post-war settlement. Even so, it is unlikely that these changes entirely determined Tory thinking, let alone the actions of Conservative governments during the Thatcher and Major years. And this is the case more generally. In both of the periods under review, prevailing macro-economic conditions set the overall parameters of the 'policy frame' within which particular options appeared more or less feasible. Looking to the 1950s, it is not surprising that Conservative governments were more favourably disposed towards forms of economic management that involved higher levels of public expenditure; nor is it surprising that governments in the 1980s and 1990s turned away from so-called 'Keynesian' solutions. However, other factors, including electoral considerations, the nature of party ideology and internal party politics, and the 'structural' difficulty of actually changing existing policies, though partly influenced by the wider economic environment, also operate with a degree of autonomy, which means that their relationship with it will be subject to overlap and slippage. It is this inevitable complexity that can make governments seem uncertain and ambivalent, despite the apparent clarity of their stated intentions.

## Conservative ideas and policies in the 1950s: a study in ambivalence

The preceding discussion suggested that the Conservatives encountered relatively benign global economic conditions in the 1950s and it was as much these as specifically 'Keynesian' economic policies that ensured full employment and a capacity to maintain levels of public spending.

But what attitudes towards public expenditure existed in the party at this time? Certainly a reading of Conservative election manifestos in the early 1950s and even a brief consideration of the party's attitude to the developing welfare state does not immediately suggest that state spending had been endorsed enthusiastically. The manifesto for the 1951 election, for example, argued that:

> Our finances have been brought into grave disorder. No British Government in peace time has ever had the power or spent the money in the vast extent and reckless manner of our present rulers. Apart from the two thousand millions they have borrowed or obtained from the United States and the Dominions, they have spent more than 10 million pounds a day, or 22 thousand millions in their six years. No community living in a world of competing nations can possibly afford such frantic extravagances. Devaluation was the offspring of wild, profuse expenditure, and the evils which we suffer to-day are the inevitable progeny of that wanton way of living. A Conservative Government will cut out all unnecessary Government expenditure, simplify the administrative machine, and prune waste and extravagance in every department. (Conservative Party Manifesto, 1951)

This strident tone was softened considerably in later manifestos. Certainly by 1959 the Conservatives, then led by Harold Macmillan, appeared more than happy to boast of their achievements in housing policy, and their success in raising the levels of old-age pensions and social security benefits, while maintaining full employment. Although both pro- and anti-state opinion is discernible in Conservative thinking at this time, testifying to uncertainty in the party, and on occasion within the leadership itself, about the role of the state and what levels of public spending were 'acceptable', the balance tipped in favour of increased spending as the decade progressed. While the ideas of convinced free-marketeers, like Brendan Bracken, Ralph Assheton and Richard Law, continued to have some currency, they found little formal support in the parliamentary party in this period (Charmley, 2008). Indeed, analyses of backbench dissent in the 1950s suggest that the Conservative governing elite enjoyed almost total backbench support up to 1959, after which time the existence of a large Commons majority allowed very small numbers of MPs to vote against the government with greater frequency and without undue risk (Norton, 1990).

More significant was the ambivalence about spending levels and the role of the state displayed within liberal Conservative and leadership circles. Those, like Iain Macleod, Enoch Powell and Keith Joseph, who were associated with the One Nation Group in the 1950s, together with others in the leadership – Macmillan being the most obvious example – struggled to produce a coherent understanding of what the 'extended state' should and should not do. Liberal Conservatives were not persuaded by the redistributive, 'collectivist' state they believed the Labour Party endorsed. And yet, influenced both by the Disraelian tradition of 'Tory Democracy' and the experience of economic depression in the 1930s, they believed that state intervention in social and economic life, and the levels of spending that this entailed, were elements of modern society that Conservatives, however reluctantly, had to embrace.

This 'reluctant' recognition of the state's role perhaps best sums up the 'One Nation' dimension of Conservative thinking. It is certainly clear in the publications of the One Nation Group, which tried to marry a commitment to full employment and welfare with an equal commitment to control public spending. *One Nation: A Tory Approach to Social Problems*, written by Macleod and Maude (1950), argued that it was important to control spending as a percentage of GDP while ensuring that the welfare state was sustained. In this way money could be found for 'tax reductions while retaining sound finance' (Walsha, 2003, p 86). Other publications produced by the One Nation Group – *Change is Our Ally*, written by Enoch Powell and Angus Maude (1954), is a good example – stressed the importance of free-market competition, relaxing financial controls and the sovereignty of the consumer. If the Group's preference for means-tested benefits and 'minimal rather than optimal levels of social provision' (Page, 2010, p 149) is added to the mix, it is possible to see why Walsha can argue that all these issues can 'be identified as the early stirrings of a line of thought which led to Thatcherism' (2003, p 87).

In fact, this verdict benefits somewhat from hindsight. It is more the case, surely, that the MPs associated with the One Nation Group genuinely recognised the potential benefits of state expenditure, but were equally aware of the opportunity costs for taxation, the value of Sterling and free enterprise if spending got out of control. The group returned to these issues in a lesser known One Nation Group pamphlet, *The Responsible Society* (1959), which expressed concerns about rising crime levels and welfare dependency, and argued that pushing public resources too far towards a collectivist state on Labour lines was not the answer. Instead remedies were to be found in the encouragement of 'voluntarism', self-reliance and the 'responsible society'. While there is little sense here of a belief that the free market should be regarded as a near-panacea for all economic and social ills, acceptance of the welfare state was plainly 'conditional' on it not consuming undue amounts of taxpayers' money, or monopolising the delivery of all goods and services. As Keith Joseph commented, 'if [social] services tend to be paid for by contribution and are only part of the pattern of personal, family, voluntary and public help available to the citizen ... there will be no danger from them to the responsible society' (quoted in Walsha, 2003, p 89). This concern about a too-powerful state extended well beyond the One Nation Group and underpinned Conservative preferences for means testing and contributory benefits and services.

Maintaining this balanced approach to the role of the state and public spending proved something of a challenge in the 1950s and early 1960s. Key Conservative figures like Butler and Macmillan, in addition to others like Powell, behaved differently at different times depending on their positions in government and the cut and thrust of electoral politics. Macmillan, for example, despite his much-heralded house-building record in the early 1950s, could be a tough Chancellor. Lowe (1989) has described how he threatened to resign in 1956 if food subsidies were not withdrawn, and also threatened to put 6d on income tax unless equivalent savings were made in public spending. As Prime Minister, Macmillan reverted to a more benign attitude towards public expenditure, best exemplified in his acceptance of the resignations of his entire Treasury team – Chancellor, Peter Thorneycroft, Powell and Nigel Birch – in 1958. A combination of electoral considerations and real disagreement about the impact of the Chancellor's proposed spending cuts, particularly on family allowances, made Macmillan and others in the leadership reluctant to accept the decidedly monetarist strategy that Thorneycroft believed necessary to offset a looming Sterling crisis.

Further evidence of the prevailing ambivalence over the extent of public expenditure is not hard to come by. Butler's approach to economic policy, and particularly his support for the Treasury's ROBOT (an acronym derived from the names of its originators, Leslie Rowan, Sir George Bolton and Otto Clarke) proposals in the early 1950s, is one example. Butler, who was associated with the wartime coalition government's far-reaching reforms to secondary education, has always been regarded as a supporter of public spending. As Chancellor in Churchill's government his continuation of the budgetary policies shaped by the outgoing Labour Chancellor, Hugh Gaitskell, led the press to coin the term 'Butskellism' to denote the similarity of economic approach between the two political parties. However, in 1952 and 1953 Butler avoided deficits even where they were deemed necessary on Keynesian calculations (Rollings, 1996) and did not display 'an overwhelming willingness to sacrifice other policies to employment' (Tomlinson, quoted in Rollings, 1996, p 100). Rollings points out, too, that Butler favoured the Bank of England's recommendations on monetary policy, rather than advice from the Keynesian-dominated Economic Section of the Treasury. His support of ROBOT – a plan to float Sterling and, in effect, to devalue the currency to protect the UK's reserves – is surprising for a supposedly 'Keynesian' Chancellor because the inevitable consequence would have been higher unemployment as imported food and raw material prices increased. In the event, ROBOT was defeated by Churchill, Eden, Macmillan and others in the cabinet, who argued that the risk to full employment was unacceptable (Gilmour and Garnett, 1998). Nevertheless, the episode demonstrates that Conservative approaches to economic management were not always consistent, and also that 'traditional' economic policy alternatives remained influential in a 'Keynesian' environment.

Symbolic of the dilemmas that confronted Conservative governments as they wrestled with the implications of rising public expenditure during the later 1950s was the pensions issue. In 1957 the Macmillan government found itself facing a pensions crisis that arose from Labour's original decision to pay the full value of pensions from the outset of the National Insurance scheme in 1948. As growing numbers of people approached retirement, however, the government recognised that something had to be done to prevent a ballooning National Insurance deficit. Awkwardly for the Conservatives, the Labour Party produced a blueprint for a state-run earnings-related pension scheme that, it was argued, would not only pay for itself over time, but would also make private occupational schemes unnecessary. Even liberal Conservatives like Iain Macleod believed that such an inclusive scheme would extend the state's welfare remit too far. The policy developed by the Minister for Pensions and National Insurance, John Boyd-Carpenter, consequently attempted to 'look both ways' by creating a limited graduated state scheme to supplement the basic state pension and to be paid for by higher contributions, while also guaranteeing the future of occupational pensions by allowing employers to retain their own schemes and opt out of the graduated element of state provision. As the 1958 National Pensions White Paper stated, the key objective of the new scheme was to underpin the finances of the National Insurance system (rather than necessarily to provide adequate pensions in old age, as Labour claimed its proposal would do; see Timmins, 1996, p 196), but it nevertheless allowed the Conservatives to make two important claims. First, pension provision had indeed been increased, but on a contributory basis, which conformed to the belief, stated by the One Nation Group among others, that individuals should pay directly towards their own welfare. Second, the preservation of occupational pension schemes meant that private-sector interests had been protected.

These examples of Conservative thinking and policymaking are inevitably selective. However, they do tell a story of a party that wanted to retain free-market, private-sector solutions while nevertheless recognising both the necessity for, and benefits of, increased public spending. In fact, for all the emphasis on increased spending, TME rose quite slowly from the mid-1950s after a marked fall in defence spending following the end of the Korean War in 1953. But growing commitments to education as baby-boomers entered the system, in addition to rising expectations about the state provision of health care, social security and pensions – all in the context of the political need to maintain full employment – meant that the Conservatives could not easily reduce what were inevitably becoming substantial cumulative demands on the public purse. Crucially, as discussed earlier, had it not been for the relatively benign macro-economic conditions of the later 1950s and early 1960s, the Conservative administrations of the period would have been confronted with considerably tougher choices.

## Rolling back the state? Conservative governments in the 1980s and 1990s

A changed macro-economy was, of course, precisely what faced the incoming Thatcher government in 1979. As discussed earlier and in Chapter 2, with Keynesianism discredited, the control of inflation now the target of economic policy, exchange rates floating and taxation viewed as a disincentive to enterprise, a very different Conservative Party claimed that the state and public spending needed to be 'rolled back'. It is not surprising, then, that the Conservative election manifesto of 1979 began with the following statements:

> To master inflation, proper monetary discipline is essential, with publicly stated targets for the rate of growth of the money supply. At the same time, a gradual reduction in the size of the Government's borrowing requirement is also vital. This Government's price controls have done nothing to prevent inflation, as is proved by the doubling of prices

> since they came to power. All the controls have achieved is
> a loss of jobs and a reduction in consumer choice.
>
> The State takes too much of the nation's income; its share
> must be steadily reduced. When it spends and borrows too
> much, taxes, interest rates, prices and unemployment rise
> so that in the long run there is less wealth with which
> to improve our standard of living and our social services.
> (Conservative Party Manifesto, 1979)

So an all-out assault on the state and public spending levels then?
In some ways yes, but this is not the full picture. If there was clearly
a marked 'adjustment' in attitudes to public spending, there were also
limits to how far an attack on state spending could be taken. As time
progressed, it became clear that electoral and policy 'reality' actually
made significant cuts to overall spending levels difficult to achieve. An
early casualty of this *realpolitik* was the fate of 'monetarism'. Despite
the enthusiasm with which monetarist policies were initially embraced,
dramatically rising unemployment and falling productivity, following
the budgets of 1980 and 1981, saw a retreat from the belief that all
that a government had to do was maintain strict control of inflation
through control of the money supply and let the market do the rest.
The existence of a direct link between inflation and the money supply
was questioned by an all-party Treasury Committee report in 1981, and
even keen monetarists such as John Biffen and John Knott questioned
the wisdom of plans to cut public spending by £5 billion because of
the potential impact on employment.

Even so, there is no doubt that the desire to reduce public spending
was a hallmark of the Thatcher governments and, operating in an
environment broadly conducive to their stated goals, they clearly
had some success in controlling expenditure – at least in certain
instances. Selling off council houses and the nationalised industries
were early examples of 'rolling back the state' and these policies saved
substantial sums on capital investment and depreciation costs, which
fell consistently throughout the period. The pensions system was also
reorganised, with the still-embryonic State Earnings Related Pension
Scheme introduced by Labour being swiftly scrapped and the basic state
pension indexed to prices, not wages – leading one commentator to
argue that 'the Thatcher government succeeded in radically reforming
British pension policy' (Pierson, 1994, p 64). Similarly, efforts were
made to control benefit levels, with John Moore, Secretary of State
for Health and Social Security, deploying US arguments about the
dangers of 'welfare dependency' to justify cuts in housing benefit and

the withdrawal of income support from 16- and 17-year-olds in 1988 (Timmins, 1996, p 449). Meanwhile, Child Benefit was also frozen in 1987 and 1988. Savings were also made in education, Glennerster pointing to a 'quite extraordinary plateau in the volume of resources available to education for two decades' (1998, p 39) – although demographic movements meant that per pupil spending actually rose slightly between the mid-1980s and mid-1990s.

By contrast, these apparent successes were offset by a number of 'structural' factors that made real savings difficult to achieve. The vagaries of Conservative economic management in the 1980s and 1990s contributed to two recessions during which it proved impossible to control spending on unemployment benefit, which tripled between 1979/80 and 1984/85, fell back in the mid-1980s and rose again in the early 1990s. The period also saw a marked increase in those claiming sickness and disability benefits, which rose from £9 billion in 1984/85 to £22 billion a decade later. Reasons for this rise are threefold. First, deteriorating labour market conditions led to increasing numbers of early retirements on grounds of poor health; second, in an effort to keep unemployment figures down, employment offices recommended claimants suffering from ill-health define themselves as incapable of work and thus eligible for sickness benefits; and, third, an ageing population meant that those with caring responsibilities themselves experienced poorer health and claimed benefits accordingly (Evans, 1998). Population ageing also meant that more resources had to be devoted to pensions, where spending increased in real terms from £26.1 billion in 1979/80 to £32.2 billion in 1989/90 and £38.8 billion in 1995/96.

Turning briefly to health, where spending rose in real terms under the Thatcher and Major governments, early optimism about injecting private money into the NHS (through a form of US-style Health Maintenance Organisations) evaporated as it became clear to the Chancellor, Nigel Lawson, and others like the young David Willetts, that the service in fact represented good value for money (Timmins, 1996), and, furthermore, that 'privatising' the NHS would have political costs. The desire to contain spending remained a key objective, of course, not least because the implications of demographic trends for health care and the expense associated with medical and technological advances set cost-effectiveness at a premium. With 'privatisation' and real terms cuts no longer regarded as serious options, Conservative governments in the later 1980s and 1990s turned to ways of reorganising health service provision (and also education to a limited extent). 'Marketisation' – the mimicking of free-market principles within key state services through the creation of 'quasi-markets' – was deemed to be more cost-efficient, although a combination of the costs associated with the bureaucratic apparatus required to administer the new system and government reluctance to pursue the market logic of its own proposals for fear of hospital closures (see Glennerster, 2007b, p 75) make it unclear whether significant savings were actually achieved (Le Grand and Bartlett, 1993; Le Grand and Vizard, 1998).

These examples demonstrate how difficult it is for governments to reduce public spending, however committed they may be to the enterprise, and explain some of the reasons why, in Charmley's (2008, p 224) words, 'the vaunted cuts did not happen' in the Thatcher years. There is one further explanation for the relative failure to achieve substantial cuts in public spending, however, and this concerns the nature of the Conservative Party, and specifically the parliamentary Conservative Party, in the 1980s and 1990s. Unlike their 1950s' predecessors, and despite their apparent domination of the parliamentary party and the cabinet, the Thatcher 'inner circle' could not rely on the unqualified support of Conservative MPs to approve the more radical aspects of their ambitions for spending cuts. Although – perfectly accurately – Gamble (1994), Kavanagh (1987) and others have detected a 'free market, strong state' duality within 'Thatcherism', this division was essentially among Thatcher supporters and did not seriously threaten to disrupt proposals for spending constraints about which all shades of Thatcherite opinion were in agreement (Norton, 1990). More significant was the division between Thatcherites of all shades and One Nation Tory 'wets', like Ian Gilmour, Peter Walker, Francis Pym and Jim Prior. On Norton's calculations, in the mid-1980s there were approximately 72 'Thatcherites' and roughly 67 'wet' or 'damp' MPs who were sceptical about the neo-liberal turn in economic policy and equally sceptical about the Thatcherite interpretation of the 'strong state', believing it to be both over-centralised and too interventionist in matters of individual 'morality' (for example, support for marriage and the traditional family, and anti-liberal measures to 'deter' single parenthood and homosexuality).

The main point, however, is that fully 217 MPs – 58% of the parliamentary Conservative Party – were 'party faithfuls'. These individuals were loyal to the party, first and foremost, and while their support for the leadership could be counted on for the most part, it could not be guaranteed. So, with 'the Thatcherites ... a minority within the party' (Norton, 1990, p 55), the leadership had to trim its wilder ambitions. Where it failed to do this, as with student grant issues in 1984, prospective threats to the NHS in the mid-1980s, the freezing of Child Benefit in 1987 and 1988, and, more significantly, the Poll Tax in 1989, support swiftly drained away. Ultimately, of course, a combination of 'wets', 'damps' and many of the party faithful unseated Thatcher when they became convinced that she had turned from an electoral asset into a liability.

During John Major's time in office, the intra-party environment changed appreciably. If the Thatcherite presence in cabinet was much reduced because key ministers had lost their seats in the 1992 general election and because Major promoted more 'wets', 'damps' and 'party faithfuls' to ministerial posts (Baker et al, 1992), the parliamentary party, conversely, was more 'dry' than its immediate predecessors. This reconfiguration could account for the fact that the Major years saw a continuation of key aspects of the Thatcherite agenda. While the deep recession of the early 1990s saw TME rise rapidly to just under 44% of GDP in 1993/94 before falling back as growth resumed, marketisation and privatisation policies continued to be pursued with fervour, and attracted relatively little overt backbench dissent. The significant fact, however, is that the debate about the role and shape of public spending that had preoccupied the Conservative Party in one way or another for over a generation, was largely displaced by the bitter factionalism within the parliamentary party over Europe (Heppell, 2002; Bale, 2010). While it is true that spending issues were an integral aspect of the argument about the UK's place (if any) in a prospective federal Europe, with sceptics questioning the degree of control UK governments would have over their own budgets, their convictions were grounded less in economic principle than in a visceral nationalism. One outcome of this increasingly febrile environment was that reasoned arguments about economic policy and the role of public spending, of the kind that marked out the One Nation Group publications in the 1950s, or, for that matter, the views advanced by the monetarists in the late 1970s and 1980s, appeared to be in short supply.

## Coda: The Cameron Conservatives – looking to the future

Other chapters in this book consider the state of the Conservatives under David Cameron, so this concluding section will do no more than note a few key points about the contemporary Conservative Party and its likely attitude towards public spending.

On the surface, certainly prior to the 2010 general election, and as noted in Chapter 1, 'Team Cameron' adopted a more ameliorative approach towards poverty and social injustice than their Majorite or

Thatcherite predecessors. Pronouncements from Cameron himself (2009a) suggested that he perceived New Labour as failing to reduce poverty and tackle associated social ills such as crime, poor education and welfare dependency. However, these failings are ascribed to the use of too much state action and the evidence to date suggests that the new government does not regard public spending per se as a necessary vehicle for the amelioration of social ills. According to Cameron, while 'we must use the state to remake society' (2009a, p 1) it would be a mistake to assume that increasing amounts of public spending are required for this purpose. Rather, it is the voluntary sector, neighbourhood empowerment and private social enterprise – the core components of the 'Big Society' – that are regarded as the key drivers of change. If there is a role for the state, it is as an 'enforcer' of social and economic discipline, an institution that ensures that all those who can work do so and that those able to contribute to society and community, but who do not, are suitably penalised.

As noted elsewhere in this book, much of the thinking behind this view of the state stems from work carried out by Iain Duncan Smith and others associated with the Centre for Social Justice (Social Justice Policy Group, 2006, 2007). Flowing from a much-disputed (see Lister and Bennett, 2010) analysis of the 'broken society' that appears to owe a good deal to older versions of the 'underclass' thesis associated with US neo-liberals such as Charles Murray (Prideaux, 2010), 'breakdown' is attributed to worklessness and economic dependency, family breakdown, addictions, education failure and indebtedness, each of which leads to poverty (Page, 2010). However, if as those such as David Willetts suggest, solutions to this state of affairs are to be found not in New Labour's reliance on the state and public spending, but on the voluntary efforts of citizens themselves, there does not on the face of it appear to be any *coherent* means by which efforts to mend the broken society can be coordinated. If the main role of the state is (somehow) to 'unlock the civic potential within society' (Page, 2010, p 155), how this objective is to be achieved is as yet unclear. The situation is not made any better by the fact that the Conservative Party under Cameron is no more – and is possibly less – a united party than its 20th-century predecessor. Evans (2008) charted the range of ideological positions that existed within the ranks of Tory MPs immediately prior to the 2010 general election and concluded that there remained a distinct appetite among Conservative MPs (such as the Cornerstone Group) for the Thatcherite agenda of tax cuts, continued marketisation and downward pressure on public spending (see also Dorey, 2009). If the new generation of Conservative MPs elected in May 2010 displays a similar predilection for these goals, Cameron is likely to find it difficult to ignore them – and recent history over the 'grammar schools incident' has shown that he and his allies are more than capable of 'trimming' where necessary (Evans, 2008, p 301).

The preceding discussion notwithstanding, the most obvious and crucial challenge to the incoming Coalition government is the current economic crisis. How the Coalition deals with the inevitably difficult budgetary issues will provide an indication of the true intent behind earlier Conservative statements about poverty reduction, disadvantage and social justice. Up to the autumn of 2010, the signs were not good. A brief account of the key measures announced to date (as also highlighted in other chapters) indicates that, despite protestations of wanting to be 'fair', the government is setting to the task of cutting public spending with a will. Spending reductions, as opposed to progressive tax rises, made up much the greater proportion of money-raising/saving policies being considered by the Treasury, despite the fact that taxation is a swifter and more efficient way of generating income. In particular, the proposed reduction of £17.5 billion from the welfare bill proposed in the Emergency Budget and October 2010 Spending Review looked draconian and cuts in public sector pension provision risked damaging the retirement prospects of those who are already on low salaries.

On present evidence then, there is nothing to suggest that the Conservative Party – even in coalition with the Liberal Democrats – has changed its historic scepticism towards public spending. Indeed, it is quite possible that the apparent success with which the Coalition government managed to transform what was originally a private-sector banking crisis into a crisis of the public sector means that the way has been cleared for a sustained assault on public spending. Even so, as this chapter has demonstrated, political ambition and the demands of ideology have rarely matched political and economic 'reality' in the history of the Conservative attitudes to public expenditure – so there remains much to play for. After all, the economic and political costs of pursuing far-reaching reductions can be high, and the structural impediments involved are little short of immense.

# FOUR

# The Conservatives, social policy and public opinion

*Andrew Defty*

In an article published shortly before the 2010 general election, Bochel and Defty (2010) observed that if Cameron was to succeed where several of his predecessors had failed, this would represent a marked shift in public attitudes towards the Conservative Party. It might also, they added, indicate a significant shift in public attitudes towards the role of the state. The uncertain outcome of the 2010 election suggests that Cameron's success in changing public perceptions of the Conservative Party is far from clear, and also raises questions about the degree of public support for significant reform of the role of the state.

This chapter examines public attitudes towards social policy in the light of the 2010 general election. The first section draws on data from *British Social Attitudes* surveys to assess whether what some have identified as a rightward shift in public attitudes may have created a climate of opinion in which the election of a Conservative government became more likely. It then draws upon more recent public opinion data to assess public attitudes towards Conservative policies in the run-up to and following the 2010 general election.

## A climate for change? Public attitudes towards welfare and the role of the state

Surveys of public opinion such as the annual *British Social Attitudes* survey, which began in 1983, suggest that since 1997 there has been a change in public attitudes towards the role of the state. A number of studies have identified a decline in public support for state provision and the redistribution of wealth, and a hardening of public attitudes towards welfare recipients in particular (Sefton, 2005; Taylor-Gooby and Martin, 2008; Curtice, 2010a). This has led some to suggest that the public's attitudes have become more closely aligned with Conservative policies than in the recent past, and may have made the election of a Conservative government in 2010 more likely. Most notably, in a series of articles in the run-up to the 2010 general election, John Curtice

(2010b, p 328) predicted that 'the 2010 election campaign will be fought against a very different climate of public opinion from that which prevailed when Labour first came to power in 1997', and that, as a result, 'the public may now be inclined to give a relatively warm reception to a traditional Conservative message of less government and less tax' (Curtice, 2009, p 179).

Central to Curtice's observations about Conservative electoral prospects was a marked shift in public attitudes towards tax and spend. This question, which has been a constant feature of *British Social Attitudes* surveys since they began, offers perhaps the most significant indication of a shift in public attitudes under Labour (see Figure 4.1). The proportion of people supporting an increase in state spending, even if this meant an increase in taxation, began to rise steeply in the 1980s, from around a third to over half, where it remained until midway through Labour's second term. Support for tax-funded increases in provision began to fall consistently from 2003; 2004 was the first year since 1986 when fewer than half of respondents supported the idea of increases in taxes and spending; and 2008 was the first time since the original survey in 1983 that over half of respondents supported keeping taxes and spending at the same level as they were at the present time.

Curtice explains this in terms of the public responding like a thermostat to the rise and fall of public expenditure. Thus, public demands for increases in expenditure rise as government spending falls, and, conversely, when public expenditure rises these demands are eventually satisfied and support for further increases begin to drop

**Figure 4.1: Attitudes towards taxation and public spending, 1983–2009 (percentages)**

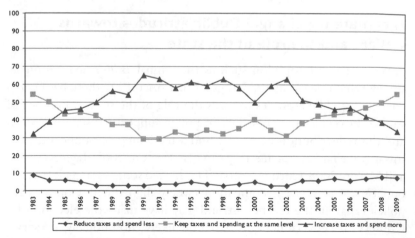

*Source:* Curtice (2009); Park et al (2010b).

off. This, he suggests, explains the rise and fall in support pictured in Figure 4.1. Support for increased expenditure rose in the 1980s as the Conservatives cut spending, at least on some areas (see Chapter 3), and then when public spending began to increase following Labour's election, the public gradually became more satisfied and support for increased spending began to fall, with the result, Curtice argues, that 'now, the balance of public preferences is almost identical to what it had been during the heyday of Thatcherism' (Curtice, 2010b, p 328).

It is not just attitudes towards tax and spend that have shifted under Labour. A number of other indicators suggest that public opinion moved to the right under Labour. When identifying their priority for extra government spending, while health and education have consistently attracted the largest proportion of public support, those claiming that these areas would be their highest priority for extra government spending in both cases fell under Labour: in the case of education from a peak of 34% in 1999 to 26% in 2008; and in the case of health from 55% in 2000 to 45% in 2008. In contrast, support for increased spending in other areas rose, most notably those who claimed that defence was their highest priority for extra spending rose from 1% in 1999 to 4% in 2008, and support for extra spending on police and prisons from 3% in 1999 to 8% by 2008 (Jowell et al, 2000, Park et al, 2010).

Looking in particular at attitudes towards spending on social welfare, although spending on benefits for unemployed people has consistently attracted less support than benefits for children, retired people and disabled people, the proportion expressing support for extra spending on the unemployed fell from 11% in 1996, the last time the question was asked under the Conservatives, to 2% in 2007, the last time the question was asked under a Labour government (Park et al, 2009). Interestingly, support for single parents, who were seen as less deserving under the Conservatives, increased under Labour, with the result that unemployed people were the group perceived as the least deserving of extra government spending. Perhaps a more significant indicator of a hardening of public attitudes towards welfare recipients is illustrated by people's responses to the question of whether they think benefits for the unemployed are too low and cause hardship, or whether they think benefits are too high and discourage people from finding jobs (Table 4.1). The proportion of those who thought benefits were too low and cause hardship rose from 46% in 1983, and was consistently over 50% from 1987 to 1995. Although support for this position had begun to fall by the time Labour was elected, it fell from 46% in 1997 to 21% in 2008. In contrast, the proportion of respondents who felt that benefits were too high and discouraged work, rose under Labour from 47% in 1998 to 61% in 2008.

**Table 4.1: Attitudes towards benefits recipients, 1998–2008 (percentages)**

| Benefits for the unemployed are | 1998 | 1999 | 2000 | 2001 | 2002 | 2003 | 2004 | 2005 | 2006 | 2007 | 2008 |
|---|---|---|---|---|---|---|---|---|---|---|---|
| ... too low and cause hardship | 29 | 32 | 40 | 37 | 29 | 34 | 23 | 26 | 23 | 26 | 21 |
| ... too high and discourage people from finding jobs | 47 | 42 | 36 | 38 | 47 | 40 | 54 | 50 | 54 | 54 | 61 |

Source: *British Social Attitudes*, 16th–25th Reports (Jowell et al, 1999, 2000; Park et al, 2001, 2002, 2003, 2004, 2005, 2007, 2008, 2009, 2010a, 2010b)

A number of studies have sought to offer explanations for these changes in public attitudes. By adopting the thermostat metaphor, Curtice (2010b) has pointed to a link between public expenditure and public support for state provision, noting that as spending increased under Labour the public became more satisfied and support for extra provision declined. Others have pointed to a link between broader economic conditions and public attitudes towards welfare recipients. Drawing on *British Social Attitudes* data, Taylor-Gooby and Martin (2008), for example, have shown that people's support for state intervention may be linked to their perception of overall economic conditions. Consequently, the drop in support for unemployed people coincided with an increase in the proportion of people who perceived poverty to be at a lower level now than in the recent past, and also an increase in the proportion of people who describe their own living standards as being 'comfortable'. As a result, while public perceptions about the number of people living in poverty have declined, sympathy for those who still remain in need has also fallen, so that in more recent surveys a larger proportion of respondents attribute individuals' poverty to a lack of willpower or laziness (27% in 2006, compared to 19% in 1986), and fewer people believe it is a consequence of injustice in society (21% in 2006, compared with 25% in 1986). In this case the relative levels of support for benefits for unemployed people may have less to do with the level of state support than the perception that some individuals are unlikely to be responsive to state intervention. In short, in times of economic growth and low unemployment people may be more likely to think that unemployment can be avoided and are therefore less supportive of state support for those who are not working, whereas in times of economic recession the perception may be that people are more likely to find themselves in need as a result of forces beyond their control, and are therefore more deserving of state support.

There is strong support for these explanations of the link between economic conditions and public support for state welfare provision, including comparative data from beyond the UK (for example, Blekesaune, 2007). However, establishing a link between attitudes towards state provision and support for political parties is somewhat more problematic. These explanations may suggest that support for political parties is largely determined by economic conditions or at least people's perceptions of economic conditions, a view that is widely embraced in the media and to some extent by political parties themselves. According to this view, Conservative governments are likely to be elected at the end of a period of economic growth in which public spending has outstripped demand and perceptions about the real levels of poverty are in decline. Then, after a sustained period of cuts, the public will rediscover their enthusiasm for state intervention, demand an increase in public expenditure and elect a Labour government.

This thesis, however, is problematic for a number of reasons. First, it assumes a more wide-ranging and in some cases dramatic shift in public opinion than can be supported by the evidence. It is also the case that while public attitudes have changed, particularly in the last decade, the positions of the political parties have also changed, so that an apparent shift to the right in public opinion may not necessarily result an increase in support for Conservative policies. While there is strong evidence for a decline in support for tax-funded increases in state provision and a hardening of public attitudes towards welfare recipients under Labour, in order to argue that this shift in public attitudes has created a climate of opinion favourable to Conservative policies one would also expect to find some element of support for significant retrenchment in state provision. However, evidence from *British Social Attitudes* surveys suggests there is little support for substantive cuts in public services, and in some areas support for state provision actually increased under Labour. For example, while support for tax and spend has declined significantly since 1997, support for cuts in taxes and public spending, while increasing from 3% in 1998 to 8% in 2008, remains at a low level relative to the alternatives of increasing taxes and spending, or keeping them at the same level. Moreover, in the absence of support for cuts to tax and spending, the high levels of support for keeping taxes and spending at the same level in the most recent surveys could be viewed as expressing support for, or at least recognition of, Labour's policies, which have involved significant increases in investment in mass public services such as health and education.

In addition while there has undoubtedly been a decline in support for spending on benefits for unemployed people, this is not indicative of a broader decline in support for public spending on social benefits. *British Social Attitudes* surveys suggest, instead, a consistent high level of support for state provision in a range of sectors, and in some cases this has increased under Labour. Between 1998 and 2008 participants were asked if they would like to see more, less or the same level of spending on social security benefits for a range of different groups. They were asked to bear in mind that an increase in spending would probably mean they would have to pay more taxes and that less spending would probably mean paying less tax. The results (Table 4.2) support the view that there has been a decline in support for spending on benefits for the unemployed. In 1998 less than a quarter of respondents favoured an increase in spending on benefits for the unemployed, and this had dropped to around one in seven by 2008. However, only in the case of benefits for unemployed people and for single parents did less than 60% of respondents support an increase in spending throughout the period. Moreover, support for increased spending on single parents, retired people and those caring for sick or disabled people, actually increased between 1998 and 2008. Throughout the period, only in the case of benefits for the unemployed and for single parents did a larger proportion of people support spending 'about the same as now'

**Table 4.2: Support for an increase in spending on social security benefits for particular groups, 1998–2008 (percentages)**

|  | 1998 | 1999 | 2002 | 2004 | 2006 | 2008 |
|---|---|---|---|---|---|---|
| Unemployed people | 21.7 | 24.1 | 21.0 | 15.0 | 15.7 | 14.2 |
| Disabled people | 72.0 | 72.2 | 69.2 | 63.0 | 61.8 | 60.7 |
| Parents who work on a low income | 68.3 | 68.9 | 69.5 | 62.5 | 66.0 | 67.5 |
| Single parents | 33.6 | 32.9 | 38.8 | 34.7 | 37.8 | 36.8 |
| Retired people | 70.9 | 70.4 | 72.7 | 72.6 | 72.2 | 72.1 |
| People who care for sick and disabled | 81.5 | 82.2 | 81.6 | 80.5 | 81.8 | 83.1 |

Source: *British Social Attitudes*, 16th–25th Reports (Jowell et al, 1999, 2000; Park et al, 2003, 2005, 2007, 2009)

than those advocating increased spending, and only in the case of spending on the unemployed did more people support spending cuts than increased spending.

Data from surveys such as these, therefore, suggest that public support for spending restraint, and especially cuts, is limited to particular groups, and there remains a high level of public support for state provision, which may call into question the level of support for a more widespread rolling back of the state. This is supported by other data, which indicate that the public remains largely wedded to the idea of state provision in a range of sectors. Public support for a broad range of state provision remained largely stable under Labour (see Table 4.3). When asked whether provision in a range of areas was mainly the responsibility of the government, the person's employer or individuals and their families, a consistently high proportion have responded that it is mainly the government's responsibility to pay for health care for the sick, ensure that long-term sick and disabled people have enough to live on, and provide for the unemployed. Only in the case of providing enough support for individuals to live on in retirement was public support below 80%, although a majority still favoured state support in this area. Even taking into account a relative lack of support for state retirement provision, and declining support for government spending on some social benefits, it is apparent that a large proportion of the public nevertheless feel that welfare provision is mainly the responsibility of the government. This may call into question the level of likely support

**Table 4.3: Public attitudes to state versus personal responsibility, 1998–2008 (percentages)**

| % saying that responsibility should be | 1998 | | | | 2003 | | | | 2008 | | | |
|---|---|---|---|---|---|---|---|---|---|---|---|---|
| | Health | Retirement | Sickness | Unemployment | Health | Retirement | Sickness | Unemployment | Health | Retirement | Sickness | Unemployment |
| ... mainly the government | 82 | 56 | 80 | 85 | 83 | 58 | 82 | 81 | 86 | 58 | 83 | n/a |
| ... mainly the person's employer | 9 | 9 | 9 | 3 | 7 | 11 | 8 | 3 | 7 | 10 | 8 | n/a |
| ... mainly the person and their family | 6 | 33 | 10 | 10 | 8 | 29 | 7 | 14 | 5 | 30 | 7 | n/a |

Source: Jowell et al (1999) and Park et al (2004, 2010).

for the Conservative idea of the 'Big Society', to the extent that it would involve rolling back the state and more particularly shifting responsibility for provision onto other providers including individuals themselves (see also Chapter 14).

Responses to more specific questions about public services being provided by a range of other providers raises further questions about the extent of potential support for Conservative policies designed to shift responsibility for provision beyond the state. Data from Ipsos MORI suggest that under Labour more than two thirds of the public believed that public services should be run by the government or local authorities rather than private companies, and that there has been a slight increase in support for state provision since 2000 (Ipsos MORI, 2008; see also Table 4.4). In particular the public remain sceptical about the ability of the private sector to provide the level of support currently provided by the state. In 2004, *British Social Attitudes* asked whether private companies would be better at running services like health and education. While 55% thought private companies would definitely or probably be able to run services more cost-effectively, and 51% thought they would provide a better quality of service, 73% thought the government would definitely or probably be better at ensuring that services go to people who need them most (Park et al, 2005). More recently, the 2007 *British Social Attitudes* survey asked whether people supported private companies running schools and hospitals and providing personal care for old people. In the case of schools and hospitals, almost three times as many people were opposed to the private sector as those who supported such a move, and in the case of personal care, where the division was much closer, 43% were opposed compared to 31% who supported private provision (Park et al, 2009).

While the public remains sceptical about the private sector, they are, perhaps significantly, much more ambivalent about whether services should be provided by the charitable or 'not-for-profit' sector. In 2007, the *British Social Attitudes* survey asked a range of questions about people's attitudes towards charities or 'not-for-profit' organisations providing services currently provided by the state. In response, 36% were supportive and 33% opposed to such organisations running schools, 36% supported and 37% opposed their running hospitals, and 53% supported and only 21% opposed their role in providing personal care for older people (Curtice and Heath, 2009). This does suggest that there may be some degree of support for Conservative policies designed to expand the role of the voluntary or third sector in the provision of services in a range of areas. Moreover, it is notable that in each case more than one in five respondents said they neither supported nor opposed the role of the private or the charitable sectors, suggesting that there is scope for building public support for a wider range of service providers, although the government would appear to need to go considerably further to change opinions about the relative merits of the private sector.

**Table 4.4: Support for state versus private provision (percentages)**

| To what extent do you agree or disagree that, in principle, public services should be run by the government or local authorities, rather than by private companies: | 2000 | 2001 | 2008 |
|---|---|---|---|
| Strongly agree | 27 | 45 | 50 |
| Tend to agree | 39 | 33 | 29 |
| Neither agree nor disagree | 14 | 10 | 6 |
| Tend to disagree | 14 | 6 | 9 |
| Strongly disagree | 3 | 3 | 5 |
| Don't know | 4 | 3 | 2 |
| | | | |
| Agree | 66 | 78 | 79 |
| Disagree | 17 | 9 | 14 |

Source: Ipsos MORI (2008).

## Responding to change: public responses to Conservative policies and Coalition government

The analysis presented so far is based on data collected prior to the financial crisis that emerged in late 2008. More recent polling data allows a more focused analysis of public attitudes towards the Conservative response to that crisis, and approaches towards social policy in particular.

The outcome of the 2010 general election suggested that the public remained to be convinced that the Conservatives were yet ready for government. Cameron's attempts to broaden the appeal of the party had arguably met with only limited success. The Conservatives had been ahead of Labour in the opinion polls almost continuously since the 2005 general election, with the exception of a short period following the election of Gordon Brown as Labour leader. However, that lead began to fall as the election approached, and rarely reached double figures during 2010. Ultimately the Conservative share of the vote rose by less than 6% between the 1997 and 2010 general elections, from a post-war low of 30.7% to 36.1%. Cameron attracted a smaller share of the vote than any previous incoming Conservative Prime Minister, although it was slightly higher than the 35% won by Blair in 2005. The Conservatives' coalition partners, the Liberal Democrats, enjoyed a remarkable bounce in the opinion polls during the election campaign, widely attributed to their leader's appearance in the televised debates. However, in the general election they managed to increase their share of the vote by only 1%, and actually won fewer seats than in 2005. Opinion polls in the months following the election indicated that support for the Conservatives increased, rising to around 41% by mid-September 2010. However, support for Labour also increased following the election, with the result that the Conservative lead had narrowed to between two and three points by mid-September. In contrast support for the Liberal Democrats fell back after the general election to the kind of level, in the mid-teens, they were at prior to the general election campaign (UK Polling Report, 2010).

In the months following the election there was some evidence of public support for the Coalition government's proposals for cutting the deficit, including an increase in support for spending cuts. This appeared to be in part a response to growing public pessimism about the state of the economy, while there is evidence that the public actually became more optimistic about the economy in the run-up to the general election. Ipsos MORI's economic optimism index is calculated by measuring those who are optimistic about the economy minus those who are pessimistic. This rose from +6 and +7 in February and March 2010 to +15 in April. Although this index had already begun to fall by the time of the election, falling to +10 by the time of the May poll, by June 2010 it had fallen to −5 with 40% of those polled thinking that the economic condition of the country would get worse compared to only 35% who thought it would get better (Ipsos MORI, 2010c, 2010d, 2010f).

This decline in optimism about the economy may, in part, be explained by a series of statements by Coalition ministers that the economic situation was much worse than they had expected prior to the election. In particular, in a speech delivered two weeks before the Coalition's first budget in June 2010, the Prime Minister stated that 'now that we have had a chance to look at what has really been going on' it was clear that the scale of the national debt was 'staggering', and 'because the legacy we have been left is so bad, the measures to deal with it will be unavoidably tough' (Cameron, 2010a). If, as was widely reported, such statements were deliberately designed to soften the public up for significant cuts in public spending in the forthcoming budget, polling data clearly indicate why this may have been necessary. Prior to the election the public was deeply divided about the need for cuts. In March 2010, Ipsos MORI reported that 49% of those polled agreed that there was a 'real need to cut spending on public services' while 45% disagreed, although acceptance of the need for cuts had risen since June 2009 when only 40% supported them. However, there was little support for substantive cuts to provision with 64% expressing the view that 'efficiencies' in public services would be enough to reduce the national debt (Ipsos MORI, 2010c). In a poll published on the eve of the budget, 58% agreed that 'there is a real need to cut spending on public services in order to pay off the very high national debt we now have', although 59% still believed that this could be achieved through efficiency savings (Ipsos MORI, 2010f).

On 22 June 2010 the Coalition government announced its 'emergency budget'. Specific measures included a public-sector pay freeze, an increase in VAT from 17.5% to 20%, a cap on housing benefit, a three-year freeze of Child Benefit, and the abolition of Child Trust Funds. The Comprehensive Spending Review which followed in October 2010 included an additional £7 billion of cuts to welfare spending on top of the £11 billion already announced, including removing Child Benefit from higher-rate taxpayers, cuts to Council Tax Benefit and Housing Benefits, and measures designed to cap payments such as time limits to Employment and Support Allowance (which replaced Incapacity Benefit), and an overall cap on benefits per family.

However, there was evidence of public concern about the speed and depth of cuts under the Coalition government. In June 2010, prior to the budget only 25% supported the statement that 'it is important to cut spending quickly even if this means immediate job losses, because it will be better for the economy in the long term', whereas 69% supported the view that 'it is better to cut spending more slowly to reduce the impact on public services and the economy' (Ipsos MORI, 2010f). Attitudes appear to have shifted somewhat following the budget, when 44% supported the view that 'the deficit needs to be cut quickly, starting this year', compared to 35% who believed the national debt 'should not be cut so soon as reducing spending may stop recovery' (Ipsos MORI, 2010g), although the wording of the post-budget poll emphasised that rapid cuts were a response to the 'national debt which is the greatest threat to the economy', rather than stressing the consequences in terms of 'job losses' as in the earlier question. Moreover, a Populus poll for *The Times*, undertaken in September 2010, suggested sustained public concern about the speed and depth of cuts. Participants were asked which deficit reduction plan they supported, without revealing which party advocated that position. Only 22% of those polled supported the Coalition's plan for dealing with the deficit by the time of the next general election. Over a third of voters (37%) supported Labour's position of halving the deficit by the time of the next general election and dealing with it over the next 10 years. The same number said that protecting the vulnerable and keeping unemployment as low as possible should be a bigger priority than cutting the deficit (Coates and Watson, 2010).

There is also some public scepticism about where the government has targeted its cuts. While the Coalition government appears to have convinced a large proportion of the public of the need for some cuts in public services, there is little evidence of support for sweeping cuts in all services, and a clear desire for targeting cuts at those most able to afford them. In a poll undertaken before the budget only one in five supported cuts to all services, while three quarters felt that the government should 'protect services for people who most need help, even if this means that other people are harder hit by tax rises' (Ipsos MORI, 2010f). This was to some extent reflected in people's priorities for cuts. Almost three quarters (74%) said that the government should cut universal benefits for the well off, such as Child Benefit, 68% supported ending tax credits for families earning over £50,000 a year, and 42% said that Child Trust Funds should only go to children from the poorest families (Ipsos MORI, 2010e, 2010f). Nearly two thirds (62%) said that the government should not cut front-line services, and 63% opposed an increase in VAT. The public were divided on the question of whether public-sector pay should be frozen, with 55% supporting a one-year freeze, and 40% opposed to such a move. Similarly, 55% thought the retirement age should be raised by one year, while 42% opposed this (Ipsos MORI, 2010f).

A further poll taken after the budget suggested that the public were divided about many of the proposed cuts. Only 32% supported the increase in VAT, while 59% were opposed, and 42% supported raising the state pension age to 65, while 48% were opposed to this. There was less support (59%) for the three-year freeze on Child Benefit, which would affect all recipients, than the support in the earlier poll for making such benefits means-tested (Ipsos MORI, 2010g).

Although polling data following both the election and the emergency budget suggested that there was a growing public acceptance of the need to tackle the deficit, and an acceptance that this would mean cuts to public services, the public nevertheless remained divided in its support for the government's approach, its long-term intentions and whether it is likely to be effective. There is a considerable disparity between what the public wants and what they expect the government will do, with a large proportion of the public appearing to believe that cuts will be more sweeping than they are prepared to support and will disproportionately affect those who are less well off. In a poll undertaken before the budget, only 33% of the public supported cuts to front-line public services, but 81% expected that the government would make such cuts. Similarly, while only 35% supported a rise in VAT, 84% expected the government to announce such a rise (Ipsos MORI, 2010f). Following the budget, 45% supported the view that the budget would 'make the rich richer and the poor poorer', and 42% felt the government had not made the right decisions about which public services would face spending cuts, compared to only 32% who felt they had. Moreover, there are significant differences of opinion about whether the government's policies are likely to be effective in cutting the deficit. Only 43% thought the budget would help to get the economy going, while 30% thought it would not. The proportion who felt the government's policies would improve the state of the economy fell from 61% in the week prior to the budget to 50% after the budget (Ipsos MORI, 2010g).

There was also, perhaps, greater scepticism about the Conservatives' broader policy agenda, which to some extent supports the data from the *British Social Attitudes* survey, which indicated consistent and relatively high levels of public support for state provision. In particular there appeared to be little public understanding or appetite for the notion of the 'Big Society'. In a poll taken shortly after the election, 57% of those polled said they did not remember hearing anything about the 'Big Society', and of those who could, 36% said they knew little about it and a further 33% said they knew nothing (Ipsos MORI, 2010e).

Looking more broadly at public attitudes towards the role of the state, there is little clear evidence for broad public support either for a smaller state or for greater public involvement, both of which are central to the vision of the 'Big Society' and have featured strongly in Cameron's speeches both before and since the election. There is some evidence of support for a smaller state, although the public is deeply divided about this. In a poll undertaken in March 2010 a large proportion (64%) agreed that the government and public services had tried to do too much in recent years and that people should take more responsibility for their own lives. However, half also said that they were worried that government and public services would do little to help people in the years ahead. Similarly Ipsos MORI found that while around half of those polled would like the state to encourage individuals to look after themselves and allow people to 'make and keep as much money as they can', a similar proportion remain wedded to the idea of a large state, which not only provides a range of services, but also works towards countering inequalities (see Table 4.5).

**Table 4.5: Divided views about the ideal society, 2009 (percentages)**

| People have different views about the ideal society. For each of these statements, please tell me which one comes closest to your ideal: | |
| --- | --- |
| A society which emphasises the social and collective provision of welfare | 48 |
| A society where individuals are encouraged to look after themselves | 46 |
| A society which emphasises similar incomes and rewards for everyone | 48 |
| A society which allows people to make and keep as much money as they can | 46 |

Source: Ipsos MORI (2010b).

Data on attitudes towards greater involvement in public services are somewhat less equivocal. The notion of individual involvement in the delivery of services, and in particular the devolution of more control to a local level, were central features of the 'Big Society' and the Conservative election manifesto, *Invitation to Join the Government of Britain* (Conservative Party, 2010e). However, Ipsos MORI found that while most people supported the principle of greater involvement in the delivery of services and more local control, many fewer said they were personally interested in getting involved in their local community. When polled, only 4% claimed that they were already involved in local services, and when asked if they would personally like to be more involved, only 5% wanted to be actively involved, 24% wanted more of a say and 47% just wanted more information about services. Similarly, apparent public support for greater local control over services such as policing and schools must be balanced against a strong public belief that 'standards of public services should be the same everywhere in Britain' (Ipsos MORI, 2010b).

## Conclusions

There is some evidence to support the view that there was a significant movement in public attitudes towards social policy under Labour. There was a decline in support for tax and spend, and evidence for a hardening of public attitudes towards benefits recipients. Curtice (2009) argues that in shifting public attitudes to the right, Blair achieved something that Thatcher had failed to do throughout the 1980s. However, evidence for a wholesale shift to the right in public attitudes is far from clear. While public support for state provision did decline in some areas, support for state provision remained strong and even increased in other areas, most notably in support for the mass public services such as health and education. Moreover, it is also far from clear that the Conservatives have been the principal beneficiaries of this shift in public attitudes. If, as Curtice suggests, Blair achieved something that Thatcher failed to do by shifting public attitudes to the right, he achieved this at the same time as effecting a similar shift in Labour Party policy away from a broad commitment to universal provision and towards a more selective targeted approach to state provision. Moreover, those groups and services targeted for support under Labour, families with children, schools and the NHS, are precisely those areas that continue to enjoy the highest levels of public support. The hardening of public attitudes towards the unemployed also to some extent reflects the policies of the Labour governments since 1997. This view is supported by the work of Taylor-Gooby (2004) and others (Curtice and Fisher, 2003), which suggests that the shift in public attitudes is most evident among those on the left of the political spectrum. In short, public attitudes have not so much moved towards the Conservatives, rather Labour has moved and to some extent taken its supporters with it.

At the same time, it would be wrong to exaggerate this rightward shift in public attitudes. There is still evidence for a strong and enduring public commitment to state provision in a range of sectors, which calls into question the extent of potential support for Conservative policies designed to roll back state provision. While there is some evidence for a growing public acceptance of the need for cuts to public services, the public appear yet to be convinced that the depth and breadth of cuts proposed by the Coalition government are necessary. Up to the general election, a large proportion of the public clearly felt that the necessary cuts could be achieved by efficiency savings. Following the election, while there has been an acceptance of the need for substantive cuts to provision, much of the public would rather see this directed at those who are better off, favouring cuts to Child Benefit, Child Tax Credits and Child Trust Funds for more well-off families, over policies that are likely to affect those in most need such as the freezing of child benefits, the wholesale abolition of tax credits and Child Trust Funds, and an increase in VAT. Public commitment to state provision may also undermine support for policies related to the notion of the

'Big Society'. While there may yet be little understanding of what this means, there is little public appetite for an expansion of private-sector provision, and there are deep divisions over the delivery of services by other organisations in the voluntary and third sector.

# FIVE

# Conservative health policy: change, continuity and policy influence

*Rob Baggott*

Health policy has long been regarded as a core Labour issue and this has been especially so since the 1980s. The Conservative Party has faced an uphill task in persuading voters and NHS staff of the merits of its policies. This would scarcely matter if health and health care were minor issues. However, between 1995 and 2007 opinion polls identified health care as one of the top issues for voters. It was the most prominent issue for most of this period, with between half and three quarters of people stating that health care was very important in helping them decide which party to vote for (see, for example, www.ipsos-mori.com). Furthermore, health has often been an issue of contention between the parties, frequently being described as a 'political football'. Individual cases of alleged health service shortcomings, such as those of David Barber, Mavis Skeet, Margaret Dixon and Rose Addis, have exploded into legendary party political battles. Health has been prominent at election time, particularly since the late 1980s, as exemplified by the War of Jennifer's Ear in 1992 and Tony Blair's call on the eve of the 1997 election of '24 hours to save the NHS'. Furthermore, health care has been an increasingly salient issue for governments since the late 1980s, as reflected in the increasing proportion of the content of Queen's Speeches devoted to it (Hobolt and Klemmemsen, 2005).

Weakness on such a vital issue presented the Conservatives with a significant problem, creating pressures for policy change. This chapter explores these pressures and how they shaped current party policy and, following the formation of the coalition with the Liberal Democrats, government policy. It begins by discussing theories of party politics that have some utility in explaining policy change and continuity. It then explores policy developments between 1997 and 2005, followed by an analysis of health policy under David Cameron's leadership of the party. The final section explores possible future directions in policy under the Conservative–Liberal Democrat Coalition.

## Theories of party politics

Within the vast literature on party politics (Montero and Gunther, 2003) lie two main bodies of theory that may further our understanding of the changes and continuities in Conservative health policy. The first concerns the adoption of policy positions by parties. It includes rational choice theories, which conceive parties as positioning themselves on an ideological continuum to maximise public votes and gain office (Downs, 1957). More recently, this approach has been superseded by 'soft rational' approaches (see Strom, 1990), which acknowledge the constraints on rational choice and party competition, such as the 'pull' of activists' views and the impact of electoral and parliamentary systems. There is also acknowledgement of political strategy, which incorporates expectations about future election results. For example, parties move to the centre if election results are likely to be close, but are less likely to compromise on ideology if they have little chance of winning (Robertson, 1976). Past election results, however, do not seem have much effect on ideological positions (Adams et al, 2004).

Parties also follow public opinion to some extent (Bara and Budge, 2001; Hobolt and Klemmemsen, 2005), being more likely to respond to public opinion when it is shifting away from them (Adams et al, 2004). Increasingly, party competition in the UK is characterised by 'issue competition' about what issues should be on the party-political agenda, rather than on ideological positions (Green-Pedersen, 2007). As ideology has become less prominent, voting behaviour depends more on perceptions of the competence of parties to govern and deliver solutions to problems (Green, 2007). Party policies tend to converge as they compete for the public vote, and they are less influenced by activists and core supporters (Bara and Budge, 2001). Parties may even adopt competitors' policies in order to increase their attractiveness to voters (Webb, 2000). This goes against the conventional wisdom that parties will seek to avoid issues where there is consensus and focus on issues where their policies are dominant (that is, where their policies are both different from other parties and are more popular) (see Riker, 1996).

The second set of theories explores the impact of changes in party government on government policy. According to some, parties have a major impact. Crossman (1972), for example, characterised parties as the 'battering rams of change'. Others have also identified party policy as a major determinant of government policy, especially in majoritarian democracies (Klingemann et al, 1994). An alternative view is that parties are only one of many influences on policy and that their impact is diluted (Rose, 1984; Rose and Davies, 1994; Webb, 2000).

Incoming governments are constrained by practical factors (such as the time and effort required to reverse previous legislation and the costs of implementing new initiatives) and political factors (such as the power of vested interests, media influence and public opinion). Rose (1984) claims that this often produces a 'moving consensus', rather than dramatic policy change. The picture is even more complex when elections produce coalition governments. Although policy is a major influence on the formation of government coalitions, it is stronger in some political systems than others (Laver and Budge, 1992).

## Conservative health policy, 1997–2005: influence without power?

The Conservatives' defeat at the 1997 general election led to a period of introspection and the gradual development of a new health policy, which is discussed shortly. However, although out of office, the Conservatives' influence over policy continued. The legacy of the policy of previous Conservative governments, implemented between 1979 and 1997, persisted, partly because of the impracticality of reversing previous health legislation in its entirety, and to some extent because the New Labour government was keen to retain some of its predecessor's policies. For example, New Labour abolished Conservative flagship policies such as GP fundholding and tax relief on private health insurance, but pressed ahead with Private Finance Initiative schemes in the NHS and extended them to primary care services. Although New Labour claimed to have abolished the Conservatives' internal market (Department of Health, 1989), the division between commissioners of health care (Primary Care Groups and later Primary Care Trusts) and providers (NHS Trusts) remained. Subsequently, Labour policy moved even further back towards the policies pursued by the Thatcher and Major governments. It adopted payment by results, a system whereby trusts would be paid for work done rather than through block service contracts, and attempted to shift commissioning responsibilities back to GPs, through practice-based commissioning. Plans to increase patient choice also resonated with previous Conservative policies. The Labour government introduced foundation trusts, a resurrection of the self-governing hospitals policy introduced by the Conservatives, but with an added element in the form of locally elected governors. New Labour extended and strengthened the performance management regime introduced by the Conservatives and increased the number of central targets. Most surprising of all, perhaps, was New Labour's endorsement of partnership with the independent health-care sector, first through a concordat (Independent Healthcare Association and Department of Health, 2000), then by encouraging private-sector management to take over 'failing' health services, and later in contracting out whole areas of NHS treatment to new treatment centres run by the independent sector.

Following John Major's replacement by William Hague in 1997, the Conservative Party began to revise its policies, including on health. Although many of its health policies were clearly reflected in those adopted by New Labour, especially after 2000, the Conservative leadership was keen to change its own policies. It felt that Labour dominated on health issues and that this would seriously affect their electoral prospects. The Conservatives sought to underline their commitment to public funding of the NHS, while also championing the independent sector. In their 2001 general election manifesto they pledged to match Labour's spending on health and to maintain a comprehensive NHS free to users (Conservative Party, 2001). The manifesto stated that a Conservative government would introduce a Patients' Guarantee, and that the NHS would be obliged to meet maximum waiting times based on clinical need, if necessary by paying for treatment in a private hospital. The Conservatives were committed to providing more information about health services, including measures based on clinical outcomes, in a system where hospitals would be paid for the care and treatment they provided. Their manifesto promised stand-alone units to deal with routine operations; the right of GPs to refer patients to a hospital of their choice; and an 'exceptional medicines panel' to address the problem of postcode rationing of expensive drugs. A new partnership between the NHS and the independent sector was proposed, alongside measures to grant tax relief on employers' private medical insurance. The party promised more autonomy for professionals at the front line, called for a greater role for nurses in health care (and for the return of matrons), and promised to reduce the influence of politicians over the day-to-day management of the NHS by creating an independent appointments body. The Conservatives' theme was a 'common-sense' approach to policy. By emphasising pragmatism, the party attempted to distance itself from the 'ideological' Thatcher era. However, this was somewhat cosmetic as overall the party's health policies differed little from those pursued in the 1980s and 1990s.

When Hague stood down following Labour's re-election in 2001, his successor, Iain Duncan Smith, was largely seen as ineffectual and himself resigned after only two years, following a loss of confidence among his backbenchers. He did, however, exert some influence on his party's policies, despite his short tenure. He initiated several policy reviews that paved the way for Conservative policies at the following general election (Evans and Williams, 2002; Williams, 2002; Conservative Party, 2003; Clark and Kelly, 2004). Viewed initially as a right-winger (not least because he inherited arch–Thatcherite Norman Tebbit's Chingford seat), Duncan Smith increasingly became interested in social policy. After resigning from the leadership, he founded the Centre for Social Justice in 2004 and exerted influence over Conservative health and social policy through his work for David Cameron on these issues, as will become clear later (see also other chapters, for example, Chapter 1).

Duncan Smith was replaced as leader by Michael Howard. Under Howard, the 2005 general election manifesto endorsed a Patient Passport scheme, developed under his predecessor. Under this scheme patients would receive half the NHS 'tariff' to pay for private health care (Duncan Smith's original plan set the subsidy at 60% of the NHS tariff). The Conservatives also stated that they would match Labour's spending plans up to 2007/08 and spend an extra £34 billion per annum from then until the end of that parliament. Independent health-care providers would secure the right to supply services on behalf of the NHS. Patients would have access to treatment in independent hospitals, which could perform operations at a standard and price acceptable to the NHS. The right to choose health-care providers would be extended to people with long-term conditions.

The Conservatives continued to argue for decentralisation. They promised that all hospitals would become foundation trusts and have greater autonomy. Commissioning would be returned to GPs. Their 2005 manifesto called for an end to centrally imposed NHS targets. These would be replaced by measures of clinical standards (based on standards set by the National Institute for Clinical Excellence [NICE], established by Labour in the late 1990s). There would be more information available to the public on hospital infection rates, waiting times, clinical outcomes and patient experience, which would be used to facilitate choice and hold providers to account. The Conservatives also promised to focus resources at the front line. They proposed the abolition of Strategic Health Authorities, a cut in the number of health quangos, a slimming-down of the Department of Health and a reduction in Primary Care Trusts and their functions.

Amid concern about hospital hygiene and antibiotic resistance to infections, the Conservatives proposed a clean-up of hospitals and a more rigorous inspection system. The 'return of matron' was reiterated. The Labour government's creation of Modern Matrons as clinical leaders managing the patient environment and standards of care was judged insufficient. The Conservatives also pledged to cut waiting lists, increase the number of beds and increase staff training places.

In addition, the Conservatives highlighted public health issues, as they had done when previously in office. The Major government had introduced a *Health of the Nation* strategy aimed at improving public health (Department of Health, 1992). This represented a considerable break with the Thatcher regime, which had opposed the idea of a health strategy. Although widely welcomed, the *Health of the Nation* policy was under-resourced and poorly implemented. The Labour government introduced a White Paper on public health, *Saving Lives* (Department of Health, 1999) and then a revised strategy, *Choosing Health*, in 2004, amid growing concerns about alcohol abuse, smoking and obesity (Department of Health, 2004). The Conservative manifesto responded to this agenda with commitments to improve cancer screening and introduce health campaigns on alcohol misuse, drug abuse and sexual health. Some ideas were innovative, including the establishment of a unified public health service to provide coherent public health messages based on evidence, and an independent public health commission appointed by parliament to undertake enquiries, commission research and recommend strategies to meet public health objectives. The manifesto also called for school nurses to be given an active role in health promotion; a 10-fold increase in residential drug rehabilitation places; the right to participate in after-school sport with trained coaches to be given to children; and pledged to help schools to retain and enhance sports facilities. However, with regard to lifestyle-related illness, such as smoking, excessive drinking and obesity, the Conservatives remained firmly in favour of greater individual responsibility for one's own health, for example, backing a voluntary rather than statutory approach to discouraging smoking in public places.

Long-term care was another issue of public concern, particularly among those worried about having to sell their homes to pay for care. The Conservative manifesto proposed a partnership scheme, whereby people paying for long-term residential care for three years would get free care for the remainder of their lives. The party also pledged to reform the existing regulatory regime for social care and to reduce bureaucracy in this field. In mental health it promised to set out standards of care in legislation, extend the right to choose to mental health patients and encourage independent provision of mental health services. Proposals to improve dentistry were also announced, in the context of widespread criticism of the government's failure to improve access to NHS dental services.

The 2005 Conservative manifesto thus continued many of the themes raised in the 2001 manifesto. However, it was more comprehensive, moving beyond the traditional concerns of primary and hospital-based health care, and backed many of the policies introduced by Labour in the field of choice, competition and decentralised management. The main difference remaining was that the Conservatives would go further down the road of markets and privatisation, as revealed by the subsidy for privately funded health care represented by the Patient Passport.

## Policy developments since 2005

At the 2005 election the Labour Party was returned for a third term of government, and in the wake of that defeat, and the subsequent choice of David Cameron as leader, Conservative health policy developed significantly. The reasons for these policy changes will be discussed later, but the first task is to outline the changes and their significance. As the next general election approached, various Conservative policy ideas on health reform began to firm up into policy commitments. A green paper on the NHS was produced in June 2008 (Conservative Party, 2008a), followed by a *Renewal Plan for a Better NHS* (Conservative Party, 2009d). David Cameron (2009b) sharpened the focus of his party's plans by setting out its top priorities for health in November 2009. This was followed in 2010 by the general election manifesto (Conservative Party, 2010e). In addition, the Conservatives produced policy documents on specific issues, such as public health (Conservative Research Department, 2007; Conservative Party, 2010a) and patient choice and accountability (Conservative Party, 2007b).

### Funding, markets and the independent sector

Cameron abandoned the Patient Passport policy and proposals for subsidies for private medical insurance in 2006. The party stated that it would seek to clarify the boundary of NHS care and access to NHS services by private patients, although this did not make it into the 2010 manifesto. The Conservatives did, however, make significant commitments on health expenditure, and NHS spending was one of only two areas exempted from planned spending cuts. Although the party promised in its manifesto to increase health spending year on year, it acknowledged that the rate of increase under Labour would not be continued. Nonetheless, even this was a substantial commitment in an age of impending austerity. The endorsement of a publicly funded health-care system, coupled with a shift in emphasis away from private health spending, was a significant move politically, as it brought the party much closer to Labour's position. However, the Conservatives made no secret of their plans to expose the NHS to competition from the independent sector. Their policy, enshrined in the 2010 manifesto, would allow patients to choose any provider meeting NHS standards and at a price acceptable to the NHS (that is, within the NHS tariff set for that procedure). This was portrayed as a more balanced approach that would enable NHS and independent-sector providers to compete on a fair basis. Even so, this was an extension of the previous Labour government's policy, rather than a radical new departure.

The Conservatives also wanted to improve the measurement of health outcomes and pay providers for success, again continuing existing government policy of 'payment by results'. The proposed improvements in NHS information would contribute to this (Conservative Party, 2009a). The Conservatives were committed to phasing out block contracts and to linking the tariff for NHS treatment more closely to specific conditions and outcomes across episodes of care. It was envisaged that contracts between commissioners and providers of care would be designed so that payments could be increased or decreased to reflect performance with regard to outcomes. The party also stated that it would consult on value-based pricing for drugs, whereby drugs companies would be paid by results (this had been already adopted for a small number of drugs, so again was largely a continuation of existing Labour policy).

## NHS organisation and management

A major theme of the Conservatives under David Cameron was to put 'front-line' health-care professionals in charge of delivering care. In opposition, they drew up an NHS independence bill and pledged to introduce this in office. This would enshrine the core principles of the NHS, such as a universal national health service for all based on clinical need, not ability to pay; the provision of comprehensive services; services based around the needs and preferences of patients, families and carers; and the need to keep people healthy and try to reduce health inequalities. Interestingly, the core principles identified by the Conservatives reflected those in Labour's *NHS Plan* (Department of Health, 2000). The Conservatives' proposals included an independent NHS board, appointed by the Secretary of State for Health on the basis of recommendations from an appointments commission and reporting to parliament. The NHS board would be responsible for securing comprehensive services in health, delivering improvement in physical and mental health and delivering improvements in diagnosis and treatment. The Secretary of State for Health would set overall objectives and outcomes for the NHS, which the board would be expected to achieve. The board would be responsible for allocating resources and setting commissioning guidelines based on NICE guidance. Subsequently, the Conservative manifesto stated that the independent board would allocate resources and provide commissioning guidelines, but there was no mention of its role in delivering objectives and outcomes (Conservative Party, 2010a). This was interpreted by some commentators as limiting the scope of the independent body (Santry, 2010). The Conservatives stated that political targets focusing on processes would be abolished. However, population health outcome targets would be retained. NHS performance would be measured against other countries' health systems, focusing on improved outcomes in areas such as cancer survival, premature mortality from heart disease and stroke, premature mortality from lung disease, and mortality amenable to health care. In addition, Conservative policy documents stated that they would seek year-on-year improvements in patient satisfaction with access and experience of health care, patient-reported outcomes for patients with long-term conditions, and a year-on-year reduction in adverse events (such as hospital acquired infections). The Care Quality Commission would be the regulator of quality standards while Monitor (the regulator of foundation trusts) would regulate competition and pricing and entry to the health care market. The party promised that all NHS Trusts would become foundation trusts. Also, GPs were promised powers over budgets and commissioning. Initially, the Conservatives proposed returning responsibilities for out-of-hours care to GPs, but this was replaced by a manifesto commitment to ensure 24-hour, seven-day-a-week, urgent care services in every area that included a GP out-of-hours service. The party also pledged to reduce health quangos and cut NHS central administrative costs by a third in four years. The Conservatives also stated that they would not reorganise the NHS, although mergers between PCTs would be 'welcomed' (Gainsbury, 2009).

In some respects the Conservatives' policies continued to mirror those of Labour, who had also proclaimed a desire to shift power to professionals, reduce management costs and reduce central targets. After 2005, these precepts became increasingly influential over government policy. The major difference was that Labour did not back an independent NHS board, but, as noted, the Conservatives' plans had already been diluted to some extent.

### Patient choice and accountability

The Conservatives aimed to create a patient-led NHS where patients would be in control of the care they receive. This meant a greater choice of secondary care provider, as indicated earlier. The Conservatives also proposed greater choice of primary care provider, and wanted patients to have control of their own health records. In addition, a manifesto commitment was made to introduce individual budgets for people with long-term conditions, a policy already adopted by New Labour on a pilot basis. The Conservatives pledged to create a national statutory watchdog, 'Healthwatch', to advocate on behalf of patients (Conservative Party, 2007b, 2010a). This body would be given statutory rights of consultation on commissioning guidelines and how care is provided in an area, and would be able to make representations to an NHS board on the planning of NHS services, such as the closure of a facility. In the 2010 manifesto, however, Healthwatch's role was confined to investigating and supporting complaints, which suggested a dilution of its role. Local involvement networks (LINkS), set up by Labour to represent service users, had earlier been promised independent inspection powers and independence from local authorities, but this was not actually mentioned in the manifesto. The Conservatives also diluted their commitment to give patients a choice of single rooms when having inpatient treatment. The 2010 manifesto only pledged to increase single rooms as resources allowed, in the context of a pledge to end mixed wards. The manifesto did, however, state that it would stop the forced closure of Accident and Emergency departments and maternity units. In addition, it promised that patient choice would be extended in maternity and mental health services, continuing existing Labour government policies. With regard to mental health, a manifesto commitment was made to increase access to effective 'talking' therapies, a policy also supported by both Labour and the Liberal Democrats.

Again, this area of policy did not represent a major difference with the Labour government. Where the Conservatives were proposing change, this was extending current policies rather than setting a new direction. Also, where the party had proposed significant changes, there was some suggestion of policy commitments being diluted.

### Public health

The Conservatives declared that the Department of Health would become the Department of Public Health, with the Secretary of State for Health taking charge of public health strategy (Conservative

Party, 2010a). This commitment, which appeared in the manifesto, was an attempt to prioritise public health issues. Earlier documents had also proposed a new Public Health Act (Conservative Research Department, 2007), but this was not reiterated in later documents, including the 2010 manifesto. However, Cameron (2009b) did commit to a new public health White Paper setting out a public health strategy. The Conservatives had argued that public health financial allocations would be ring-fenced and over time transferred to a new structure, separate from health-care resource allocation. The manifesto stated that 'separate' public health funding would be provided to local communities (Conservative Party, 2010e). Previous commitments to a strengthened Chief Medical Officer's department, independent of ministers, and jointly appointed local directors of public health (DPHs), were not mentioned in the manifesto. The party did, however, commit to recruiting a further 4,200 Sure Start health visitors and introducing minimum service guarantees for this service, specifying what level of services should be delivered to families with children. The manifesto also pledged to tackle health inequalities, with a 'health premium' weighting public health funding towards the poorest areas with the worst health outcomes.

The Conservatives had promised to implement a range of measures to improve diet, increase levels of exercise and reduce smoking and alcohol abuse (Conservative Research Department, 2007; Conservative Party, 2010a). However, they reiterated that lifestyles were ultimately an individual responsibility and that legislation would be a last resort. Their 'responsibility deal' set out a 'non-bureaucratic' relationship with business to promote health. This approach, based on self-regulation, voluntary agreement and corporate social responsibility, included several components. With regard to diet and obesity, the Conservatives proposed a single mandatory food labelling system based on guideline daily amounts (GDAs) as opposed to the 'traffic light system' preferred by the Food Standards Agency (FSA). They also backed industry-led initiatives to reformulate food products and reduce portion sizes. The Conservatives endorsed 'proportionate' regulation of food advertising and positive campaigns by government and industry to encourage healthy diets and promote healthy living. They supported a bigger role for business in local partnerships and local area agreements to promote better diet and active lifestyles. With regard to alcohol misuse, the Conservatives endorsed a responsible drinking campaign, matched with community action projects to address drug abuse, sexually transmitted infections and alcohol misuse, using a proportion of the drinks advertising budget. The Conservatives had also backed clear labelling of alcoholic drinks and effective local partnerships to tackle alcohol misuse. However, they went further in their manifesto and proposed a range of measures, including: banning off-licences and supermarkets from selling alcohol below cost price, raising taxes on drinks linked to anti-social behaviour, overhauling the licensing acts to strengthen powers to control outlets causing problems, increasing powers to close outlets persistently selling alcohol to children and increasing the fine for underage sales to £20,000.

The Conservative health spokesman, Andrew Lansley, established a Public Health Commission in 2008 to advise on the long-term health of the nation and to comment specifically on the sharing of responsibility for health. Members included senior people drawn from the food and drinks industries (including alcohol), advertising and the retail sector, nutritional experts (including some with links to industry), doctors, scientists, consumer representatives, charities and the fitness industry. Its report (Public Health Commission, 2009) emphasised social marketing approaches to public health. It backed a partnership approach involving government, the NHS, the voluntary sector and employers and business. It urged government and the NHS to give prevention a higher priority than it had hitherto enjoyed. The Commission was not in favour of extending enforcement and regulation, but agreed that enforcement of existing laws should be improved. It identified ways of incentivising healthy lifestyles through the tax system (such as reducing VAT on gym membership), and also called for more evaluation of interventions to improve public health. The Commission broadly agreed with the Conservatives' responsibility agenda, but was critical of some proposals, notably that advertising budgets should fund responsible drinking campaigns.

As was the case in other policy areas, most Conservative policies on public health did not differ radically from the Labour government. However, there were some interesting departures, notably with regard to proposals for a Department for Public Health and a separate funding system for public health.

## Social care

The Conservatives promised legislation to create a home protection scheme that would enable elderly people to insure themselves against the costs of residential care. They also promised to pilot schemes that enabled people to be looked after in their own homes (such as telecare, home adaptation and self-care). Their election manifesto reiterated that they would introduce a voluntary insurance scheme for long-term care, and also pledged to improve access to respite care for carers. Although there was much agreement across the main parties for greater support for carers and assisted living schemes, there was deep disagreement over how to fund long-term care (see Chapter 10 for more detailed discussion of this policy area).

## Explaining policy developments

It is possible to identify a number of factors behind developments in Conservative policy after 2005. Indeed, the impact of the election defeat itself cannot be underestimated. As with Labour after 1987, this prompted a fundamental rethink of strategy and policy. It also led to the choice of a relative newcomer as leader. David Cameron, though a political advisor to Conservative ministers in the 1990s, had only been elected to parliament in 2001. His election as party leader represented a significant break with the past (Dorey, 2007). Although Eton-educated and affluent, Cameron was seen as more open than his predecessors to socially inclusive welfare policies (Lee and Beech, 2009). Given the party's poor performance in recent general elections, he was given leeway to experiment with policy. In addition, there was a personal factor that many believed had political significance for David Cameron's perspective on health and welfare. His son, Ivan, was born with a rare and severely disabling medical condition that required round-the-clock care and treatment. Tragically, in February 2009, he died at six years of age. Cameron has placed on record the impact of his family's experience on his views of the NHS: 'I believe that the creation of the NHS is one of the greatest achievements of the 20th century. When your family relies on the NHS all the time ... you really know how precious it is' (quoted in Elliot, 2009).

The combination of personal perspective, political viewpoint and the opportunity afforded by the Conservatives' weak standing with the electorate, particularly on health and welfare issues, created the conditions for change in policy. As discussed in Chapter 1, on taking up the leadership of the Conservative Party, Cameron launched a series of policy reviews, which included people with expertise from outside the party and invited evidence from external groups. Those most relevant to health were: the final report on public services (Public Services Improvement Policy Group, 2007); the public services subcommittee report on health (Public Services Improvement Policy Group, 2006); and the social justice reports on family breakdown, addictions, gambling and the third sector (Social Justice Policy Group, 2007). These reports made many detailed recommendations, including some at odds with recent Conservative policies. They contributed to the process of policy development, not only by making specific recommendations that were incorporated into party policy, but by highlighting specific areas for policy development. However, their fundamental purpose was to reinforce Cameron's control over policy (Lee, 2009).

There are many examples of recommendations from the policy reviews being accepted in whole or in part. For example, the Social Justice Policy Group's reviews made recommendations to strengthen the health visiting service, move towards an abstinence-based addiction treatment service and use taxation to curb alcohol misuse, all of which appeared in the Conservatives' 2010 manifesto. The Public Services Improvement Policy Group also had some of its recommendations accepted, particularly with regard to strengthening the emphasis on outcome measures, the need to address health inequalities, the commitment to make all secondary providers into foundation trusts, the publication of performance data, the engagement of professionals in local decision-making, and insulating the NHS from day-to-day political interference. Of course, many other recommendations were not taken up, at least not explicitly, and those that were adopted tended to be consistent with the leadership's views.

The recommendations of the policy reviews meshed with party consultations (on public health, public involvement and NHS independence) and shadow cabinet commitments on IT (Conservative Party, 2009a) and NHS funding (McSmith, 2006). Meanwhile ideas on health policy emanated from various pro-market and Conservative think tanks and advocacy groups. These included those that had influenced Conservative health policy in the past, such as the Conservative Research Department, the Centre for Policy Studies (Mason and Maxwell, 2008) and the Adam Smith Institute (Ramsay and Butler, 2001; Brown and Young, 2002), and other more recently established think tanks active in this area including Policy Exchange (for example, Hamblin and Ganesh, 2007; Barlow et al, 2008; Featherstone and Storey, 2009), Reform (Smith, 2006; Bosanquet et al, 2007, 2009; Charlson et al, 2007) and the Social Market Foundation (Furness and Gough, 2009). In addition, the Centre for Social Justice has made pronouncements on health issues, such as mental health and addictions. Furthermore, a number of market-oriented health advocacy groups were active in seeking to influence Conservative policy. One of the most prominent is Nurses for Reform, which advocates placing all health provision in the independent sector, more decentralisation of decisions about investment in local health facilities, more information about health services (including freedom to advertise services), an end to collective bargaining for health professionals, and strict limits on tax-funded public health information.

It is difficult to measure the influence of think tanks and advocacy groups. It is rare that a single recommendation is exclusive to one organisation, and in most cases similar proposals are backed by other policy actors. Nonetheless, as noted elsewhere in this book (see Chapter 6, for example), these organisations have provided a source of policy ideas that have been taken up to some extent by the Conservative leadership. These include: devolving responsibility for the NHS to local clinicians and managers, reducing the burden of central regulation and targets, the importance of retaining commissioning, the need to encourage employers and individuals to take more responsibility for health, and the imperative to tackle public health problems such as alcohol abuse and obesity. Not all recommendations emanating from pro-market and Conservative think tanks have been welcomed by the Conservative leadership, however. Proposals to introduce new charges for NHS services (Charlson et al, 2007; Furness and Gough, 2009) or to introduce social insurance systems (Brown and Young, 2002) have so far fallen on stony ground. Even so, now the Conservatives have gained office, it is possible that such ideas might gain support from within government, particularly in an era of austerity.

Notably, the leadership's position on health policy has contrasted with that of many Conservative MPs. According to one survey, before the 2010 election two thirds of Conservative MPs supported tax relief on private medical insurance, a policy rejected by the Cameron leadership (Sky News, 2009). Moreover, there are elements within the party that remain strongly opposed to the core principles of the NHS and who support alternative models of health care. In 2009, these views were publicly aired by Conservative MEP Daniel Hannan in the context of debates on health-care reform in the USA. Hannan described the NHS as a '60-year-old mistake' adding that he 'wouldn't wish it on anybody' (Summers and Glendinning, 2009). His comments produced a swift defence of the NHS from the UK government and the Conservative leadership. However, although rebuked by Cameron, who described him as 'eccentric', the suspicion remained that Hannan was not a lone figure on this issue. Indeed, Hannan was linked to senior figures on the Conservative frontbench, some of whom were reportedly sympathetic with his perspective (Helm and Syal, 2009).

Other factors may also have shaped the Conservatives' policies. For example, special interests, such as the private health-care industry and the food, alcohol and tobacco industries are traditionally close to the party and have good links with MPs, including shadow health ministers.

Indeed, in January 2010, the *News of the World* revealed that senior Tory MPs in charge of health policy had accepted donations from private health-care companies (Kirby, 2010). Others had undertaken consultancy work or accepted benefits in kind. While these payments were declared, and there is no impropriety attached to them, this does at the very least reveal the links between the Conservatives and these interests, which may provide a useful platform for lobbying senior politicians when in office. Similarly one would imagine that powerful interests connected to the Conservative Party, notably the food and drink industries, may perhaps seek to weaken the government's resolve to tackle issues such as obesity and alcohol misuse, even more so than under Labour, which had also been influenced by these special interests.

## Coalition politics

Following the 2010 general election, with the outcome a hung parliament, the Conservatives, as the largest single party, did a deal with the Liberal Democrats, forming the first formal coalition government in Westminster for almost 70 years. The Coalition produced a programme for government, which revealed the compromises made by both parties. An analysis of the programme reveals that 55 commitments related to health (see Table 5.1): 26 to the NHS, four to social care and 25 to public health policies (excluding policies on climate change, which have health implications). Twenty-two came directly from the Conservative manifesto (including the commitment on spending, a panel on cancer drugs, changes to drug pricing, an independent NHS board, individual budgets for health and social care, a health premium for disadvantaged areas, the expansion in Sure Start health visitors, and measures to restrict alcohol availability). Nine came from the Liberal Democrat manifesto (including greater choice of GP, prioritising dementia research, a review of social care and measures to protect school playing fields). Fifteen were derived from proposals found in both (for example, support for carers, greater access to 'talking therapies', banning alcohol sales below cost price, cutting management costs and quangos, changing the GP contract, and giving the professions more autonomy). Six elements in the government's programme were the product of compromises between the two parties (partial election of Primary Care Trusts, measures to increase openness and public information about health services, and a review of alcohol taxation). Three were not mentioned in either manifesto (although some had been heralded to some extent in previous Conservative policy documents, for example, the reform of NICE). Seventeen health policy proposals mentioned in the two party manifestos did not appear in the government's programme (12 Conservative and 5 Liberal Democrat commitments). Conservative manifesto proposals not included in the programme included: spreading the use of the NHS tariff to reflect patient choices and quality of service; the establishment of Healthwatch; ensuring all secondary providers become foundation trusts; and turning the Department of Health into the Department for Public Health.

**Table 5.1: Conservative and Liberal Democrat manifesto commitments and the Coalition's *Programme for Government*: health policies**

| Manifesto/source | NHS | Social care | Public health | Total |
|---|---|---|---|---|
| Conservative | 9 | 1 | 9 | 19 |
| Liberal Democrat | 5 | 2 | 2 | 9 |
| Both | 6 | 2 | 7 | 15 |
| Compromise | 4 | 0 | 2 | 6 |
| Neither | 4 | 0 | 1 | 5 |
| Total | 28 | 5 | 21 | 54 |

The Coalition programme, although a useful indication as to what policies will be pursued, cannot be relied upon as a definitive guide. Previous Conservative policy proposals and manifesto commitments are likely to resurface as the details of policy are hammered out. This will also tell us more about the actual balance of power between the partners and their priorities. At the time of writing, there have been significant developments already. A White Paper on the NHS (Department of Health, 2010a) surprised many, not only by proposing the abolition of Strategic Health Authorities (which had been trailed in media reports), but by scrapping Primary Care Trusts (which had not). The White Paper proposed that commissioning would be undertaken by GP consortia within a framework set by a national commissioning board; that all trusts would become foundation trusts; and that Healthwatch would be established as the guardian of patients' interests (but located within the Care Quality Commission, rather than as a free-standing body). The White Paper confirmed that a new public health service would be established with ring-fenced local budgets. But few envisaged the transfer of key public health functions to local government on the scale proposed. These plans were to be detailed further in a separate public health White Paper, *Healthy Lives, Healthy People* (Department of Health,

2010b) published in November 2010. Other unheralded changes affecting health care arose from a review of government agencies, which led to decisions to abolish a number of key public bodies including the NHS Appointments Commission, the Health Protection Agency, the NHS Institute for Innovation and Improvement, the National Patient Safety Agency, and the Audit Commission. Some bodies were to be merged with others or removed from the public sector entirely. In contrast, a small number of agencies were strengthened, with proposals that NICE and the Health and Social Care Information Centre, for example, would expand their remit and be placed on a statutory footing.

## Conclusions

During their long spell in opposition, the Conservatives' policies on health changed and developed significantly, especially after 2005, becoming more comprehensive and giving more attention to issues such as public health, public involvement and social care. Clearly the NHS remained a key battleground, but the Conservatives, like Labour, realised that these other issues were increasingly important and that they had to respond with policy proposals. Conservative policy, therefore, became more detailed and specific, although many of the party's ideas and commitments did not appear in the 2010 manifesto. However, this does not mean that they will not resurface now that the party is in government.

Several key themes of past Conservative policy remained, however, such as their criticism of NHS bureaucracy, calls for decentralisation and the preference for choice and competition. At the same time, their pronouncements on the NHS were more careful to defend the core principles of the service, including the need to acknowledge inequalities. This acknowledgement was a major shift from the position during the 1980s and 1990s, where Conservative governments refused even to use the term (preferring 'health variations'). Support for private medicine, a long-standing principle of Conservative policy, was not as explicit as it had been in the past. The party committed itself to a public funding model and rejected plans to subsidise private purchasing of health care. In addition, the Conservatives committed themselves to substantial NHS spending, promising to increase the budget in real terms, even as an era of massive public spending cuts loomed. However, it should be noted that 'real terms' relates to general levels of inflation, rather than the rising cost of health services – which is generally higher. Moreover, the NHS, like other public services, is expected to make significant efficiency savings. Although independent provision of NHS services was endorsed, the party was keen to emphasise that this would not undermine the principles of the NHS.

In many respects Conservative and Labour policies became more similar from 2000, as Labour moved closer to the Conservatives in some areas. After Cameron's accession, this proximity was increased further as Conservative policies began to move closer to Labour's positions. Some differences remained, however, such as the commitment to NHS independence and the abolition of targets, although even these may be less significant than they might seem, as Labour began to reduce the number of central targets from 2007 onwards. Moreover, early signs were that in government the Conservatives had begun to dilute this policy as they clarified their plans for the NHS commissioning board. Although some key targets have now been abolished – notably with regard to waiting times – it is likely that some form of target setting, focused on improved health outcomes, will remain.

The coalition with the Liberal Democrats adds a further level of complexity. As noted earlier, some compromises have been made. As a result, some Conservative policies may not be implemented or may have lower priority than would have been the case under a majority Conservative government. The pressing economic situation and the imperative to reduce public spending will also shape policy choices, for example by increasing pressures for NHS reform (despite commitments to increase health spending in real terms). There are also countervailing pressure, with some commentators arguing that the government will face great difficulties in implementing its ambitious reform programme (for example, Ham, 2010). It is extremely difficult at present to predict how these various forces will affect health policy. There have already been some big surprises, such as the abolition of PCTs (which was not envisaged in the Coalition agreement, given the proposal therin to directly elect individuals to PCT boards). Indeed, the Coalition agreement appeared to rule out substantial reorganisations, stating that 'we will stop the top-down reorganisations of the NHS' (Cabinet Office, 2010, p 24). The extent of the transfer of public health functions to local authorities also came as a surprise to many.

Finally, to return to the discussion at the start of the chapter, the weakening of ideological factors in relation to voting behaviour has made it easier for the Conservatives to change their policies and become closer to Labour in an area where Labour has traditionally been strong. Meanwhile, as noted, Labour had already adopted policies with which the Conservatives agreed (such as choice, foundation trusts, plurality of provision and payment by results). Another factor was that the Conservatives' victory at the 2010 election was far from guaranteed (as the result indeed showed). The leadership, therefore, felt obliged to reassure the electorate on the NHS, particularly given the party's weakness on this issue in recent decades.

# SIX

# Something old, something new: understanding Conservative education policy

*Sonia Exley and Stephen J. Ball*

Since the Thatcher era, Conservative education policy, like many areas of Conservative policy, has been fraught with tensions. Looking back over 30 years conjures memories of some familiar figures and contradictions. We remember Keith Joseph and his neo-liberal zeal over freedom for schools and vouchers for parents, but we also remember Kenneth Baker and his introduction of a prescriptive National Curriculum with national testing at age seven or indeed Kenneth Clarke, his abolition of HMI and his creation of Ofsted in an unprecedented shift in relations between government and the educational establishment. As far back as 1998, William Hague sought to disassociate his party from past perspectives, arguing that 'there *is* such a thing as society' (Rafferty, 1998b). However, Gillian Shephard told us that policy on education should not concern itself with class–envy 'dogma' because such is the enemy of 'excellence' (*Hansard*, 2 June 1997, cols 28–9).

On the one hand, within Conservative education policy a belief in markets and a minimal state, basic tenets of neo–liberalism, have meant a push for privatisation, the 'liberation' of schools to innovate and diversify, and an enhanced role for parents as consumers in an educational marketplace. On the other, strong distrust of a 'left–wing' teaching profession, coupled with firm Conservative beliefs in 'real subjects' and that 'the old methods are the best' when it comes to teaching, discipline and the curriculum, have meant the imposition of strong accountability measures, detailed instruction over what should be taught in schools and a great deal of surveillance imposed from above. Conservative education policy is also associated with a strong view that the route to tackling poverty and educational underachievement lies in greater personal responsibility. Where pupils succeed, it is thanks to ability, hard work and traditional teaching methods. Where they fail, it is because they, their families or their teachers have not tried hard enough, or have come under the influence of misguided progressivism. A long history of individualisation and decontextualisation of educational success and failure within the Conservative Party – despite academic research linking educational attainment and deprivation – has lent legitimacy to support for private and selective schooling, evidenced by past Tory initiatives such as the Assisted Places Scheme (subsidising private schooling for high-achieving non-privileged pupils), and periodic calls for a return to selection.

## The 1997 general election

In the wake of the 1997 general election, humbled by defeat and under the new leadership of William Hague, the Conservatives in Britain promised a period of 'listening and learning', admitting on education that during the election 'there had been nothing more depressing than people who merely gave their profession – as a teacher or nurse – as the reason they would not be voting Conservative' (Rafferty, 1998a).

Plans introduced by John Major to ensure 'a grammar school in every town' were soon abandoned. Attempts to block Labour's abolition of the Assisted Places Scheme were made by some MPs, but these failed and the scheme was soon consigned to history. As in other policy areas, electoral unpopularity in 1997 suggested it was time for the Conservative Party to rethink its associations with Thatcherism on education. The major problem here was that 'education, education, education' had been a key factor in Labour's victory in the 1997 general election and one of the policy areas in which the 'Third Way' notion of pairing economic competitiveness with social justice was to be pursued. Faced with difficulty in gaining a toehold in the political centre where Labour appeared to have a monopoly, the Conservatives had little choice but to focus first on a gradual shift in educational policy 'image'.

Early attempts to shift the party away from Thatcherism and support for private and grammar schooling were helped by William Hague as leader. Educated at Wath-on-Dearne school in Rotherham, Hague was the first Conservative leader to have been educated at a comprehensive, and he hailed the benefits of this education. He appointed as Shadow Education Secretary Stephen Dorrell, known as being on the left of the party, who talked about the need to redistribute education to those who needed it most, and avoided in his speeches any talk of grammar schools. Contrite attempts to win the support of teachers could be seen in lamentations over poor staff morale in schools and policies such as increased protection for teachers during pupils' allegations of abuse.

However, despite nods in the direction of a more centrist stance after 1997, specific policies and promises on education were strategically avoided. Formal working parties were eschewed and the Conservatives sought instead to develop and focus on a set of core themes, which were outlined in the 2001 manifesto. Nonetheless, these core themes remained remarkably close to those underlying past policy – parent power, shrinking the state, 'independence' for schools, opposition to Labour's control from the centre (despite calls for increasingly tough accountability measures), and vehement opposition to a role for local government in education. Ideas for 'free schools' – that is 'state-independent' schools to be set up by parents, trusts and governors and run outside local authority control – were presented as new. However, they sounded remarkably like earlier Conservative moves to set up Grant Maintained (GM) schools and City Technology Colleges (CTCs). Principles also remained remarkably socially conservative. There were reactions against inclusive education with policies for enhanced exclusion of 'thugs' and 'disruptive, unruly pupils'. Support for extending grammar schools floated in and out of party rhetoric, with Hague often contradicting his Education Secretaries and taking a traditional pro-selective party line.

Following the resignation of William Hague as party leader in 2001, despite or possibly because of the subsequent election of Iain Duncan Smith and then Michael Howard as Conservative leaders, and a revolving door of Shadow Education Secretaries – Theresa May, Damian Green, Tim Yeo, Tim Collins – between 2001 and 2005, the Conservatives changed little on education. Party rhetoric overall shifted in the direction of a new 'compassionate Conservatism'. There were discussions about a need to return to One Nation Conservatism, a need for greater positivity about public services and a new focus on social justice (as discussed in several chapters, the Centre for Social Justice was established by Iain Duncan Smith in 2004) and on the socially vulnerable. However, problems that were now at least being acknowledged and discussed by the Conservatives – the huge attainment gap in education between rich and poor, and the lack of social mobility for those from disadvantaged backgrounds – continued to be viewed as not the place of the state to fix. Instead these were to be fixed by a revival of personal responsibility, family, community, a voluntarist 'civil society' (all perceived as being 'broken'), social enterprise and the market. Traditional Conservatism was alive and well, also, with pledges in the 2005 manifesto to 'root out political correctness' in the curriculum, to give teachers full control over exclusions while protecting them again from 'malicious allegations of abuse' (Conservative Party, 2005, p 8) and to stop a minority of '"difficult pupils" ... ruining education for others'.

## The Conservatives under Cameron

An arguable step change for policy creation, building on rhetorical shifts towards 'compassionate Conservatism', came with the appointment of Eton-educated David Cameron as Conservative Party leader in December 2005 (see also Chapters 1 and 2). Prior to becoming leader Cameron had spent seven months as Shadow Education Secretary. He declared education to be his 'personal and political obsession' and as leader he appointed David Willetts as his Shadow Education Secretary, then later Michael Gove, with Willetts as Shadow Secretary for Innovation, Universities and Skills. Over the course of four years, Cameron, Willetts and Gove expanded and diversified the Conservative rhetoric on education. Speeches about poverty, educational inequality, inclusion, mobility and 'the education gap' took centre stage. Within an explicit mission of helping 'the very poorest' and 'making opportunity more equal', Gove argued:

> The central mission of the next Conservative Government is the alleviation of poverty and the extension of opportunity. And nowhere is action required more than in our schools. Schools should be engines of social mobility. They should enable children to overcome disadvantage and deprivation so they can fulfil their innate talents and take control of their own destiny. (Gove, 2009a)

Regarding gaps in GCSE and A level attainment between the most and least disadvantaged, he commented that, 'It is an affront to any idea of social justice, a scandalous waste of talent, a situation no politician can tolerate. And we are pledged to end it' (Gove, 2009a).

Claims by Gove over the education gap form part of a wider Tory response to 'evidence-based policy' under New Labour. In 2008 he published *A Failed Generation: Educational Inequality under Labour* (Gove, 2008a), in which he spoke about educational inequality since 1997 and its causes, deploying detailed data from the Department for Children, Schools and Families, UCAS, the Higher Education Statistics Agency, the Sutton Trust, the British Cohort Studies, evaluations of Sure Start, and research by academics at the London Institute of Education in order to indicate a failure of government policy to prevent educational inequality from (allegedly) growing. As Crace (2008) put it in *The*

*Guardian*, 'It is meant to hit Labour where it hurts most'. In a speech to the Institute for Public Policy Research, Gove (2008b) criticised Labour policy for creating inequality in society, and said it was a 'national disgrace' that almost half of children from deprived backgrounds leave school without a single good GCSE. However, Gove's report was criticised by academics for its 'extreme carelessness or disregard for truth and accuracy' (see Crace, 2008; Lupton and Heath, 2008), feeding into a broader impression of Conservative education policy as lacking foundation in academic evidence (discussed further later).

What do 'modern, compassionate Conservatives', then, see as being the solutions to the education gap about which they are now concerned? Reading policy in detail, beyond the surface rhetoric there is little that is different from past approaches. A rebranded form of neo-liberalism incorporating elements of communitarianism is now presented as a 're-imagining' of the state; that is, cutting back and changing its role and size at both local and central levels. Quangos are to be cut as part of the move towards a 'post-bureaucratic state'. The state as provider of schools is to be replaced by the private sector in combination with social enterprises and the voluntary sector. This is part of what David Cameron calls the 'Big Society': 'a new focus on empowering and enabling individuals, families and communities to take control of their lives so we create the avenues through which responsibility and opportunity can develop' (Cameron, 2009a).

However, it is also part of broader social change towards what has been termed 'polycentric governance' (Ball, 2009) – a shifting of responsibility for education away from the state, with increasingly blurred lines between public and private and complex 'heterarchies' of participatory relationships between educational stakeholders – funders, providers and users.

The Conservative vision for education is one where individuals, families, school staff and communities will be given 'freedom' to 'take responsibility' for the education system. The 2010 manifesto built on earlier proposals for 'free schools', and past initiatives, such as GM schools and CTCs, with plans for hundreds of new Academies to be set up by independent providers of different sorts. Such a model, it is claimed, draws on policy from US and Canadian (for example, Alberta) Charter Schools, but mostly on a Swedish policy model for state-independent schools, which are claimed to 'improve standards faster'. Existing surplus places in English schools are to be ignored – it is believed shutting down undersubscribed schools and replacing them with between 500 and 2,000 new, small and diverse schools will solve the 'problem of educational quality'. However, how new schools will be funded in a period of cuts to public service budgets is not clear. Critical questions highlighting the relationship between educational quality and social deprivation in undersubscribed schools are answered by plans for a 'Pupil Premium' (first suggested by American pro-marketeers Chubb and Moe [1990]), providing extra money per head where pupils come from 'poorer homes', 'making schools work harder' for pupils in these circumstances.

Schools will be subject to market accountability. Parents will choose schools, with all schools, state and otherwise, liberated to innovate and set teacher salaries. Academies will also be free to set their own curriculum. Where schools attract pupils, they will be permitted to expand (this was attempted in 1992 by Kenneth Clarke, with little success). Where they do not and/or where standards decline, they will face closure or tendering, a promise reflected in the 2010 manifesto commitment to turn into Academies any schools classed as being in 'special measures' for over a year. The Academies Act, introduced to parliament just 14 days into the new Conservative–Liberal Democrat government, enabled not just secondary schools, but also primary and special schools classed as 'outstanding' to become Academies without barriers such as a requirement to consult local authorities. Michael Gove expects that Academies will become the norm among English schools (Paton, 2010). Regulation over school admissions in the form of the School Admissions Code (brought in by Labour in 1998) has so far not been targeted for reform as part of the deregulation project. However there is little support for the Code, and Gove has expressed derision towards a 'bureaucracy which has allocated school places in such an antique command and control fashion and which now seeks to criminalise parents who simply want the best for their children' (Gove, 2009a) while praising deregulative practices in the commercial world:

> We will reduce the number of staff at the DCSF [Department for Children, Schools and Families], and the number of things they regulate, monitor and issue decrees on.... The most successful commercial organisations in the world now are delegating more and more control to the front line and slimming their central offices. Some multi-nationals now have as few as 100 employees in their headquarters. One, Dana, has matched its slimming down of the management structure with a thinning out of bureaucratic control. It has replaced twenty-two and a half inches of policy manuals with a one page statement of the company's aims and values. (Gove, 2009a)

Similarly, David Willetts had previously argued that 'There are commonsense limits to what you can do. You can't micro-manage the admissions policies of 20,000 schools. You can't have the government inspector sitting on the shoulder of the admissions panel as they decide individual cases' (Willetts, 2007).

Opening up the system in this way also extends to the teaching profession and its recruitment. Conservative plans to support the 'anti-bureaucratic education charity' Teach First, will, it is proposed, see growing numbers of graduates from Oxbridge spending time teaching upon leaving university before they move on to different careers (although Teach First is already the largest graduate recruiter at Oxbridge). Graduates participating in the Teach First scheme will not be required to undertake full teacher training, raising questions over educational quality, despite the Conservatives' rhetorical focus in this area. Plans extend beyond Oxbridge, too, with intentions to broaden the base of teacher recruitment to include those in the military and those with 'high-flying careers' in other areas (the Teach Now programme). Again, a 'rigorous application process' will stand in place of a full Postgraduate Certificate of Education (PGCE) training:

> We'll expand Teach First – which has helped recruit the highest performing graduates into teaching.... We'll develop a Troops to Teachers programme – to get professionals in the army who know how to train young men and women into the classroom where they can provide not just discipline – but inspiration and leadership.... And we'll ensure that experts in every field – especially mathematicians, scientists, technicians and engineers – can make a swift transition into teaching so our children have access to the very, very best science education. (Gove, 2009b)

Such notions are not new. They are strongly reminiscent of Conservative ideas from the early 1990s for a 'mums army' of non-graduates with only minimal training who would teach the under-sevens in primary schools, and further moves towards school-based teacher training and flexible entry into teaching.

## Policy and evidence

Plans for continued prescriptive and centralised accountability measures characteristic both of New Labour and the 'old' Conservatives also remain, however, highlighting the classic unstable mix of freedom for schools and surveillance over them – a version of autonomy and responsibility. There have been proposals for national testing which would begin even younger than before (age six), 'no notice' Ofsted inspections for schools with lower examination results (in contrast with 'earned autonomy' for high-performing schools), and more extensive centralised publication of league tables on maths, English and science, with exam scores no longer adjusted for deprivation (Stewart and Vaughan, 2010). Despite intentions to broaden the base for teacher recruitment, teachers will be required to hold at least a second-class university degree. Moving against curricular innovation and despite claims that 'we will stop the constant political interference in the curriculum that has devalued standards' (Gove, 2009a), Michael Gove has indicated strong views on what the curriculum should include, and objections to Facebook and Twitter, even the use of Google. In Gramscian fashion, the Conservatives believe that a return to traditional teaching methods in primary schools will raise the attainment of working-class students, claiming that 'Employers and universities are increasingly unhappy with students who have qualifications in subjects they regard as soft. They especially prize passes in rigorous scientific subjects' (Gove, 2009a) and that:

> In GCSE science we ask students whether a better argument for nuclear power is the fact it creates jobs, or the fact it creates waste. In GCSE English the satisfying study of whole novels and plays has been replaced by extracts, worksheets and freeze-dried fragments of literature. And in exam scripts we award marks for candidates who write nothing but expletives. In GCSE modern languages there is no proper translation, and in A level modern languages no requirement to study any literature. In History students are left with a disconnected and fragmentary sense of our national story while in mathematics subjects such as calculus which were once studied by fifteen and sixteen year olds have been erased from their curriculum. (Gove, 2009b)

On similar lines, Gove has argued that science should be divided into physics, chemistry and biology, that 'too much of the curriculum was about "airy fairy" goals rather than hard facts', and that 'teaching literature should concentrate on the classics rather than contemporary fiction and poetry' (Sylvester and Thomson, 2010) so that 'You can have Browning, Wordsworth and Byron introduced to children at a relatively early age. Learning poetry by heart is an immensely powerful way of ensuring you have your own private iPod, a stock of beauty you can draw on in your own mind' (Sylvester and Thomson, 2010).

Such policy tends to be based more on gut instinct rather than a weight of evidence over academic traditionalism, and replays the Conservative think-tank offensive in response to the National Curriculum legislation in 1988 (see Ball, 1990; and later) again showing a lack of real concern with evidence-based policymaking. Within the politicised promotion of certain teaching content and methods over others there is very little to suggest that academic work is considered. Synthetic phonics in reading provides a good example, cited confidently in the Conservative manifesto as being the way forward for primary school literacy but with reference only to very limited and selective evidence (for critiques of this evidence, see Ellis, 2007; Wyse and Styles, 2007):

> So we will provide training and support to every school in the use of systematic synthetic phonics – the tried and tested method of teaching reading which has eliminated illiteracy in Clackmannanshire and West Dunbartonshire. (Gove, 2009a)

Within a 'post-bureaucratic' age, an anti-Whitehall stance and a stripping down of the functions of the former Department for Children, Schools and Families (and central government more broadly) under Coalition rule, it is unlikely that comparable levels of commissioning of academic research to those seen under Labour will continue, suggesting again a shift away from trends in the last decade towards evidence-based policy. Such an approach is likely to feed into increased reliance on non-academic or even anecdotal evidence, selectively interpreted and understood, feeding into a decontextualisation of educational success or failure:

> [Academies'] success now is powerful, incontestable, proof that it is not intake which makes a school outstanding – but independence – it is not conformity with bureaucratic diktats which drives success but accountability to parents.... Standards in private schools are so high because fee-paying schools are independent from bureaucratic control and accountable to parents not ministers. (Gove, 2009a)

The Sutton Trust has been carrying out research into whether bright pupils from comprehensive schools are missing out on degree places. This led the Conservative Education Society to suggest that 60,000 such pupils had missed out, but not because of bias against them by top universities, simply because they are let down by poor education (Conservative Education Society, 2008).

Policy-borrowing by the Conservatives from 'the Swedish model' seems divorced from context and based on a highly selective reading of outcomes, and claims about the model 'improving standards faster' seem again without basis in academic research. References to Sweden may represent an attempt at 'posturing' to link the party with a traditional social-democratic country,[1] in line with 'modern, compassionate Conservatism', but they ignore the greater levels of general equality between schools in Sweden, the commitment of 6.4% of Swedish GDP to education (compared with cuts by the Coalition government) and the regulatory role of local government over free schools in Sweden. Free schools in Sweden display many characteristics that stand in direct contradiction with other elements of Conservative education policy: they are required to follow a national curriculum (as would not be the case in England); testing for any pupil is eschewed entirely until pupils reach their mid-teens. It should be noted that lower proportions of school staff hold qualified teacher status in Swedish free schools than in state municipal schools (Skolverket, 2009, Table 4A). New schools created through the free school movement, based in office blocks and warehouses, often have no space for 'traditional' teaching in science labs, or for sports fields – possibly not very attractive for the middle-class voters the Conservatives hope to impress. Moreover, studies have shown that in Sweden free schools and competition have coincided with some slipping of Swedish standards in international comparisons of exam performance (Sharma, 2010). This is despite claims by Michael Gove such as:

> New providers [of schooling in Sweden] have not only created schools with higher standards than before, the virtuous dynamic created by the need to respond to competition from new providers has forced existing schools to raise their game. There is a direct correlation between more choice and higher standards – with the biggest improvements in educational outcomes being generated in those areas with the most new schools. (Gove, 2008c)

Far from educating pupils from the most disadvantaged backgrounds, free schools in Sweden may well have contributed to patterns of increasing segregation and decreasing equity in the Swedish education system (Sharma, 2010).Typically, free schools are a magnet for children from educated, urban, middle-class families and have a higher proportion of girls than municipal schools. Pupils from immigrant backgrounds are also over-represented, although these tend to be second-generation immigrant pupils (Allen, 2010), often living in affluent or gentrifying areas. This reality is glossed over in anecdotal claims made by Gove that Swedish free schools educate 'higher than average' proportions of immigrant and ethnic minority pupils, as in the following:'There have been claims that the Swedish reforms have increased social segregation but I saw all-ability comprehensives with a higher than average number of ethnic minority pupils' (Gove, 2008c).

Similar increases in segregation have coincided with a growth of free schooling in Denmark (see Wiborg, 2009). Indeed, should the Conservatives take a fully evidence-based approach, they might consider the case of Finland, where an entirely comprehensive state education system has resulted in topping OECD international exam performance tables in maths, literacy and science since 2000.

Finally, in keeping with the theme of continuity, strong elements of social conservatism remain within current Conservative policy. Echoing and extending promises from previous manifestos, plans include greater power for teachers to use physical force against unruly pupils 'without fear of legal action':

> We will give headteachers a general legal power to ban, search for, and confiscate any items they think may cause violence or disruption (which the [Labour] Government opposes on 'human rights' grounds). We will reverse the legal obligation on teachers to prove that their search and confiscation is legal. We will abolish the Guidance whereby the Government 'strongly advises' teachers not to search children if they object to being searched. (Gove, 2009a)

There have been nostalgic calls for greater 'adventure' and competitive sports in school, defying the regulations of 'health and safety bureaucrats'. While old favourites of the party faithful such as grammar schools and the '11-plus' have been formally denounced, they have been replaced with promises of 'aggressive setting by ability' (Cameron, 2007c). Long-standing plans remain for 'no nonsense' exclusion of troublemaking pupils, while attempts at the inclusion of pupils with special educational needs in mainstream schools are dismissed on the basis that they are 'ideologically driven'.

## Policy networks

Ideas underpinning policy commitments of the 'new' Conservatives in education are supported and reinforced by the existence of a sprawling and highly interconnected policy network. Centre-right organisations undertaking extensive policy activity nationally and internationally have expanded hugely in number in the same way that numbers of centre-left organisations expanded around New Labour (Ball and Exley, 2010). Ideas heard in Conservative speeches and seen in policy documents are the same ideas flowing through organisations within the network. They are spread and reinforced by the network, feeding into normative discursive shifts in the media and public mind, influenced by and influencing policy. Organisations on the right are not just connected by 'key players' with membership and connections across multiple organisations, they are linked by new and well-funded 'gateways' of centre-right thinking – websites such as Conservative Home, Conservative Intelligence and the Conservative Education Society – where policy activity across hundreds of organisations is monitored, updated and brought together in one place.

Think tanks influencing Conservative education policy include some old and some new. 'Old' organisations such as the Centre for Policy Studies, the Adam Smith Institute, the Institute of Economic Affairs and Politeia have enjoyed recent press interest after more than a decade of centre-left think tank dominance in the media. The Centre for Policy Studies has written on the abolition of quangos in a 'post-bureaucratic' age (Burkard, 2009). Its contacts are strong, with David Willetts on its council and journalists such as *Spectator* editor Fraser Nelson on its board. New think tanks also have an influence. As with other policy areas, the Centre for Social Justice has been central to changing Conservative rhetoric on education and social justice, and its policy group has produced literature assessing the extent to which Labour has failed to increase social mobility (Centre for Social Justice, 2006a). On the 'Big Society', David Cameron has been heavily influenced by 'Red Tory' or 'progressive Conservative' Phillip Blond – former member of Demos and founder of think tank ResPublica in 2009 – and his ideas for 'popular capitalism', 'mutualism', social entrepreneurialism and local community ownership of public services. The think tank Policy Exchange is highly influential and has been described by Conservative Chancellor, George Osborne as 'a wellspring of new ideas throughout this decade'.[2] Policy Exchange has Michael Gove as one of its key founders (together with Nicholas Boles and Francis Maude). Sam Freedman, Head of the Policy Exchange Education Unit, moved to be

Conservative Party advisor on 'poverty and opportunity'. The Policy Exchange report, *Blocking the Best*, challenged local authorities over the barriers they present to new school providers (Fazackerley and Wolf, 2010). The report recommended that new schools should be entirely exempt from local authority planning controls and that, more broadly, authorities should have no power to stop new schools from being created. The New Schools Network (NSN) – jointly responsible for *Blocking the Best* along with the Policy Exchange – was set up by Rachel Wolf in 2009 in order to promote 'free schools' and Academies across England in line with the Swedish model and US Charter Schools. Aged just 24, Wolf has advised Michael Gove and also Boris Johnson. She is known to have contributed to the 2010 Conservative manifesto.[3]

Complex 'heterarchies' and polycentric governance in relation to educational delivery can be seen as extending into the processes of policymaking itself. Networks of knowledge and ideas connect diverse and 'enterprising' state, private- and voluntary-sector actors in the creation of educational policy, with complex, fluid and codependent relationships between actors. Companies and charities involved in 'the business of education' – whether for profit or not – form alliances with political parties who promote through policy their ideas and services. Examples can be seen in Conservative connections with private Swedish education provider Kunskapskollan and the promotion of Teach First in the 2010 Conservative manifesto, signalling plans that the government will work with this charity to ensure its activities are expanded under Conservative rule. The Conservatives' idea for teachers to hold degrees of no less than lower second-class standard comes from McKinsey's work on the comparative status of teachers in other countries (Barber and Mourshed, 2007). Think tanks are often 'do tanks'. They are part of the 'Big Society', stakeholders participating in education – funding, piloting, undertaking media publicity and evaluating initiatives, then becoming authoritative voices, advising politicians and undertaking further commissions to deliver initiatives. The New Schools Network has among its trustees Sir Bruce Liddington – former head of Academies in the DCSF and current Director General of EACT, a foundation opening chains of Academies across England. It also has as a Trustee Amanda Spielman from Absolute Return for Kids (ARK) – a philanthropic organisation funding multiple Academies. The 'do tank', Civitas, runs independent extra-curricular educational programmes for children from underprivileged backgrounds (fitting in well with 'compassionate Conservatism'). It also provides low-cost independent schooling through its 'New Model Schools Company', praised in the right-wing press (Fox, 2009). It produces publications advocating the 'Swedish model' of independent schooling (Cowen, 2008) and, as in the case of the New Schools Network, Civitas had input into the 2010 Conservative manifesto.[4]

## Conservative and New Labour education policies: continuity or change?

Any analysis of Conservative education policies needs to understand their continuities with New Labour as well as and alongside their differences. This was equally the case in reverse when considering New Labour education policies in 1997, and in the case of Labour very little policy from before 1997 was directly dispensed with (with the exception of the Assisted Places Scheme, Neighbourhood Nursery Vouchers and Grant Maintained schools), although there was also plenty of new policy. The 1998 Labour Party conference briefing paper on education listed 47 initiatives, although a good number of these were based upon an elaboration of previous trends or initiatives introduced by the Conservatives. In some areas of policy Conservative ideas were taken much more seriously by New Labour – for example Specialist Schools, CTCs/Academies and business participation in education more generally (as in Education Action Zones and Academies, and later Trust schools), in addition to surveillance over educational standards. According to Novak (1998, p 2), 'the triumph of Tony Blair may in one sense be regarded as the triumph of Margaret Thatcher'. And as John Major saw it, 'I did not, at the time, appreciate the extent to which he would appropriate Conservative language and steal our policies' (1999, p 593).

Nonetheless, the policy dynamics around these areas, and arguably what made them so prominent under New Labour, apart from Tony Blair's education mantra, is also a major point of difference, or two points of difference, a difference then and a difference now. That is, New Labour were willing to spend money and to drive their policies by investment, intervention and direction (for example, on the one hand, Building Schools for the Future, class sizes and the national strategies, and, on the other, national performance benchmarks, 'naming and shaming' and the National Challenge). New Labour took the Conservative infrastructure and gave it meat and teeth. While Conservative education policy from 1988 to 1997 had involved many changes of direction and many new ideas, to a great extent (the National Curriculum and national testing aside) it had remained locked into Thatcherite 'small state' thinking, and in thrall to free-market neo-liberalism. New Labour, initially through the political trope of the 'Third Way', moved on to a post-neo-liberal policy phase in which the state became the powerhouse of public sector reform and a 'transformer' and market-maker (see Cabinet Office, 2006). In a sense New Labour 'did' many of the Conservative policies but 'did' them differently, although the nuances (or perhaps rhetoric) of some of these policies were also different.

Gamble and Kelly have argued in a Nexus forum debate that instead of merely a revision of social democracy the Third Way could be: 'a new and heterodox alignment of ideas (which some are bundling under the rubric of the radical centre) which recognise that there has been a sharp break of political continuity [and] which render many former certainties obsolete' (Halpern and Mikosz, 1998).[5] While Labour sought after 1997 to reform education by regulation and through centralised programmes, the Conservatives from 2010 intend to achieve change by reducing and stripping out regulation, giving schools and head teachers more autonomy, and allowing greater diversity (of some sorts) and a much greater emphasis on consumerism. Supply-side measures are to be put in place to set education 'free' by introducing new providers and new choices, cutting excessive red tape, scrapping unnecessary quangos, and creating a streamlined funding model where government funding follows the learner:

> We will change the laws – on planning, on funding, on staffing – to make it easier for new schools to be created in your neighbourhood, so you can demand the precise, personalised, education your children need…. The money currently wasted on red tape and management consultants instead invested in books and teachers…. This is step one in a revolution which will see more and more of our schools run by professionals – who are accountable to parents not central or local bureaucracy. (Gove, 2009b)

But despite all this, there is still a good deal of direction in Conservative policies, around 'order' in schools, around exclusions and around teacher pay, qualifications and sackings. The increased juridification of teacher–pupil relations that took place from 1997 to 2010 (Ball et al, 2009) will continue further under Conservative plans to enable the physical removal of pupils from classrooms by teachers, plans for formal home–school agreements on behaviour, and plans to give teachers more power to search pupils. Moreover, Conservative plans to spare schools already judged as 'outstanding' from Ofsted inspections – unless their results fall dramatically, scores of teachers leave or huge numbers of parents complain – while putting out to tender the management of schools believed to be 'failing' and subjecting them to 'no notice' inspections, also echo Labour policy. The Conservative attack on and response to 'failing schools' sounds remarkably like Labour's first-term policies for 'naming, blaming and shaming' and 'Fresh Start' schools. Under Labour, schools within the National Challenge were subject to being turned into Academies, Trust schools or becoming part of a Federation. Here again the differences seem a matter of a more managed Labour response as against a more libertarian Conservative one, and the Conservative rhetoric of reform sounds remarkably like that surrounding Labour's first iteration of Academies run by 'hero' entrepreneurs:

> We will – in our first hundred days – identify the very worst schools – the sink schools which have desperately failed their children – and put them rapidly into the hands of heads with a proven track record of success…. We will remove the managements which have failed and replace them with people who know how to turn round schools. (Gove, 2009b)

While Labour's Ed Balls talked of primary school mergers and 'executive heads', Michael Gove has suggested celebrity advisors like Carole Vorderman and Goldie Hawn. Thus, to some extent Conservative policy can be understood in terms of previous Labour policy, taking it further in particular directions by different means.

However, as described earlier, 'new' Conservative policy is also influenced by the party's pre-1997 policy and its contradictions. In 1990 Ball identified the influence of 'neo-liberals', 'neo-conservatives' and 'industrial-trainers' within Conservative education policies, and Jones (1989, 2003) uses similar distinctions. These different strands are still in evidence, hence Ryan's view that:

> One day Michael Gove is extolling the virtues of free schools, liberated from the shackles of Whitehall, with the touchy-feely charms of Goldie Hawn jostling alongside Swedish companies to deliver. Days later he is laying down the level of detailed knowledge that every youngster should have of their kings and queens, their classical poetry by heart and their algebra under the tutelage of the Tories' Maths mistress Carol Vorderman. Gove's confusion on education policy, one of the few areas where the Tories have at least done some homework, seems to mirror his party's wider

confusion as it wobbles in the polls. This is exemplified in planning, where Gove has pledged to railroad through new local school plans in Whitehall regardless of local objections while his shadow cabinet colleague Theresa Villiers apparently wants every parish council to have its say on any high speed rail link. (Ryan, 2010)

As suggested earlier, Conservative education policy is not of a piece. Rather it is a bricolage of often incoherent international 'borrowings', the input of a diverse set of 'think tanks' ranging from the Centre for Social Justice through to the Red Conservatism of ResPublica, the acceptance of many of Labour's 'good ideas', and the underlying tensions of traditionalism ('real' subjects), liberalism (school diversity and choice) and economism (vocationalism).

Even here it is perhaps a matter of emphasis rather than distinction. Ideas around gifted and talented pupils, ability grouping, discipline and school uniforms were also very evident in New Labour policies and are distinct trends within the Academies programme (for example, ARK, Mossbourne and Knowledge in Power Programe (KIPP)). Several of the specific policy initiatives favoured by the Conservatives were founded or flourished under New Labour, such as Academies and Teach First.

The area of vocational education also seems marked by differences in emphasis rather than principle. The New Labour infrastructure of Diplomas and new vocational routes for 14- to 19-year-olds, and ideas like Kenneth Baker's University Technical Colleges, a new kind of Academy (the first to be set up in Birmingham, sponsored by Aston University), will also be taken up and taken further but through specialist vocational schools set up in 12 cities across England funded from the Academies budget and a tripling of Young Apprenticeships – also introduced by New Labour – rather than Diplomas. Both versions involve a reinvention of technical education and a separation of students into different curricula routes at age 14.

Even in areas where we might expect significant differences, at least in rhetoric, there are convergences, continuities and overlaps. Over and against Labour's muted, meritocratic version of social justice, the convoluted avoidance of an end to grammar schools and attempts at widening participation, the Conservatives' manifesto planned to fund an extra 10,000 university places, although in the event these did not materialise. They have been critical of New Labour's 'failure' to reduce social inequalities, as described earlier, and have put forward policies of their own purporting to tackle inequalities.

In practical terms, the policy and legislative infrastructure for a great deal of Conservative education policy already existed before May 2010, particularly those aspects that focus on getting more providers and greater diversity and choice into the state school system. This was illustrated in Michael Gove's response to a question at the *Spectator* conference, 'The Schools Revolution', in March 2010. When asked if the Conservatives would allow for-profit providers to run state schools, he replied that they would, but 'within the framework of existing legislation'. There is a plethora of 'policy texts', existing legislation, regulations, guidance, frameworks, procedures and reports (see the Department for Education website) enabling Conservative 'new' and 'free' school initiatives to take off immediately. Academies already existed under Labour, and in mid-2010 there were 321 Trust schools in existence,[6] for example:

- Monkseaton High School, England's first Trust school, run by The Innovation Trust, a partnership between Monkseaton, North Tyneside Council, Microsoft, and Tribal Education.
- The Futures Learning Trust, made up of three primary schools, had the Life Channel, Burnley Football Club and Liverpool John Moores University as partners.
- The Lodge Park Technology Trust had Dell Computers and Land Securities as partners.

Under Labour, within the former Department for Children, Schools and Families, there already existed a unit guiding school competitions: the School Organisation and Competitions Unit (SOCU). Some early competitions had been in Southampton (Oasis Trust, a Baptist group), Northamptonshire (Woodnewton – a Learning Community [a state primary school] and The Brooke Weston Partnership), Kent (The Homewood Trust and another local school), Lincolnshire (British EduTrust [an Academy Sponsor] and the Gainsborough Educational Village Trust) and West Sussex (The Bolnore School Group and a parent/community group). Four schools had been contracted out to private providers, three in Surrey, and the most recent, Salisbury School in Enfield (now Turin Grove), on a three-year contract to the UK subsidiary of the US Edision Corporation. The Labour government had already established a scheme to vet and recognise new providers: Accredited School Providers and Accredited Schools Groups.

All of this points to a new kind of policymaking. It is policymaking by increments and by experiment, a process of 'ratcheting' (see Ball, 2008), making more things thinkable, possible and doable, through a series of small moves (the first two terms of New Labour saw eight separate Education Acts) rather than moments of 'big' legislation, although the rhetoric, as expressed by David Cameron, 'I don't want anyone to doubt the size, scope and scale of the changes we want to bring' (Cameron, 2010c), indicates differently. Conservative education policy wants to let many flowers bloom, from Goldie Hawn to the Church of England. Still, how freedoms and requirements will be managed and balanced under Conservative rule, and which principles of policy will emerge as being paramount, remains unclear.

## What does all this portend?

The disarticulation of the state education system in England is already well under way, and the Coalition's programme will perhaps take this process further and faster. Trends established by New Labour towards a system of 'fragmented centralisation' will continue as 'new' schools are set up, new providers enter the system and more Academies are created. Within all of this, the teaching workforce will experience further 'flexibilisation', and the role of local authorities in service delivery and administration will be increasingly replaced by commissioning work.

It is always dangerous in policy discussions of this kind to make assumptions about coherence or the ultimate resolution of policy contradictions. Nonetheless, we can ask what the outcomes or consequences will be of the tensions and contradictions of principle noted earlier. Will schools really have freedom to innovate without government intervention? How will this fit with plans for strong surveillance over teaching and an insistence on old-fashioned teaching methods? When plans for funding cuts are major and imminent, how will funding be found for 2,000 new schools? Given financial constraints, will new schools emerge 'on the cheap'? If so, what will happen to Conservative assurances over educational quality – good school facilities, sports fields and science labs and (perhaps most importantly of all) highly qualified teachers? Given the Teach Now programme, will it always be possible to ensure teacher quality? On the question of quality more broadly, and given indications that the Conservatives will embrace the technocracy of school improvement, will funding remain for commissioning research on 'what works' (and perhaps more importantly what does not) within the re-established Department for Education?

There is a particularly important question to be answered around how educational equality might be reconciled with an attack on bureaucracy and an emphasis on weakly redistributive voluntarism or indeed 'society not the state'. To borrow from Rutherford (2008), Conservative philosophy focuses on liberty and 'fraternity', but not equality. Freedom is conceptualised in Hayekian terms as negative 'freedom from', but it might be considered that only through state 'assertion' of some sort can any semblance of educational equality be ensured. Without state regulation of education, will it be possible to protect fully the needs of the least advantaged in society and guarantee comparable educational quality for all (particularly where parents and private providers are setting up schools)? Will parents have genuine empowered involvement in running 'free schools' or will they simply act as commissioners, passing on control of schools directly to businesses and philanthropic organisations? With an absence of local authority control over school admissions, will it be possible to ensure (as opposed to just creating mild financial incentives) that schools do not reject the pupils who are hardest to teach? In 1999 an initial review by Power and Whitty of New Labour policies and Education Action Zones concluded that 'a mixed economy of schooling, developed on a local basis and dependent on the amount of local capital available is likely to reinforce variations between disadvantaged areas' (1999, p 545). This may be even more the case from now on. The Coalition's Pupil Premium assumes that additional money for deprived pupils will be sufficient to secure entry for these pupils into high-achieving schools, but can this be assumed in a context where schools are under pressure to maintain high examination scores? Will 'successful' schools risk alienating middle-class parents who do not want their children to be educated alongside disadvantaged pupils? Finally, can a strong Conservative commitment to excluding 'troublemakers' ever be reconciled with a commitment to narrowing the education gap?

Which principles matter most will become clearer over time, and these will determine how modern or indeed 'compassionate' Conservative education policy turns out to be. Within the new Coalition government, and with Michael Gove as the new Secretary of State for Education, which promises on education will be kept – particularly given earlier manifesto clashes between the Conservatives and the Liberal Democrats – remains to be seen. Still, what is clear now is that we may well be at the beginning of the end of state education.

## Notes

[1] Similar posturing can be seen in the frequent Tory referencing of school choice schemes endorsed by US President Barack Obama, including the 'Swedish model' and Charter Schools across the US and Canada.

[2] See http://www.policyexchange.org.uk/about/

[3] See http://conservativehome.blogs.com/conference/2010/01/conservativeintelligences-guide-to-the-tory-manifesto-is-now-available-to-buy.html

[4] See note 3.

[5] See also www.thirdway.eu/2008/01/30/the-third-way-an-answer-to-blair/ (accessed 19 March 2010).

[6] See http://www.trustandfoundationschools.org.uk/parents/trustschools.aspx

# SEVEN

# Conservative housing policy

*Peter Somerville*

Current Conservative housing policy emerged rather later than their other policies. In *Breakdown Britain* (Social Justice Policy Group, 2006), for example, which proposed new policies for families, education, debt management, tackling poverty and substance misuse, and promoting the third sector, there was no mention of housing at all. Housing policy, did, however, appear in *Breakthrough Britain* (Social Justice Policy Group, 2007), and we can see this as the embryo of the housing policy that followed. However, Conservative housing policy has continued to be overshadowed by wider debates about welfare reform and the so-called 'Big Society' and the relationship of housing to these debates is not entirely clear.

## The genesis of Conservative housing policy

At first, the Conservatives' approach to housing policy was distinguished by an emphasis on family. On this, *Breakthrough Britain* (Social Justice Policy Group, 2007) made four recommendations:

- To create asset-owning families through extensions of the right to buy, rent-to-own and shared equity schemes, with the aim being 'for all social housing tenants to be able to build up capital within (and ultimately be able to purchase) the property they occupy'.
- To reform housing benefit so that it 'could move from being arrears-based to credit-based', with the implication being that the benefit being paid to tenants could be capitalised in order to enable tenants to acquire assets such as housing.
- To make it easier for social housing tenants to move, through 'a more flexible tenancy arrangement which takes changes in circumstances into account'. The text here gives the example of families who are under-occupying because their children have 'flown the nest', so the implication appears to be that it is changes in family circumstances that the Conservatives have in mind.

- To help vulnerable families move towards self-sufficiency through increasing the provision of supported housing projects.

These recommendations suggested a general policy approach of capitalising lower-income families, increasing their residential mobility and enabling them to improve the management of their own housing circumstances. Of these, however, it is only the idea of flexible tenancies that has been taken forward into policy.

By the time of the publication of the Centre for Social Justice's (2008b) report on *Housing Poverty*, thinking within the Conservative Party had moved on considerably. This report advocated a wide range of measures including:

- a 'localised revolution in housing supply' (2008b, p 3);
- the immediate implementation of mortgage rescue schemes;
- the expansion of the private rented sector;
- more vigorous action on empty homes and under-occupation;
- ending 'the stifling requirement that social housing tenancy be secure for life' (2008b, p 7);
- freeing local authorities to use new housing or empty housing as they see fit;
- a tariff on housing developers to pay for community services;
- housing benefit reform so that it takes the form of an 'undifferentiated subsidy' (2008b, p 10) (or voucher) that tenants can spend as they choose including on purchasing housing within their area that meets their needs;
- compulsory commitment contracts whereby new working-age tenants agree actively to seek work and their landlord agrees to provide or access support (such as training or childcare) for them to do so;
- extension of housing support services to all older and disabled people, regardless of their tenure; and
- for housing services generally to become more differentiated, with housing organisations being run as social enterprises.

This is an interesting list to consider. Some proposals, such as on private renting, more freedom for local housing authorities and turning housing organisations into social enterprises, reflect the concerns of the previous New Labour governments, namely, to make housing markets work better by increasing diversity among providers and choice among consumers. Other proposed policies, however, such as on mortgage rescue, empty homes, under-occupation, developer tariffs and commitment contracts, appear to conflict with the Conservative Party's long-standing aim to increase freedom for local authorities and for housing markets generally, because such policies involve intervention in the housing market and the imposition of new restrictions on the contractual relationship between landlord and tenant. Perhaps it is not surprising, then, that these proposals have not yet translated into government policy.[1] The most important one that has been adopted by the Coalition government is that of ending secure tenancies (Department for Communities and Local Government, 2010b).

What emerges most clearly from the more interventionist policies is the emphasis on capitalisation, and not just of the poor. Capitalisation is a recurrent theme of what has been called 'progressive Conservatism' (see, for example, Blond, 2010), and which is summed up in the phrase 'property-owning democracy'. The right to buy, for example, was hailed as the flagship of Conservative government policy in the 1980s, not so much because it involved a massive transfer of public assets into private hands, as because it involved an unprecedented extension of the ownership of (housing) wealth. In the case of the proposals in *Housing Poverty*, it can be seen that: mortgage rescue means safeguarding the mortgagor's capital asset; proposals on empty homes, under-occupation and developer tariffs are designed to maximise housing capital values; housing benefit reforms involve direct capitalisation of subsidy; and commitment contracts and housing support aim to make tenants ideally into capital owners but, failing that, at least into efficient and effective managers of capital assets (namely, their homes).

## Conservative housing policy

The reports from the Centre for Social Justice were followed by three important 'Green Papers': *Control Shift* (Conservative Party, 2009b), *Strong Foundations* (Conservative Party, 2009e) and the *Planning Green Paper* (Conservative Party, 2010g). It is these three papers that form the basis for current Conservative housing policy. The proposals in these papers all found their way into the Conservative manifesto, published on 13 April 2010 (Conservative Party, 2010e) and have mostly been confirmed since the election by Coalition government leaders (see, for example, Cabinet Office, 2010). Many of them now appear in the Localism Bill.

Much of *Control Shift* sounds identical to New Labour's thinking, as with the example that 'Conservatives want to build a stronger, safer society where opportunity and power are spread much more widely and fairly' (2009b, p 3). However, the papers contained a powerful indictment of Labour's failure to deliver the housing that people need and can afford, the causes of which they attributed mainly to Labour's 'centrally planned and controlled system' (Conservative Party, 2009b, p 7), citing the government's own statements in their support (Ministry of Justice, 2007). To counteract this over-centralisation, they proposed to abolish the regional tier of government in England – all regional planning and housing powers including those of the Regional Development Agencies. Instead they advocated a new localism:

> Our vision of localism is one where power is decentralised to the lowest possible level. For services which are used individually, this means putting power in the hands of individuals themselves. Where services are enjoyed collectively, they should be delivered by accountable community groups; or, where the scale is too large or those using a service too dispersed, by local authorities themselves, subject to democratic checks and balances. (Conservative Party, 2009b, p 8)

This seems an important interpretation of the principle of subsidiarity, according to which decisions over public services should be devolved to the lowest level possible that is consistent with their effective and fair implementation. It is also a principle that lies at the heart of the idea of the 'Big Society' (Conservative Party, 2010c; Norman, 2010; see also Chapters 1 and 14, this volume): it calls for a substantial devolution of power from government to local community groups and local authorities, which New Labour never seemed to be either able or willing to achieve.

The three Green Papers proposed specific measures:

- First, to free local authorities from central control – ending capping powers,[2] giving them a general power of competence (to conduct any lawful activity in the best interests of their electorates), abolishing process targets and the comprehensive area assessment, and allowing them to devolve unlimited funding to ward councillors.
- Second, to give local communities a share in local growth by providing a financial incentive to build new affordable housing (specifically, funding from government to local authorities that matches the council tax payable on each new home). In the *Planning Green Paper*, this financial incentive was quantified at 125% of the council tax raised by each home built, annually for a period of six years.

- Third, to provide a 'community right to build', according to which a community will be able to award themselves planning permission for a development in their area, provided that no more than 10% of the community (that is, residents on the electoral register within the area of a parish or town council) are opposed to it (Conservative Party, 2009e). Development here can mean the building not only of homes, but also of shops, business space and other commercial properties.

These measures have now been largely incorporated, along with many others (some of which are discussed below), in the Localism Bill. The proposal in the 2009 Green Papers to issue incentives to councils to build new affordable housing also went ahead as planned in the autumn of 2010. It is important to note, however, that this subsidy (now known as the New Homes Bonus, and amounting to £350 per year for each new home – see Department for Communities and Local Government, 2010a) does not represent any new money for councils, and will actually be top-sliced from the annual block grant that the government makes to them. Considering also that the Coalition's emergency budget of June 2010 froze council tax for two years and cut £600 million from the budget for the Homes and Communities Agency, which was primarily responsible for funding social housing, and that, as announced by HM Treasury on 14 July 2010, the cap on local authority borrowing would not be removed, it is tempting to conclude that very little housing, if any, is likely to result from this particular proposal.

The *Planning Green Paper* contained further proposals for the local planning system, which were new and more radical than the policies in any of the other papers. Rather than increasing the freedom of local authorities to make their own planning decisions, these proposals introduced major new curbs on municipal power in favour of the power of residents and the 'Big Society'. The curbs fell under three main headings:

- First, a presumption in favour of sustainable development. It proposed to give individuals and businesses the right to build homes and other local buildings that conform to national environmental, architectural, economic and social standards, and to the local plan, provided that they pay a tariff that compensates the community for the loss of amenity and costs of additional infrastructure. This tariff would be a single unified local charge applicable to all development except affordable housing, varying according to the size of the development.

- Second, all significant local projects would have to be designed through a collaborative process that has involved the neighbourhood (village, town, estate, ward or other relevant local area) prior to submitting a planning application. Local authorities themselves must also use collaborative democratic methods in drawing up their local plans (Conservative Party, 2010b), which must be completed within a prescribed period. This proposal is now incorporated in the Localism Bill.
- Third, local residents would be given new powers to object to planning applications and to appeal against local planning decisions. If more than a small minority of the immediate residential neighbours (a parish council area could count as a set of immediate neighbours) raise an objection, a planning application must be formally assessed by the local planning authority for its conformity with the local plan. Otherwise, it can be approved as it is. Where an application has been approved, local residents as well as developers will be allowed to appeal, but only on the grounds that correct procedure was not followed in assessing the application or that the decision reached contravenes the local plan (Conservative Party, 2010b).

These proposals sparked considerable controversy. Regeneration professionals and house-builders expressed serious concerns that the proposals, if enacted, would exacerbate delays in the planning process – the opposite of their intention (see Hayman, 2010). In the Isle of Man, where a third-party right of appeal already exists, most developers see it as a recipe for delay. Another problem was that the proposed reliance on the local plan removed the room for discretion on the part of the local planning authority: planners might want to approve applications that fall outside the scope of the plan, for example, because of their potential economic benefits, but, if they did so, local residents who objected to the application might be able to launch a successful appeal. John Slaughter, the policy director for the Home Builders Federation was reported as saying:

> While we welcome the Conservatives' commitment to increase housing supply, their proposals pose some significant concerns for developers. Scrapping regional targets and devolving power to local communities is a high-risk strategy, because, while most people recognise the general need for more housing, acceptance of that principle is often lacking when planned housing is on their doorstep. A key question is whether the proposals for incentives to

reward housing supply and for the early adoption of new-style local plans are effective enough. (Carpenter, 2010)

Understandably, Grant Shapps, then Shadow Housing Minister (and now Housing Minister), argued that the council tax incentive scheme would be sufficient to ensure that more homes were built (Hayman, 2010). Williams (2010), however, took a different view, arguing that the Conservatives had failed to understand the real reasons for the problems with the planning system:

The difficulty of getting a planning approval has increased. It has become so difficult and costly that small developers have been squeezed out and the big six housebuilders favoured. The barriers to entry to this market have been raised too high by bad regulation. The result has been anti-competitive behaviour, provider monopolies, little design choice and high prices. But the answer is not to destroy the planning system or give vetoes to the Nimbys. The answer is to find out why it costs so much to get approval and why planning refusals have increased. Then fix things. The former is easy: too much planning guidance and policy has been created, so that 20 years ago an application was only 20 pages long and today it is 200. Transaction costs are too high, so cut them. Keep the planning system, just take an axe to the amount of paper and process required for an application. Planning refusals have risen because of a perverse consequence of an otherwise sensible reform. The introduction of the cabinet system of government in the 1990s led to a division between 'strategic planning' and 'development control', and the placing of planning application determination in the hands of the backbenchers. Planning rejections went off the scale after this because, frankly, party leaders no longer sat on planning committees exercising discipline and strategic oversight. If cabinet members were once again to sit on planning committees, even *ex officio*, planning sanity will be restored. (Williams, 2010)

Here Williams identifies the key problems in the planning process as not so much the time it takes to process an application as the cost of an application and the high rates of refusal. Further, he argues that the cost problem has been caused by a deluge of planning policy and guidance, and the refusal problem has resulted from allowing decisions to be made by backbench councillors. If this analysis is correct, it would seem to follow that the Conservative proposals would be likely to make both problems worse, because more collaborative processes are likely to increase the amount of paperwork and therefore costs, and the local people who are given the right to object to a planning application may well be supported by their local councillor. There is no evidence as yet that the Coalition government acknowledges such problems, let alone intends to respond to the arguments made. Indeed, during the summer of 2010 a wide-ranging group of 29 national bodies concerned with planning issues wrote to Eric Pickles, the Secretary of State for Communities and Local Government, because they were concerned about the possible consequences of the Coalition government's planning reforms (Royal Town Planning Institute, 2010). More recently, the Rural Coalition (2010) has argued strongly that a parish-led collaborative planning process should be sufficient on its own to secure the provision of affordable housing to meet local need, without any need to give local residents a right of veto.

Finally, the Localism Bill proposes a right for communities, working through parish councils or neighbourhood forums, to draw up neighbourhood development plans, consistent with national and local government planning policy. The plans come into force if they are approved by a majority of residents in a referendum. Under such plans, groups of residents will be able to undertake small developments without having to seek permission (the so-called 'community right to build'). Perhaps in response to the objections discussed above, the Localism Bill contains no new powers for residents to object to planning applications or to appeal against planning decisions.

A final comment to make about the *Planning Green Paper* is that it perhaps contained a trace of the 'nasty party' (see Chapter 1) in its proposal to repeal the Human Rights Act, mainly, it seems, in order to address the problems of evicting trespassers from private and public property: '[the Human Rights Act] has overridden planning law by allowing travellers to go ahead with unauthorised development' (Conservative Party, 2010g, p 18). Organisations working with Gypsies and Travellers have already pointed out that this will only increase the problem of illegal sites. This is because, as Emma Nuttall, Advice and Policy Manager at Friends, Families and Travellers, has said: 'Some Travellers don't know you need planning permission to live in a caravan on your own land. If they can't do this they will camp on fields and parks and potentially cause more problems to the community' (Twinch, 2010; see also Brooks, 2010; Stockdale, 2010).

*Strong Foundations* contained several further important new policies. These can be grouped under the three dimensions of localism identified in *Control Shift*, namely, services to individuals, services to local communities and services to a wider public.

## Services to individuals

Proposals under this heading related only to social housing tenants and were aimed at improving their choice and strengthening their rights. The idea that their rights might be weakened in any way (for example, by ending security of tenure) was implicitly rejected. The main proposals were:

- A 'right to move'. This meant giving social tenants with a record of five years' good behaviour the right to demand that their landlord sell their current property and use the proceeds, minus transaction costs, to buy (and thereby bring into the social rented sector) another property of their choice anywhere in England (Conservative Party, 2009e). The origin of this policy seems to lie in a paper by Tim Leunig published by the Conservative-leaning think tank, Policy Exchange, three months earlier (Leunig, 2009a).[5]
- A new national mobility scheme, to replace the one abandoned by the Labour government. Accordingly, on 4 August 2010, Grant Shapps, the Housing Minister, launched a so-called 'Freedom Pass', which will allow all social housing tenants in England to see details of all other social housing tenants wishing to move to another social housing home. This is now known as the National Homeswap Scheme (in the Localism Bill).
- A free 10% equity share in their rented property for social tenants with a record of five years' good behaviour. This could be cashed in when they leave the social rented sector. They would continue paying the same rent and would have to maintain good behaviour, that is, pay their rent on time, and not breach their tenancy agreement (Conservative Party, 2009e). This proposal seemed to fit well with the Conservatives' aim to capitalise the poor – the paper argued that such asset transfers could lift people out of poverty.

There are serious practical problems, however, with the first and third of these proposals. The right to move could entail significant costs for landlords, not only arising from the transaction itself, but also in terms of the diseconomies of scale resulting from the wide dispersal of ownership that would inevitably result from such a policy. Perhaps for this reason, it was proposed that the policy be piloted first, to establish the extent of such implications. Grant Shapps later announced (4 August 2010) that he would work with two London councils to pilot a right to move scheme.

The equity-sharing proposal has been criticised as potentially wasteful, for example, if a tenant puts the money towards buying a house and the purchase goes wrong, or if the tenant would have moved out anyway. Leunig (2009b) has argued that this shows a need to pilot the scheme first. It could be suggested, however, that problems with the proposal go deeper than this. Indeed, there is an interesting parallel to be drawn between this proposal and the previous Conservative government's policy on rents-to-mortgages back in 1991 (see Department of the Environment, 1992; and the evaluation of the pilot scheme by Park and Smith, 1994). The principle of that policy was that the ownership of the property could be transferred to the tenant without requiring them to pay any more for their housing – that is, their new mortgage payments would not exceed their former rent payments. This was achieved by means of an additional charge on the property, which was payable on disposal of that property. Discounts were available as under the right to buy, but at a lower rate.

The equity shares on offer under the current proposal are similar to the discounts available under rents-to-mortgages, only less generous and simpler because the latter varied according to how long they had been tenants and how much rent they paid (the discounts could be as much as 40% of the purchase price). From the tenant's point of view, the main difference would appear to be that under rents-to-mortgages they became responsible for repairs and maintenance to the property. Evaluation of the pilot scheme showed that take-up was extremely low (around 0.6%); tenants did not apply, or applied but did not go ahead with the purchase, because of concerns about the financial implications of home ownership, in particular the upkeep of the property. The equity-sharing proposal is different from this because the tenant is not given any extra responsibilities at all in return for the equity given to them.[4] It is simply an incentive to move out, and it is assumed that they will not want to come back.

Perhaps the main problem with the equity-sharing proposal is its assumptions that social tenants do not move because they cannot move (see Conservative Party, 2009e) and that a 10% share of the equity will be sufficient to enable them to move. The first assumption is called into question by research for the Tenant Services Authority (which the Conservatives are committed to abolishing), which found that nearly three quarters of social tenants said they wanted to stay in the sector for the next 10 years. This suggests that they do not want to move rather than that they are unable to move. Indeed, levels of satisfaction were so high that 80% said being a social tenant was better than owning your own home or living in the private rented sector (see *Inside Housing*, 25 September 2009, p 5). The second assumption is also highly dubious, particularly in a housing market where deposits of up to 20% are commonly required for house purchase.

All of these factors, taken together, can perhaps explain why the Coalition government has been completely silent about the equity-sharing proposal (it does not figure in the Localism Bill), although it would be rash to conclude from this silence that the idea is now dead and buried.

## Services to communities

The key proposal in *Strong Foundations* for improving services to communities was that for Local Housing Trusts (LHTs). LHTs are based on Community Land Trusts (CLTs), in which land and other fixed assets are acquired by a community and held in trust to enable community members to benefit in the form of affordable housing and other facilities built on that land, and to ensure that the land and housing are not disposed of to the detriment of the community. As with CLTs, it was envisaged in the paper that all non-market housing built by LHTs would remain in local ownership in perpetuity.

This proposal seems to have been overtaken by events. Originally, the community right to build required 90% support from local people but over the course of 2010, this figure was reduced to 80%, then 75%, and finally, under the Localism Bill, 50% of residents. This now accords closely with the findings of a survey of 1,000 adults for *Inside Housing* which found that most respondents would object to new developments of more than 100 affordable homes in their area but would support development that involved small numbers (only 9% would object to developments of up to 25 affordable homes) (Thorpe, 2010). Further, it is arguable that the concept of neighbourhood planning introduced in the Localism Bill makes LHTs unnecessary because the plan itself, owned by a parish council or neighbourhood forum, provides a basis on which community assets can be developed and safeguarded for the benefit of the community as a whole.

It is also worth noting that the previous Labour government had already proposed, on 5 April 2010, to consult on allowing parish councils to approve applications for up to 15 affordable homes to be built in their areas (the Conservative proposals originally envisaged only 5–10 properties), with no need for LHTs or ballots of residents. The Coalition government's policy, therefore, now looks very similar to that of the outgoing Labour government, with a referendum on the neighbourhood plan taking the place of a vote by the parish council.

### Services to a wider public

The only proposals in *Strong Foundations* beyond those for individuals and communities related to the need to move towards a low carbon economy. The paper cited Friends of the Earth (press release, 27 November 2007) as saying that carbon dioxide emissions from the housing sector currently account for 27% of the UK's carbon footprint. Reducing such emissions, therefore, is now a key challenge for housing policy. There is, however, only one new policy here that is of any significance. This is the proposal, confirmed by the Coalition government on 2 July 2010, to give all householders a right to a £6,500 interest-free loan for energy efficiencies in their homes, with repayments being recovered automatically through household energy bills over a period of up to 25 years. At an estimated cost of £90 billion, this proposal looks more generous than the former Labour government's piloted 'pay as you save' proposal that allowed for loans of an average of £10,000 per home but which were not interest-free (HM Government, 2010c). Both proposals, however, as part of a wider approach emphasising energy efficiency, take no account of what householders might do with the savings made from such efficiencies – they could buy more goods whose production has used up energy, or they could travel by energy-using transport. When it comes to achieving a low-carbon economy, housing cannot be considered in isolation.

Looking at all these further proposals, it seems that, in some respects, they can be regarded as a logical progression from some of the recommendations in *Breakthrough Britain*.[5] The equity-sharing proposal, for example, can be seen as helping to capitalise lower-income families, while the right to move is clearly intended to increase residential mobility. Building new affordable housing could also be argued to be essential if poorer families are to have any opportunity to progress. Other proposals seem to fit well with the vision of the 'Big Society', for example, removing central restrictions on local authorities. Interestingly, the proposals as a whole suggest a change in policy approach from that of New Labour, from one of coercion and regulation to one of encouragement and incentivisation. This impression is reinforced by the character of some of the new policies that the Coalition government has announced which were not in the Conservative manifesto (or anywhere else for that matter), such as scrapping the previous government's plans for further regulation of the private rented sector (including the licensing of private landlords) and abolishing the Audit Commission.

## The Big Society and housing policy

The idea of the Big Society derives from the 'compassionate Conservatism' of Jesse Norman (2006) and the 'progressive Conservatism', of Phillip Blond (2010). It is a vision of a 'connected society' (Norman, 2010, p 104), held together by affection and personal ties. It believes that horizontal organisation works better then either vertical, top-down direction or a free-for-all (which Norman likens to a Hobbesian state of nature). It is opposed equally to state authoritarianism, which assumes that government knows best, and to laissez-faire capitalism, which allows the strong to dominate the weak (Blond, 2010, p 22). It criticises traditional Conservatism for both its paternalism (which lacked a critique of the state) and its libertarianism (which lacked a critique of the market) (Norman, 2010, p 179).

The 'Big Society' idea was launched by the Conservatives on 31 March 2010 and developed in a paper published on 19 May (Conservative Party, 2010c). The key elements of the idea are: to support an unprecedented expansion of the third sector, for example, through the creation of a Big Society Bank that will fund bodies that support social enterprises; to encourage the formation of neighbourhood groups, for example, through the training of 5,000 community organisers,[6] and to give neighbourhood groups a range of powers, in particular a right to bid to take over certain assets and services in their areas, and a right to develop their own services such as schools and housing; and to promote more engagement in neighbourhood groups and social action projects.

In some ways, the idea can be understood as a continuation and development of New Labour's emphasis on the third sector, community participation, civil renewal and 'active citizenship' (Ministry of Justice, 2008). The Labour government, however, tended to expect citizens to do something in return for what the state was doing for them, for example, 'a hand up not a hand out', accepting 'responsibilities' in return for being given 'rights'. It launched numerous strategies, projects and programmes, in which citizens were encouraged to participate, but such participation was typically subordinated to the government's own purposes (see Somerville, 2011). In the 'Big Society', however, it seems to be envisaged that the government will support and encourage, but it will not take the lead, and, more importantly, it will devolve real power to citizens. In a major speech on 27 July 2010, Greg Clark, Minister of State at the Department for Communities and Local Government, stated that building the 'Big Society' requires three rights: a right to know, particularly how public money is being spent; a right for public service users to challenge how public resources are deployed wherever and whenever a better way can be found; and, perhaps most importantly, 'turning Government on its head', by which he appears to mean a distinctively more 'bottom-up' approach, with government as servant rather than as master, distributing resources directly to communities to help them solve their problems, including the problems that are caused by government itself (Clark, 2010).

The most obvious models for the Big Society in housing are those of cooperatives and community-based housing associations (and, more widely, what used to be called the voluntary housing movement), along with social enterprises and voluntary action generally. This is an area where the outgoing New Labour government was already developing new ideas (see HM Government, 2010b). The Conservatives have continued down this road (see, for example, Blond, 2010; Boyle et al, 2010; Maginn, 2010; Norman, 2001; Wyler and Blond, 2010). In principle, it seems that they want to see a wide range of cooperatives: both producer cooperatives, where public-sector workers take over the services in which they work, and consumer cooperatives, where the users of the public services assume responsibility for them. Different kinds of cooperative are seen as appropriate in different circumstances. In education, for example, their proposals for parents to run their own schools (see Chapter 6) suggest a preference for consumer cooperatives, whereas in health their proposals to devolve power to GPs (see Chapter 5) indicate a favouring of producer cooperatives. However, neither the Conservatives' manifesto nor the Coalition government's latest consultation paper (Department for Communities and Local Government, 2010b) has contained any word of support for housing cooperatives or recognition of the ways in which social housing can currently be run along cooperative lines (for example, through exercise of the Right to Manage)[7] or transferred into cooperative ownership (such as through Community Gateway – see the Confederation of Cooperative Housing website[8]). Under the community right to build in the Localism Bill, however, it will be possible for community groups to acquire community assets, which could include housing, potentially in tenant takeovers of housing estates.

Within the Conservative Party, however, the voices of both traditional authority and of market freedom remain powerful. This traditional

Conservatism is expressed in the drive to discipline the poor and weak, primarily through the deployment of market mechanisms. It harks back to the Conservative heyday of the 1980s and seeks to rekindle the flame of Thatcherism – to re-establish the authority of bosses over workers, parents over children, landlords over tenants and so on (see Chapter 2). Its vision of a 'Big Society' looks back to the Victorian era of strong local government and philanthropy, a society where (allegedly) everyone knew their place. Progressive or compassioniate Conservatism, on the other hand, involves a critique of Thatcherism, not only for its divisive, 'two-nation' stance, but also for its worship of private wealth accumulation. Progressive Conservatives' vision of a 'Big Society' is inclusive and forward-looking, a society of free and equal citizens, caring for themselves and for others, without their efforts being hindered or hijacked by the machinations of 'big government'. The implications of these differing strands of thought for housing policy are in some respects quite different.

## Traditional Conservatism

In housing policy, traditional Conservatism is perhaps most clearly revealed in attitudes to social housing. *Housing Poverty: From Social Breakdown to Social Mobility* (Centre for Social Justice, 2008b) is a key text here. It recognised that the problems of social housing areas (unemployment, crime and so on) are related to long-term processes of residualisation, whereby over the years better-off households moved out of social housing and poorer, more needy, households moved in. It made no specific proposals, however, to reverse these processes or to counter their effects. Instead, it proposed to exacerbate these processes by reinforcing the low status of social housing as housing of last resort – a Conservative view of social housing that goes back at least to the 1920s.[9] Thus it stated:

> the period in which a tenant finds themselves in social housing must be used to build aspiration, not stifle it. This can mean that, wherever appropriate, social housing is a step on the property ladder, used for shorter periods of time, to help people in crisis or to overcome homelessness. It should be a dynamic resource, playing a part in helping people to get back on their feet, either by working their way from social tenancy to private tenancy, then to shared equity and finally outright ownership, or through altering the tenants'

> relationship with the state so that they become, not a tenant, but a part owner. (Centre for Social Justice, 2008b, p 7)

This statement made it clear that a social tenancy is to be seen as inferior not only to ownership, but even to a private tenancy. There was also the patronising suggestion that social housing tenants were not paying their way as they needed 'to get back on their feet'.[10] For the Centre for Social Justice, the most important thing for a social tenant to do was to exit the tenure as quickly as possible, in order that their 'aspiration' would not be 'stifled'. The problem with this is that the exit of more aspirational tenants is the main reason why social housing became residualised in the first place, so further encouragement of such aspirations is likely only to serve to increase the plight of those who remain. Removing 'the stifling requirement that social housing tenancy be secure for life' (Centre for Social Justice, 2008b, p 7) will simply seal the fate of these poorer, less 'aspirational', tenants.

In an interview for *Inside Housing*, Iain Duncan Smith (26 March 2010, pp 23–4) defended the proposal to abolish secure tenancies on the following grounds: 'It doesn't do them any good, because the lifelong right to tenure they have is in the house that they're in, so it doesn't reflect changing circumstances'. One might have thought that having such a right would put them in a stronger position to get what they need if their circumstances were to change. For him, however: 'A sense of security is "I have a house over my head and I don't want to be here forever". We talk to most social tenants and they don't want to be there forever. They want to move on.' Needless to say, perhaps, he did not explain how removing their security of tenure can help them to do this.

These negative views of social housing and social tenants are not confined to the Conservative Party. For example, from a Labour standpoint, Gregory (2009) argued that social housing estates were a factor in reducing the life chances of their residents, because they are correlated with unemployment, poor health, lack of educational qualifications, crime and single and teenage parenthood. Such arguments, however, suffer from a deep lack of logic. Basically, they mistake correlation for causation. Just because social housing estates are associated with all these problems, it does not follow that they cause these problems. The association is, as stated earlier, the consequence of residualisation processes. No doubt some social housing estates are badly designed, badly maintained and so on, but these may comprise only a small proportion of all social housing. To say that social housing estates cause unemployment and poverty because so many of their residents are poor and unemployed is like arguing that hospitals cause people to die because so many people die in them. There is actually some truth in the latter argument because of the surgical errors, superbugs, malnutrition and so on, that occur in hospitals, but for the most part people are taken to hospital for treatment that is intended to cure them and often does so. Similarly, so it could be argued, social housing on the whole provides decent homes for those who need them. And where social housing estates are failing, the causes of this need to be properly investigated before deciding what needs to be done, rather than jumping to the conclusion that it must be the fault of the tenure itself.

Unfortunately, it is possible to display a traditional and patronising attitude to social tenants without resorting to such illogical arguments. The Chartered Institute of Housing (CIH), for example, which claims to represent housing professionals, takes a more 'pragmatic', less 'ideological', view than the Centre for Social Justice or Gregory for the Fabian Society, but managed to come to policy conclusions that were remarkably similar to those in *Housing Poverty: From Social Breakdown to Social Mobility* (Centre for Social Justice, 2008b). In the interests of fair rationing, it proposed 'moving towards a system of flexible tenure in which all new lets can be reviewed after set period of time [sic]'; and if it turns out that a tenant's circumstances 'have improved, and have changed in a sustained way, we would suggest that it is right and fair that there is a menu of options to choose from, but that the existing terms and conditions are not an option' (CIH, 2008, p 22). The menu of options included advice about how to exit social housing or else face the prospect of 'rent increase towards a more market level' (CIH, 2008, p 23). In other words, pay up or get out! As with the other proposals to remove tenants' rights or drastically increase their rents, it is difficult to see what positive benefits this could bring either for social tenants or for social housing estates. It can, however, be represented as an attempt to reassert the power of housing managers over those whom they are supposed to manage.[11]

A final key publication for understanding traditional Conservatism in housing policy was that by Greenhalgh and Moss (2009).[12] This remains an important paper, not only because Greenhalgh is the leader of the London Borough of Hammersmith and Fulham, but also because it contains a much clearer statement of a traditional Conservative position. The paper proposed to abolish security of tenure and increase all rents to near-market levels, and to restrict housing benefit so that it would pay for housing costs only in excess of 40% of household income. Local authorities and housing associations would be free to do what they liked with their housing, with local authority housing duties being reduced to housing only those who are deemed incapable of housing themselves, to help others to find housing in the market and to fix broken neighbourhoods. The paper is full of unsubstantiated claims, which there is not space to discuss here. Although entitled *Principles for Social Housing Reform*, the main principle that seems to guide its arguments is that of ensuring a better return on the capital invested in the public housing stock.[13] There is nothing in this paper that takes forward the Conservative principles outlined earlier: nothing about how lower-income families might be capitalised, nothing that would increase their ability to move, nothing that would enable them to manage better themselves. The paper is also inferior to the three Conservative Party policy papers discussed earlier, in that it does not effectively place social housing within a wider housing, planning and social system. In the main, it appears to be an attack on social tenants in the pursuit of greater power and freedom for landlords. Hence the reaction from Maxine Bayliss and Shirley Cupitt, from the Hands Off Our Queen Caroline Homes Action Group (based in Hammersmith and Fulham), in a letter to *ROOF Magazine* (Nov/Dec 2009, p 15):

> This council [the London Borough of Hammersmith and Fulham] holds a distorted, stigmatising view of council tenants. The leader Stephen Greenhalgh described estates as 'broken neighbourhoods' and 'ghettos' where a 'dependency culture and culture of entitlement predominates' [see Greenhalgh and Moss, 2009, p 6]. How insulting to the thousands of us who live in decent, tolerant communities, not ghettos, which house public service and retail sector workers and provide a vital safety net to other, more vulnerable individuals.

## Progressive Conservatism

The Progressive Conservatism Project, chaired by David Willetts, who became Secretary of State for Universities and Science on the creation of the Coalition government, states that the principles of progressive Conservatism are as follows: 'something for something'; 'children should have a fair start'; and 'ownership is good' (Wind-Cowie, 2009, p 12). The first two of these are very much in tune with New Labour, namely, first, that the state should intervene to provide the poor with opportunities and in return the poor should be responsible for taking up these opportunities; and, second, that the state should intervene to reduce unfairness resulting from inequalities in socio-economic background.

What is distinctive about progressive Conservatism, therefore, is its emphasis on ownership for all, and specifically the ownership of assets. The opportunities that are to be provided to the poor are, crucially, opportunities to acquire assets (such as housing), and the reduction in inequality is directed mainly towards a fairer distribution of assets, because 'in our capitalist society it is counter-productive for ownership to be concentrated in the hands of the few' and, in general, 'Ownership has positive behavioural effects on individuals and families, gives people a stake in their community and their society and promotes democratic engagement' (Wind–Cowie, 2009, p 12). Consequently, it is the Conservative Party's proposals that involve capitalising the poor that can be said to count as progressive Conservatism.

There are three points that can be made about this project for capitalising the poor. First, as already suggested, this is a direction in which Labour was already moving, with their continued emphasis on home ownership, welfare-to-work (which involves acquisition of assets such as skills and other human capital), social capital and asset based welfare more generally (this is recognised by Wind–Cowie, 2009, p 16). In this sense, New Labour would also count as progressive Conservatives. Second, capitalism inevitably generates winners and losers, resulting in inequalities in asset ownership. Consequently, the state is bound to be fighting a losing battle for more equal asset ownership unless it has policies to reform capitalism itself, but such policies are notable by their absence in both Conservative and Labour literature. It is not clear, anyway, why 'private property is central to the health of society' (Wind–Cowie, 2009, p 22). Is public property or social property not just as central? More radically, why do assets have to be owned by anyone at all? Why can they not be held in trust, for example, for future generations or for the benefit of the planet?[14] Third, some of the key Conservative housing policies both now and in the past (for example, right to buy) do not involve something for something, but rather something for *nothing*. An incentive is not a reward for doing something in the past, nor does it oblige the recipient to act in a certain way in the future; rather, it induces or encourages or influences the recipient to act in a certain way. Wind–Cowie's essay is entitled *Recapitalising the Poor*, as if the poor are to be paid back for capital they have lost, but the truth is that the poor never had this capital in the first place. So the progressive Conservative principle of 'something for something' is flatly contradicted by the proposal to transfer assets to the poor without the poor having to do anything particular in return. Progressive Conservatism can, therefore, be argued to look in some respects similar to 'Old' Labour, who also believed in the unconditional redistribution of wealth from the rich to the poor.

There is, however, one significant housing policy proposal in Wind-Cowie (2009), and that relates to housing benefit. It proposes that anyone on housing benefit or working families tax credit for more than two years should be able to capitalise their expected next five years of benefit or credit as a deposit to buy their home with a sub-market fixed rate mortgage from a state-owned bank: 'At the moment housing benefit is literally dead money for the state. By allowing those who wish to build their way to ownership to use money they are already entitled to, progressive conservatives can help to end the culture of dependency that dominates poor communities' (Wind-Cowie, 2009, p 13). This is an interesting suggestion, which is bound to look attractive to a government of progressive Conservatives. Realistically, however, it is likely that few tenants would be willing to take up such an option. One could ask: if a family cannot afford to pay the rent (which is presumably why they are receiving housing benefit), how is it that they will be able to afford to buy?[15] More generally, the suggestion fails to recognise that a tenancy is already an asset of a kind and assumes that, when it comes to housing, freehold is the only asset worth having. The whole project of capitalising the poor, therefore, becomes exposed as simply another way of privileging home ownership within the housing system. This in turn entails a failure to recognise that it is the privileging of home ownership, operating according to market forces, that is largely responsible for the plight of poorer households in the first place (including by pushing up the price of land and housing beyond the reach of those on low and even middling incomes, and encouraging them to borrow beyond their means to pay for it).

One of the most notable protagonists for progressive Conservatism is Phillip Blond (2010). While Blond has little to say on housing policy specifically, he is a strong supporter of the right to buy, arguing that: 'Evidently it was progressive – it was an asset sold at less than it was worth to many of the poorest in the land' (Blond, 2010, p 120). Here Blond refers to the fact that the right to buy offers an incentive in the form of substantial discounts on the purchase price, but only 10 pages earlier he criticised incentivisation policies as regressive, because incentives are more likely to be taken up by those who are already better off (Blond, 2010). So it appears that, for Blond, the right to buy is progressive as well as regressive, and for the same reason, namely that it provides an incentive to acquire an asset. It only needs to be added that right-to-buy purchasers are mainly not the poorest in the land because they have to be able to afford to make the required mortgage repayments, which the poorest in the land would not be able to do. Blond's statement therefore reveals what is perhaps the key flaw in the whole programme of progressive Conservatism, namely that it is progressive mainly for those who do not actually need to progress because they are already reasonably well off. The principle is, as with Wind-Cowie (2009), that all tenants should have the same opportunities to acquire assets, but in practice only the better off are in a position to take up these opportunities. So the poorest have lost out and will continue to lose out.

Blond also emphasises free association, 'the revival of the associative society' (Blond, 2010, p 153), but for him this must be 'built around the practice of virtue and exploration of the good' (Blond, 2010, p 154). The virtuous are those who 'put different points of view before us with integrity and after careful consideration of alternative positions' (Blond, 2010, p 169). The implications for housing policy of such arguments are, however, significant, not necessarily to promote the nation of homeowners preferred by Blond and his fellow progressive Conservatives, but rather to encourage the formation of associations of different kinds, including ones that develop, own and manage housing together, in which decisions are made through processes of democratic deliberation. In other words, the way forward lies with organisations such as self-build housing associations and housing cooperatives, using legal vehicles such as trusts (by law, the trustees would play the part of the virtuous). Blond does indeed say that he favours 'mutualist or co-operative structures of ownership and reward' (Blond, 2010, p 197), but he does not mention housing cooperatives.

In the end, therefore, Blond's Conservatism looks potentially progressive in a number of ways – for example, the renewal of civil society, the expansion of cooperative enterprise, a morally and socially responsible private sector, a state that serves its people and invests more in its poorer citizens and so on. It seems, however, that Blond has no serious proposals that will directly reduce economic and social inequality (except perhaps in relation to pensions). All of these points apply equally to Norman (2010). Instead, it is argued that:

> any natural talent is surely a potential benefit for all which should be developed and not suppressed through forcible equalisation. In this respect one can also defend certain kinds of inherited privilege to the degree that what is passed from parents to child is a tradition of honourable duty as well as material comfort and social status. (Blond, 2010, pp 182–3)

In other words, investing in natural talent is justified in so far as it provides benefits to all, but somehow, for Blond, this means that it may also be acceptable for these benefits to be passed on exclusively to one's descendants. Such inheritance of benefits, however, can only serve to perpetuate the inequalities of wealth and welfare that Blond criticised in the introduction to his book. One counter-argument to Blond is that inheritance tax is precisely a way of ensuring that, where the state has invested in such 'natural talents', the benefits from that investment really do pass to all.

To sum up on progressive Conservatism: first, it is simply not based on any clear progressive principles. Instead of the avowed principle of mutuality ('something for something') we have incentives to own ('something for nothing'), which may be progressive to an extent, but are not embedded in any clear approach to wealth redistribution. Instead of a stated principle of intergenerational justice ('children should have a fair start'), we see (at least in the case of Blond, 2010) a clumsy and unconvincing attempt to defend the privileges of inherited wealth. And instead of developing a clear programme for capitalising the poor, we find a reinforcement of the traditional (unequal) pattern of wealth or asset ownership, particularly of housing ownership. It can be concluded, then, that progressive Conservatism is not quite what it claims to be.

## Is the Coalition government's housing policy traditional or progressive?

Returning to the distinction between traditional and progressive Conservatism, it can now be seen that they have much in common. Both are concerned primarily to maintain established authority of one kind or another – the family, private property, capitalist work, established religion and state power – what Norman (2010) refers to, vaguely, as institutions. The core institutions of British society are viewed as basically good and not in need of major reform – society may be 'broken', as some Conservatives affirm, but they are confident that it can be mended using traditional, well-tried and trusted methods. All Conservatives now also seem to agree that social problems are best solved not by government, but by society itself, acting either on its own or with the support of government. In this particular respect, the Coalition government's approach differs from that of New Labour, who saw government as playing a key or leading role in solving all or nearly all social problems.

Where progressive and traditional Conservatives differ, then, is not on the vision of the 'Big Society' or the role of government, but on the best ways of realising that vision: whether to rely more on incentives or on coercion; to support and extend civil rights or remove some of these rights; actively to ensure a wider and fairer distribution of wealth or allow the outcome to be decided more by market forces, and so on. In these terms, as regards housing policy so far, it seems that the Coalition government is looking more traditional than progressive. This is because: none of the proposals in *Housing Poverty: From Social Breakdown to Social Mobility* (Centre for Social Justice, 2008b) to intervene in the housing market have been carried forward into government; none of the proposals to capitalise the poor have yet been adopted by the Coalition partners; the incentives to councils, for example, to build new affordable housing, look unlikely to have much impact; and, perhaps most importantly, the government now proposes to abolish security of tenure for social housing tenants, as recommended by the Centre for Social Justice (2008b).

This latter proposal came as a complete surprise, being announced by Cameron in response to a question at a public meeting (BBC News, 2010b). (With hindsight, it appears that the manifesto commitment to retain security of tenure actually related only to existing tenants, not future tenants.) It was justified 10 days later by Shapps (2010), on the grounds that it will increase the number of lettings that can be made to those in need. He declared: 'surely it is right to ask: just because somebody is in need at some point in their life and, therefore, gets a council home, do they necessarily need it forever?' To which one could reply 'no', they do not necessarily need it forever, but surely it is right for them to decide when they need to go, not for their landlord to decide when they should go? A number of critics have pointed out that, rather than motivating tenants to improve their circumstances, this new coercive policy actually creates a perverse incentive for them not to seek better-paid jobs and so on, because they could end up losing their homes (see, for example, Sweeney's [2010] response to Shapps: 'we risk creating ghettos of workless poor, with little incentive to better their situation for fear of losing their home'); the proposal has been developed further in a consultation document, *New Homes Bonus: Consultation* (Department for Communities and Local Government, 2010a). It proposes radical reform of the social housing system, including restoring powers to private landlords that have been eroded by previous legislation. In spirit, the proposals reflect those of Greenhalgh and Moss (2009). Localism here appears to mean increased control for local housing providers, rather than for tenants and residents. The argument that the reform will increase the supply of affordable housing is unconvincing as the new 'flexible' tenants will still have a right to buy, which they may be expected to exercise in large numbers in order to be able to continue to live in their chosen homes.

Perhaps the main worry with the Coalition government's housing policies is that they will increase inequality, not only between rich and poor, but also between different areas. In particular, the increased emphasis on (home) ownership and on local control will inevitably privilege owners above tenants and better-off areas above poorer areas. There are no Conservative proposals that recognise these regressive effects or do anything to counteract them, and it does not seem realistic to expect the 'Big Society' to play such a role. There may certainly be a need for an alternative to New Labour's command-and-control approach, but it is unlikely that sufficient people will be able and willing to participate to the extent required to ensure the effective and fair co-production of services envisaged by the 'Big Society' idea (see also Chapters 4 and 14). On the strength of the latest consultation paper (Department for Communities and Local Government, 2010b), it seems that the progressive vision of the Big Society has already been eclipsed by a reactionary emphasis in which service users (that is, tenants and residents) will be assigned a subordinate, consultative role.

Finally, the Coalition has no clear strategic role for government in relation to housing policy, no clear vision of how housing can contribute to the good society and no understanding of the need to achieve a balance between private property and social property or where that balance might be drawn (for example, how much social housing do we need or want?). The Conservatives appear to genuinely believe that, if local authorities, for example, are freed and incentivised to develop new affordable housing as proposed, then the lot of those in housing need will be improved. When this fails to happen, however, what will the Coalition government do then?

**Notes**

[1] Although it should be noted that, under the Localism Bill (published on 13 December 2010), the government proposes to continue New Labout's community infrastructure levy (a tariff on developers) and extend it to enable funding of infrastructure maintenance.

[2] Interestingly, in the Localism Bill, local authorities will be allowed to raise taxes above the centrally prescribed ceiling if local people approve this in a referendum.

[3] For students of the policy process, this represents an excellent example of the seemingly arbitrary way in which policy is so often made. Someone has a bright

idea, gets it published through a medium that is accessible to key policymakers and, then, if the latter like it, it can become policy almost overnight.

[4] It is basically something for nothing – a reward for doing what they should be doing anyway.

[5] Only in some respects, as there are no specific proposals on housing benefit or supported housing services. Housing benefit is not discussed in this chapter, but it should be noted here that the Coalition government's emergency budget contained major cuts in housing benefit that are certain to result in severe hardship and homelessness for many households. For further details see the Department for Work and Pensions website at www,dwp.gov.uk

[6] Citizens UK has since been appointed to organise this training.

[7] Under the Leasehold Reform, Housing and Urban Development Act 2003.

[8] www.cch.codp

[9] This relates to the Conservative idea of a 'property-owning democracy', which sounds innocent enough until you realise that it could imply the disenfranchisement of those who do not own property.

[10] The Centre for Social Justice (2008b, p 2) assumes that, because social tenants are paying below market rents, they must be subsidised in some way (in addition to the housing benefit subsidy that some of them receive towards their rent). This is a common misunderstanding. In fact, many of these tenants will have paid for their homes many times over and are effectively cross-subsidising other tenants. Many local authority housing revenue accounts do not receive any subsidy from government apart from housing benefit subsidy.

[11] For an earlier example of such 'professional' opinion, see Dwelly and Cowans (2006). For the latest such thinking from the CIH, see Thornhill (2010, p 33), who claims to be 'going beyond the argument made by CIH' in 2008, wanting to evict tenants not only for not paying the higher rents demanded of them, but also for refusing to accept any changes in their conditions of tenancy that their landlord deems to be necessary in the light of changes in the tenants' circumstances.

[12] It is also important to note that much of the thinking in this paper comes from leading housing professionals such as Julie Cowans, David Cowans (the same Cowans as in Dwelly and Cowans, 2006), Nick Johnson and Kate Davies.

Needless to say, perhaps, these are not the front-line professionals whom Blond (2010) wants to see running housing services – see later.

[13] Greenhalgh and Moss (2009, p 7) complain that: 'A conservative estimate values public sector housing stock at around £300 billion and yet the return to [Registered Social Landlords] and councils on this capital investment is barely 1 per cent'. And then they ask: 'So what should we do?'.

[14] In any case, it can be argued that Wind-Cowie's (2009) project to capitalise the poor exaggerates the importance of wealth compared with other kinds of assets in realising this project. For example, he cites the motto, 'Give a man a fish and he will eat for a day, give a man a fishing rod and he will eat for life', as an appeal for an asset-based development policy (Wind-Cowie, 2009, p 32). This misses the key role of education: people have to be taught how to use a fishing rod, what bait to use, where to find the best fishing spots and so on. Wind-Cowie is actually alluding to the old Chinese proverb: 'Give a man a fish and you feed him for a day. Teach a man to fish and you feed him for a lifetime'. So, for human nourishment, the acquisition of a fishing rod is actually secondary to the development of the necessary human capital; and analogously, for abolishing poverty and achieving a fair society, education is more important than what is actually a very modest asset transfer.

[15] Wind-Cowie (2009, p 61) admits that 'There are significant risks – of people finding themselves unable to maintain ownership or of such a scheme entrenching inequality between the waged poor and those who are wholly dependent on benefits'. But he sees such risks as worth taking. There may be some tenants who would agree with him but they are likely to be very few.

# EIGHT

# Social security and welfare reform

*Stephen McKay and Karen Rowlingson*

Radical reform of the social security system is rare as it affects the lives of so many people. Spending on social security was anticipated as being £196 billion in 2010/11, an increase from £143 billion (real terms) in 1997/98. This may be expressed as an increase from 12.6% of GDP to 13.4%. A sizeable rise, therefore, but smaller than had been seen in either the NHS (5.2% to 8.7%) or in education (4.6% to 6.1%) over the same period. The extensive reach of the system, therefore, makes it difficult to reform, but it also makes it a target for those hoping to make public expenditure cuts.

This chapter argues that the Coalition government looks set to have important aspects of continuity with the approach of New Labour, but also some important areas of difference. Following on from previous work assessing Blair's legacy in relation to social security policy (McKay and Rowlingson, 2008), this chapter assesses the kinds of reforms proposed against the yardstick of Hall's (1993) orders of change. Hall characterises 'third-order' change as involving changes to *policy goals* and also involving a *paradigm shift*. The next, 'second-order', level of change involves keeping the same policy goals but changing *policy instruments* and 'first-order' change involves keeping the same policy instruments but changing the *levels or settings*. Early indications from the Coalition government suggested that while there was likely to be much first- and second-order change, there would be little third-order change.

In assessing the Coalition's approach, we divide social security into a number of key areas. First, we look at poverty, a policy issue that clearly distinguished New Labour from the previous Conservative government. The Coalition government are still using the 'p' word (poverty) but explain it even more in terms of individual attitudes and behaviour, requiring slightly different tools to fix the problem. Second, we look at making work pay. Since 1997, a key aspect of policy within social security has been to move people from unemployment (and some other kinds of inactivity) into paid work, and to ensure that having a paid job is financially rewarding. This overall strategy reflects Labour's original vision of 'work for those who can', or alternatively of work being the best form of welfare. The Coalition's policy here seems set to continue on the path laid down by New Labour. The sanctions may harden, the names of programmes may change, but the approach set out by the Conservatives and Liberal Democrats seems to be an intensification of existing policies rather than a new direction. There is, however, one potentially more radical change on the table: the Universal Credit. This is the 'Holy Grail' of social security policy: an integration of the tax and benefits system that would simplify the system and make work incentives much clearer. But it would be expensive, and likely to cause tension between the Department for Work and Pensions and with the Treasury. In November 2010 a White Paper, *Universal Credit: Welfare that Works* (Department for Work and Pensions, 2010g), set out the government's position on this topic. Third, we look at pensions and income security in retirement. While most political and public attention towards social security is devoted to those of working age, around half of social security spending is on older people. Here we find that the framework established by the Pensions Commission still appears to be holding, at least for now, and that, again, the policy direction is one of intensifying some existing changes – such as the age at which people may receive their state pension, with recent confirmation that the state pension age will rise to 66, for both men and women, by 2020.

There are of course other important areas of social security – including disability benefits, child support policy and asset-based welfare – where Labour made a number of reforms. Some of these policy areas have barely been mentioned, but one, asset-based welfare, appears to have been wiped off the policy map with the abolition of Child Trust Funds and the Saving Gateway.

Overall, then, the Coalition government appears to be implementing mainly first- and second-order change, but with some signs of more radical change (the abolition of asset-based welfare and proposals for a Universal Credit). But before completing our assessment of Coalition proposals and policies in this field, we first briefly review New Labour's legacy so that we can then judge the extent of continuity and change since Gordon Brown left Downing Street in May 2010. One important terminological aspect is that policy now refers to 'welfare' rather than 'social security'. It used to be a distinctive feature of the United Kingdom that all benefits, whether income-related or contributory, were referred to as 'social security' and not 'welfare', a term often seen as pejorative. Now the Coalition, largely following New Labour it must be said, happily call both contributory and means-tested benefits by the term 'welfare'. We continue to follow the older usage in most of this chapter.

# The inheritance from New Labour

## Poverty

McKay and Rowlingson (2008) concluded that Tony Blair achieved a 'paradigm shift' when he pledged to eradicate child poverty by 2020. Under the previous Conservative governments, the word 'poverty' rarely appeared in any official literature and there was great disagreement about its definition, and scepticism about its existence within government circles. Labour's focus on child poverty led to a raft of measures including an increase in Income Support rates (especially for those with younger children), the Sure Start programmes, the introduction of tax credits, a national minimum wage, a childcare strategy, and welfare-to-work measures. But the reduction in levels of child poverty was slow and, indeed, started to reverse from 2004, moreover, poverty among childless adults of working age increased (MacInnes et al, 2009). The fight against pensioner poverty was more successful, partly due to the introduction and expansion of support through Pension Credit.

## Making work pay

New Labour put great stall by moving people from welfare into work (see Chapter 9) and 'making work pay'. The introduction of the National Minimum Wage was a high-profile policy in Labour's 1997 manifesto and one that was opposed by the Conservatives at that time. Alongside the 'right' to a minimum wage, New Labour also insisted that those receiving Jobseeker's Allowance acted responsibly in relation to availability for work, and actively seeking it. These obligations were gradually extended to most groups of working age who would previously have been regarded as 'economically inactive'. The obligation to seek work was thus extended to lone parents, apart from those with younger children, and more of those previously on Incapacity Benefit were transferred to an Employment and Support Allowance (ESA) with more restrictive testing of those who were deemed unable to work. Much of this found favour with the Conservatives, who came to support Labour's welfare reforms. Their opposition to the National Minimum Wage was also dropped as this became widely supported.

Perhaps the major element of policy towards making work pay was the introduction of a variety of tax credits. These attracted both praise and critique. Praise because they were used to channel considerable extra resources towards families with children, but, in addition, criticism because they were viewed as complex, and with incomplete take-up.

Another important benefit for making work pay, while also one feature that may increase the perceived financial barriers to employment, is housing benefit (for social tenants, and Local Housing Allowance [LHA] for private tenants). Some reforms were enacted, including linking maximum levels of LHA to the median local rent, but housing benefit always seemed to remain at the bottom of the ministerial reform 'to-do' list.

## Pensions

Most attention to social security has tended to focus on moving people into paid work, and the links to reducing poverty and worklessness. Policy towards pensions has figured less prominently in recent years, perhaps owing to the consensus-building approach of the Pensions Commission, established in 2002 following a pensions Green Paper. Nevertheless the Pensions Policy Institute perceives that some key differences of approach have opened up, suggesting in a pre-election briefing that 'The outcome of the election is likely to have some major ramifications for pensions policy' (Pensions Policy Institute, 2010, p 4).

## Asset-based welfare

McKay and Rowlingson (2008) have argued that the introduction of the Child Trust Fund and the plan to introduce the Saving Gateway were among the most radical policies of New Labour in relation to social security. These policies signalled a shift from income-based measures to tackle poverty towards 'asset-based welfare'.

## Vulnerability to reform

New Labour's commitment to ending child poverty was a major change from the previous regime, but the government never backed up this commitment with open support for redistribution through benefits. Any redistribution was carried out 'by stealth', through tinkering with particular parts of the means-tested benefit system. The failure of the government to make a case for redistribution fed through to the general public with the public becoming increasingly negative towards benefit recipients and the role of the government in redistributing incomes (McKay, 2010; see also Chapter 4, this volume). Even among core Labour supporters, there has been decreasing backing for moves to redistribute income. This lack of support for redistribution left New Labour's reforms vulnerable. A second source of vulnerability is an increasingly complex and increasingly means-tested system of benefits (and especially tax credits). A little-understood system, with key elements unreformed, with little by way of political or popular support, is a potential target for those looking to make cuts.

## The Conservatives in opposition:'compassionate Conservatism'

As Page (2010) argues, the Conservative Party sought to turn from the 'nasty party' to 'compassionate Conservatism' during the 2000s as a way of distinguishing itself from the unpopularity of the Thatcher legacy at that time. This 'modern Conservatism' was, perhaps, a form of One Nation Conservatism. Both appear to see poverty and inequality as a problem, although 'modern Conservatism' is perhaps more sceptical about state intervention as a means to solve this problem.

In 2004 the former Conservative leader, Iain Duncan Smith, established a think tank, the Centre for Social Justice (CSJ). The CSJ carried out extensive consultation and Duncan Smith himself made high-profile visits to deprived areas to investigate the causes of poverty. Following on from this, the CSJ has produced a large number of social policy reports, including on subjects such as family law, policy, prisons and asylum. For our purposes, three reports have particular significance: *Breakdown Britain* (Social Justice Policy Group, 2006), *Breakthrough Britain* (Social Justice Policy Group, 2007) and *Dynamic Benefits* (Centre for Social Justice, 2009). The first report, released in five volumes plus a lengthy executive summary, identified five key pathways to poverty:

*   family breakdown;
*   educational failure;
*   worklessness and economic dependence;
*   addictions; and
*   indebtedness.

The Centre for Social Justice concluded that the solution to 'the broken society' was to strengthen marriage and informal childcare (through the tax and benefit systems) in a bid to make families stronger.

A further volume from the same collection, 'Second chance', looked to the potential role of the third sector in implementing solutions to poverty, with Duncan Smith suggesting that the voluntary sector was 'significantly underused and under supported in our fight against poverty' (Centre for Social Justice, 2006b, p 5).

As argued earlier, New Labour's pledge to end child poverty and emphasis on pensioner poverty marked a paradigm shift from the previous Conservative governments. This shift is not being fundamentally challenged by the 'compassionate Conservatives', who also use the 'p' word and indeed have accepted that poverty is a relative rather than an absolute concept (Page, 2010). There is also agreement about the role of work as the best route out of poverty. New Labour and compassionate Conservatism diverge slightly when it comes to the focus on income in relation to poverty. The Conservatives, perhaps, take a wider view of poverty and criticise Labour for seeming to think that simply raising income levels will solve the problem. The Conservatives also place even more emphasis, perhaps, on individual responsibility, although they do seem to be less prone to the kind of judgemental moralising that was expressed in the previous Conservative government, notably in the 'back to basics' campaign of 1993. Recruiting the Labour MP, Frank Field, to review poverty measures, as noted later, seems consistent with this view.

## The Coalition government

So far, this chapter has considered the Conservatives in opposition and, in common with the overall approach of this book, paid less attention to the Liberal Democrats. The Coalition between the two parties in government, however, requires that we now give some consideration to the Liberal Democrat perspective on these areas, even though they are the more junior party in government. The Liberal Democrat manifesto was based around the key theme of 'fairness'. A central element of their proposed fiscal reforms was a huge increase in the personal tax allowance, to £10,000 (Liberal Democrats, 2010). The main elements of social security policy were:

- restoring the earnings link for the state pension immediately, with a longer-term aspiration of a citizen's pension;
- ending government payments into the Child Trust Fund; and
- restricting tax credits, and having awards fixed for six months at a time (avoiding the need to retrospectively deal with under- and overpayments).

It is also worth acknowledging important divisions in the approach of the Liberal Democrats, as partly exemplified by the publication of *The Orange Book: Reclaiming Liberalism* (Marshall and Laws, 2004). This attempted to move the party towards a greater accommodation of free markets, as a part of the liberal heritage. Contributors to this book were well-represented among high-profile Liberal Democrats joining the cabinet of the Coalition government.[1]

## The ministerial team

The direction of social security policy is likely, of course, to be heavily affected by the ideas and experience of ministers, particularly those in the Department for Work and Pensions (DWP). Under the new DWP, established in 2001 by New Labour, there had been eight Secretaries of State in just nine years. Given the complexity of the social security system, this may not have led to the strongest leadership and may have given the Treasury (led, of course, by Gordon Brown, for much of that period) much more power in relation to policy. However, the new Coalition ministerial team comes with considerable relevant experience of this role while in opposition, and before that.[2] For example, the Secretary of State at the DWP, Iain Duncan Smith, was Shadow Social Security Secretary from 1997 to 1999, and, after ceasing to be party leader, established the Centre for Social Justice, which developed many new Conservative approaches towards tackling poverty. He has also appointed Philippa Stroud, the CSJ Director and member of the Social Justice Policy Group Secretariat, as a special advisor. His Conservative colleague, Chris Grayling MP, may have been shifted from his Home Office shadow role to become a DWP minister of state, but had also recently served as Shadow Social Security Secretary (2007–09).

One of the most interesting appointments within the government has been that of the Pensions Minister, Steve Webb. Webb had previously been an economist at the Institute for Fiscal Studies and a social policy academic at the University of Bath, prior to his political career with the Liberal Democrats as an MP from the 1997 general election. He was also a member of the Commission on Social Justice, established by the then Labour leader, John Smith, in 1992 to help inform Labour's thinking while in opposition. While this might suggest a stark difference in political ideology, those looking to what unites rather than divides this group might notice that all three of these ministers appear to have significant religious convictions.

They are joined by Lord (David) Freud, who had previously advised the Labour government on welfare-to-work programmes, and Maria Miller as Minister for Disabled People. Another surprising appointment, though not part of the ministerial team, is the Labour MP, Frank Field, formerly Minister of Welfare in the Blair government (1997–98), to lead a major review of poverty. Field was well known for his support for insurance-based benefits rather than means testing, not least because he felt that means testing encouraged people to behave less responsibly (for example, because it may discourage work and encourage fraud). In common with all three of the new ministers in the DWP, Field shares religious convictions as a significant part of his make-up.

The make-up of the ministerial team may play a major part in shaping social security policy, but the Treasury is also likely to play a major role. It certainly did under New Labour when Brown was Chancellor of the Exchequer, and saw himself as having overall control of domestic policy. The tensions between the DWP and the Treasury look set to continue under the Coalition government. As we have seen, the DWP under Iain Duncan Smith interprets social security as having trapped people in poverty by reducing incentives for self-provision – overall reducing incentives to take work, to save and to marry. This position aims at long-term reductions in spending on social security but sees these more as a secondary aim or even a result of pursuing other goals (tackling the 'broken society'; see Pickles, 2010). The DWP also believes that upfront spending may be needed to turn the system around. It also sees policy in this area as being able to transform work incentives and move people back into paid work. The Treasury, however, under George Osborne, is committed to reducing the volume of spending, viewing social security as constituting a large burden on the public finances (and, by extension, the economy as a whole), and perceiving such spending as growing at an unsustainable rate. The Treasury (the 'Cutters') see spending reductions as a key goal of policy, the DWP (the 'Reformers') see it as an important by-product of reform and one that may not be realised in the short term. The Treasury approach had already generated a slight increase in rates of benefit withdrawal in the 2010 emergency budget, the anathema of the DWP approach.

These two forces (the Reformers and the Cutters) have been reported as having inevitably clashed, and compromised (Martin, 2010). The development of social security policy will depend a great deal on how this conflict plays out over time. So, in June 2010 the budget announced around £11 billion of cuts (HM Treasury, 2010), with a further £7 billion cuts coming in the October 2010 Spending Review.[3] The pace of reform on the more structural changes is necessarily slower, and a subject of greater consultation (Department for Work and Pensions, 2010a).

## Poverty

The latest figures on low incomes, poverty and material deprivation appeared on 20 May 2010, just two weeks after the general election (Department for Work and Pensions, 2010d). They related to the financial year 2008/09, thereby including part of the effects of the recession within the data. Poverty fell very slightly, while it had increased in each of the preceding three sets of figures. Joyce et al (2010, p 2) explain that benefits uprating may lead to a further reduction in poverty visible in the 2009/10 figures, rounding off the New Labour government record. They also characterise the last Labour term as being associated with higher inequality, the second term as reducing inequality, and the first term as having only a limited impact on inequality. It will be another two years, and more, before the effect of any Coalition policy changes is covered within this series of data.

What is perhaps more interesting than the figures is the reaction of ministers within the DWP. To date, this provides the only opportunity to gauge their views about poverty and their dedication to meeting the past commitments to eradicate child poverty as enshrined in the Child Poverty Act 2010. The accompanying press release (Department for Work and Pensions, 2010b) set out aspects of a concern for poverty reduction and, perhaps, a scepticism about the role of cash transfers in tackling that goal. Iain Duncan Smith noted that while 'Such levels of poverty are unacceptable', 'Vast sums of money have been poured into the benefits system over the last decade in an attempt to address poverty, but today's statistics clearly show that this approach has failed'. He therefore stated that, 'A new approach is needed which addresses the drivers behind poverty'. Most of the rest of his views show a high level of identification with the policies of New Labour, 'Work, for the vast majority of people, is the best route out of poverty.... It is not right that someone can actually be worse off by taking work, we should be rewarding such positive behaviour by making work pay.'

Within the same press release, Steve Webb welcomed the small drop in pensioner poverty but worried about take-up issues: 'We must look to create a simpler system of financial support that works for pensioners, as opposed to one where too many feel it is hard work to get the help they need'. On the subject of disability, the Minister for Disabled People, Maria Miller, returned to the same theme as Duncan Smith and agreed that policy would need to move towards 'tackling the causes of poverty; not just giving out cash payments which do not tackle the real underlying problems'. Clearly, while the goal here is generally the same as was that of New Labour, the analysis of the problem is slightly different and this leads to the use of slightly different tools in an attempt to resolve the situation.

In late May 2010, the government published a 'state of the nation' report, looking at levels of 'poverty, worklessness and welfare dependency'. We were told that 'The Coalition Government is committed to building a fairer society, where opportunity is more equally distributed' (HM Government, 2010d, p 6). This is also a government that has no qualms whatsoever about describing the receipt of benefits, or at least some benefits, as 'welfare dependency' (2010d, p 10). The emphasis is also clearly on helping those with the greatest problems under the current arrangements, 'Our core goal will be to improve the quality of life for the worst off' (2010d, p 3). The concerns expressed about inequality also lean towards a concern with the gap between the middle and the bottom: 'the gap in income inequality between the middle and the bottom, measured in terms of the 50:10 ratio, has not improved in the past decade, and it appears that incomes of the bottom 5% have fallen on average in real terms' (2010d, p 21). This report also places a focus on those with incomes below 50% and 40% of the median, not just the 'standard' relative poverty line of 60%, and towards those facing multiple disadvantages.

The emergency budget of June 2010 gave another opportunity to scrutinise the Coalition approach to social security. One of the key changes was in the rate at which benefits are increased each year. Many benefits are increased in line with movements in prices each year. The measurement of prices is generally taken as the Retail Prices Index (RPI), although for means-tested benefits an index that uses the RPI stripped of the costs of housing is more generally used, and sometimes known as RPIX. The so-called Rossi index also strips out council taxes. The most significant change announced in the 2010 budget was a switch to indexation by the Consumer Price Index (CPI). This reform alone is expected to save almost £6 billion in spending in 2014/15. Whatever the technical merits on either side of different measures of inflation, unless interest rates are falling (and currently they are at historic lows), the RPI will generally yield a higher rate of price increases than the CPI. As at July 2010, the annual rate of change in the CPI was running at 3.1%, while for the RPI it was 4.8% (the annual rate of change in RPIX was also 4.8%). This difference in indexation approaches translates over time into quite sizeable differences in rates of benefits. Taking Jobseeker's Allowance (JSA) as an example, Table 8.1 shows that within 15 years this difference would effectively be taking almost £30 a week out of the level of JSA, although the differences in the earlier years would be rather smaller. Those on the lowest levels of income will see their position worsen compared to others in society. It is also worth noting that the indexation of benefits and tax credits applies from April of each year, based on the relevant price index in the preceding September. But it has been announced that VAT is rising from January 2011, and this may add 1.47% to the CPI, or 1.24% to

**Table 8.1: Effect of CPI versus RPI uprating on the weekly rate of Jobseeker's Allowance**

| | With RPI uprating (4.8%) | With CPI uprating (3.1%) | Difference |
|---|---|---|---|
| Now | £65.45 | £65.45 | – |
| After 5 years | £82.74 | £76.24 | £6.50 |
| After 10 years | £104.60 | £88.82 | £15.78 |
| After 15 years | £132.33 | £103.46 | £28.77 |

*Note:* In practice amounts are rounded to the nearest 5p each year. These calculations use the inflation rates for July 2010, which, of course, may be higher or lower in subsequent months.

the RPI (Morgan, 2010, p 4). This set of price increases, resulting from the VAT increase from January 2011, will therefore not feed through into higher benefits until April 2012, some 15 months after the initial VAT increase. CPI indexation is also being proposed for occupational pensions.

Another rapidly growing area targeted for reform is housing benefit. A large number of reforms will be introduced in 2011, which are expected to be saving close to £2 billion by 2014/15. The key changes include:

- Capping rates of LHA depending on property size, and irrespective of local market conditions. Rates will be capped at £250 per week for a one bedroom property, £290 per week for two bedrooms, £340 per week for three bedrooms and £400 per week for four bedrooms or more.
- Setting the rates of LHA at the 30th percentile of local rents, rather than the 50th percentile (the median) as at present.
- Increases in rates of deductions for non-dependants.
- Housing benefits entitlements for working-age people in the social sector will reflect family size (from April 2013), rather than the size of the accommodation.
- Housing benefit awards will be reduced to 90% of the initial award after 12 months for claimants receiving JSA (from April 2013).

These changes, like the changes in benefit uprating, are likely to affect those on the lowest incomes, the most 'vulnerable' in Coalition-speak. The introduction of caps on rates of LHA – with an absolute maximum entitlement of £400 per week – is projected to save £65 million by 2014/15. However, changes to non-dependant deductions, a little-recognised part of the system, are projected to save six times as much

(£390 million). The restriction of housing benefit entitlements in the social sector by family size by the same year will save £490 million. These latter two large changes have not attracted the kind of media rhetoric related to private tenants.

In a similar vein, the changes to disregards within tax credits, and the new disregard for income drops (i.e. lower wages do not mean higher tax credits) save more money than removing the family element for better-off families. Again, the latter point was emphasised rather than the apparently more technical reforms. The government has also announced that it will restrict the Sure Start Maternity Grant to the first child only, and abolish the Health in Pregnancy Grant (in 2011). We may also note that while the Coalition government is still formally 'signed up' to the previous government's child poverty commitments, they are having a review, led by Frank Field, to consider how child poverty might most appropriately be measured.

This discussion suggests, therefore, that while one part of government (the Reformers) are talking about protecting the most 'vulnerable', the other part (the Cutters) do not appear too concerned about who is affected by spending cuts.

## Making work pay

An analysis by Crisp et al (2009, p 67) argued that 'a Conservative Party election victory would presage continuity rather than change'. Indeed, it is clear that Labour's approach to welfare reform had taken on board a great deal of previous Conservative thinking about the benefits system. Crisp et al identify as key differences only the Conservatives' (a) emphasis on rewarding marriage, (b) greater concern with the effects on immigration, and (c) willingness to go further in sanctioning those of working age who refuse jobs. But the record of New Labour showed a wholesale adoption of workfare-style reforms, and, moreover, in the autumn of 2010 it remained unclear, even following the election of Ed Miliband as Labour leader, what direction the party would take on these issues in opposition.

Under New Labour, tax credits were a key means of making work pay, and reducing levels of child poverty. They succeeded a system of in-work benefits. However, by 2014/15, changes made by the 2010 budget are expected to reduce spending by around £3 billion, through a series of steps. There will be a restriction in entitlement, so that better-off families do not receive them (above £40,000 from April 2011), and a higher rate of withdrawal of tax credits for higher incomes. The higher rates for children under one, and persons over 50, are also to be abolished.

In the past, only substantial increases in incomes led to reduced tax credit entitlement, and income drops could mean an increase. The allowance for higher incomes is being reduced from £25,000 to £10,000 in 2011 and then to £5,000 in 2013. While, from 2012 the first £2,500 of any drop in income will be disregarded, backdating of entitlements is also being reduced from three months to one (2012).

These are all changes in the settings of the policy levers rather than major changes in the levers themselves. They therefore count as first-order change in Hall's classification even though they may have an effect on a very large number of people.

The Coalition is also following on from New Labour in extending conditionality for lone parents. Lone parents with no children under the age of five will be moved to JSA rather than Income Support (from 2011/12). This continues the changes from having no job requirements to step reductions to children of 14, 11 and most recently seven years of age. And there will be new medical tests for recipients of Disability Living Allowance (DLA), expected to save around £1 billion annually.

## Pensions

The Conservative manifesto set out a number of proposals in relation to state pensions, the pensions of civil servants and towards private pensions and the new NEST (National Endowment Savings Trust, formerly Personal Accounts). The Coalition agreement accepted many of these, not least restoring the earnings link for the basic state pension from April 2011 with a 'triple guarantee' that state pensions will rise by the higher of earnings, prices or 2.5%. This, again, was broadly in line with New Labour plans. The Coalition has also agreed to phase out the default retirement age; review the long-term affordability of public-sector pensions while protecting accrued rights; and protect key benefits for older people including the winter fuel allowance, free TV licences, free bus travel and free eye tests and prescriptions. So far, it seems, there appears little difference in policy between New Labour and the Coalition in this area of policy.

## Other key changes

A number of other important changes were announced as part of the 2010 budget, including a freezing in the value of Child Benefit for three years, from 2011/12. This will save about £1 billion in 2014/15, and smaller amounts in the preceding years. Media stories in the run–up to the budget suggested that means testing was also being considered, though that may have been to lessen the political impact of this freeze. However, at the Conservative Party conference in October 2010 George Osborne announced that Child Benefit would no longer be paid to families with a higher rate taxpayer.

McKay and Rowlingson (2008) have argued that New Labour's commitment to asset-based welfare was a major development. It was also one that most commentators assumed that the Conservatives would support, given its emphasis on encouraging people to save for their own future welfare. However, the Liberal Democrats had never supported the Child Trust Fund, and at a time when cuts are considered vital, the Coalition has stopped contributing to Child Trust Funds. The proposed Saving Gateway, originally planned to start from July 2010, will not now proceed. Hence, both tranches of 'asset-based policy' have been abolished.

Apart from the abolition of asset-based welfare (which was only a minor part of the system anyway) much of this chapter has emphasised continuity rather than change from New Labour. However, one proposal for policy change, if implemented, could result in one of the most radical changes in the social security system since Beveridge. This is the proposal for a Universal Credit, which, it is argued, would remove the confusing complexity of the benefits system and ensure that people see a gain when entering work (see also Chapter 9, this volume). The Universal Credit would also reduce the scope for fraud and error by making the benefits system simpler, and reduce the unnecessary and costly administration of benefits. Currently people can have overlapping entitlements or switch between different benefits – around 200,000 people a year cycle between Jobseeker's Allowance and Incapacity Benefit or Employment and Support Allowance.

The Universal Credit is, it seems, the 'Holy Grail' of social security reform and it is close to the heart of Iain Duncan Smith. Duncan Smith has claimed that previous Labour DWP ministers had wanted to introduce a similar system, but that this ran counter to Gordon Brown's tax credit empire. The White Paper on Universal Credit has provided further detail. It will bring together means–tested benefits and tax credits, and introduce a uniform taper of 65% of net earnings. These design features represent something of a compromise between reform and financial expediency, the 65% taper saving money and being rather higher than envisaged in opposition (when 55% was proposed).

## Overarching themes

Throughout all these areas of policy, there is an emerging emphasis on individual responsibility and behaviour from the Coalition government. The 'root' causes of poverty are seen very clearly in terms of individual factors, such as family breakdown, drug addiction and worklessness, rather than in terms of structural constraints and inequalities. This, again, is an intensification of a theme followed by New Labour rather than a new backdrop to policy.

A second emerging theme is a refocusing of support on the worst off, and a general distrust of universalist policies. Thus we have seen an ending of the Child Trust Fund, removal of tax credits from higher earners, changes to Child Benefit and considerable speculation about the future of benefits that are not means-tested. The budget pointed out that those with the greatest needs were protected against such changes, as it was 'protecting those who are most vulnerable and have the highest level of need' (HM Treasury, 2010, p 33), but while the government certainly talk about protecting the 'most vulnerable', some of the changes to uprating and housing benefit look set to make this group worse off.

A third theme is that the Coalition are looking in particular at workers on lower levels of pay (Department for Work and Pensions, 2010a, p 6), arguing that the system should 'establish a fairer relationship between the people who receive benefits and the people who pay for them *and, as crucially, between the people on out-of-work benefits and the people who work in low-paid jobs'* (emphasis added). This is perhaps most clearly found in the reforms to housing support for tenants discussed earlier.

Most of the cuts have also been targeted at those of working age; older people are (for now) spared most of the changes. The budget report (HM Treasury, 2010, p 33) even stated that 'The Government is committed to reforming the *working age* benefit and tax credit system so that it is fair and affordable.' (emphasis added). Older people enjoy guaranteed higher rates of increases in the basic state pension through the 'triple lock'. Thus far, election promises to maintain some of their universal benefits (winter fuel payments and bus passes) have been maintained, although press speculation on their future continues. Restrictions to entitlement would certainly be consistent with other aspects of the strategy of cutting the cost of social security benefits elsewhere in the system.

## Conclusions

It is not surprising that a government committed to reducing the growth of total public spending will closely scrutinise the highest-spending department and other fiscal transfers related to it. Even so, the larger part of spending is received by older people and pensioners, and these groups have so far been spared any serious reforms – albeit changes to uprating may have an effect, and future workers may be retiring rather later.

The reforms announced to date strongly reflect the cost-cutting agenda, with measures aimed at areas where spending has been growing rapidly – including tax credits and support for rents in the public and private sector. Those cuts have meant a more means-tested system, and no reduction in the numbers facing high marginal rates of tax on moving from benefits and into paid work. The second stream of Conservative thinking is that welfare must be reformed to enable people to move into paid work, and to guarantee that such a move will be financially rewarding. This aspect of reform, associated with the work of the Centre for Social Justice (and Iain Duncan Smith) may require some upfront changes in benefit structures that increase rather than reduce the benefits spend, at least in the short run. They run counter, at least in some respects, to reforms that increase the number facing higher benefit withdrawal rates. From 2013 the new Universal Credit will attempt to simplify the means-tested parts of social security – for those of working age. This may be seen as a victory for the reform element of the Coalition government, but the relatively high taper rate shows that the cutting agenda continues to be extremely important in directing reform.

### Notes
[1] The contributors to the *Orange Book* included Vince Cable, Nick Clegg, Ed Davey, Chris Huhne, David Laws and Steve Webb.

[2] The team has been described by Shirley Williams, in *Total Politics* magazine, in the following way: 'in ministerial terms, the Department for Work and Pensions has the strongest team of the whole government', available online at: http://www.totalpolitics.com/magazine_detail.php?id=1038

[3] As reported at: http://www.bbc.co.uk/news/uk-politics-11569160

# NINE

# A new welfare settlement? The Coalition government and welfare-to-work

*Alan Deacon and Ruth Patrick*

'Change' was the leitmotif of both the Conservative and Liberal Democrat campaigns in the general election of May 2010. The Conservatives urged the electorate to 'vote for change' and to sign up to a 'contract for change' (Conservative Party, 2010e), while the Liberal Democrats promised 'change that works for you' (Liberal Democrats, 2010). In the field of welfare reform, however, the opposition parties offered not change, but more of the same. As Lister and Bennett have noted, the Conservatives' Work Programme, which was to become a central feature of the Coalition agreement between the two parties, did not 'break out of the policy paradigm established by Labour', but rather took it 'further and faster in what has become a process of policy leapfrog' (2010, p 102).

Television viewers were presented with the rhetorical equivalent of this policy leapfrog during the third of the prime ministerial debates. In this, Gordon Brown declared, 'No life on the dole. That's my policy. We've got to get people off unemployment benefit and they're going to be forced to work if they've been on benefit for a period of time.' For his part, David Cameron promised that the Conservatives would 'do everything we can to help' people willing to accept work or training but that those who refused 'should lose [their] entitlement to benefits for up to three years'. In direct response, Nick Clegg claimed that 'we actually all agree with that. We agree that benefits should be conditioned [sic], we all agree that benefits shouldn't be just dished out for free if people refuse to take up work' (BBC News, 2010a).

The '*Sturm und Drang*' of electioneering is not, of course, conducive to a measured debate about the details of policy. Nor does this level of agreement offer any guarantee that the measures in question will have the effects envisaged. On the contrary, it makes it even more important that they be subject to independent scrutiny and analysis.

There are, then, three questions that need to be addressed in this chapter. First, what are the central features of the welfare-to-work programmes that were developed by New Labour and will now be expanded and intensified by the Coalition government? Second, what explains the apparent consensus around these programmes? Third, what impacts are they likely to have upon different groups of claimants? To these questions may be added a fourth: does this apparent consensus on welfare reform reflect something distinctive about this policy area, or is it part of a broader 'welfare settlement' comparable to that of the late 1940s or the Butskellism of the 1950s?

## From the New Deals to the Work Programme

Welfare-to-work concerns the policy mechanisms by which all those not currently working are encouraged, enabled and, where deemed necessary, compelled to enter paid employment. From its arrival in office, New Labour had consistently declared its intention to 'rebuild the welfare state around work' (Department of Social Security, 1998, p 23). The centrepiece of its strategy was the New Deal programmes, which were to 'break the mould of the old passive benefits system' and form the basis of a new contract between claimants and government: 'It is the Government's responsibility to promote work opportunities and to help people take advantage of them. It is the responsibility of those who can take them up to do so' (Department of Social Security, 1998, p 31). Over time the scope of this contract was widened to include groups of claimants who had not previously been expected to seek paid work, most importantly lone parents and disabled people. In 2006, for example, a Green Paper said that the government wanted to challenge 'the assumptions that people with health conditions and disabilities, women with dependent children, and older people cannot work or do not want to work' (Department for Work and Pensions, 2006, p 19).

This emphasis upon so-called workless households was reinforced in 2007 when the then Prime Minister, Tony Blair, asked a former city banker, David Freud, to 'review progress on the welfare-to-work programme since 1997'. Freud reported that the government's record on employment was 'genuinely impressive' – the numbers claiming unemployment benefit had fallen to a 30-year low in 2004 – and that 'by any measure' the New Deals 'had been a success'. He went on, however, to recommend that more now needed to be done to help 'the least advantaged into work' (Department for Work and Pensions, 2007, p 1). This would require 'intensive, individualised support', which should focus on 'assisted job search'. This support 'could in principle' be provided for 'all benefit recipients, including people on incapacity benefits, lone parents and partners of benefit claimants, but excluding carers'. He further argued that this work should be contracted out to private- and voluntary-sector agencies, which would become 'responsible for intensive case management, and for providing individual tailored help for individuals to re-engage with the labour market' (Department for Work and Pensions, 2007, p 6). Moreover, these agencies should be paid by results, with the level of payment reflecting the degree of difficulty presented by individual claimants.

The government's initial response to the Freud Report was lukewarm, but in 2008 he was invited back by the Secretary of State for Work and Pensions, James Purnell, to advise on what became the 2009 Welfare Reform Act. This Act incorporated many of Freud's proposals. In particular, it introduced a requirement that lone parents whose children were over seven had to register for work as a condition for benefit and extended the level of work-based conditionality for some groups of disabled people receiving Employment and Support Allowance, a new benefit launched in 2008 (see later). Notably, the Act also provided for the piloting of workfare, a development that Freud had previously advised against in his report. By the time the Act was passed, however, David Freud had joined the Conservatives, becoming, as Lord Freud, a frontbench spokesman on welfare reform, and subsequently Minister for Welfare Reform in the Coalition government.

In opposition, the Conservatives had described the 2009 Act as a 'half-hearted' attempt to implement Freud's report, and had promised a 'full-blooded version' if returned to power. This was to take the form of the aptly, if rather uninspiringly, named 'Work Programme' (WP) due to be launched in the summer of 2011 (Department for Work and Pensions, 2010f). WP is now at the forefront of the 'welfare revolution' promised by the new Secretary of State for Work and Pensions, Iain Duncan Smith (Wintour, 2010b). It will replace all existing welfare-to-work programmes and will provide a single point of access to specialist provision. Everyone who is out of work, and of working age, will be eligible for entry to the programme, encompassing all unemployed people, lone parents whose children are over five, and many disabled people. Participation will be mandatory (Conservative Party, 2009c).

All disability benefit claimants still on Incapacity Benefit (IB) will be migrated over to the Employment and Support Allowance (ESA) introduced by the 2007 Welfare Reform Act. All existing IB claimants, many of whom have been on disability benefits for years, will be required to attend a Work Capability Assessment (WCA), which determines eligibility for ESA. Those whose impairments are found to be so severe as to prevent them from doing any formal work are guaranteed a higher-level benefit, and placed on the 'support' component and not subject to work-related conditions. Those found capable of doing some work, however, will be placed on the 'work related activity' component of the benefit, and will be required to participate in WP as a condition of continued benefit receipt (Conservative Party, 2008b). Many more will be found fit to work and thus transferred instead onto the Jobseeker's Allowance (JSA) regime.

WP will be designed so that benefit claimants can enter the specialist provision at different time points, depending on how far they are from being 'work ready'. Adopting the rationale that those with the greatest needs require the most immediate help, the programme will be structured so that early intervention is prioritised for disabled people, young unemployed people and those with other complex needs. Young people under 25 will be provided with the support that WP can offer, and will be compelled to participate, after nine months on benefit (Department for Work and Pensions, 2010f). All eligible claimants are to be transferred onto WP within 12 months of their benefit claim (Freud, 2009; Conservative Party and Liberal Democrats, 2010; Department for Work and Pensions, 2010f).

The Government is taking what is describes as a 'black box' approach to the tendering of welfare-to-work services, giving WP providers the freedom to personalise their support and programmes in ways which they believe will enable them best to support their 'customers' into work. Thus, the Government will not dictate the forms and types of support to be provided, although it has committed to establishing comprehensive minimum service standards (Department for Work and Pensions, 2010f). Nonetheless, there is a notable absence of detail on the proposed content of the Work Programme in relevant policy documents, with virtually no discussion of how the programme will support people into work, or what particular mechanisms and tools it will draw on.[1] This can be contrasted with much more discussion and focus on how sanctions will be applied to those who fail to participate in WP (Department for Work and Pensions, 2010f).

The Conservatives are clear that benefit claimants must make real efforts to seek work as a condition of benefit receipt. Mimicking and replicating New Labour, the Conservatives promise to be 'fair but firm', to offer a 'hand up, not a hand out', and to ensure that benefit claimants keep their side of the bargain (Conservative Party, 2010b). Launching the welfare reform White Paper, Iain Duncan Smith warned '... this is a two way street. We expect people to play their part too. Under this

Government choosing not to work if you can work is no longer an option' (Duncan Smith, 2010).

While we have heard this rhetoric before, the proposals announced in the White Paper do deepen and extend the reach of work-related conditionality and the possible sanctions for failing to keep to the terms of a new 'claimant commitment' (Department for Work and Pensions, 2010f). Those on Jobseeker's Allowance who fail to apply for a job, reject a reasonable job offer, or refuse to participate in Mandatory Work Activity when so directed (more on this below) will face the complete withdrawal of benefit (2010f). A first failure to comply with these conditions will result in three months' benefit loss, a second, six months' loss, while a third incidence could result in an individual's losing eligibility for benefits for up to three years.

Importantly, the White Paper also announces a deepening of conditionality for those disability benefit claimants placed in the 'work related activity' ESA group. These benefit claimants, who are assessed as having some 'limited' capability to work, are expected to participate in work-related activity and attend Work Focused Interviews. They are also required to participate in the WP when assessed as likely to be 'fit for work' in three months' time – although how this threshold will be assessed remains unclear (Department for Work and Pensions, 2010f). Failure to comply with these conditions without good cause will result in a complete withdrawal of ESA until the claimant re-engages, with fixed minimum penalties of one, two and four weeks' loss of benefit for first, second and third occurrences of non-engagement respectively (Department for Work and Pensions, 2010f). This is a marked extension of the conditionality applicable to disabled people in this claimant group, who previously faced the threat of benefit reductions but not the complete withdrawal of benefit.

The 'welfare that works' White Paper also proposes the introduction of Mandatory Work Activity for those whom it is felt would benefit from a four-week compulsory work-experience placement. This programme of workfare is presented as a paternalist intervention which will assist claimant to acquire 'the habits and routines of working life' and to develop experience in 'attending on time and regularly ... and working under supervision' (Department for Work and Pensions, 2010f, p 29). At the same time, however, it is also expected to help reduce benefit fraud by flushing out those who are simultaneously working and claiming. Participation in the scheme will be at the discretion of Jobcentre Plus advisers, and it seems that previous Conservative proposals for a one-year 'community work programme' for long-term benefit claimants have now been shelved (Conservatives, 2008, 2009; Department for Work and Pensions, 2010f).

In addition to the Work Programme, the Conservatives had promised a number of associated programmes and interventions that were designed to help claimants to return to the paid labour market. These have all been adopted by the Coalition government. They include an initiative to promote locally led and community-based Work Clubs, where people can come together to network and share their experiences of seeking work, and a 'Work Together' programme which seeks to develop skills by promoting volunteering (Conservative Party, 2009c; DWP, 2010h). The government has also introduced a 'New Enterprise Allowance' to provide loans and support to unemployed people who want to start their own business (DWP, 2010h). There are also to be a number of Service Academies, which will provide pre-employment training for unemployed people in areas where there are identified vacancies and associated skills shortages (Conservative Party, 2010e).

As proposed by David Freud, WP will be delivered by third-sector and private organisations, which will bid for regional contracts to run the programme. Critically, payment will be mainly outcomes-based, meaning that providers will be paid for results in getting people back to work rather than for simply providing requested services (Department for Work and Pensions, 2010f). In a recent retreat from the repeated commitment to pay providers *only* on the outcomes they obtain for their 'customer' group, the Employment Minister, Chris Grayling, has announced that WP providers will be given an initial payment in the 'low hundreds of pounds' for each benefit claimant entering their programme (Timmins, 2010). To ensure that payments reflect sustainable results, WP will only count entering a job as an outcome if it is retained for at least six months, with larger payments provided if employment is sustained for longer (Conservative Party, 2010d; Lister and Bennett, 2010; Timmins, 2010). This should motivate programme providers to deliver post-employment support to ensure that their customers keep their jobs, as this becomes contingent on their receiving payment. Again following the Freud Report, differential or 'disadvantaged-based' payments will seek to ensure that 'providers will be incentivised to help those furthest from the labour market, not ignore them in favour of easier to place candidates' (Conservative Party, 2009c, p 9).

A technical and rather complicated element of the Conservatives' welfare-to-work policy package involves a change to the Treasury accounting systems to enable benefit savings from getting people into work to be re-channelled into paying for WP. Called the DEL:AME switch, this involves allowing money saved in Annually Managed Expenditure (AME) budgets through benefit savings to be used to pay welfare-to-work providers, who were traditionally funded solely through Department Expenditure Limit (DEL) budgets (Conservative Party, 2009c; Freud, 2009). This change in the accounting rules is important because WP is expected to be very costly, especially for a Coalition government whose raison d'être is said to be the need to reduce the UK's budget deficit.

Contrary to Conservative rhetoric, which depicts the WP as a fresh departure that represents a 'new' way of dealing with worklessness (Conservative Party, 2010f), in fact it has much in common with New Labour's Flexible New Deal (FND). FND was being phased in from October 2009 to provide personalised support for jobseekers and to incorporate and amalgamate the various New Deals. It too was delivered by third-sector and private organisations, and included sanctions for non-engagement. FND also included an element of outcomes-based payments, and New Labour had planned to pilot the DEL:AME switch (Department for Work and Pensions, 2009, 2010e; Smith, 2009b). Moreover, New Labour had their own version of workfare in development and was planning to pilot a 'work for your benefits' scheme from October 2010.[2]

The main notable difference between the two programmes lies in the treatment of disabled people. WP will apply to those disabled people on the 'employment' component of ESA, whereas under New Labour this group were dealt with separately through Pathways to Work and other dedicated forms of support. Also possibly significant is the Coalition's decision to end the Future Jobs Fund, a New Labour job-creation programme that sought to create 170,000 jobs for young people (Conservative Party, 2009c; Smith, 2009a)

Traditionally, New Labour's welfare-to-work promise included a commitment to 'making work pay' so that those who played the game and kept their side of the bargain would be rewarded (Driver, 2009b). In seeking to make work pay, New Labour delivered some of the most social-democratic and redistributive policies of its tenure in government, which included the introduction of a national minimum wage, tax credits and assistance to make childcare more affordable and accessible. This commitment endured, and their 2010 election manifesto included a proposal to increase the minimum wage in line with rises in earnings; to pay everyone working in Whitehall a living wage; and to provide a 'better off in work guarantee' that people would be at least £40 a week better off in work than on benefits (Labour Party, 2010).

Importantly, the Coalition seems similarly concerned to ensure that work always pays more than welfare and has recently announced potentially radical reforms to the benefit system in this regard (Department for Work and Pensions, 2010g). Their welfare reform White Paper details the planned introduction of 'Universal Credit', a benefit designed to wrap up in-work and out-of-work support and increase work incentives. The proposals, which are influenced by previous work done by Iain Duncan Smith whilst Chair of the Centre for Social Justice, aim to simplify the benefit system and reduce the punitive marginal participation rates (the combined effect of benefit withdrawal and taxation) often faced by benefit claimants making the transition from welfare to work (Centre for Social Justice, 2009). To this end, the Universal Credit will feature a single benefit withdrawal rate or 'taper' of 65%, meaning that claimants will be able to keep 35 pence of every extra pound that they earn (Department for Work and Pensions, 2010g). Furthermore, earning disregards will be increased and made sensitive to family circumstances so that, for instance, a household with two children will be able to earn more before any benefit is withdrawn than a single-person household.

While a full critique of the Universal Credit proposals cannot be attempted here, it is important to note that in persuading the Treasury to fund this expensive programme of benefit reform for which £2 billion has been set aside, Duncan Smith had to acquiesce to swingeing welfare cuts, which will see the welfare budget fall by £18 billion by 2014/15 (Watt, 2010). Furthermore, the simplicity that the Universal Credit seeks to deliver has long been the 'holy grail' of welfare policy and there are unanswered questions regarding whether this ambitious objective will be achieved by these reforms (Ramesh, 2010). There is a also a tension and inconsistency between the government's much-stated determination to increase work incentives and the measures announced in the 2010 Comprehensive Spending Review to reduce elements of working tax credits and cut the proportion of reclaimable childcare costs from 80% to 70% (Lawton, 2010).

Work incentives can be increased by either improving the rewards attached to paid work, or reducing those linked to benefit receipt (Stanley, 2010), and it is still possible that the Coalition will opt for the latter approach. Significantly, the 2010 Conservative Party Conference included the announcement that the government will introduce a benefits cap so as to ensure that households can never receive more on welfare than the 'average working household' (Osborne, 2010). Furthermore, the Emergency Budget in June 2010 suggested a preference for further residualising welfare since it included changes to benefit indexation rules that will reduce the real value of welfare over time, and cuts to housing benefit (HB) for those on JSA for over

12 months (Centre for Economic and Social Inclusion, 2010). Notably, the Budget Red Book explicitly justified the HB measures in terms of increasing work incentives, arguing that:'excessively generous payments …damage work incentives'. The Treasury promised reform to 'remove payments that trap benefit claimants in poverty instead of providing incentives to work as well as being unfair to the millions of families on low incomes who do not depend on welfare' (HM Treasury, 2010). Taken as a whole, thus far there seems to be a marked reliance by the Coalition on efforts to reduce welfare entitlement and ensure that all benefits are strictly tied to efforts to seek work, alongside a notable commitment to simplify the benefits regime and improve the rewards of paid employment via the proposed Universal Credit.

## Explaining the consensus

The reasons why the major political parties have adopted a common approach to welfare-to-work are clear. First, all believe in the transformative power of paid work. In the words of Theresa May, then Shadow Minister for Work and Pensions, 'having a job gives you so much more than just a wage. In giving someone a purpose and a routine it can improve health, self-esteem and social inclusion' (May, 2010). Similarly, the former Labour minister James Purnell has recently written that 'work is what works.… It is as close to a silver bullet in policy as I've come across' (Cooke and Gregg, 2010, p 10). Second, all believe that employment offers the most effective route out of poverty (Page, 2010). According to the Freud Report, for example, a child living with a workless lone parent is five times more likely to be poor than one living with a single parent in work. Similarly, the risk of poverty for a child in a couple household is 61% if no adult works, 14% if one adult works and 1% if both adults work (Department for Work and Pensions, 2007, p 81). Third, all believe that active labour-market policies are an effective mechanism for helping people into such employment, and justify this belief by reference to the experience of other countries – most notably Australia and the United States (Conservative Party, 2008b). It is now common ground that the effect of long-term unemployment is to deskill and demotivate people, and to make them less attractive to employers. It follows that if employment programmes can counter these effects, then they can, in Richard Layard's (1997) words, expand the 'universe of employable people' (p 336). Moreover, this logic holds even in a recession, when, if anything, it is even more important to ensure that claimants are equipped to take advantage of the recovery when it eventually arrives (Department for Work and

Pensions, 2008). Despite the inevitable cross-party sniping during the election campaign, all accept the verdict of the Institute for Fiscal Studies that Labour's New Deals have reduced unemployment, albeit by less than was claimed in the Freud Report (Brewer and Shephard, 2005). And all implicitly acknowledge that the former government's labour-market policies can take some of the credit for the fact that unemployment rose less during the recession of 2008/09 than may have been anticipated given the severity of the economic downturn. Fourth, and most important, a majority of MPs in all parties agree that the benefits of paid work and the value of the opportunities created by employment programmes justify the use of sanctions and penalties upon those who fail to take advantage of them.

The extent to which this agreement over labour-market policies is part of a broader welfare settlement is discussed in the conclusion to this chapter. Before doing so, however, it is important to examine the criticisms that have been made of the welfare-to-work approach adopted first by New Labour, and now the Coalition.

## Troubling the consensus

Both the legitimacy and the effectiveness of welfare conditionality have been the subject of a long-standing academic debate (Deacon, 2005; Fitzpatrick, 2005; Dwyer, 2008; Cooke and Gregg, 2010). Within that debate, particular attention has been paid to the question of whether or not it is reasonable to talk of a contract between governments and those in receipt of out-of-work benefits, and, if so, what prior obligations have to be fulfilled by governments before they are entitled to compel claimants to participate in welfare-to-work programmes (White, 2003, 2005; Stanley and Lohde, 2004). Space does not permit a full discussion of that debate here. Nonetheless, it is important to examine the argument of those who have challenged the current approach. In addition to some scholars, these critics include voluntary bodies such as the Child Poverty Action Group and the Disability Alliance, as well as a relatively small number of dissenting MPs. Perhaps surprisingly, one of the most forceful of the parliamentary critics has been Steve Webb, a former Liberal Democrat spokesperson on work and pensions and now a junior minister in the DWP. Thus, this section of the chapter outlines key potential snagging points with the current approach, first by exploring broad issues of concern before, then focusing on two groups of benefit claimants particularly affected: lone parents and disabled people.

The first point of criticism is that the arguments advanced in support of work-first, mandatory employment programmes rest upon a narrow and exclusionary understanding of personal responsibility and commitment. In effect, individual responsibility is equated with preparing for and engaging in paid work. While the architects of welfare-to-work claim to recognise the special position of carers, and promise to treat with respect those disabled people unable to work, the reality is that work in the formal labour market is construed as the central obligation of the responsible adult citizen. Valorising paid work as the marker of adult citizenship has profoundly exclusionary consequences for those unable or unwilling to participate in formal employment (Lister, 1999). Many disabled people, those lone parents not in paid work and elderly people become implicitly excluded from the community of responsible citizens. While provisional membership might be provided to those unable rather than unwilling to work, it is likely that those outside the formal labour market find themselves similarly excluded from the citizenship community. Indeed, where work is posited as the solution to every problem and the key to personal fulfilment, those who cannot work may find themselves forgotten and ignored. They may be supported financially by the state, but may be tacitly dismissed as passive non-workers as opposed to the model, responsible, active worker-citizens. Where people actively refuse to keep to the terms of the welfare contract, and 'choose' not to take up the responsibilities that welfare-to-work policies demand, their exclusion from citizenship seems supposedly unproblematic.

The important point is, of course, that the elevation of paid work as the responsibility of the dutiful citizen neglects all other forms of contribution that people can and do make, not only as carers, but also as volunteers, service users or parents. An inclusive approach to citizenship would encompass the many forms of socially useful contribution, rather than focusing on paid work alone (Lister, 1999). Worryingly, the provision of care is most often construed as a barrier to work, rather than being conceptualised as an activity of value in its own right (Duncan and Edwards, 1999). This is in stark contrast to the arguments of care theorists such as Joan Tronto (2001), who argue that the central obligation of citizenship is the acceptance of a commitment to care for others. Arguably, then, the adult worker model of citizenship, which the current welfare-to-work settlement adopts, has profoundly exclusionary potential and this is an enduring weakness of the approach.

A second line of criticism is that paid work does not always confer the benefits that are claimed for it. Although workless families are more vulnerable to poverty, having someone in employment does not guarantee that a household will not be poor (Driver, 2009b). Those lone parents who feel compelled to enter work rather than care for their children, or long-term unemployed people participating in workfare as a condition of continued benefit receipt, may find their self-esteem does not improve as a result of their new relationship with the labour market. Further, while having a well-paid job in stimulating work environments may deliver on the promised outcomes, there is a question as to how far these also apply when the work one is doing is menial, badly paid and repetitive. Tony Blair once famously stated that 'work must be made to pay if welfare is to be made to work' (1997, p 6), and the justice of the work-first approach critically depends upon the quality of the jobs that people are required to take.

A third criticism is that the Coalition government – like its predecessor – pays too little attention to the potentially damaging effects of the sanctions that are imposed upon those who are judged to have failed to keep their side of the contract. Although hardship payments and crisis loans are available to those with dependants, there is an enduring question of the appropriateness of applying financial penalties that can result in worsening poverty for those affected. Further, sanctions are too often applied a long time in arrears, meaning that the original behaviour for which one is penalised has long since taken place (Department for Work and Pensions, 2007, p 95). This may well undermine the behaviour-changing potential of sanctions, and weakens the clarity of the terms of the welfare contract.

The issue of sanctions also relates to a fourth, broader, criticism: that the emphasis within the welfare-to-work discourse upon the personal responsibility of the individual benefit claimants to find work neglects the structural factors that affect their ability to do so. Certainly, active welfare-to-work policies have long been criticised for their concentration on the supply-side of the labour market, with energies centred on improving the employability of welfare claimants and with less attention paid to demand-side issues, such as the availability of jobs and the inclusiveness, or otherwise, of the labour market. Implicitly justifying a supply-side focus, the political defences for welfare-to-work too often employ a language of welfare dependency that characterises benefit claimants as passive dependants who look upon welfare as a way of life, and even a lifestyle choice. The Freud Report, for example, spoke of 'the difficult heritage of the passive labour market policies of the 1970s' as being 'one of welfare dependence rather than self-reliance' (Department for Work and Pensions, 2007, p 46). More recently, Iain Duncan Smith has argued that 'the nature of the life you lead and the choices you make have a significant bearing on whether you live in poverty' (Centre for Social Justice, 2009). It is all too easy to lose sight of the social, economic and political causes of unemployment and to depict an underclass of 'broken Britons' who need activation and conditionality to shift them off welfare and back to work (Scott and Brien, 2007; Conservative Party, 2009c, 2010b).

Indeed, the onset of the recession has led some long-standing advocates of conditionality to point to just such a danger. In a parliamentary debate on the previous government's Welfare Reform Bill in March 2009, for example, Frank Field claimed with some justification that very few people 'think that I am not tough enough on the group who do not genuinely want to seek work'. He went on, however, to point to the 'new poor: people who are already registering at job centres and who are desperate for work, scrambling for jobs, and willing to downsize in terms of the jobs and wage packets that they accept' (*Hansard*, 17 March 2009, col 874). Field's contribution highlights the importance of structural factors in a time of recession, and the consequent limitations of an approach that focuses upon the activities of individual claimants. As the Institute for Public Policy Research argued in August 2010, the Coalition is now 'forging policy in a very different world, where unemployment is expected to remain at 8 per cent amid bleak economic growth forecasts' and in such a context 'welfare-to-work must be reconfigured to meet the complex needs of employers as well as clients' (Laming, 2010, p 28), hinting at the possible limitations of a conditional approach that emphasises individuals' responsibilities to find work when jobs are simply not available.

A further set of criticisms relates to the position of lone parents, who are increasingly expected to work once their children reach primary school age. From October 2010, a lone parent whose youngest child is seven or older will no longer be entitled to income support, and will instead have to claim Jobseeker's Allowance and participate in work-related activity as a condition of continued benefit receipt. In 2011, lone parents will be transferred onto JSA when their eldest child is only five to ensure that all those with school-age children are participating in welfare-to-work programmes (Tickle, 2010). These changes have been criticised by many lone-parent and poverty charities, who worry about the consequences of an elevation of paid work that seems to neglect and even reject the independent value of parenting. Most recently, research by the single-parent charity Gingerbread has presented evidence that lone parents now on the JSA regime are feeling pressurised, stigmatised and are struggling to fully understand the conditions and flexibilities of JSA (Peacey, 2009).

There is a fundamental question as to the appropriateness and justness in obliging lone parents to participate in paid work, given that this restricts their choices, effectively preventing them from actively choosing to prioritise the parenting work they provide to their children. While married mothers can still choose full-time parenting, providing their partners earn a sufficient salary, this choice is effectively closed off to benefit-dependent lone parents. In an important contribution to this debate, Duncan and Edwards (1999) introduced the idea of 'gendered moral rationalities' to explain the decisions parents make in deciding whether or not to participate in paid work. These personal, situated decisions do not prioritise economic factors, but instead relate to individualised perceptions of responsibilities to children and how these can best be discharged. Many lone parents see their responsibilities as a parent as incompatible with significant paid work, meaning that in enforcing work–related conditionality politicians may effectively be forcing people to do what they consider to be morally wrong (Barlow et al, 2002).

In a parliamentary debate in January 2009, Steve Webb supported this position, claiming that while the Liberal Democrats had no issue with the idea of providing more help to lone parents who wanted to work, they had 'grave concerns about pressurising lone parents with young children into paid work when they would not otherwise choose to take up paid work'. Instead they supported the 'principle that mothers and fathers make their own choices about their family arrangements, child care, work, and the balance between those things. We do not believe that the state should make that decision on behalf of parents, especially when children are young' (*Hansard*, 27 January 2009, col 212).

Here again it should be acknowledged that there is a large body of evidence regarding the positive outcomes that can result from encouraging and supporting lone parents into work, with particular success often noted in terms of lifting lone-parent families out of poverty (Millar, 2006). The point, however, is that if these outcomes are to be achieved, then efforts to support lone parents from welfare into work must attend to the flexibility of the jobs available, as well as ensuring that good, affordable and accessible childcare is available. Financial support and practical help with the transition into employment must be provided, as must training to ensure that lone parents can enter rewarding and stimulating jobs. Again, this hints at the importance of the government looking to its side of the contractual relationship. As well as imposing responsibilities on individuals to seek and retain work, it must also ensure it meets its own responsibilities, to support and reward people entering employment.

A final group of criticisms are directed at the growing focus of welfare-to-work measures upon disabled people. There is an increasing expectation that many of those with physical impairments and mental health issues will enter the labour market. The migration of all Incapacity Benefit claimants onto Employment and Support Allowance is expected to result in many thousands of claimants being transferred off disability benefits onto JSA, with many more placed in the 'work related activity' ESA group, which includes work-related conditions. From 2012, eligibility for contributory-based ESA for those in the 'work related activity' group is to be time-limited to 12 months, further increasing the pressure on this group of disabled people to find paid work (Watt, 2010). Those judged incapable of participating in paid work will continue to receive benefits unconditionally, but there is concern here regarding the exclusionary potential of the work-first approach. The Coalition may promise 'respect' for those who cannot work, but whether this will be delivered in a society that elevates paid work as the primary responsibility of the active adult citizen is questionable. Further, the separation of disabled people on ESA into either a 'support' or 'work related activity' group could revive old and pernicious distinctions between the deserving and undeserving poor, with those in the 'employment' group potentially construed as work shy benefit claimants who need conditions to activate them off benefits and back into work.

Critics argue that efforts to encourage disabled people into work focus almost entirely on the employability of disabled people, with the use of conditionality implying that benefit conditions are necessary to alter disabled people's behaviour (Houston and Lindsay, 2010). Applying this logic to disabled people is problematic, they claim, given that they face a job market that is all too often unwelcoming and inaccessible (Barnes, 1999; Barnes and Roulstone, 2005; Puttick, 2007). Indeed, it is seen as more than a little perverse to compel disabled people to participate in work-related activity and accept 'reasonable' job offers, given the reality of a discriminatory, disabling workplace. This, of course, is not to discount the many positive steps that have been taken to improve the accessibility of the workplace for disabled people – which include anti-discrimination legislation, anti-stigma campaigns and funding to provide workplace adaptations through the Access to Work scheme.

Nonetheless, critics would still argue that the work-first approach focuses too much on the supposed deficits of a disabled individual, rather than turning the critical lens towards the disabling society in which we all live. For nearly 30 years, disability activists have been calling for a social model of disability that locates disability and its exclusionary potential as a societal problem, rather than an individual, medical issue. Thus, disability is defined as 'the loss or limitation of opportunities to take part in the normal life of the community on an equal level with others due to physical and social barriers' (Disabled People International, cited in Oliver, 1996, p 4). Social model thinking demands that society change, rather than individual disabled people, but this is a way of thinking that seems not to have permeated the welfare-to-work domain, which fails to adequately address discrimination and disabling barriers in the labour market.

What is more, there is concern that the new Work Capability Assessment (WCA), which determines eligibility for ESA and whether work-related conditions are attached to its receipt, is failing to properly assess disabled people's capability to participate in work (Citizens Advice Bureau, 2010). Figures have shown that the majority of benefit claimants applying for ESA are being found 'fit for work' by the WCA, and are thus being placed on JSA, rather than receiving the greater support and less intensive welfare-to-work conditions that the ESA regime provides (Wintour, 2010a). When introducing ESA, the New Labour government estimated that around 50% of new claimants would be found fit for work through the WCA, but, in fact, this figure is closer to 66% (Department for Work and Pensions, 2010c). Of those who complete the ESA claim process, only 10% are placed in the 'support' group (for whom no mandatory activity is required), with 24% allocated to the 'work related activity' group. Importantly, some 37% of claimants are not completing their benefit claim and more research is required to explore the reasons for this high drop-out rate (Department for Work and Pensions, 2010c).

Given these figures, there is concern, particularly among disability charities and pressure groups, that the WCA is tending to overestimate individuals' 'fitness for work' by underplaying the impact of the benefit claimant's health conditions and/or impairment(s) (Disability Benefits Consortium, 2010; Mind, 2010). Health conditions, particularly mental health issues, often fluctuate, and someone could perform well in a medical examination one day, and fail it the next. Further, the WCA's determined focus on capabilities may lead it to neglect to give sufficient attention to an individual's difficulties and impairments, which could make their participation in paid work problematic. Inappropriately making someone subject to work-related conditions could have profoundly negative consequences on their health and well-being. Recent research for a BBC documentary, on the operation of the WCA to date, revealed that many found fit to work in their WCA are challenging this judgement, resulting in over 8,000 appeals each month. Worryingly, almost 40% of those who appeal have the original decision reversed. Commenting on this, Danny Alexander, then a backbench Liberal MP, and now Chief Secretary to the Treasury, described a 'system close to meltdown', one 'working against many who are in genuine need' (BBC Scotland, 2010).

The Department for Work and Pensions recently published an independent review into the operation of the WCA, which highlighted fairly major problems with its performance, most notably around the treatment of people with mental health issues and fluctuating conditions, as well as a lack of empathy in its application (Harrington, 2010). The independent reviewer, Professor Malcolm Harrington, concluded: 'I have found that the WCA is not working as well as it should', declaring that he had uncovered problems with each stage of the assessment process (Harrington, 2010). While the government has promised to implement all of the report's recommendations, it has ignored calls from disability charities to delay the planned migration of Incapacity Benefit claimants onto ESA while the WCA is reformed (Disability Benefits Consortium, 2010b; Department for Work and Pensions, 2010i). Indeed, October 2010 saw pilots of this migration launched in Aberdeen and Burnley in preparation for a national roll-out from April 2011 (Disability Alliance, 2010). Clearly, the government believes, as Iain Duncan Smith put it, that: '*The WCA is the right test for the future ...*' (Department for Work and Pensions, 2010i, p 4).

## Conclusions

Commenting on the Coalition's welfare reforms, the Blairite former minister, James Purnell, outlined a 'covert consensus in Britain on welfare', describing the new government as being in 'continuity mode' (Purnell, 2010). Certainly, the level of agreement around welfare-to-work measures is widely recognised (Brewer and Joyce, 2010) and can be readily explained. What is much less clear, however, is how far the consensus around welfare-to-work is carried over into other areas of welfare. Is it the exception within an otherwise contested policy terrain? Or is it simply one manifestation of a new post-Blairite welfare politics, in which the Coalition accepts the central tenets of much New Labour thinking just as New Labour had itself modified but not overturned its legacy from Thatcherism?

The first, and most obvious, response to this question is that it is too soon to tell. As Lawson has written, it is not possible to 'look into David Cameron's heart and tell what sort of man he is' (2010, p 8).

There is no way of telling whether his statements on poverty and social justice represent a dramatic shift in Conservative Party thinking, or are instead what Lister and Bennett have called a 'cheeky piece of political cross-dressing' (2010, p 84) that will not survive the also-promised retrenchment of the state.

In this context, it is helpful to return to the notion of a welfare settlement, defined by Hughes as occurring when:

> a kind of framing consensus becomes established which sets the limits within which compromises over what and how, and by whom and for whom, welfare services and benefits are delivered.... The concept of 'settlement' as used here refers to a set of arrangements that create a temporary period of stability or equilibrium, even while they remain complex, contested and fragile. (1998, p 4)

We suggest that it is possible to identify such a 'framing consensus' in respect of welfare reform, anti-social behaviour and parenting. This 'framing consensus' is characterised by a common moralist or behavioural approach, which is itself grounded in a conservative communitarianism that shapes the thinking of David Cameron, David Willetts and Iain Duncan Smith as fully as it shaped that of Tony Blair, Gordon Brown, David Blunkett and Frank Field.

In contrast, other chapters in this book demonstrate quite clearly that there is no comparable 'framing consensus' in respect of the relative roles of the state and voluntary and private sectors in the delivery of benefits and services in many areas of social policy. In these policy realms, disagreement between the main parties over the mechanisms of welfare delivery is often matched with ideological differences over the appropriate objectives and nature of state intervention.

It follows from this that what makes the consensus over welfare-to-work distinctive is not just the ubiquitous rhetoric about rights and responsibilities and welfare contracts with which the programmes are justified, but the agreement over the use of voluntary and private agencies to deliver those programmes. Talk of 'combining public and private provision in a new partnership for the age' had always featured in New Labour claims for its 'third way' (Department of Social Security, 1998). Even so, it was the adoption of the Freud Report by James Purnell in 2008 that now looks to have been the crucial factor in laying the foundations for a new settlement over welfare-to-work, a settlement that may well be cemented by the enactment of the Coalition's proposed reforms.[3]

## Notes

[1] There has, however, been considerable discussion of the so-called 'personalisation' of welfare regimes and of the implementation of welfare conditionality by think tanks such as the IPPR and Demos (cf. McNeil, 2009; Ben-Galim and Sachrajda, 2010; Cooke and Gregg, 2010).

[2] New Labour's workfare pilot is discussed in *Welfare Reform* (Department for Work and Pensions, 2010e). A further striking example of policy convergence is provided by the work of the Open Left project at Demos, headed by James Purnell and his former policy advisor at the DWP, Graeme Cooke. A central plank of their proposed *Liberation Welfare* is a 'single employment programme with support targeted not by benefit category but by length of time out of work', with their proposals sharing many other features of the Work Programme (Cooke and Gregg, 2010, p 43).

[3] This new settlement also extends to the principles that should underpin a reform of in-work benefits. Compare, for example, those set out in *21st Century Welfare* (Department for Work and Pensions, 2010a) and *Liberation Welfare* (Cooke and Gregg, 2010).

# TEN

# The Conservative Party and community care

*Jon Glasby*

The Conservative governments of 1979–97 were responsible for a series of major changes in the conceptualisation and delivery of community care services (see Box 10.1 for a summary). In particular, this period saw the introduction of a series of private-sector approaches and terminology, as well as the gradual transition of social workers and social services departments into purchasers rather than necessarily the providers of care. As a result of these changes, the community care landscape changed dramatically. Between 1982 and 1991, places in private-sector care homes increased from 46,900 to 161,2000, while the independent sector provided 60% of home care contact hours in 2001 compared to just 2% in 1992 (Means and Smith, 1998; Means et al, 2003). At the same time, the role of social workers began to shift, with practitioners increasingly recast as 'care managers' – assessing need and designing care packages from a much more mixed economy of care. With hindsight, many front-line workers seem to have found these changes profoundly deskilling, claiming that current practice is focused much more heavily on administration and bureaucracy than on traditional social work skills such as counselling, group work and community development (personal communications).

At the same time, such changes may also have led to some positives. While many commentators have argued that consumerism is an insufficient basis for reforming community care services (see, for example, Barnes and Walker, 1996), these reforms arguably helped to concentrate the mind of senior managers and leaders and may well have contributed to greater responsiveness and efficiency, up to a point. The concept of care management, moreover, has the potential at least to shift thinking away from very service-led approaches (where the person is assessed with what is currently available very much in mind) towards much more needs-led approaches (where the person's need is identified separately from the subsequent process of finding ways to meet that need) – albeit that this has proved difficult in practice.

## Box 10.1: Conservative community care policies, 1979–97

- Changes in social security regulations in the late 1980s meant that people entering independent-sector residential and nursing homes could seek support from the social security system, based solely on their finances and with no assessment of their care needs. As a result, expenditure on this form of provision spiralled from £10 million per year in 1979 to £459 million by early 1986 (Means and Smith, 1998).

- In response, the 1990 NHS and Community Care Act made local authority social services departments the lead agency in the provision of community care. While some saw this as the natural role for local authorities to take on, others complained that the responsibility for tackling this rapidly rising central budget within local cash-limited budgets was 'the only thing Thatcher ever gave local government' (personal communications, local government employees). While initially there was probably enough money in the system to reduce the impact of these changes, it seems clear that the community care reforms of that period lie at the heart of more recent funding difficulties in local authority adult social care – and that this may have been a deliberate attempt by central government to pass responsibility for bringing this budget under control to local government (for an overview, see Lewis and Glennerster, 1996; Glasby and Henwood, 2007). Perhaps as a result of this, the funding of long-term care remains a long-term and contentious political issue – and one that the Conservative Party may find comes back to haunt them, as discussed later in this chapter.

- In the process, the 1990 Act accelerated the trend towards increased use of the private sector and the introduction of commercial techniques and language into the provision of care. Thus, there was a requirement for 85% of the funds given to local authorities to meet their new responsibilities (the Special Transitional Grant) to be spent in the independent sector, while service users became increasingly badged as 'clients' or 'consumers'. The role of front-line social workers also changed as they became 'care managers' – responsible for assessing needs and securing relevant services from a mixed economy of care.

- With changes in the nature of service provision came a growing need to regulate and inspect the myriad of providers involved in the delivery of community care. Under the 1990 Act, a new inspection system was introduced, initially at arm's length from the management of services and, over time, increasingly independent. These arrangements evolved yet further under New Labour, and the best way of monitoring and driving up service quality remains a key issue.

> • The 1996 Community Care (Direct Payments) Act enabled service users (initially aged 18–65) to receive the cash equivalent of directly provided services with which to purchase their own support or to hire their own personal assistants. Interestingly, this change had been campaigned for by both civil rights activists in the disabled people's movement and by neo-liberals committed to rolling back the boundaries of the welfare state (see later for further discussion).

## The inheritance from New Labour, 1997–2010

Following 18 years of Conservative rule, the election of New Labour seemed to offer an alternative way forward for community care. Under the mantra of 'Third Way politics', the incoming government stressed the need to move beyond what they portrayed as polarised ideological approaches to the respective benefits of the state and of the market, arguing that 'what matters is what works'. While this sounds like a clear statement of intent on first hearing, with hindsight such an approach seems to be clearer about what the government was not in favour of (not the market and not the state), and is rather less clear on what a Third Way for community care might actually entail. This has been described by Ham (2004) as 'eclectic', and acknowledged (in a more positive fashion) by the government itself as 'building on what has worked but discarding what has failed' (Department of Health, 1998, p 10).

Under New Labour, policy with regard to health and social care for disabled and older adults was described initially in terms of 'modernisation', with more recent policy emphasising the importance of 'personalisation' (for example, Department of Health, 1998; HM Government, 2007). As Means et al (2003, p 75) suggest, New Labour's approach to 'modernisation' included:

• a focus on outcomes;
• partnership across agency boundaries and between sectors;
• greater use of evidence and research;
• greater consultation with service users;
• the use of targets and performance monitoring to improve quality;
• additional investment conditional upon improved results;
• greater valuing of public services by developing skills and rewarding results; and
• the development of IT throughout government.

As with the concept of a 'Third Way', these descriptions imply something potentially distinctive to previous approaches, but are nevertheless difficult to define precisely in a meaningful way. For present purposes, however, there are five main themes and issues from the New Labour inheritance that seem likely to be of particular significance to the Coalition government:

1. *Funding*: with significant funding increases in the NHS and (to a lesser extent) in social care, the early 21st century was a time of relative plenty for community care. This injection of much-needed funding was a major departure from the previous Conservative administration, and a key challenge from 2010 onwards will be how the new government and local services respond to a much more difficult financial context.

2. *Long-term care*: New Labour's 1997 manifesto promised a Royal Commission on Long Term Care, which reported in 1999. Although the Commission's central recommendation of free personal care was implemented in Scotland, it was rejected by Whitehall, essentially on the grounds of cost. Following continued and increasing pressure, however, in 2009 a Green Paper reviewed this issue again (HM Government, 2009), and decisions about how best to fund support for growing numbers of older people are likely to be a key test for future governments. In practice, the subsequent 2010 White Paper proposed creating an independent working group to reconsider the issue of funding – with many wondering how this differs from the 1997 Royal Commission (HM Government, 2010a).

3. *The social care infrastructure*: in an attempt to raise the profile and improve the quality of social care, New Labour established a series of new national bodies. At the time of writing, these included the Social Care Institute for Excellence (to identify and disseminate good practice), the General Social Care Council (to register the workforce and maintain professional standards, now to be merged into a bigger organisation including health) and Skills for Care (focusing on workforce development). A previous organisation – the Commission for Social Care Inspection – was merged with other health-care regulators to create a new inspectorate – the Care Quality Commission – in 2009. However, there are likely to be further organisational changes (particularly in a period of financial difficulty), with both parties in the Coalition having members who have been vociferous in their concern about the cost and bureaucracy associated with such 'quangos' and pledging to reduce the number of such bodies. New Labour was also responsible for the separation of children's and adult social care following the tragic death of Victoria Climbié and the subsequent Laming review.

*4. Personalisation:* 'personalisation' has been described in the following terms:

> Across Government, the shared ambition is to put people first through a radical reform of public services. It will mean that people are able to live their own lives as they wish; confident that services are of high quality, are safe and promote their own individual needs for independence, well-being, and dignity.... Personalisation, including a strategic shift towards early intervention and prevention, will be the cornerstone of public services. This means that every person who receives support, whether provided by statutory services or funded by themselves, will have choice and control over the shape of that support in all care settings. (Department of Health website, accessed 15 June 2009)

As part of the *Putting People First* vision (HM Government, 2007), New Labour committed itself to transforming adult social care through support for all via universal services and better information and advice, greater focus on prevention and early intervention, and greater choice and control for people using services. A key mechanism here was the advent of personal budgets (Glasby and Littlechild, 2009), which allow the person and those close to them to know how much money is available in advance, thereby enabling them to be more creative in designing support to meet their needs.

*5. Specific policy commitments:* having often been seen as something of a 'Cinderella service', support for a range of previously marginalised user groups (including people with dementia, people with learning difficulties, mental health services and carers) received additional emphasis via a series of national strategies and frameworks. Particularly important was the growing recognition that mainstream health services had tended to focus too heavily on hospital care for people in crisis and the subsequent need to rebalance the system in favour of providing ongoing support to the growing number of people with multiple long-term conditions.

## What next for community care policy?

Following the 2010 general election it was far easier to understand where current policy priorities have come from and what previous administrations have done than what the new government might do in practice. Thus, in June 2009, the first 10 health news stories on the Conservative Party website contained six highly critical and negative stories, for example: 'Lansley Attacks Labour's Failure to Tackle Alcohol Abuse', 'Lansley Slams Labour for Fall in Dental Check-ups for Children', 'O'Brien Attacks Labour's "Confused" Child Protection System', and 'Lansley Slams Johnson's "Complete Failure" as Health Secretary'. In contrast, only three of the 10 seemed to be attempting to put forward an alternative. Of course, such tactics are often adopted while parties are in opposition, as they have the relative luxury of critiquing the current government's policies without necessarily having to provide the same level of detail about their proposed alternatives. However, in many policy areas the Conservative Party's strategy for the 2010 general election could be seen as being almost to say as little as possible that they could later be held to account for, simply letting New Labour run out of steam and/or implode in the process. While this might seem a slightly cynical interpretation, it was certainly considerably easier to find Conservative statements that various aspects of policy had been mishandled by the Labour government and that things would be better under the Conservatives, and there was relatively little detail as to how things would be better or what they might do that would be different to what had gone before. Nowhere is this more true than in the realm of community care – never traditionally a vote-winner and always difficult and controversial to explain properly to the general public.

For example, in April 2008, the Conservative Party website had no separate section under 'policy' for social care, adult services or children's services. Although there were a number of policy papers available on the NHS, none was produced for social care. While there was a section on families, this referred mainly to issues such as financial help, flexible working and health visiting. Similarly, the schools section referred primarily to education. Also at this time, the party had 13 campaigns. Of these, two focused on the NHS ('Save your local GP' and 'Stop Brown's NHS cuts') while others sought to save 'the great British pub', save local newspapers and keep post offices open. None related to adult social care or to community care. Where social care and social work were mentioned on the website, many were very brief news items and a significant proportion were focused on children's services following a series of child protection scandals. Where community care did appear, it tended to be in a very brief comment on current events, critiquing New Labour's record without articulating a potential alternative. Thus, in January 2008, the Shadow Health Minister responded to a review of eligibility criteria for adult social care by suggesting that 'there is no evidence that the Government are going to do anything more than talk about social care' (Conservative Party website, News, 29 January 2008). Around the same time, the same person saw a negative Public Accounts Committee report on dementia as evidence of 'the Government's ongoing failure to bring forward wider solutions for social care' (24 January 2008). In both cases, it was harder to find a more positive proposal for the future put forward as an alternative to the New Labour approach being critiqued. In the Conservatives' defence, the websites of the other two main political parties, Labour and the Liberal Democrats, did not feature community care issues in a prominent manner either.

Despite this relative lack of focus, there are a number of clues and trends that suggest possible approaches. First and foremost, a number of policy papers on NHS reform provide something of an insight into future priorities (see, for example, Conservative Party, 2007a, 2007b, 2008a, 2008b, 2009a), albeit that some lack detail on practical implementation. In legislative proposals published in 2007, the Conservatives committed themselves to the NHS as 'the Conservative Party's number one priority':

> We share Britain's pride in the values which underpin it and we are confident about its future. We have made an unambiguous commitment to provide the NHS with the funding it needs to deliver European standards of health care to all, free at the point of use, and according to need and not ability to pay. (Conservative Party, 2007a, p 3)

However, the same document was equally clear that the Conservatives do not feel that extra investment under New Labour has been well spent, and the paper points to 'a combination of falling productivity, excessive bureaucracy and lamentable leadership and management by Ministers' (2007a, p 3). Since then, a number of key themes have continued to emerge (see Box 10.2; see also Chapter 5 this volume) and it is possible that similar approaches might be apparent in other areas of state welfare – for example, those working in or managing community care services.

## Box 10.2: Key themes in Conservative health policy

- Full commitment to a comprehensive NHS free at the point of delivery, funded by general taxation.
- Rejection of regular reorganisations.
- NHS Board, independent of day-to-day 'interference' from ministers and greater autonomy for front-line professionals.
- Emphasis on clinician-led primary care commissioning with real budgets.
- Stronger emphasis on public health.
- Greater use of choice, competition and a mixed economy of care (including individual budgets for people with long-term conditions).
- Focus on patient outcomes rather than on more narrow process-based targets.
- Commitment to protect NHS spending in current financial climate.

Of course, as is also clear from the discussion in Chapter 5, there are considerable similarities to the policies of the previous Labour government. Indeed, while there are differences of emphasis, the underlying concepts and approaches seem largely the same (with the possible exception of an NHS Board). This has been usefully explored in an editorial in the *British Medical Journal* by Ham (2009, p 338), who argues that:

> The many similarities between the health policies of the opposition and those of the government should come as no surprise given that the Labour government has pursued market based reforms for almost a decade. The main challenge for the Conservatives will be to show that their policies are ready for implementation if they are elected to office.... Having set out the broad outline of their health policy, the Conservatives now need to add the missing detail if they are to justify their claim to be a credible government in waiting. At a time when trust in politicians is at a low ebb, the public has a right to expect full disclosure of policy intentions and detailed plans for implementation as the election draws closer.

The financial context meant that any party elected in May 2010 would face a very challenging economic situation, and would be forced to re-examine current spending commitments, irrespective of their politics. In the run-up to the 2010 election, New Labour tended to reaffirm their three-year approach to public expenditure (the Comprehensive Spending Review), with public finances relatively protected until 2011. In contrast, the (then) Shadow Health Minister, Andrew Lansley, created something of a political storm in June 2009 when he seemed to pledge to protect and increase funding for the NHS, international development and schools, leading to an alleged 10% reduction in the expenditure of other departments (*The Daily Telegraph*, 2009). This was then seized upon by Labour as apparent evidence of Conservative commitments to cutting public services (contrasted with Labour's desire to invest). In response the Shadow Chancellor, George Osborne, claimed that New Labour was failing to be honest about the reality of the current economic climate:

> We've all been tip-toeing around one of those discredited Gordon Brown dividing lines for too long. The real dividing line is not 'cut versus investment', but honesty versus dishonesty. We should have the confidence to tell the public the truth that Britain faces a debt crisis; that existing plans show that real spending will have to be cut, whoever is elected. (Osborne, 2009)

Above and beyond the rhetoric, this debate made clear that future public spending would be very tight whoever was in power. However, any decision to prioritise spending on the NHS would clearly mean greater reductions elsewhere, and it seems unlikely that social care spending would be protected to the same degree. As a result, there seemed the distinct possibility of future cuts in community care under any government.

Of course, the Conservatives' 'silence' on community care was to change to some extent in April 2010 with the publication of the Conservatives' manifesto, their *Invitation to Join the Government of Britain* (Conservative Party, 2010e). Here there were pledges to: create a single health and social care personal budget (to some extent already happening as part of Labour's personal health budget pilots); provide direct payments to carers (already policy under Labour); and to reject Labour's 'death tax' to fund long-term care (see later for further discussion), instead enabling people to protect their home with a voluntary one-off insurance premium, with the potential to top this up voluntarily to cover the cost of care at home.

Other than this, there remained little detail about the policies that would be pursued and about how this would differ in practice from ongoing Labour policy. The one exception to this – discussed further later – was the issue of funding long-term care.

## Key policy dilemmas

Against the background of the previous government's policies and the relative lack of clarity from the Conservatives, the current policy context suggests a number of dilemmas to which the Conservative Party and the Coalition government will have to respond.

First and foremost is the issue of the future funding of long-term care for older people. While dissatisfaction has been growing with the current system for some time, future governments will have to find ways of responding to the growing mismatch between the money available to fund community care services and increasing levels of need in an ageing society. In many ways, this is an issue that Labour failed to address, having rejected the main recommendation of the Royal Commission on Long Term Care (1999) and, arguably, having failed to give due attention to the future funding requirements of adult social care. Thus, although the Wanless Review presented a series of options for future funding (Wanless, 2006), it is notable that the study was commissioned by an independent think tank following the Labour government's refusal to give social care funding the same attention as health-care spending (which was twice reviewed by Wanless at the government's request). However, there would be an added irony if in government the Conservative Party finds itself responsible for tackling a long-term funding issue that its predecessor did not resolve, given that many of the current funding tensions within the system may well date back at least in part to the reform of community care spending from 1990 to 1993, discussed earlier in this chapter.

To date, the signs that the Conservatives will be able to rise to this first challenge are not good. While one of the first actions of the incoming Coalition government was to establish a Commission on the Funding of Care and Support to report by July 2011, many commentators found it hard to see what this could recommend that had not been identified in previous reports. In addition, the debates between the parties on this problem in the years prior to the 2010 general election had been far from fruitful.

In 2007, something of a political storm arose over the future of inheritance tax, with the Conservatives quick to respond to the unpopularity of this source of funding by engaging in a debate that quickly led parts of the media to label this as a form of 'death tax' (Mitchell, 2007). Whatever one's views on the strengths and limitations of inheritance tax, there is an important issue about how we collectively pay for public services (either while we are alive, or after we are dead, or both), and framing this as a debate about the 'death tax' was probably not the best way to engage in serious debate about these issues. When Labour's 2009 Green Paper on care and support (HM Government, 2009) was published, moreover, debates in the House of Commons tended to focus on the alleged shortcomings of the government rather than a positive and proactive Conservative vision for the future. In particular, there were criticisms that the government had taken too long to react and that its proposals were too vague and insufficiently costed. As the Shadow Health Secretary, Andrew Lansley, suggested:

> The Secretary of State has been wandering around the television studios this morning telling us that the standards of adult social care have gone down and down. He tells us how cruel the lottery of support for the elderly is. He tells us how unfair it is that people are forced to sell their homes to fund their long-term care. Which Government does he think has been in charge for the past 12 years? Which Government promised 12 years ago to stop people being forced to sell their homes to fund their long-term care? Which Government rejected the findings of their own royal commission? Which Government sidelined the King's Fund review? Which Government kicked the issue into the long grass in their 2007 spending review? Frankly, we do not need simply to start another debate. One debate always seems to roll into another with this Government. We need a decision, and we need serious, costed proposals to be the basis for that decision. (*Hansard*, 14 July 2009, col 160)

While many commentators might agree with this diagnosis, the Health Secretary, Andy Burnham, was quick to criticise the tone of this contribution, arguing instead for a more detailed debate instead of 'the usual slanging match' (*Hansard*, 14 July 2009, col 160). When briefly summarising his own proposals, moreover, the Shadow Health Secretary's response was to state a series of principles that many would support, but which had no detail about how the proposed vision might actually be achieved:

> Four years ago we made it clear that there needs to be a partnership approach. We made it clear that we need a system whereby people can be sure that their care needs are supported, a system that raises the quality of care provided in people's homes as well as in residential and nursing care, reverses the decline in productivity in the social care sector,

and ends the scandal of people being forced to sell their home or lose their lifetime savings simply because they are unfortunate enough to need long-term care. We will build a system that guarantees our older citizens the care and dignity they deserve. (*Hansard*, 14 July 2009, col 161)

Following this initial debate, more details emerged about the Conservatives' commitment to a one-off upfront payment at the age of 65 to enable people to insure themselves against future care costs (Lansley, 2009; Conservative Party, 2010e). Again, however, there was very little detail and the measure also looked very similar to one of the options already debated by New Labour (albeit that the Conservatives seemed to think it would cost a lot less than Labour). Under the Coalition there is instead a commitment to review all the funding options via the Commission on the Funding of Care and Support – with some seeing this as a helpful way of promoting political consensus, and others seeing this as a means of putting off a difficult political decision that is unlikely to turn up anything not already considered in previous debates in 1999, 2006 and 2009. Taken together, debates about inheritance tax and about the 2009 Green Paper seemed to suggest that a future Conservative government would need to demonstrate its ability to engage in a much more nuanced and mature discussion of the many issues at stake if it is going to successfully resolve the funding of long-term care.

That this might be the case became even more apparent in early 2010 when the funding of long-term care suddenly re-emerged as a key electoral issue. In many ways, much of the furore was caused by a speech given by Gordon Brown at the 2009 Labour Party conference, which surprised virtually all commentators by announcing plans for free personal care at home for those with the greatest needs. To many people this seemed completely unconnected to the recent green paper, and there were significant doubts that the proposals had been fully costed and thought through before being announced. Indeed, the policy concerned was so out of the blue that it was widely interpreted as an early attempt to make long-term care a key political issue in the run-up to a general election, forcing the Conservatives to set out their own proposals in public.

To some extent this tactic seemed to work. After several months of the main political parties trying to establish some sort of consensus behind the scenes, the Conservatives responded to Brown's challenge in kind. Interpreting the speech as a blatant attempt at scoring some fairly cheap political points, the Conservative hierarchy responded with a poster campaign (once again) portraying one of the funding options allegedly being considered as a form of 'death tax' alongside an image of a tombstone (see Figure 10.1). Very quickly, New Labour responded by holding a national event for leading charities and very publicly not inviting the Conservatives, with the whole issue descending into something of a pre-election farce. While it is difficult to know exactly what was going on here, or who (if anyone) was to blame, it seems fair to conclude that no one really came out of these events well – with professional groups and key voluntary organisations despairing of a political system seemingly incapable of having a sensible long-term debate about a key issue.

**Figure 10.1: Conservative poster campaign, 2010**

The second major issue facing the Coalition is that of personal budgets. Although, prior to the general election, all three main political parties seemed supportive of the roll-out (and potential extension) of personal budgets, there remain a series of ambiguities about the motives of different stakeholders. One of the reasons why both direct payments and personal budgets enjoyed such initial support was partly because they appealed to different groups across different parts of the political spectrum – with different people supporting these concepts for potentially different reasons. Whereas some people are supportive of these ways of working because they see them as part of a campaign for greater civil rights, choice and control for disabled people, others see them as an essentially market-based mechanism for rolling back the boundaries of the welfare state and as a form of 'privatisation by the backdoor' (see Glasby and Littlechild, 2009). Now they are in power, a key task for the Conservatives is to make clear the underlying aims of their community care policy and the value base on which they are operating. Interestingly, in the course of the election campaign, Conservative leader David Cameron specifically mentioned the importance of direct payments during the prime ministerial TV debates, with brief reference to his own experience as the parent of a disabled child.

In many ways this links to a third issue about the future of welfare services more generally (particularly in a period where there may well not only be greater need as the population ages, but also much tighter public finances with which to respond). To date, many have seen self-directed support and personal budgets as a potential means of starting to square this circle – possibly achieving better outcomes for either the same or sometimes less money. This also links to some of the key issues debated as part of the 2009 Green Paper – essentially this revolves around what we will be expected to prepare for and pay for ourselves, and what the state will provide on our behalf. Answers to these issues are often highly personal, philosophical and political, with scope for any government to make itself extremely unpopular. To date, it is not yet fully clear how any of the main political parties may respond to these challenges, and the task of this government may well be to spell out in more detail what they will actually do in practice to respond to such pressures and dilemmas. A little like New Labour's commitment to a 'Third Way', it is hard to know what David Cameron's vision of a 'Big Society' might mean in practice for community care, and for other services, until the detail emerges. And while the Commission on the Funding of Care and Support is considering these issues, that is a further year during which they will remain unresolved.

## Conclusion

Often seen as something of a 'Cinderella service', community care policy has arguably not received the attention it deserves from the main political parties. After significant reforms in the early 1990s, the New Labour governments of 1997–2010 developed a range of new approaches that often tended to continue previous themes, rather than breaking decisively with the past. The one exception to this – the personalisation agenda – was at an early stage and it remained to be seen how genuinely radical policymakers would allow this approach to be in practice (Glasby and Littlechild, 2009). In the build-up to the 2010 general election, the Conservatives said relatively little about community care (certainly compared to other policy areas, such as the NHS), although this is not uncommon for a party in opposition, or indeed given the often neglected nature of social care more generally.

Although there has been high-profile disagreement about the future funding of long-term care, the tone of this debate in the run-up to the election left few confident about the ability to generate a genuine cross-party consensus about such a long-term challenge, while the creation of the Commission on the Funding of Care and Support further postponed any major decisions. In the absence of detailed policy proposals, however, the two key issues seem to be how best to design and fund support for older people with long-term care needs, and what value base to promote when rolling out concepts such as personal budgets. However the relationship between the Conservatives and the Liberal Democrats in the new Coalition government plays out, these seem set to be two key dilemmas that are unlikely to go away.

# ELEVEN

# Conservative policy and the family

*Paul Daniel*

Speaking at his party's Spring Forum in 2008, David Cameron signalled his intention to place the family at the heart of Conservative social policy: 'My ambition is to make Britain more family friendly.... Not just because it is the right thing to do, not just because my family is the most important thing in my life, but because families should be the most important thing in our country's life' (Cameron, 2008c). Of course, it has become more or less mandatory for political parties in Britain to proclaim themselves as 'the party of the family'. Arguably, no other aspect of social policy in recent times has been so suffused with rhetoric and empty platitudes. For those on the right of the political spectrum, in particular, 'family' conveys an image and an emotional resonance that politicians are keen to exploit. Beyond the rhetoric, however, Cameron went on to emphasise that this was a policy issue where he believed that there was a clear differentiation between contemporary Conservatism and its predecessors – both New Labour and the governments of Margaret Thatcher and John Major – claiming that British politics had 'got the family wrong for decades'.

More specifically, the theme that Cameron's Conservatives have chosen to make the central theme of their family policy is support for marriage. Drawing upon Iain Duncan Smith's analysis of the factors contributing to the 'broken society' (Social Justice Policy Group, 2007), family breakdown has been highlighted as a key issue, so that 'Sticking together and raising our children together has shifted from being seen as just part of the natural order to being thought of as more like climbing Mount Everest – a triumph of heroism and endeavour accomplished by few' (David Cameron, quoted in *The Daily Mail*, 2009). In Cameron's view the policy of successive governments has for too long failed to address, or even actively contributed to, a decline in marriage. New Labour, in particular, he accused of a 'pathological opposition to supporting marriage' (quoted in *The Daily Mail*, 2009). This issue then, above all others, was to become the most high-profile and contentious topic of the period running up to the election campaign – at least until the collapse of the banking system and the economic crisis came to dominate all else.

At first glance it would seem surprising, and possibly foolhardy, for the Conservatives to have chosen marriage as a key social policy battlefield. For a start, it can be argued that there is, in reality, very little disagreement between the main political parties on this issue. The following passage, taken from the Labour government's 1998 Green Paper, *Supporting Families*, would support this view:

> But marriage is still the surest foundation for raising children and remains the choice of the majority of people in Britain. We want to strengthen the institution of marriage to help more marriages to succeed. (Home Office, 1998)

Second, there are inherent dangers for politicians in this issue, and, as we will see in the next section, Conservative politicians from Keith Joseph to John Major have fallen victims. As Polly Toynbee (2008) has suggested, once politicians move beyond the 'motherhood and apple pie rhetoric' when it comes to marriage and try to interfere in intimate family relationships then they are entering a 'vipers nest'.

This chapter considers the genesis and development of current Conservative attitudes to marriage and the family. It examines the extent to which they differ from those of New Labour as well as the earlier Conservative governments of Margaret Thatcher and John Major. Finally it reflects upon the possible implications for future social policy arising out of Cameron's commitment to supporting marriage.

## Broken Britain: Broken families

As has been made clear earlier in this book (see, for example, Chapter 1 and others) much of the basis for Cameron's thinking on social policy derives from the work of his predecessor as leader of the party, Iain Duncan Smith. The new think tank established by Duncan Smith after stepping down from his leadership post, the Centre for Social Justice, produced two reports, *Breakdown Britain* (Social Justice Policy Group, 2006) and *Breakthrough Britain* (Social Justice Policy Group, 2007), which became influential in setting the social policy agenda for the Conservatives in the period up to the 2010 election. Leaving aside the contentious and hyperbolic suggestion that British society is 'broken', much of the analysis and even many of the policy proposals flowing from the Centre for Social Justice are very familiar. The focus on poverty, benefit dependency, teenage pregnancy, school failure, crime and disorder are the same indicators that the Labour government had used as measures of social exclusion (for example, Office of the Deputy Prime Minister, 2004). Similarly, the emphasis on early prevention and support for very young children could come straight from New Labour social policy manuals. Indeed the fact that one of the publications produced by the Centre for Social Justice was a joint effort between Iain Duncan Smith and Labour MP Graham Allen helps indicate the extent of the congruence of thinking on this issue (Allen and Duncan Smith, 2008).

However, where the emphasis of the Centre for Social Justice differs from that of Labour's Social Exclusion Unit is on the primacy it gives to the promotion of marriage as a means of countering the social problems both organisations had identified, so that:

> A child not growing up in a two parent family is 75 per cent more likely to fail at school, 70 per cent more likely to be a drug addict, 50 per cent more likely to have an alcohol problem, 40 per cent more likely to have serious debt and 35 per cent more likely to experience worklessness.... Yet, despite evidence clearly demonstrating the importance of stable, healthy and, in particular, married families, current policy does not reflect this. (Centre for Social Justice, 2010, p 4)

The argument of the Centre for Social Justice is that governments have ignored demographic data that indicate not only that children do better in two-parent rather than single-parent households, but also that marriage is more stable than cohabitation, in an attempt to avoid being seen as judgemental. They suggest that 'Politicians and policy makers in Britain have typically shied away from distinguishing between family structures. They have become scared that they may upset someone if they talk of two parent families. Too many hide behind the mantra that it is just about personal choice' (Centre for Social Justice, 2010, p 8).

Of course, the Centre for Social Justice is by no means the first or only pressure group or think tank in or around the Conservative Party to promote support for marriage. As Durham has shown, there have been a number of influential and long-standing organisations campaigning on this issue (Durham, 2001). Two of the oldest, the Institute of Economic Affairs (IEA), founded in 1955, and the Centre for Policy Studies, established by Keith Joseph and Margaret Thatcher in the mid-1970s, have between them produced a stream of reports highlighting the harmful effects of family breakdown. Among the most influential was the publication in 1992 by the IEA of *Families without Fatherhood* (Dennis and Erdos, 1992). In this, two ethical socialists, Norman Dennis and George Erdos, argued that society's ills were in large part attributable to the absence of fathers from children's lives. Along with the work of the American sociologist Charles Murray, on what he termed the 'underclass' (Murray, 1990), this played a significant role in academic, media and political debate around the family throughout the early 1990s. Particularly prominent, in terms of media exposure, were Patricia Morgan, writing principally in *The Daily Mail* and in a series of polemical pamphlets (Morgan, 1995, 2000), and Melanie Phillips, writing in *The Times*. Other voices from outside the Conservative Party that have contributed to the pro-marriage lobby are Christian Action, Research and Education (CARE) and Family and Youth Concern, both established in the early 1970s. Within the party, the Conservative Christian Fellowship has enjoyed considerable influence (Durham, 2001).

Between them, these various groups and individuals constituted a powerful and constant 'pro-marriage' influence on Conservative Party thinking. However, in the heart-searching that followed electoral defeat in 1997, attitudes within the parliamentary party became less clear-cut, or even polarised, on this issue. On the one hand, Theresa May's much-quoted conference speech in 2002, where she warned Conservative delegates that they had come to be seen by the public as the 'nasty party', prompted a desire to be more inclusive and less judgemental, not least in terms of personal and family relationships. Similar sentiments were expressed in a number of key speeches by senior Conservatives such as Michael Portillo and David Willetts. On the other hand, traditionalists such as Ann Widdecombe continued to promote the idea of the traditional family. This theme was also prominent in a number of speeches made by the then party leader, William Hague, in 1998 (Durham, 2001).

So for David Cameron to have chosen to place support for marriage at the centre of Conservative policy on the family was a far from obvious move. Yes, there was a powerful and long-standing lobby on this issue, together with a strong recommendation from Iain Duncan Smith's Centre for Social Justice. However, he will also have been aware of the difficulties that this has caused the Conservative Party in the past. He may also have considered whether such a policy was consistent with his aim of modernising and, in particular, encouraging greater tolerance of diversity within the party (as discussed in Chapter 1). Arguably, this was a high risk strategy. What, then, were the reasons for adopting it?

There are several factors that must have made this an appealing policy for the Conservatives prior to the 2010 election. One is that it enabled David Cameron to draw a clear distinction, although whether real or imagined is open to discussion, between Conservative and Labour policy towards the family. The New Labour agenda of support for early years services, promotion of family-friendly working practices and even the elimination of child poverty have been broadly adopted by the Conservatives. Leaving aside the emphasis on marriage, there would be very little difference between the two parties in either philosophy or policy.

A second, and perhaps more important, advantage to David Cameron of the emphasis on marriage lies in the fact that it gave him an issue around which he could appeal to the more traditional supporters within his own party. Given that much of his emphasis since being elected leader of the party had been to make it more modern, diverse and socially liberal, there was a great danger that he would alienate large swathes of its membership and electoral support in the process. The main Conservative supporting newspapers, *The Daily Telegraph* and *The Daily Mail*, had been lukewarm at best, and sometimes openly scathing in their judgement of Cameron's brand of Conservatism. So, in placing marriage and personal responsibility at the heart of family policy not only did he tap into more traditional conservative values, but he gave *The Daily Mail* an issue that they could wholeheartedly get behind, as the following headline demonstrates:'Now it's War: David Cameron in Savage Attack on Labour's "Pathological" Refusal to Accept Marriage IS Key to Happy Families' (*The Daily Mail*, 2009).

Nor is it only the traditionalists within the party that have found this aspect of Cameron's thinking to its liking. Alongside David Cameron's drive to shift the Conservatives towards social liberalism, there has been a parallel development at grass-roots level. As the philosopher John Gray observes, 'There can be little doubt that Christian fundamentalism has become a growing force in the party and the strand of thinking that is emerging has much in common with the theo-conservatism that has divided and paralysed the Republicans in the US' (Gray, 2010). Prominent among the evangelical Christians currently playing a significant role within the Conservative Party is Philippa Stroud. As a co-founder and chief executive of the Centre for Social Justice, she was one of the main architects, with Iain Duncan Smith (himself a convert to Catholicism), of the policy on marriage and the family. Subsequently, as a parliamentary candidate for Sutton, Cheam and Worcester Park, she attracted notoriety following allegations of involvement in a church that ran prayer sessions to 'cure' gay people (*The Observer*, 2 May 2010). On the one hand, then, the emphasis on marriage within his family policy was perhaps of strategic importance to David Cameron in winning support from large sections of his party, particularly at a time when he was in danger of alienating these same groups with his emphasis on diversity. On the other hand, however, the sight of Conservative candidates in the run-up to the 2010 general election 'preaching the sanctity of marriage and some letting slip their belief that being gay is sinful' (Gray, 2010) demonstrates the political tightrope that Cameron has to walk.

In promoting marriage and identifying alternative family arrangements as causes of social problems, the Conservatives have, in the past, encountered serious political difficulties, as discussed in the next section. Clearly Cameron and his senior colleagues were well aware of this danger. In a speech to the National Family and Parenting Institute in 2006, he sought to distance himself from the mistakes of the last Conservative government when he claimed 'not only is the war against lone parents over, but the weapons have been put permanently beyond use' (Hoggart, 2006). This was echoed by Michael Gove, speaking at the Institute for Public Policy Research. Making the case for putting marriage at the centre of family policy, he acknowledged that 'we need to be clear about where we [the Conservatives] have gone wrong in the past. I think the Right was wrong to get hung up on homosexuality. I think we indulged prejudice in the eighties and missed the point.... I also think the Right was wrong in its rhetoric about single mothers' (Gove, 2008b). Such a frank admission of past mistakes brings us to a consideration of policy towards the family during the Thatcher and Major governments.

## Conservative policy and the family, 1979–97

Two years before becoming prime minister, Margaret Thatcher addressed the 1977 Conservative Party conference with the claim that 'we are the party of the family'. At the same conference, one of the party's other frontbench spokesmen, Patrick Jenkin, gave an indication of the model of the family that the Conservatives had in mind when he declared that, 'Quite frankly, I don't think that mothers have the same right to work as fathers do. If the good Lord had intended us to have equal rights to go out to work he would not have created men and women. These are biological facts' (cited in Abbott and Wallace, 1992, p 117). In this respect the Conservatives were tapping into a growing concern over the family within academic and public debate at this time (see Durham, 1991; Abbott and Wallace, 1992). Writing in 1991, Durham described the context within which the Thatcher government came into office as follows: 'In article after article in recent years, the family in Modern Britain has been described as in crisis. Rising divorce rates, one parent families, abortion, homosexuality, pornography – all have been cited as indices of a nation facing social collapse' (Durham, 1991, p 5).

This gave rise on both sides of the Atlantic to a powerful coalition of individuals and organisations campaigning on issues of morality. Dubbed the 'moral new right', this movement was undoubtedly more concerted and influential in the United States. However, the Thatcher government was also the target of protracted activity by a number of moral crusaders, such as Mary Whitehouse's National Viewers' and Listeners' Association, which was an almost daily voice in the media throughout the 1980s, and Victoria Gillick, who campaigned on the issue of government policy in relation to contraceptive advice to teenagers. Yet, despite her rhetoric on family values and the pressure from a wide range of campaign groups, Margaret Thatcher's period of government was not one that put the family, traditional or otherwise, high on its policy agenda. Indeed, the Conservatives came under fire from a number of the moral campaigners for their timidity or duplicity on this issue. Anderson, for example, writing in *The Times* in 1985, regretted the weakness of the United Kingdom's family lobby and argued that neither the Church nor the Conservative Party had defended traditional family values. Gillick reacted even more strongly, saying of the Tories that 'traditional values ... family stability ... parental choice were all electioneering humbug' (both cited in Durham, 1991, p 168).

There are several possible explanations as to why the Thatcher government was reluctant to take a strong policy stance in defence of 'the traditional family'. One is that the Prime Minister had herself received a personal lesson of the political dangers inherent in the politics of the family. In 1974 her friend and close political ally, Keith Joseph, made a speech in which he warned against the danger to 'our human stock' of the increasing number of children born to lone mothers in social classes 4 and 5 (semi- and unskilled working class). The furore that this caused led to Joseph withdrawing from the contest for the leadership of the Conservative Party, to be replaced by Margaret Thatcher. Apart from the somewhat eugenicist emphasis in the speech, with its reference to a decline in the quality of 'the national stock', Joseph was voicing a concern over the breakdown in marriage and the traditional family that was being widely promoted at the time, and one that was later echoed by Iain Duncan Smith and the Centre for Social

Justice. The outcry and the political damage to Keith Joseph, however, were such that it may well have given Thatcher pause for thought.

The second, and perhaps more significant, factor that inhibited the Thatcher government from pursuing a more active role in relation to family policy is to be found in the conflict within New Right thinking at that time between economic liberalism and traditional conservatism. As a number of commentators have pointed out (for example, Fox Harding, 1999), the economic liberal strand within the New Right and what has come to be known as Thatcherism, advocated a free market and a minimum role for the state. This extends to a strong emphasis on individual freedom. On the other hand, traditional Conservatism placed more emphasis on a strong and authoritarian state to enforce law and order and traditional values, including within the family. Although Thatcherism did manage to accommodate these two strands (Gamble, 1994), there are potentially significant tensions between them, particularly when it comes to family policy. One of the clearest examples of this was to be found in the attitude of the Thatcher government to women's, and especially mothers', employment in the labour market. On the one hand, the family traditionalists, epitomised by Patrick Jenkin's views cited earlier, saw the role of mothers as lying within the home. For the economic liberals, on the other hand, the unprecedented increase in the number of women, including mothers, in the workplace during the 1980s was simply a function of the operation of the market. A product of this unresolved tension was that the record of the Thatcher government on supporting mothers in the workplace, through childcare or flexible employment, was very poor compared to comparable European countries (Randall, 2000).

On the specific issue of support for marriage, which has become such a central element of Cameron's Conservatism, the record of the Thatcher era was equally indifferent. For all the rhetoric about support for 'the traditional family' this was by no means a policy priority. Divorce was actually made easier as a result of the 1984 Matrimonial Proceedings Act, which allowed husbands and wives to petition for divorce after one year rather than the three years that had previously been required. Throughout the 1980s and early 1990s, divorce rates rose steadily and were the highest in Europe. Similar increases were to be seen in the numbers of lone-parent families and cohabitations (Somerville, 2000). At the same time, as Durham has pointed out, there were a number of unsuccessful private members' bills attempting to reform the law on homosexuality, pornography and abortion, none of which were given official backing by the Thatcher government (Durham, 1991).

The one high-profile and controversial example of legislation that was in line with the rhetoric on traditional family values was Clause 28 of the 1988 Local Government Act, which prohibited local authorities from 'promoting homosexuality'. In practice, however, for all its notoriety this legislation was a little used and largely superfluous piece of window dressing. Certainly it pales into insignificance with the main thrust of policy during the Thatcher government, which was the shift away from the state in the direction of family responsibility. When Margaret Thatcher made her infamous remark in an interview with a women's magazine that 'There is no such thing as society. There are individual men and women and there are families' (Thatcher, 1987), she set out a theme that united traditionalists and market liberals. The belief that welfare policies of successive governments had undermined the role of the family was a dominant theme in New Right thinking in Britain and the US.

Thus withdrawal of state support for the family was a consistent policy motif in the 1980s. Perhaps the most blatant, and in the event the most politically damaging, example of this was the 1991 Child Support Act. Although this reached the statute book only after she had left office, this was very much a product of 'Thatcherism'. Portrayed principally as an Act to benefit children by requiring irresponsible fathers to meet their obligation to provide financial support, in reality it made many poor children worse off and was rather a means of transferring the costs of child support from the Treasury to families (Garnham and Knights, 1994). Not surprisingly, the effect of policies that placed responsibility for children squarely on families, from whom state support was being progressively withdrawn, at a time when increasingly deregulated labour markets were moving in the direction of poorly paid and part-time employment, led to a dramatic increase in child poverty (Bradshaw, 2002).

Overall, then, the approach towards the family during the government of Margaret Thatcher has been well summed up by Abbott and Wallace (1992, p 130) as follows:

> A moral agenda was implemented under Thatcherism, but it was not one explicitly concerned with improving the living conditions of families or even of consistently prioritising the needs of the patriarchal nuclear family. Rather it has been concerned with constructing a new form of citizenship – active individualism that places the emphasis on individuals being resourceful in providing for their own welfare and that of others.

It was only towards the end of her time in Downing Street, as her memoirs reveal, that she became increasingly convinced, in language that was later echoed by the Centre for Social Justice, that strengthening marriage and the 'traditional family' was the only way to tackle crime and other social problems (Thatcher, 1993). However, it was left to her successor, John Major, to take this theme forward.

In policy terms the Major government continued along the lines set by its predecessor. There was, however, a softening in the government's stance on Child Benefit. Frozen since 1987, its future was widely seen as bleak leading up to the 1992 general election. However, the personal commitment of John Major to the benefit ensured that the Conservative election manifesto contained the promise that 'child benefit will remain the cornerstone of our policy for all families with children' (Conservative Party, 1992). Slightly more sympathetic noises were made in relation to early years childcare provision and, following the appointment of Gillian Shephard as Employment Secretary, on the difficulties faced by working women. But at the same time, the Major government blocked European Union directives on parental leave and on limiting working time. As with the Thatcher government, there was no overt attempt to support and promote marriage. Indeed, in 1993 the then Chancellor, Norman Lamont, began the process of reducing the value of the Married Couple's Allowance within the tax system, culminating in its complete abolition in 2001. Lamont's advisor at the time was David Cameron – a fact that appears to have gone largely unremarked upon when, as leader of the party, he made support for marriage within the tax system such a key element in Conservative family policy leading up to the 2010 election.

If the family continued to be neglected in relation to policy, the rhetoric of the Major government shifted, at least from 1993 onwards. One external event that played a large part in changing the discourse on the family in the UK at that time was the murder of two-year-old James Bulger by two 10-year-old boys. The outpouring of soul-searching in the media about the state of British childhood and family life was reflected within the Conservative Party in a return to the themes voiced by Keith Joseph 20 years earlier. The 1993 party conference set the tone. Under John Major's conference-rallying cry of 'Back to Basics', ministers such as John Redwood and Peter Lilley vied with each other in their attack on 'the permissive society', attributing a whole range of social ills to the breakdown of the family. Although Major himself did not join in the orgy of lone-parent bashing, there followed several years when this was widespread within the party and in large sections of the press. This has been vividly recalled by the author of the Harry Potter series, J. K. Rowling, herself a lone parent in the early 1990s:

> I had become a single mother when my first marriage split up in 1993. In one devastating stroke, I became a hate figure to a certain section of the press, and a bogeyman to the Tory Government. Peter Lilley, then Secretary of State at the DSS, had recently entertained the Conservative Party conference with a spoof Gilbert and Sullivan number, in which he decried 'young ladies who get pregnant just to jump the housing list'. The Secretary of State for Wales, John Redwood, castigated single-parent families from St Mellons, Cardiff, as 'one of the biggest social problems of our day'. (Rowling, 2010)

However, for all the sound and fury on this issue, there was no new policy thinking. Indeed, in a more reflective mode than when he sang to the party conference, Peter Lilley concluded that government was essentially helpless in relation to family breakdown, so that:

> The idea that government could impose family values by edict or exhortation is authoritarian and impractical. Likewise the idea that the state can strengthen the family by undertaking most of its functions is equally objectionable. It amounts to nationalising parental responsibility, making fathers redundant and mothers dependent. (Lilley, 1994)

In the event, the Major government was to find that not only was this an area of policy where the government's scope for action was severely limited, but it was also one that contained serious risk of political embarrassment, as a series of sexual indiscretions involving prominent Conservative politicians came to light. The ultimate moment of *Schadenfreude* was provided when one of the main scourges of lone parents, John Redwood, subsequently left his wife and children in acrimonious circumstances.

## New Labour, 1997–2010

No less than the government of John Major, Labour in opposition was profoundly influenced in its social policy thinking by the murder of James Bulger. As Durham has pointed out, as early as October 1993 Tony Blair, then Shadow Home Secretary, was arguing for Labour policy to acknowledge the importance of the family. Later, in 1995, as leader, he went on to warn that a strong country could not be 'morally neutral about the family' (Durham, 2001). However, when it came to Labour's particular view of the nature of the family, and on marriage in particular, difficulties were apparent. Anxious to avoid the judgemental approach of the Major government, Labour was careful to show its support for a diversity of family types. At the same time, it appeared to wish to clearly signal its preference for marriage. In truth, as Driver and Martell have argued, there was a divergence within New Labour thinking on this issue. For while Tony Blair laid emphasis on the advantages of the stable, two-parent family as a basis for promoting the welfare of children, the leading academic figure within New Labour, Anthony Giddens, was much more sanguine about the benefits of family change in terms of the choice and autonomy of individual adults (Driver and Martell, 2002). The earliest indication of Labour's stance on the family was to be found in its Green Paper *Supporting Families* (Home Office, 1998). This contained a chapter entitled 'Strengthening Marriage', which set out the new government's position as follows:

> This government believes that marriage provides a strong foundation for stable relationships. This does not mean trying to make people marry or criticising or penalising people who choose not to. We do not believe that Government should interfere in people's lives in that way. (Home Office, 1998, p 30)

The Green Paper then went on to set out a number of policy proposals to support marriage, including the setting up of an Advisory Group on Marriage and Relationship Support within the Lord Chancellor's Department. It suggested that couples planning to marry should be given guidance on their rights and responsibilities and, in the event of divorce, they would be expected to attend counselling sessions.

This rather uneasy compromise between support for marriage and reluctance to be judgemental in relationship matters predictably attracted criticism from both flanks. On the one hand, it was attacked for its advocacy of marriage from outside the party by groups such as the lone-parent organisation, Gingerbread, and the Lesbian and Gay group, Stonewall, and from inside by ministers such as Tessa Jowell. On the other hand, it came under fire from Christian organisations, such as CARE, on the grounds that it was too lukewarm in its support for marriage (Durham, 2001). To some extent Labour was able to sidestep this tension in its approach by shifting its focus away from the family and onto children. Blair's momentous pledge to abolish child poverty, made in 1999, ensured that the government's focus was less on marriage and the family, and more on children and their life chances. Nor was Labour's interest in children confined to the concern over child poverty, historic though this was; investment in children was also pivotal to Labour's social and economic policy. Again and again, both Blair and the Chancellor, Gordon Brown, hammered home the message that children were the key to Britain's future prosperity. In their respective speeches to the party conference in 2003, for example, the Prime Minister made 23 references to children, and the Chancellor no fewer than 40 (*The New Statesman*, 20 October 2003).

The focus on childhood was marked by the establishment of the Children and Young Persons Unit within the Cabinet Office in 2000, and the creation of the post of Minister for Children in 2003. Above all, though, it was demonstrated by the unprecedented range and scale of policy initiatives and resources focused on children, including universal services such as enhanced Child Benefit and expanded early years services as well as more targeted provision, such as Sure Start centres and Child Tax Credits (Daniel, 2010). Given this focus on the child, it has been suggested by Iain Duncan Smith and his colleagues at the Centre for Social Justice that Labour ignored the importance for children's well-being of parents' relationships with each other, and the significance of marriage in particular (Social Justice Policy Group, 2007). However, the claim that Labour failed to recognise the importance of family relationships is inaccurate. For example, in *Support for All: The Families and Relationships Green Paper*, it clearly states that 'an extensive literature shows that the quality of the relationship between parents is linked to positive parenting and better outcomes for children too' (Department for Children, Schools and Families, 2010, p 17).

The difference between Labour's thinking and that of the Centre for Social Justice lies in the fact that the former put much less emphasis on the structure of the family unit and much more on what goes on within it. Thus the Green Paper just cited quotes from a research paper produced for the Department for Children, Schools and Families by the Thomas Coram Institute, as follows: 'It is clear from the evidence that how the family functions, rather than family type is more relevant to understanding the impacts associated with family breakdown' (Department for Children, Schools and Families, 2009, p 21). This, together with the view expressed a number of times throughout the Green Paper that 'marriage is a personal and private decision for responsible adults, with which politicians should not interfere' (2010, p 3), explains Labour's pragmatic approach to family form. While it would be wrong to claim, as the Centre for Social Justice does, that the Labour government was anti-marriage (Social Justice Policy Group, 2007), it certainly did not promote it above other forms of relationship. The abolition of the vestigial married couples' tax allowance, in favour of extra support for children via tax credits, and the repeal of Part 11 of the 1996 Family Law Act, which aimed at rescuing failing marriages, can be cited as evidence of its indifference to marriage. So too can the fact that the 2002 Adoption and Children Act enabled same-sex and cohabiting couples to adopt for the first time. The common thread in all these measures, however, is not a negative or indifferent attitude towards marriage, so much as a determination to put children's welfare first and an acceptance of the fact that families come in all shapes and sizes.

A more substantial criticism perhaps, which was directed against Labour's approach, is that it produced an excessive increase in state involvement in family life. Kirby has referred to it as 'the nationalisation of childhood', suggesting that it derives from Marx's and Trotsky's aim for 'the functions of the family to be absorbed by the institutions of the socialist society' (Kirby, 2006, p 2). While this is arguably a wildly over-the-top analysis of Labour's childcare policy, other critics have made similar points in a more measured fashion. For example, Fawcett et al, while recognising the considerable benefits to children arising out of Labour's extensive programme of action, note that it has involved a degree of 'hyperactivity which can make the wealth of initiatives exhausting … as one set of initiatives, zones, targets, standards and performance indicators follows quickly on the heels of the previous set' (Fawcett et al, 2004, p 164). Also, alongside the undoubted gains for children in being seen in 'social investment' terms, they argue there are costs in that 'there is a greater use of regulation and surveillance of both parents and children' (2004, p 165).

Michael Gove, then Shadow Education Secretary and one of the Conservatives' most thoughtful and influential critics of Labour government policy, also tapped into these sentiments when addressing the Institute for Public Policy Research in September 2008. He used a speech delivered by ex-president Clinton to the Labour Party conference in 2006, where he proposed *ubuntu* as a political mantra, in order to mount a critique of the government's social policy. *Ubuntu* is a Bantu word that broadly translates as 'I am because you are'. Gove went on to suggest that Labour had lost sight of the importance of relationships in its approach to policy:

> Under Labour there is really only one relationship which
> matters. The relationship between the individual and the

state.... The quality of the relationships we enjoy – with the teachers who might inspire us, with the employers who might shape our career, with the partners who're helping us raise children, with friends and neighbours in the community we inhabit – are all neglected. Because they can't be measured, directed and controlled from the centre. (Gove, 2008b)

Marking a clear departure from the Thatcher and Major years, Gove acknowledged that there were many aspects of Labour's policy on the family that needed to be preserved. Specifically he accepted that a commitment to childcare and family-friendly working should be an essential part of the Conservatives' family policy. However, he sought to distinguish Conservative thinking from what he regards as the impersonal central control in Labour policy, 'We want state help to be as personal, intimate, human and responsive as possible, reinforcing relationships and working with the grain of human nature. There when you need it, not when it suits the government. Freely mentoring, not on your case monitoring' (Gove, 2008b). An example of a light-touch service that can strengthen relationships at a time when they are often under greatest stress, and which the Conservatives would wish to expand, he suggested, was health visiting, concluding that what drives Conservative thinking in relation to childcare is 'the need to see everything through the prism of stronger, healthier relationships'.

Gove's touchy-feely language has a certain appeal, and phrases such as 'mentoring not monitoring' may strike a chord in their critique of some of Labour's more bureaucratic or authoritarian features. It is not clear, however, that it is anything more than a Panglossian flight of fancy in its emphasis on relationships. What it reflects is that the contemporary politics of the family is as much about language as actual policy. In a Fabian essay Horton has suggested that the problem of the left is that, for all that it can credibly claim to have done most of the things which bring greatest benefit to the family, it has 'no story of the family'. He suggested that the then Labour government did not talk about 'the family' any more:

> Talking about 'children' and 'families' isn't enough. 'The family' is an incredibly important and resonant ideal in society. While that ideally may be vaguely (though decreasingly) attached to an image of a nuclear family, its strongest images and resonances are less about family structure than about duties of care, nurture, love and all that

is dear to us in our personal relationships. The word 'families' does not tap into that imagery or emotional resonance: 'the family' does. (Horton, 2010, p 20)

## The future of family policy under David Cameron

It seems unlikely that the broad direction of family policy will change under the Coalition government. The preceding Labour government moved the goalposts in relation to a range of issues, including tackling child poverty, the provision of early years services and family-friendly employment. From a position where, during the Thatcher years, the Conservatives denied the existence of poverty in contemporary Britain, under David Cameron they have signed up to the commitment to eliminate child poverty launched by Blair in 1999. Similarly, whereas the Conservatives when last in government believed that responsibility for the care of pre-school children should be left to the family, and that working arrangements were determined by the free market, they entered the 2010 general election campaign committed to extend existing state support for young children and their working parents. Whether childcare will be delivered by the same means as under Labour, however, is not certain. Given their emphasis on the 'Big Society' rather than the state, and the major cuts in public expenditure, the Conservatives may be tempted to turn to grandparents and other voluntary providers. The one specific promise in relation to family support in the Conservative election manifesto was to increase the number of health visitors by 4,200. However, no timescale was placed upon this and doubts have been raised that it can be achieved without a radical overhaul of training and recruitment (*Children and Young People Now*, 9 March 2010).

As has already been made clear, the striking point of departure in the Conservative Party's approach to the family is its attitude towards marriage. Initially it was not made clear how this might translate into policy. In 2008 David Cameron talked about 'bringing an end to the couple penalty in the tax and benefit system' (Cameron, 2008a). The 'couple penalty' is generally taken to be the change in entitlements to benefits and tax credits and in liability to taxes that occurs when two single people marry, or start to live together as husband and wife. As such, it does not actually distinguish between married and cohabiting couples. It would also be prohibitively expensive to eliminate – estimated by the Institute for Fiscal Studies at £34.3 billion at 2010 tax and benefit rates (Adam and Brewer, 2010). What followed in the build-up to the election was a struggle to make policy match the rhetoric.

Cameron constantly alluded, especially in the pages of *The Daily Mail*, to a 'tax bonus for married couples' in order to send out a strong signal of approval. Depending on the audience, couples in civil partnerships were included too. This commitment gradually unravelled in the face of the cost implications as well as the many pitfalls involved, such as the question frequently voiced by Polly Toynbee over the justification for allowing an abandoned wife to lose her bonus while her ex-husband takes it with him to a second and third marriage (Toynbee, 2010).

In the event, the Conservative election manifesto contained two much more modest commitments. The first was for a partial transferable tax allowance for married couples (and those in civil partnerships). Briefly stated, this would allow non-working spouses to transfer £750 only of their unused personal allowance to their husband/wife/civil partner providing that they are below the higher rate tax band. In other words, it would be worth £150 per year to such families. It has been estimated that it will apply to four million couples, one third of whom will be pensioner families and only 35% will be families with children (Brewer and Greaves, 2010). The second proposal was the much vaguer intention to abolish the couple penalty in the tax credit system. No timescale or mechanism was spelled out for this and in view of its estimated cost of £18 billion, it would seem to be a long-term goal.

Overall, it is difficult to reconcile a proposal on transferable tax allowances, described by the Institute for Fiscal Studies as 'complicated, confusing and untransparent' (Institute for Fiscal Studies, 2010b), with the 'celebration' of marriage within the tax system that David Cameron promised in December 2009 (*The Daily Mail*, 2009). Moreover, and somewhat ironically given the widespread use of metaphors involving marriage and civil partnership to describe the Coalition government, and the relationship between David Cameron and Nick Clegg in particular, family policy has proved to be one of the most contentious areas for the new government. Before the election, Nick Clegg had been scathing in his assessment of the Conservatives' flagship policy of recognising marriage in the tax system, dismissing it as 'patronising' and an 'expensive bribe' that would be unfair to many families. The choice of a Liberal Democrat, Sarah Teather, for the post of Minister for Children and Families, and the fact that the Liberal Democrats were granted the right to abstain on the issue of transferable tax allowances, suggested that the Conservatives were eager to avoid potential conflict. The sting was further taken out of the issue, at least for a time, by establishing a taskforce on childhood and families. Despite the inclusion of Iain Duncan Smith on this taskforce, the participation of the Liberal Democrats may mean that it is less likely to reproduce the narrow emphasis on marriage that has characterised much of the work of the Centre for Social Justice. More generally, the Coalition appears to have pushed Cameron, possibly gratefully, in a more socially liberal direction, and has weakened those within the Conservative Party, the lobby groups and the media who have advocated a return to 'traditional family values'.

# TWELVE

# Crime and criminal justice

*Mike Hough*

It would normally be quite straightforward to summarise and appraise the law-and-order policies of an incoming administration six months into its term of office. As others in this volume have also pointed out, times are far from normal, for two reasons. We have a Coalition government for the first time since 1945 (discounting the less formal Lib–Lab pact of 1977/78) and we are entering a period of unparalleled cuts in public-sector expenditure. These factors substantially curtail each of the Coalition parties' freedom of manoeuvre to implement the criminal justice policies that appeared in their manifestos – which only months after the election already had a somewhat historic feel to them.

At the time of writing it had been announced in the new government's spending review that criminal justice agencies, like the majority of the public sector, would receive cuts of around 25% over a four-year period. Clearly, given such pressures, there are unlikely to be any new initiatives that carry a significant price tag, or even ones that have significant set-up costs. Offering a commentary on the criminal justice policies that we can expect to see over the lifetime of this administration is therefore more a question of divination than of manifesto content analysis. The approach that is taken here is, first, to summarise the key thrust of criminal justice policy over the last 30 years; and then to 'read the runes' to see what sorts of continuity or discontinuity we can expect.

## The context: criminal justice policy since 1979

This summary of criminal justice policy over the last 30 years is impressionistic. It makes no claims to be definitive, but it should provide an adequate benchmark against which to examine emerging Coalition policies. In some policy areas readers might reasonably expect an analysis broken down by different political parties. In criminal justice policy, however, one can differentiate clearly between the period from 1979 to 1992, when the Conservatives pursued a surprisingly liberal set of policies, and the period from 1993 to 2010, when the main parties seemed consistently locked in a competition to 'out-tough' each other on law and order. The differences between the two periods are greater than the differences between the two main parties. The obvious question to ask is whether the Coalition government will carry on in this combative tradition, or whether it might revert to what seems, in hindsight, a more benign era – for criminal policy at least – under the Conservative administration up until 1992.

## 1979–92

While under the Thatcher administrations most government departments were exposed to spending cuts and demands for 'value for money', the Home Office and its criminal justice agencies were largely left alone – probably because the Conservatives had established themselves at the 1979 election as the 'party of law and order', and this claim might be undermined by reductions in police spending. Nor, in this period, were criminal justice agencies exposed to New Public Management (NPM) performance targets. Paradoxically, successive 'One Nation' Home Secretaries adopted policies that one would not immediately associate with social Conservatism. William Whitelaw, Leon Brittan and Douglas Hurd each introduced legislation and policies that aimed to increase police accountability, reduce the use of custody, and youth custody in particular, stimulate the use of community penalties, and broaden responsibility for crime prevention, ensuring that local authorities played a greater role. Douglas Hurd famously characterised imprisonment as an expensive way of making bad people worse in his 1990 White Paper (Home Office, 1990).[1] These policies culminated in the 1991 Criminal Justice Act, which tested to destruction an approach to criminal policy that liberal commentators have characterised as 'doing good by stealth' (for example, Green, 2009).

## 1993–2010

The 1991 Criminal Justice Act was the most explicitly decarceral of the Criminal Justice Acts of this period, placing a series of hurdles in front of sentencers that they had to surmount before they could pass prison sentences. It was implemented in late 1992, at a time when New Labour was beginning to mount a credible challenge to the Conservatives as the party of 'law and order'. Tony Blair famously promised in early 1993 that a New Labour government would be 'tough on crime, tough on the causes of crime' (Blair, 1993). In the face of this challenge, and under growing media criticism for their liberal policies, the Tories retreated rapidly from the policies embedded in the 1991 Act.[2] Since then, both parties have taken care to ensure that their penal policies resonate with public opinion, at least as it is constructed in, and reflected by, the popular press. Many criminological commentators have described the malign impact of this penal populism (for example, Hough et al, 2003; Millie et al, 2003), which has seen the doubling of the prison population over a period where overall crime has undoubtedly fallen (see, for example, Flatley et al, 2010). Notable developments have included:

- the introduction of long presumptive sentences for repeat burglars and drug dealers;
- the near-doubling of tariffs for life sentences; and
- the introduction of the indeterminate sentence of Imprisonment for Public Protection (IPP), with manifestly unjust consequences.

It was in this period, too, that forms of governance associated with NPM started to be imposed on the criminal justice system. Initially Michael Howard, Home Secretary from 1993 to 1997, and then a succession of Labour Home Secretaries from 1997, imposed increasingly more elaborate numerical performance targets on the police and on other parts of the system. I have argued elsewhere (Hough, 2003, 2007) that politicians' populist orientations to criminal justice interacted with NPM forms of governance to grossly simplify political conceptions of justice policy (whether or not politicians preserved a richer and more textured understanding privately of the issues is irrelevant: they became trapped in the logic of NPM). The need for a set of politically plausible, publicly comprehensible, targets resulted in a system that took for granted that the function of the criminal justice system is to reduce crime through strategies of deterrence, rehabilitation and incapacitation (keeping offenders out of circulation by imprisonment). In other words, controlling crime was to be achieved through strategies of narrow instrumentality, involving adjustments to the costs and benefits of lawbreaking.

Trapped in this narrowly instrumental discourse, politicians overpromised on what they could deliver in terms of crime control. Perhaps the clearest example of this was Michael Howard's assertion in his 1993 speech to the Conservative Party conference that 'prison works'. What was ignored – by all sides – was the fact that commitment to the rule of law involves normative as much as instrumental considerations, and that the normative systems that control moral (and legal) behaviour fall largely outside of political control (for discussion, see Hough, 2007; Hough et al, 2010). What also emerged – predictably – over time was that the NPM regime brought with it many perverse effects. Notably, the police as a disciplined organisation imbued with a fair degree of occupational cynicism, achieved the targets set for them rather than the goals behind the targets (FitzGerald et al, 2002).

If penal populism and NPM were the hallmarks of penal policy over this period of almost two decades, some other related features are worth a mention. First, governance through NPM was heavily *centralising* in its effects. Power moved to Whitehall, and within Whitehall from spending departments to the Treasury and the Cabinet Office. In theory, local agencies retained – or could earn – autonomy over the means that they could use to meet their targets, but they lost (or ceded) the scope to exercise their professional judgement about the goals that they should be pursuing.

Second, NPM brought with it a commitment to *responsiveness* to citizen preferences. Responsiveness has been a consistent feature of NPM, which may make sense when the state is providing a service that can also be purchased from the private sector, health and education being the obvious examples. Whether such a consumerist orientation is as appropriate for systems of justice is questionable, of course, but undoubtedly there has been an increasing trend to permit local communities to exercise greater control over the priorities of criminal justice agencies. This tendency towards 'responsiveness' is in tension with the centralising tendencies inherent in NPM; and showed signs of waxing as the enthusiasm for NPM governance through targets waned from 2005 onwards.

Third, despite their penal rhetoric, neither the Conservatives nor Labour ever abandoned rehabilitative ambitions. Probation services expanded rapidly, and with them the use of community penalties. Labour invested a great deal of effort to reform the probation and prison services to form a single National Offender Management Service (NOMS), although they probably overestimated the scope for reducing crime through tougher and more disciplined rehabilitative programmes; they certainly underestimated the costs of the changes – both financially and in terms of morale – that were associated with the establishment of NOMS. However, the commitment to rehabilitation remained firmly in place.

This *tour d'horizon* of crime politics over 30 years poses three key questions about the policies that we can expect of the Coalition government:

- Can we expect continuity with the trend over the last two decades to penal populism and the narrowly instrumental crime-fighting focus?
- What balance will be struck between centralisation (and centrally set targets) and responsiveness to local preferences?
- How much weight will be attached to rehabilitation, and can we expect a rehabilitation revolution?

These questions are considered in turn next.

## Penal populism and the 'war on crime'

The logic of penal populism has been to sympathise with public concerns about crime, and then to offer tough, decisive action in response. The populist politician assumes a capacity, and promises a commitment, to tackle 'wicked issues' that their predecessors have failed to solve. Many of the 'tough', 'decisive', strategies on offer in crime politics have not withstood much critical scrutiny (the use of an indeterminate sentence of Imprisonment for Public Protection [IPP] being an obvious example), but they may have yielded some electoral advantage. The scale of the 1997 Labour election victory has been attributed in part to the decision to be 'tough on crime'. The consequence has arguably been a needlessly punitive – and expensive – penal system. Politicians to date may recognise this privately, but have been reluctant – especially when in power – to admit it in public. Will the Coalition government be any different?

There is some room for cautious optimism. First and foremost, the fiscal crisis imposes intense pressure on the Coalition government to 'talk down' the prison population, taking precisely the opposite approach to Michael Howard in the mid-1990s and David Blunkett in the early 2000s, when they were Home Secretaries (the rapid increase in the use of imprisonment in the 1990s and early 2000s can be attributed, at least in part, to politicians 'talking up' the prison population by fostering a more punitive climate of opinion; see, for example, Hough et al, 2003; Millie et al, 2003). Second, the disciplines of coalition politics, and the need for pragmatic negotiation, may make it harder for politicians to place electoral advantage over the intrinsic value of a given set of policies. Although the Liberal Democrats are the junior partner in the Coalition, one might expect them to exercise a brake on any tendency to penal populism. Third, the ideas behind the 'Big Society', rather than 'big government', are somewhat inconsistent with any claims that the government exercises tight control over the levers for crime reduction.

Admittedly the section of the 2010 Conservative manifesto on crime reads – as indeed do those of the other main parties – very much like a continuation of the 'Punch and Judy' competition between the two main parties to be tough on crime – including a claim about increases in violent crime under New Labour, which is hard to construe as anything but disingenuous (Conservative Party, 2010e). Neither, too, does the Liberal Democrat manifesto read as if that party was planning to introduce a form of 'new politics' for law and order: coverage of crime was brief, the main promise being to provide a more effective deterrence by putting 3,000 more police officers on the beat – a promise that in retrospect seems ill-informed if not naive. However, they also offered greater public accountability and less bureaucracy – more traditional Liberal Democrat offerings, but also themes that were consistent with Conservative policy (Liberal Democrats, 2010).

Even if the manifestos showed little sign of a change in the style of criminal justice politics, there have been, more recently, signs of a shift. The apocalyptic 'broken Britain' narrative favoured by the Conservatives before the election has become submerged, and in 'Big Society' policy documents there has been some appreciation of the complexities involved in building and maintaining civil society (for example, Conservative Party, 2010c). Although little is said specifically about crime in these documents, there is a sense that the authors understand the lack of quick fixes to crime problems.

Even more significant, perhaps, is the 'mood music' coming from the Ministry of Justice. Kenneth Clarke, the unexpected appointment as Justice Secretary, used his first major speech in June 2010 to suggest that imprisonment is now overused:

> I said soon after I was appointed that I am amazed that the prison population has doubled since I was Home Secretary in the early 1990s. It stands at more than 85,000 today. This is quite an astonishing number which I would have dismissed as an impossible and ridiculous prediction if it had been put to me as a forecast in 1992. (Clarke, 2010)

A month later, this was followed by a further speech from the Justice Minister, Crispin Blunt (2010), noting with approval the famous quote from Winston Churchill that, 'The mood and temper of the public in regard to the treatment of crime and criminals is one of the most unfailing tests of the civilisation of any country'. The implication of the speech was that there was room for a shift away from the 'prison works' policies that were associated with the last Conservative administration.

At the time of writing the Ministry of Justice had just published a Green Paper on sentencing, setting out a more detailed statement of penal policy (Ministry of Justice, 2010). This indeed reflected the tenor of the ministerial team's earlier statements, and included a range of proposals to promote rehabilitative sentences both in the community and in prison, to reform and simplify sentencing and to further curtail the use of the indeterminate IPP sentence. It remains to be seen whether the principles of transparency and of earned remission can be implemented in a way that manages to be both fair and affordable. More generally, the commitment to honesty in sentencing – with courts passing sentences whose terms accurately reflect reality – is to be welcomed; the difficult task is to achieve the transition from an opaque to a transparent system without at the same time introducing a costly (and needless) step-change in sentence severity.

Nor has the Ministry of Justice been the only government department to introduce a new tone to their policies post-election. The Home Secretary, Theresa May, announced – again in July 2010 – that it was 'time to move beyond the ASBO', with simpler sanctions that were 'rehabilitating and restorative rather than criminalising and coercive' (reported in *The Guardian*, 28 July). This marked something of a departure from the Conservatives' hard-line pre-election rhetoric on anti-social behaviour.

Whether these statements represent a real or durable shift remains to be seen. It is one thing for a new administration with no track record to defend to challenge the orthodoxies held dear by their supporters, it is quite another to do so in the period of 'mid-term blues' when the electorate starts to become disenchanted and the next election looms into sight. A key factor will be crime trends. We have seen a sharp fall in crime followed by a levelling off over the last 15 years (Flatley et al, 2010). A reasonable assumption – though one not yet borne out by events – is that the trend will be reversed as the recession and the subsequent public expenditure cuts increase income inequality. Whether the Coalition – and in particular its Conservative members – could continue a self-denying ordinance against crowd-pleasing tough talk under these circumstances remains to be seen.

## Centralisation or responsiveness to local pressures?

In the period from 1993 until the 2010 general election it was the political attachment to forms of governance associated with NPM that linked crime-fighting rhetoric and practice. According to NPM, the job of central government was to set the direction of policy using a framework of performance targets, leaving it to agencies at local level to find ways of achieving these. Simple numerical targets necessarily lacked subtlety, and thus mirrored the crudity of political rhetoric. There were many examples of performance targets distorting organisational behaviour, especially in policing, with people being swept needlessly into the criminal justice system for very minor offences in order to secure targets – and, in some police forces, performance-related pay – for 'bringing offenders to justice'.

We now see considerable disenchantment with this approach to governance across the political parties, and across the public sector, and as a corollary, a much greater commitment to greater local autonomy – a commitment that can be comfortably embraced by both Coalition partners. The move away from governance through NPM in the criminal justice system is – assuming that it continues – to be warmly welcomed. Whether the mechanisms for giving voice to local preferences are adequate or appropriate is untested, however.

Some would argue that the centralising tendencies of governments towards the police over the last two decades or more have been a response to the weaknesses of the 'tripartite structure' that shares control over policy between the Home Secretary, police authorities and their chief constables. For example, it could be argued that successive Home Secretaries filled the policy vacuum created by police authorities' failure to fulfil their statutory role adequately. The contrary viewpoint is that the centre never allowed police authorities enough space to develop in ways that allowed them to provide effective political oversight at local level.

Insofar as plans for improving local policing accountability have been spelled out, they comprise the replacement of police authorities with locally elected commissioners, on the one hand, and, on the other, the continuation or extension of public engagement at the very local level, through neighbourhood policing structures. Both the Conservatives and the Liberal Democrats appear committed to the idea of greater local accountability achieved through systems of local election. Thus it seems likely that *something* will be put into place to achieve this. Whether a system of local commissioners will provide a more effective alternative than police authorities remains to be seen. Leaving aside the resistance that can be anticipated from chief officers – which could turn out to be a serious distraction – there are two obvious concerns. The first is whether there is a pool of potential candidates with the capacity and skills to serve as commissioners across the police forces in Britain. The second is whether sufficient checks and balances can be introduced to ensure that those commissioners who are skilful enough to effect real change are genuinely accountable and do not pursue maverick agendas.

Community engagement in policing at a more local level appears to offer continuity with the previous administration's neighbourhood policing strategy. This is to be welcomed, as the strategy has firm intellectual underpinnings and is supported by evaluative research. The main risk – as with all attempts at community engagement (and indeed with much of the government's 'Big Society' agenda) – is whether people can be found who will competently and honestly represent community viewpoints, rather than pursuing their own ideas and opinions. It would also be likely to be a positive development if the new administration could reframe the strongly consumerist perspective that the community engagement agenda has had to date in criminal justice. There are important differences between the services provided to citizens in health and education, for example, and those provided in justice. Unlike the former, the latter cannot, generally, be bought in the marketplace. The criminal justice system polices us all, despite political rhetoric that implies that it provides a service that protects the 'law-abiding majority' against 'criminals'. Community engagement should be reconceptualised as a means of testing whether local police enjoy legitimacy in the eyes of local communities, and of finding ways of correcting deficits in legitimacy.

This perspective, derived from procedural justice theory (Tyler and Huo, 2002; Tyler, 2003, 2007; Hough et al, 2010), would place less emphasis on getting local people to task their police to pursue specific priorities, and more emphasis on ensuring that the police perform their duties fairly and respectfully, in the eyes of those who they police. It would involve a recognition that the police are accountable first and foremost to the law, and second to the citizenry, and that effective policing involves strategies for nurturing and sustaining public consent to the rule of law. It is muddle-headed to think of community engagement as being a process that achieves police obedience to the (local) popular will, when in reality an effective police service is one that works in a style designed to ensure public obedience to the law.

## The rehabilitation revolution?

The Coalition's apparent commitment to the rehabilitation of offenders is to be welcomed. It is to be hoped also that this administration learns the lessons of the last in attempting to over-reform the structures through which rehabilitation is provided. The prison and probation services were subject to successive organisational changes from 1997 onwards, which in the latter's case substantially constrained its capacity, and damaged its morale and its resilience. Whatever changes in practice the Coalition aim to introduce, their success could be compromised if these were accompanied by yet further structural change.

The rehabilitation revolution relies on the deployment of two sorts of incentive: financial incentives for those providing services for offenders, and incentives for offenders, such as earned remission. Incentives for providers were being considered by the Ministry of Justice prior to the election, and schemes are now being piloted. Financing rehabilitation through Social Impact Bonds (Loder et al, 2010) involves payment to investors in third-sector programmes according to results, with low levels of reoffending resulting in high rates of return. This is an intriguing approach, born of the idea that some providers have much more success than others, and that this is probably a function of organisational ethos. So if organisations can be motivated more effectively to achieve real results, these may genuinely turn out to be achievable.

There are, however, several possible obstacles to programmes involving payment by results. The obvious one is the problem of measurement. Reconviction rates are only a proxy for reoffending rates, and in any case may reflect the success of other agencies, such as the police, either in preventing crime (which would provide a 'free ride' for the investors), or in detecting crime (which would unfairly penalise investors). Behind these problems lie further ones, about the distortions to policing and prosecution practice that might occur when one partner within the criminal justice system has a powerful vested interest in preventing other agencies from taking formal action against offenders. Finally, if the performance of new programmes is to be benchmarked against the norm, what happens when new programmes *become* the norm? This is not to say that these problems are insurmountable. Finding new ways of harnessing organisational energy to prevent reoffending seems a good principle – provided, of course, that the practical problems can be ironed out.

Whether the ideas for incentivising offenders to reform in 'prisons with a purpose' can take root is another issue. Certainly the idea of earned remission resonates with public opinion. People tend to think that it makes more sense to make release conditional on progress towards rehabilitation than to have automatic and fixed release dates. However, this presupposes that those who attract prison sentences are responsive to the costs of non-compliance and the benefits of compliance. In reality, a large proportion of those who end up in prison have a long track record of unresponsiveness to the deals offered to them by agencies of social control. They will have become inured to the threats held out by parents, social workers, school teachers, workers from youth offending teams and probation officers. Realism should tell us to be pessimistic about the outcome of a final set of decisions about costs and benefits attached to compliance with programmes in prisons.

This is not to say that rehabilitation can never be achieved. It is simply to suggest that expectations must be tempered by experience. Most persistent offenders emerge at some stage from their criminal careers, but – in common with dependent drug use – persistent offending is a habit that takes a long time to break. Achieving rehabilitation is a slow process that can sometimes be accelerated by the support of probation and prison staff – or third-sector staff – who offer the right sort of support at the right time.

Critical to this process is the establishment of a relationship of trust. It is a mistake to think that those with long records of persistent offending – who absorb a large proportion of the capacity of the criminal justice system – will respond any differently than they have in the past to a new set of decisions about the costs and benefits of offending. What is needed to achieve a genuine 'rehabilitation revolution' is some hard thinking about the forms of political leadership and institutional structures that are most likely to support the 'people-changing' craft within criminal justice (see Hough, 2010, 2011).

## Conclusions: new directions for criminal policy?

This discussion of the Coalition's policies on criminal justice is inevitably tentative. There are already some marked differences in tone and substance from the prospectus set out in the election manifestos of each party. It is too early to speak with any certainty, but it seems just possible that the fortuitous collision of a Coalition government and a fiscal crisis may benefit justice politics. On the one hand, the populist stridency that we have grown used to from the main political parties since the early 1990s may be on the wane, at least for as long as the pressures of coalition act as a restraint. On the other hand, expansion of the justice system is simply unaffordable. This may turn out to be a positive moment in the history of British justice.

If the conjunction of a spending crisis and the Coalition government has created a moment of openness in policy, in what direction should we aim to push this administration? The key objective should be to discourage a return to that crude discourse about crime control that emphasises:

- 'common sense' strategies for securing instrumental (or situational[3]) compliance from 'criminals';
- sharp distinctions between 'criminals' and the 'law-abiding majority';
- greater responsiveness to the wishes of the 'law-abiding majority' as consumers of criminal justice; and
- greater responsiveness to the needs of victims.

It may be possible to help the Coalition develop a subtler and more nuanced discourse about the role of the criminal justice system, which places more emphasis on normative considerations and less on instrumental ones. The criminal justice system is one of those secondary systems of formal social control that support less formal and more culturally rooted systems of control. A successful system is one that promotes normative compliance with the law.

Both the previous and the current administration appear to value community confidence in justice, but arguably for the wrong reasons. In an oversimplified discourse about crime control – as we increasingly see in the United Kingdom – the rationale for improving 'confidence in justice' is that greater consumer satisfaction on the part of the 'law-abiding majority' will secure their cooperation with the authorities – through reporting of crimes, acting as witnesses and so on – thus enhancing the deterrent effectiveness of the system.

A more subtle approach, grounded in procedural justice theory, would direct attention to the building of *trust* in justice – as distinct from consumerist confidence – among those parts of the population whose commitment to the rule of law is more tentative, the primary purpose being to secure compliance first, and cooperation second. It would also allude to the fact that the 'law-abiding majority' also commit crimes, and that in any case they too care more about fair procedure than effectiveness narrowly defined. All available evidence suggests that fostering trust and legitimacy via fair and decent treatment would pay dividends across the population. It is also a significant consideration, in the current fiscal climate, that getting criminal justice officials to treat people fairly and respectfully is not necessarily a costly strategy.

Some might feel that these are narrow, academic distinctions, and that we are all 'on the same page' in wanting to improve 'confidence' in justice. However, there is an important difference, which is worth emphasising. The consumerist rationale for improving confidence is based on *reciprocity*, where responsive justice buys public cooperation, but offers no guidance about the treatment of lawbreakers and those at risk of lawbreaking. The procedural justice rationale by contrast focuses attention precisely on these groups whose compliance with the law is problematic, and actually provides a rationale for explaining why the criminal justice system should actually treat *justice* as the central product of the system. It provides a vocabulary for explaining why fairness and rights – for everyone – are important. People need to trust in justice, if the system is to work.

## Notes

[1] Although the quote, in the foreword to the White Paper, was signed by his successor, David Waddington, the drafting was his.

[2] By April 2002 Kenneth Clarke had taken over as Home Secretary from Kenneth Baker. Kenneth Clarke oversaw the retreat from the 1991 Act before handing over in 1993 to Michael Howard.

[3] It makes sense to view incapacitative or preventative sentencing as a way of securing situational rather than instrumental compliance.

# THIRTEEN

# The Conservatives and social policy in the devolved administrations

*Richard Parry*

Conservative policy development in Scotland and Wales has, in recent years, been structured by the weak position of the parties in the two nations. The formation of the Conservative–Liberal Democrat Coalition on 10 May 2010 had many unanticipated by-products, not least the partial resolution of the dilemma of territorial politics faced by a Conservative Party nearly all of whose parliamentary strength comes from England. The addition of Liberal Democrat votes and MPs took the Coalition presence in Scotland to 35.6% of the vote and 12 seats out of 59, and in Wales to a healthy 46.2% and 11 seats out of 40. Conservatives in Wales contributed 26.1% of the vote and eight seats, a stronger surge than in England; but in Scotland the painful outcome of only one seat and 16.7% of the vote, less than a 1% increase from the 2005 general election, threw into relief the role and distinctiveness of the Conservative Party in Scottish politics. In Northern Ireland the Conservatives' attempt to win seats in alliance with the Ulster Unionists failed. At these levels of support the party's task is survival, in terms of its activist and voter base, and also of its capacity to generate distinctive ideas about policy. The scope for new Conservative policies authentically of the nations, and expressing divergences of circumstance and attitude from England, is the central focus of this chapter and forms part of any well-rounded appraisal of a party that claims unionism as a core belief.

The role of the Conservative Party in Scotland and Wales has been affected profoundly by the collapse in the size of the constituency wanting no devolved legislative body at all, the Conservatives' position up to 1997. Polling evidence suggests that in Scotland this group declined from 17% in 1997 to 10% in 2007 (40% among Conservative voters in 2007) (Curtice, 2008, p 40), and in Wales from 37% in 1997 to 14% in 2009 (All-Wales Convention, 2009, p 85). Although there is a residual anti-devolution vote to be mobilised, much of it still goes to Labour, and there is little political potential for the Conservatives in being a refusenik party on the constitutional issue.

Indeed, the paradoxical legacy of New Labour's constitutional project was that the Conservatives, wiped out in their Scottish and Welsh Westminster seats in 1997, were given a lifeline back to elected office and influence on government through the proportional voting system of the devolved bodies, whose main tasks fall into the social policy area. Despite frequent discussion of policy divergence between the UK government and the devolved administrations, the position of the Conservatives, the one major party never to have held office in any of them, is less well explored. The Conservatives' two traditional roles of opponents to Labour and defenders of the United Kingdom have to be managed and prioritised, especially in election years. The link between the two is the coalition-building strategy of the party, including hitherto surprising relations in Wales (the abortive rainbow coalition of May 2007) and Scotland (the Conservatives' support for Scottish National Party [SNP] budgets since 2008).

Organisationally and financially, the Scottish and Welsh Conservatives are components of the UK party, although with a separate leader (their leader in the devolved legislatures), annual conference and recognition of policy autonomy on devolved functions. Over the years their statuses have converged from opposite directions: the once fully distinct Scottish party (until 1965 known as the Scottish Unionist Party) was largely integrated at the organisational level in 1977. After the 1997 defeat commissions under Lord Strathclyde and Sir Malcolm Rifkind fused the parliamentary and voluntary wings of the party and the Scottish Conservative and Unionist Association ceased its separate existence. In Wales, the party was always fully integrated into England and Wales structures and developed its distinct identity alongside the growth of Welsh devolution from the 1970s.

## Conservative electoral fortunes in Scotland and Wales

The general election of 2010 revealed an important divergence in political behaviour. Comparing Conservative performance with the last time they formed a government in 1992 (Table 13.1), Wales has strengthened its relative position in the Conservative ranks, reducing the gap between its Welsh and British performance to a historically low 11%, and increasing its number of seats to eight. Scotland has moved in the other direction; the vote gap widened to over 20% and only one seat was held.

**Table 13.1: Conservative electoral performance in Scotland and Wales, 1992 and 2010**

|  | 1992 votes (%) | 1992 seats | 2010 votes (%) | 2010 seats |
|---|---|---|---|---|
| Scotland | 25.7 | 11 | 16.7 | 1 |
| Wales | 28.6 | 6 | 26.1 | 8 |
| GB | 42.8 | 336 | 37.0 | 307 |

*Source*: Butler and Kavanagh (1993,Table A1.2); data from BBC News Election 2010 website (including the delayed Thirsk and Malton poll).

At the devolved level, the trajectory of Conservative support since 1999 shows the generally low level of support for the party and the opening up of a gap between flatlining in Scotland and recovery in Wales (Table 13.2; because the Greens do not contest constituency seats the regional list vote is the best indicator of party support).

**Table 13.2: Conservative Party fortunes in Scottish and Welsh devolved elections**

|  | Scotland | Wales |
|---|---|---|
| **1999** |  |  |
| % list vote | 15.3 | 16.5 |
| Constituency seats | 0 (out of 73) | 1 (out of 40) |
| List seats | 18 (out of 56) | 8 (out of 20) |
| Total seats | 18 (out of 129) | 9 (out of 60) |
| **2003** |  |  |
| % list vote | 15.5 | 19.2 |
| Constituency seats | 3 | 1 |
| List seats | 15 | 10 |
| Total seats | 18 | 11 |
| **2007** |  |  |
| % list vote | 13.9 | 21.0 |
| Constituency seats | 4 | 5 |
| List seats | 13 | 7 |
| Total seats | 17 | 12 |

At the levels of support they enjoy, Scottish and Welsh Conservatives gain little more than symbolic benefit from winning constituency seats, as when they do so they tend to lose regional list seats in order to maintain the overall proportionality of their representation. But they have partly rebuilt their fortunes from the wipeout of 1997 and 1999. In Scotland in 2003 they won David McLetchie's seat in Edinburgh, held a by-election gain in Ayr and edged out the SNP in the very marginal Galloway and Upper Nithsdale (with Alex Fergusson, already a list MSP and since 2007 Presiding Officer of the Scottish Parliament). In 2007 they added Roxburgh and Berwickshire, an area of former strength that had seemed lost to the Liberal Democrats. But the larger Westminster constituencies reduce their prospects, as became evident in the 2010 general election when only the single seat of Dumfriesshire, Clydesdale and Tweeddale was retained; its MP, David Mundell, became Minister of State for Scotland under a Liberal Democrat Secretary of State, initially Inverness MP Danny Alexander (a low-profile figure in Scotland who owed his advancement to being Nick Clegg's chief of staff) and after David Laws' resignation, the slightly better-known Michael Moore, who had repelled the Conservative targeting of his Borders seat.

Wales has shown stronger Conservative performance (culminating in their topping of the poll in the 2009 European elections, when they, Labour and Plaid Cymru clustered at about 20% of the vote). In the Assembly elections of 2003 and 2007 they ran Plaid Cymru close, in the latter making four constituency gains from Labour to re-establish themselves in their former heartlands of Pembrokeshire, seaside North Wales and suburban Cardiff. Wales has what Scotland does not, a party occupying the bourgeois political space and rising alongside improved Conservative fortunes in England. In December 2009 the Conservatives gained a 13th member with the floor-crossing of Plaid Cymru AM Mohammad Asghar (a list member from South Wales East), the first such defection in the Welsh or Scottish elected bodies. In the 2010 general election, on new boundaries, the Welsh Conservatives converted four hopes in their strong areas into wins in line with the UK swing (Cardiff North, Vale of Glamorgan, Aberconwy, and Carmarthenshire West and Pembrokeshire South).

The possibility of being both a constituency and a regional list candidate has given Conservative leaders in Scotland an insurance policy against failure (David McLetchie in 1999 and Annabel Goldie in 2007 were returned despite constituency defeat; McLetchie won a notable victory in Edinburgh Pentlands in 2003, repeated in 2007); and has allowed younger talent such as Murdo Fraser and Derek Brownlee to have reasonably safe berths in the parliament. Although Labour succeeded in outlawing dual candidacies in Wales in the 2006

Government of Wales Act, the Conservative heavyweights, led by Nick Bourne since 1999, have had safe list positions.

## The provenance of the Scottish Conservatives

Theoretical and empirical work on political parties is one of the Cinderella subjects of devolution – for the Conservatives the most distinguished exception being James Mitchell, with his doctoral and subsequent work on party history (Mitchell, 1990). David Torrance's recent contributions on the Conservative Party are also of note (Torrance, 2006, 2008) and his account of Margaret Thatcher's influence is a compelling blend of academic and journalistic talents, including the use of interviews and public archive material (Torrance, 2009). He emphasises that, contrary to popular views, Thatcher's policy towards Scotland was cautious, as she slowly reversed the pro-devolution position she had inherited and appointed non-ideological Secretaries of State in George Younger and Malcolm Rifkind. She suffered a notable setback when her acolyte Michael Forsyth was eased out of the chairmanship of the Scottish party in 1990 (Torrance, 2009). The debacle of the Poll Tax came late in her tenure, and the biggest industrial closures and free-market social policies came after she had departed.

Conservatives in Scotland and Wales have to operate as minority partners in a four-party system. The Scottish Conservative Party that is left is a shadow of the once-dominant political force (called Unionists from 1912 to 1965) that outpolled the UK average of the party from 1945 to 1955, won a majority of Scottish seats and votes in 1955, and then at least 24% of the vote and 10 seats in UK elections up to 1997, despite a clear weakening from 1959 onwards. Although typically second best to the Liberals in the 19th century (never outpolling them until 1923) and Labour in the 20th, Scottish Conservatives could mobilise a potential coalition of rural interests, the professional middle classes and working-class Protestants. Even in Glasgow, 10 one-time constituencies had some post war Conservative representation until the party was finally seen off by Roy Jenkins' by-election victory in Hillhead in 1982 (Jenkins often expressed his fascination with his highly educated constituency and the opportunities for centre-left forces in an apparently Tory area). In rural Scotland, the Conservatives were hit hard by the rise of the SNP in the 1970s, who knocked out seven MPs in 1974. By 1997 every Conservative constituency was in the sight of Labour, Liberal Democrat and SNP challengers who swept up the anti-Conservative forces in tactical voting.

The gradual relative weakening of its position during Conservative governments since 1955 trapped the party between its potential role as a clear right-wing party or a moderate, inclusive version of One Nation English Conservatism. Devolution provided another dimension of ambivalence, with support for an elected Scottish body embraced by Heath in 1967, but repudiated by Thatcher in 1976. In 1959 Labour advanced in Scotland against the national swing, and subsequent UK Conservative governments were on the defensive, promoting regional economic policy and deferring to Scottish professional interests on education, health and social work. The Thatcher years were difficult and the Major years even more so as right-wing policies that had been held at bay took over. In the Scottish Office, the grandee (George Younger) gave way to the liberal-minded urban professional (Malcolm Rifkind) and then to the right-wing political operator (Michael Forsyth). All Conservative seats were lost in 1997; former Scottish Secretaries Rifkind, Forsyth and Ian Lang lost their political base and showed no interest in rebuilding it in the Scottish Parliament. The post-devolution leaders, David McLetchie and Annabel Goldie, both lawyers who worked their way up through the voluntary side of the party, have never been Westminster MPs and have been relative strangers to the national Conservative leaders. Proportional representation gave the party a lifeline, but it has never developed a clear ideology in relation to either public policy or the constitution. There are periodical suggestions that it is a broken party without a viable policy or local organisation and in need of reinvention with a new name as a distinct right-wing party standing in the same relation to the UK party as the Christian Social Union (CSU) in Bavaria does to its Christian Democratic Union (CDU) allies.

## The provenance of the Welsh Conservatives

Under Nick Bourne (a legal academic who, unlike his predecessor Rod Richards, has never sat at Westminster) the Welsh Conservatives have been more prepared than their Scottish colleagues to transform their previous opposition to devolution (an element of the massive referendum defeat of proposals in 1979 and near-defeat in 1997) into support for greater powers on the grounds of clarity and accountability. With Welsh national and civil society institutions much less well-developed than their Scottish counterparts, the Conservatives have seen an opportunity to spin themselves off into something distinctive, a process tolerated by the national Conservative leadership as long as they continue to show potential to deliver Westminster seats. The opportunistic and the principled unite in what Bourne came to see as a near-duty to explore cooperation with Plaid Cymru 'both to hold Labour to account and to fight off continuous Labour government in Wales' (quoted by Osmond, 2005, p 44).

A telling analogy is the way that the (Anglican) Church in Wales was disestablished and split off from the Church of England in 1920 and slowly rebuilt itself as authentically Welsh (Osmond, 2004). Similar processes have been evident in civil society bodies that were initially organised on a British or England and Wales basis, with Wales as a region (and sometimes not even that). Until the 1970s the Welsh party held no conference and was administratively a region of the London-based party; now it is an authentic part of Welsh civil society. A problem has been that only one of the seven Conservative Secretaries of State for Wales has sat for a Welsh constituency (Nicholas Edwards); three others, including the present incumbent, Cheryl Gillan, were at least Welsh-born. David Melding, the party's policy director and manifesto writer and the most prominent thinker on the Welsh Conservative frontbench, has become associated with a maximalist position in which Welsh Conservatives stay in the vanguard of Wales's nation-building in a functionally federalist British state (Melding, 2009). This 'Welshification' strategy is seen by some Scottish leaders as an approach that needs to be replicated in order to achieve comparable electoral success (Settle, 2010).

In both Scotland and Wales, with political weakness came the loss of a power base in local government. Conservatives (until the 1970s known as Progressives) formed the administration in Glasgow as late as 1967, and usually controlled Edinburgh until 1984. They legislated for the reorganisation of Scottish local government into regions and districts in 1975, and controlled the Grampian, Tayside and latterly Lothian regions until 1986. A further reorganisation into 32 single-purpose authorities in 1995 led to a failure to win any of them, despite carefully drawn boundaries. In Wales, Conservatives controlled Cardiff in the late 1960s, late 1970s and mid-1980s, and a handful of other councils, but again failed to win any of the 22 new single-purpose authorities in 1995. An important consequence was that comprehensive education became universal in Scotland and Wales, and the Conservatives were in no position to advance a distinctive social policy agenda at the local level. But in Scotland proportional representation (the single transferable vote), introduced for local government elections in 2007 as a concession by Labour to the Liberal Democrats, again gave the Conservatives a lifeline back to some power. As at 2010 they were the largest single party in two councils and had a share in the administration in a total of nine.

## The Conservatives in Northern Ireland

By the 20th century pro-union elected members in Ireland became confined to the nine counties of the province of Ulster, and an Ulster Unionist Council of local unionist associations was formed in 1905 (Rose and McAllister, 1982). It later became clear that a unionist majority existed in only six counties, which were constituted as Northern Ireland in 1920 and remained within the United Kingdom when the rest of Ireland was granted independence in 1921. Northern Ireland's (under-represented) 12 seats in the UK parliament were dominated (and monopolised between 1955 and 1966) by Ulster Unionists, who took the Conservative whip. In 1951, when Labour outpolled the Conservatives, it was this that allowed the Conservatives to gain an overall Commons majority.

The situation changed after the Northern Ireland 'troubles' started in 1968. Ulster Unionists supported the Conservatives in the 1970 parliament and one of them, Robin Chichester-Clark, became a junior minister. In 1974 unionism fragmented and groups opposed to Conservative policy won 11 seats and maintained freedom of action in their parliamentary votes. United Kingdom Conservatives were reluctant to become involved in Northern Ireland politics, but in 1991 they eventually allowed local associations to organise and stand in Westminster elections; they never came close to winning a seat but made some impact, especially in 1992 when they gained 32% of the vote in Down North and 15% in Strangford.

In the 2010 election the Conservatives made a formal alliance with the Ulster Unionists under the banner of the 'Ulster Conservatives and Unionists – New Force', which gained only 15.2% of the vote. Embarrassingly, the only sitting Ulster Unionist MP, Sylvia Hermon in Down North, declined to run under this banner and won re-election as an Independent with 63% of the vote. The Ulster Unionist leader, Sir Reg Empey, came 3.5% short of winning in Antrim South, with 30% of the vote, but the experience of intervention in Ulster politics was disappointing for the Conservatives, especially when David Cameron got into trouble in a BBC interview with Jeremy Paxman on 23 April for saying that in parts of the UK – 'the first one I would pick out is Northern Ireland' – the 'state accounts for a bigger share of the economy than it did in the communist countries of the old eastern bloc – it is clearly unsustainable ... in Northern Ireland it is quite clear, almost every party, I think, accepts that the size of the state has got too big, we need a bigger private sector' (BBC News, 2010d). As in previous administrations, an English MP (Owen Paterson) became Secretary of State for Northern Ireland.

## The Conservatives and social policy

The basic dilemma of Scottish and Welsh Conservatives – are they a Tory-lite, kinder and gentler version of their English colleagues, or a clear right-wing alternative to the soggy consensus of the other parties in their nations – recurs in social policy. Policy development is heavily constrained by the dynamics of devolution: policy is either set at UK level (with little or no opportunity for non-English input), or is devolved in distinctive institutional arrangements (in which case the party in England would not wish to interfere). In the former category fall pensions, benefits, employment law, immigration and drugs policy; in the latter are education (at all levels), health, social care and housing (but not housing benefit or the finance of owner-occupation). In devolved areas, where there was administrative devolution to an integrated Scottish Office since 1939 and a Welsh Office since 1964, the tone had long been that of a less ideological application of Conservative policies to Scotland and Wales.

An important intermediate area under devolution is about charging within the welfare state (student fees; drug prescriptions; means testing of the costs of non-medical social care). Although the Conservatives have favoured prescription charges, they were prominent in the coalition behind the implementation of the Sutherland Commission (Royal Commission on Long Term Care, 1999) on non-means-tested personal care, to which the main opposition came from Labour. Conservatives have favoured choice and non-state input into health, education and social care, but their ability to take these ideas very far has never recovered from the experience of harder-line Conservative Secretaries of State in the mid-1990s (Michael Forsyth and John Redwood) and their electoral punishment in 1997.

In terms of overall ideology the main symbol of a 'new' Conservative social policy has been the Centre for Social Justice (CSJ), chaired by former leader Iain Duncan Smith, who was born in Edinburgh and became Work and Pensions Secretary in the 2010 government. Duncan Smith's personal journey into UK social reality was launched in Glasgow in 2002 and the CSJ has given disproportionate attention to Scotland; urban Glasgow attracted particular attention for its low life expectancy and high rate of worklessness through unemployment or incapacity (Centre for Social Justice, 2008a). A press release in May 2008, 'Sanity from Scotland on Drug Treatment – Will England and

Wales Follow Suit?' (the issue being alleged over-use of methadone) is an example of resonance between UK and devolved policy that the CSJ has promoted (Centre for Social Justice, 2008c).

However, the devolved Conservatives have had nothing comparable. One prominent Scottish think tank, Reform Scotland, run by merchant banker Ben Thomson, presents itself as non-partisan but is seen as vaguely pro-Conservative, with its researcher, Geoff Mawdsley, having once worked for the party. The party itself lacks the financial resources to engage in much policy development, and had to discontinue the appointment of its media chief, ex-television journalist Michael Crow, after the 2010 elections.

## The Conservatives and the nationalists

In a way unknown in England, Conservative statecraft in Scotland and Wales has been dominated by their relation with the nationalist parties: the Scottish National Party and Plaid Cymru – the Party of Wales. It had not been at all clear how either nationalist party could win power. At their peak they gathered 30% of the vote, but seemed marginalised in a constitutional ghetto in which none of the other parties would deal with them. In Scotland this position has persisted: the only party willing to do a deal with the SNP after 2007 were the Greens, and this was of a limited character, not committing the Greens to support any particular SNP policy or even their budget. But the Conservatives, unreceptive to a pan-unionist coalition, embraced the principle that the largest party after the election (the SNP by one seat over Labour) was the 'winner' and should be allowed the chance to govern as a minority.

In Wales, Plaid Cymru's more nuanced constitutional policy enabled a better rapport with the other opposition parties during the years of Labour minority government and ensured that none of them were unduly constrained in their coalition tactics after the 2007 elections. As Plaid was marginally ahead of the Conservatives in both seats and votes, one precondition in the negotiations – that Plaid would not serve under a Conservative First Minister – was not an obstacle. A Plaid–Conservative–Liberal Democrat rainbow deal was put together, but did not come into effect because of a temporary but fatal wobble by the Liberal Democrats that put Labour back in the picture, first as a minority government and then as a coalition partner with Plaid Cymru. In the event, the Labour–Plaid deal was widely seen as a better, less contrived fit, offering Plaid and Labour maximal devolutionists clear support for the activation of the 2006 Government of Wales Act's provisions for full lawmaking powers through the promise not just of a referendum, but of a campaign for a 'yes' vote. The Conservatives became the opposition in the Assembly and had an easier time with their own supporters. But in policy terms the deal was done, the drafting accomplished and the way that a disparate trio of parties could at least start out in government defined.

## Party interactions: policy lines

In Scotland, SNP government since 2007 has given us an unbroken look at what happens when a nationalist party runs public policy. As well as a shared distaste for Labour, there is also some consonance between Conservative and SNP policies. Despite clear differences in justice and energy policy, there has been a broad area of compatibility defined by the SNP's being more pro-small business and pro-local government than was Labour. Several Conservative pledges in 2007 were consistent with what the SNP promised or has done (see Table 13.3).

**Table 13.3: Conservative 2007 manifesto pledges consistent with SNP 2007 pledges and policies**

| |
|---|
| More autonomy for local government, reduce ring-fencing. |
| Grants for first-time homebuyers. |
| Abolish Communities Scotland. |
| Eliminate bridge tolls. |
| More police officers on streets. |
| Reduce council tax (halved for pensioner households). |
| Single Skills Agency, including careers service. |
| Reduction in business rates for small businesses. |
| Preserve local accident and emergency facilities. |
| Reduce NHS waiting times. |
| Promote Scottish brand. |
| Grants for new farmers. |

A rare instance of a Conservative–Labour alliance on social policy came with shared opposition to minimum alcohol pricing as proposed in the SNP's Alcohol (Scotland) Bill; in the stage 1 vote on 9 June 2010 a Conservative amendment suggesting that there was no evidence to support such a policy passed 54 to 49 with SNP and Green opposition and Liberal Democrat abstention. The Conservatives, but not Labour, abstained on the stage 1 vote on the amended bill. Conservative reasoning on the issue combined free-market principles, concern about adverse economic impacts and a wish to let the UK government take a lead on alcohol pricing issues.

Because the structure of devolved powers does not include pensions and benefits, it accentuates the possibility that the Conservatives will support pro-welfarist policies either as matters of investment (education and housing) or in support of the iconic NHS ('Conservatives are passionate supporters of the NHS', as their 2007 manifesto declared [Scottish Conservative and Unionist Party, 2007, p 30]). The basis for programmatic collaboration takes shape and is there for the right political conditions to arise. On the constitution itself, the Conservatives moved in step with other unionist parties to resist SNP proposals to call a referendum on opening negotiations over independence and develop new constitutional policies through the Calman Commission, set up by them and the UK government, proposing in June 2009 adjusted financial and legislative competences that the UK Labour government largely accepted. The most important of these was a transfer of 10 percentage points of income tax, with the grant cut correspondingly, in order to force the Scottish Parliament to set its own income tax rate. The Conservatives did not commit themselves fully to Calman, promising only their own White Paper after the UK elections, but in the event the coalition deal with the Liberal Democrats did promise full implementation and legislation in 2010–11.

## The Conservatives in the politics of the devolved budgetary process

The most characteristic expression of party positions, but one traditionally absent from UK systems, is a proposal for additional expenditure or reallocation of existing expenditure. The devolved legislatures have budgetary protocols similar to Westminster, in that the budget is proposed by the administration and members cannot make line-item alterations to it. But in a non-majority situation the same practical effect can be obtained by a threat to vote against the Budget Bill, knowing that abstention would probably guarantee passage of the budget without the need to support it. In this way, Plaid Cymru, with Conservative support, obtained free eye tests for many groups in 2000 (Osmond, 2000). During their minority government periods in 1999–2000 and 2003–07, budget-making was always a fraught process for Welsh Labour. It was inevitable that from time to time all the opposition parties would make common cause on some item of education or health spending. The highest-profile event occurred in November 2003 when the illness of a Labour AM and the negative casting vote of the Presiding Officer caused the voting down of the government's health plans, though this was reversed the following week (Osmond, 2003).

In the Scottish Parliament, since taking power in 2007 the SNP has had to fight for its budget – but it has done so with the support of the Conservatives on all key votes. The way this has happened can be illustrated by the way that the Finance Committee divided in its report on the Budget Bill for 2008/09, the SNP's first (Table 13.4). These votes did not alter anything in themselves – they were recommendations to the parliament – but they showed how the Conservatives, in return for an inside track to the government and concessions on justice and business rates, would decline to support even palatable Labour priorities that, if pressed, might have defeated the budget. In 2007/08 the process worked smoothly: the SNP won a key vote 64 to 62 with Conservative and Green support, and in the final vote Labour abstained, in a messy tactical decision after an aspirational amendment about youth apprenticeships was accepted by the SNP.

In 2009 the basic strategic forces continued but the tactics did not work on the day of the vote: the Greens declined to be bought off on their pet energy conservation measures and the vote was tied – and so the budget lost – despite Conservative support. After a round of concessions to all the parties, a new Budget Bill was agreed by all parties except the Greens. Labour, reluctant to abstain for a second year, went along with the bill. The consistent tacticians, working in the backrooms, were the Conservatives. In 2010 the Conservatives were again on board and the Liberal Democrats abstained. The Conservative UK campaign in 2010 made a virtue of their collaboration and implied that Labour, not the SNP, were their principal opponents.

## The rainbow text: The All-Wales Accord

In Scotland, SNP–Conservative agreement has been on budget-making through some policy congruence; in Wales there has been the abortive rainbow coalition document, the All-Wales Accord, to set alongside the UK deal with the Liberal Democrats as an example of how the Conservatives can reconcile their policies with other parties. The document is more detailed than Labour–Plaid Cymru's One Wales (where many of the policies reappeared) and seems more characteristic of Plaid Cymru than of the other two parties, but marked the systematisation of many of the common policy lines developed in opposition to Labour between 1999 and 2007. It offered seven 'thematic pillars':

**Table 13.4: Coalition-building in the Scottish Parliament
Finance Committee, January 2008: Votes on proposed spending
transfers in report on Budget Bill**

**a) Proposed by Labour**

| | |
|---|---|
| £20m from roads improvement to Modern Apprenticeships | Lost 4–3. Con supported SNP, Lib Dem abstained |
| £15m from capital works to create Skills Academies | Lost 5–3. Con and Lib Dem supported SNP |
| £10m from winter maintenance to support for air services | Lost 4–3. Con supported SNP, Lib Dem abstained |
| £10m from police support services to recruitment of additional police | Lost 4–3. Con supported SNP, Lib Dem abstained |
| £75m from support for water borrowing to eliminate water charges for pensioner households | Lost 5–3. Con and Lib Dem supported SNP |
| Five specific grants from local government to health budget | Lost 4–3. Con supported SNP, Lib Dem abstained |
| Two specific grants from local government to rural affairs budget | Lost 4–3. Con supported SNP, Lib Dem abstained |
| £12.5m from health information to primary care | Lost 4–3. Con supported SNP, Lib Dem abstained |
| £20m from local government efficiency found to create town centre turnaround fund | Tied 4–4. Con and Lib Dem abstained, lost on casting vote of SNP convener |
| £10m from local government resource grants to new fund for children with special needs | Lost 4–3. Con supported SNP, Lib Dem abstained |
| £23m from local government resource grants to provide nursery places for vulnerable two-year-olds | Lost 4–3. Con supported SNP, Lib Dem abstained |

**b) Proposed by Conservatives**

| | |
|---|---|
| Scottish Government to consider further scope for business rate reductions | Won 4–0. SNP supported Con, Lab and Lib Dem abstained |
| Consider further scope for business rate reductions | Won 4–0. SNP supported Con, Lab and Lib Dem abstained |

*Source*: Scottish Parliament Finance Committee (2008, annex A).

1. A set of measures to promote the nation's constitutional development, the achievement of a bilingual society in a country that is unified while culturally diverse.
2. A new focus on encouraging an enterprising, innovative economy and a highly skilled workforce.
3. Concerted action on climate change, energy efficiency and sustainable development.
4. A forward-looking programme of investment in health care and well-being.
5. Major commitments on social justice, including childcare, affordable housing, council tax and student debt.
6. A range of actions to promote Wales in the international context.
7. A deep commitment to developing a new style of governing.

In Welsh circumstances, the final pillar is the decisive one as it would have marked the end of Labour rule. That apart, the content of the programme has echoes of the Conservative–SNP overlap in Scotland – enterprise, investment-based social policy like housing and childcare, and workforce skills. The most difficult area was health, where the Conservatives had favoured more English-style market and choice mechanisms, in line with the criticism that Welsh failure to embrace English reform policies had resulted in longer waiting times. The document emphasised opposition to hospital closures and promised a Charter of Patients' Rights, without saying what they would be and how they would be enforced. The debate about waiting times was sidestepped.

On governance matters, the agreement did not specify how ministries would be shared out, but did state that the leader of Plaid Cymru would be First Minister, and the leaders of the two other parties both Deputy First Ministers, the leader of the larger one (the Conservatives) having precedence in deputising. Processes were to be developed for 'ensuring appropriate credit for and recognition of the policy contribution of each party' (a provision found in similar terms in One Wales).

The Labour–Plaid Cymru coalition set up an All Wales Convention under Sir Emyr Jones Parry (returning to Wales after a diplomatic career culminating as ambassador to the United Nations). The Welsh Conservatives, along with the other political parties, nominated one of their executive committee members, and so were implicated in the recommendation to proceed to a referendum. It should be noted, though, that the referendum was presented by many as substituting a clear primary lawmaking power (Part 4 of the Act) for the present cumbersome mix of framework laws and legislative competence orders endorsed by Westminster; it was not necessarily a vote for 'more devolution'. In the event many Conservatives, including Nick Bourne, spoke in favour of the Assembly's endorsement on 9 February 2010 of the Convention recommendation, and on a free vote the whole group voted for it in the 53 to 0 outcome. The Conservative position in their 2010 manifesto was that 'we will not stand in the way of the referendum on further legislative powers requested by the Welsh Assembly. The people of Wales will decide the outcome and Conservatives will have a free vote' (Conservative Party, 2010e, p 67). While Conservatives could still be expected to play a prominent part in an umbrella 'no' vote campaign, they were no longer seeking to be dismantlers of devolution in either Wales or Scotland.

## Party positions in 2010

The party manifestos (Invitation to join the government of Britain) issued by the Conservatives in Wales and Scotland in 2010 are so similar in layout, typography and content to the English manifesto as to make the differences of emphases intriguing (Table 13.5). The Northern Ireland Ulster Conservative and Unionist New Force manifesto substitutes 'the United Kingdom' for 'Britain' but is also a clone. In general, the social policy sections of the Scottish version look like a manifesto for the 2011 Holyrood elections, seeking credit for some influence on SNP policy but delineating alternative approaches to others.

Issues mentioned in Scotland only included the maintenance of Accident and Emergency facilities; more funding for drugs approved in Scotland (by a system separate from the English and Welsh National Institute for Health and Clinical Excellence, NICE) to be allowed. Wales-only items included better neonatal care and action against violence in NHS facilities. The strongest distinction is on prescription charges, supported in Wales and Scotland, but opposed in Northern Ireland.

In general it is hard to find differentiated policy lines distinct from decisions on drafting – the introduction to the NHS chapter for Wales is:

> We will back the NHS. We will increase health spending every year in England, protecting funds for Wales and working to ensure that the NHS in Wales has the resources it needs. We want to give patients more choice and free health professionals from the tangle of politically-motivated targets that get in the way of providing the best care. We want to give patients better access to the treatments, services

**Table 13.5: Social policy issues mentioned in at least two Conservative devolved nation manifestos, 2010**

| | Wales | Scotland | Northern Ireland |
|---|---|---|---|
| Relationship support | We will work with the Welsh Assembly Government (WAG) to put funding for relationship support on a stable, long-term footing (p 34) | | We will put funding for relationship support on a stable, long-term footing and make sure couples are given greater encouragement to use existing relationship support (p 44) |
| Sure Start and equivalent schemes | We will work with the WAG and Conservatives in the Assembly to ensure the most disadvantaged children get the help they need (p 35) | We have identified funding in the Scottish health budget to increase the number of health visitors. This would allow all parents to get a guaranteed level of health visitor support before birth and in each of the first five years of their child's life (p 43) | We will take Sure Start back to its original purpose of early intervention, increase its focus on the neediest families, and better involve organisations with a track record in supporting families (p 44) |
| NHS funding | Conservatives in the Assembly want to ensure that any increase in funding [in England] is allocated to NHS services in Wales (p 36) | If the Scottish Government shares our priorities, it will have more money to spend on the NHS (p 45) | Urge increased health spending year-on-year in Northern Ireland in line with what is proposed in England by Conservatives (p 46) |
| Prescription charges | Conservatives in the Assembly will re-introduce prescription charges for those who can afford it, saving more than £20 million a year that will be used to fund hospices, nursing care, stroke units and speech therapists. But we would not ask those under 25, the elderly, cancer patients and all those who were previously exempt to pay (p 37) | We also oppose the phasing out of prescription charges.... We will campaign for this money to be spent on front-line care instead, while at the same time securing the future of free prescriptions for those who cannot afford to pay (p 46) | We have also introduced free prescriptions. The abolition of these charges is an investment in the future of the health and well-being of all the people in Northern Ireland. It's also an investment in the economy, enabling people to get back to work earlier if they have the right medication (p 47) |

**Table 13.5:** continued

| | Wales | Scotland | Northern Ireland |
|---|---|---|---|
| Single budgets | Conservatives in the Assembly believe that people with a chronic illness or a long-term condition should have the right to shape the care they receive and want to offer people access to a single budget that combines their health and social care funding, which they can tailor to their own needs (p 38) | We will preserve disability living allowance and attendance allowance and would expand the use of direct payments by removing the barriers which stand in the way of their uptake (p 46) | |
| Examinations | Conservatives in the Assembly want to restore the integrity of our examination system and would scrap the targets that encourage grade inflation. And Conservatives in the Assembly want to ensure that A-Levels are rigorous and challenging (p 41) | We will campaign to ensure standards are maintained within the Scottish examination system and that there are more opportunities for our brightest pupils to sit Advanced Higher examinations (p 52) | |
| 'Free' schools | Conservatives in the Assembly have pledged to break down barriers to entry so that any good education provider can apply to take part in a 'free schools pilot' – free, non-selective, high-quality state schools that are open to all (p 42) | We have called for charities and not-for-profit trusts to be allowed to set up new schools, which would receive funding from the state based on the number of pupils that they attract (p 53) | |

*Sources:* Conservative Party and Ulster Unionist Party, 2010; Scottish Conservative and Unionist Party, 2010; Welsh Conservative Party, 2010.

and information that improve and extend lives and boost the nation's health. (Welsh Conservative Party, 2010, p 36)

For Scotland it is:

> We will back the NHS. We will increase health spending in real terms at Westminster, which will generate consequential funding for the Scottish Government, which we want spent on the NHS. We will campaign to give health professionals more autonomy and patients more choice. We will push for the NHS to be refocused on improving standards of care and for the dogma and wastefulness that have held it back to be taken away. (Scottish Conservative and Unionist Party, 2010, p 45)

And for Northern Ireland:

> Conservatives and Unionists back the NHS. We support the plans of Conservative colleagues in England to increase health spending every year and will seek the same in Northern Ireland. (Conservative Party and Ulster Unionist Party, 2010, p 46)

The eventual UK Coalition agreement (Cabinet Office, 2010) was properly deferential about the rights of the devolved administrations to set policy, and also of Conservative–Liberal Democrat Party competition in the 2011 elections. On devolution substance, it agreed to 'implement the proposals of the Calman Commission' and 'introduce a referendum on further Welsh devolution' without the qualifications in the Conservative manifesto (Cameron subsequently got into trouble by suggesting [later confirmed] that the vote would be delayed until 2011, a position previously associated with Labour opponents of a 'yes' vote). It offered financial sweeteners to all three nations: for Northern Ireland a government paper examining potential mechanisms for changing the corporation tax rate; for Scotland, a promise to 'review the control and use if accumulated and future revenues from the Fossil Fuel Levy in Scotland' (money from, energy utilities to fund renewable alternatives that could be added to devolved spending); and for Wales, progress on the Sustainable Homes Legislative Competence Order and a recognition of 'the concerns expressed by the Holtham Commission on the system of devolution funding'. Wales was offered its version of the Calman process, but the general rubric that 'at this time, the priority must be to reduce the deficit and therefore any change to the system must await the stabilisation of the public finances' (Cabinet Office, 2010, p 28) might seem to compromise Calman-type changes in Scotland as well.

## Conclusion: ideologically ambivalent multi-party politics

Almost unnoticed by their English colleagues, Conservatives in the Scottish and Welsh devolved bodies have come to embrace US-style party behaviour, in which party differentiation is unpredictable and without ideological anchors. Parties go into elections with compatible programmes that express loyalty to the devolved system by being critical of some of the UK public service norms that have developed under both Conservative and Labour governments in London. From bridge tolls to student fees to personal care, it has been possible for a more general and universalistic approach to be put before the electorate. This creates the basis for post-election negotiation. A key variable is that the Conservatives are now involved in this process. In Wales they were prepared to enter a rainbow coalition; in Scotland they have discreetly but clearly propped up the SNP government and celebrated this in their 2010 manifesto. Denied the spoils of devolved office, they have eventually repositioned themselves as an available coalition partner with congruent policies.

Whether Scotland, Wales and Northern Ireland offer a distinctive approach to Conservative social policy is much more problematical. There is no evidence of any distinctive manifesto positioning by the party in Wales, Scotland and Northern Ireland. The Conservatives have acquiesced in national-based innovation promoted by other parties. They were part of coalitions behind free personal care and free university tuition, positions that did have an influence at the UK level as the party searched for voter-friendly policies, but in government deemed them unaffordable. By reinforcing points in SNP policy that tended towards the Conservative position (more police on the streets, small business taxation, local Accident and Emergency facilities) the party opened up a tacit arrangement with the minority government; in Wales they used economic development and social justice as a thematic bridge with Plaid Cymru and the Welsh Liberal Democrats in a striking but ultimately abortive coalition deal. The two nations already had the cohesion to offer something like the 'Big Society' approach of David Cameron, and as time has gone by the Conservatives have tended to embrace rather than challenge this dominant political culture. When

David Cameron raised in Northern Ireland the Thatcherite bogey of the over-large public sector the electoral risk became clear.

None of this is surprising, as the Conservatives in the three nations have been in a historic fight for survival. Given that there is no other centre-right bourgeois party, they should be well-placed to gain a quarter of the vote even when nationalist parties are in the frame: in Wales they achieved that in 2010 (26%), but in Scotland they underperformed (17%) and in Northern Ireland, enlisting the Ulster Unionists, they did even worse (15%). With underperformance comes a lack of organisation, a lack of new talent, a lack of policymaking capability and a lack of risk-taking (leadership of a post-election 'modernisation' review by the Scottish Conservatives was entrusted to a 77-year-old former Thatcher minister, Lord Sanderson, to widespread derision; see Settle, 2010). The UK Conservative Party values its non-English colleagues not for their policies, but for their votes, and when these yield virtually no strength at Westminster – in 1997 zero out of 130 available seats, in 2010 nine out of 117 – it has little interest in learning from them about social policies or making their protection an element in its social policy decisions.

# FOURTEEN

# The Conservatives and the governance of social policy

*Catherine Bochel*

The Conservative governments of the 1980s and 1990s introduced major changes not only in the nature of social policies, but also in the ways in which such policies were made and implemented, with a more centralist and managerialist approach combined with a preference for markets and competition in the delivery of policies. Under the Labour governments from 1997 to 2010 there were further significant changes, including, for example, devolution to Northern Ireland, Scotland and Wales (see Chapter 13), and the placing of significant emphasis on attempts to improve the processes of policymaking and delivery.

Under David Cameron the Conservatives, when in opposition, put forward a variety of proposals that might impact upon the ways in which social policy is made and delivered, including for changes to the ways in which legislation passes through the House of Commons, some devolution of power to local authorities (although at the same time proposing to allow local residents to veto high council tax rises), reducing the number and power of quangos, replacing the Human Rights Act with a Bill of Rights, and emphasising a significant role for voluntary and community groups, rather than the state, in the provision of social policy. This chapter, therefore, considers the possible implications for the governance of social policy of the Conservative Party under the leadership of David Cameron, including the coalition with the Liberal Democrats.

## Why the governance and mechanisms of policymaking and implementation matter

From the 1990s there has been a growing awareness of the importance of the processes of formulation, implementation and evaluation in the development and management of policies. Prior to this period 'government' and 'governance' tended to be seen as synonymous, so that Finer (1970, pp 3–4), defined government as: 'The activity or process of governing' or 'governance'; 'A condition of ordered rule'; 'Those people charged with the duty of governing' or 'governors'; and 'The manner, method or system by which a particular society is governed'. More recently there has been a greater emphasis on the differences between the two terms, with Rhodes (1997, p 15, original emphasis), for example, noting that 'The term "governance" refers to a change in the meaning of government, referring to a *new* process of governing'. 'Governance' therefore 'tries to make sense of the changing nature of the state' (Richards and Smith, 2002, p 14), recognising that we no longer live (if indeed we ever did) in a society where everything is controlled by a government at the centre. Instead there are many different actors, organisations and centres of power at local, regional, national, transnational and global levels all linking a less coherent and more fragmented process of policy- and decision-making.

The notion of governance is itself complex. Rhodes, for example, notes that 'There are many uses of governance', and that 'It has too many meanings to be useful' (Rhodes, 1997, p 15). Much has been written on 'governance' and it is not the intention to explore this further here. For present purposes, Stoker's observation that 'Governance recognises the capacity to get things done which does not rest on the power of government to command or use its authority. It sees government as able to use new tools and techniques to steer and guide' (Stoker, 1998, p 18, cited in Newman, 2001, p 12), is perhaps appropriate (see also Pierre and Peters, 2000; Newman, 2001; Richards and Smith, 2002).

## Governance under the Conservatives, 1979–97

Between 1979 and 1997 the Conservatives introduced a wide range of changes to the ways in which policy was made and implemented, reinforcing the perception of a shift from government to governance. Many of these directly impacted upon social policy. These included internal markets in the NHS and education, privatisation, the use of performance measures and standards, the increased use of arm's length government, including quangos and Next Steps Agencies, reform and residualisation of local government, and the introduction of a range of mechanisms designed to give consumers a greater say in the operation and delivery of services.

In addition, the general style of governance changed under the Conservatives. Until 1988, their approach arguably reflected an emphasis on 'managerialism', based on a belief that private-sector performance tools could benefit the public sector in order to make central and local government more efficient and effective. From 1988, however, there was a shift in style towards approaches based on 'the new institutional economics' with 'incentive structures' being introduced into public service provision, with 'Greater competition through contracting out and quasi-markets; and consumer choice' being central to this (Rhodes, 1997, pp 48–9). These changes were underpinned by New Right beliefs that bureaucracies were lacking in central control, self-interested, inefficient and wasteful of public resources (Niskanen, 1971, 1973). The Conservatives, therefore, took a top-down approach in an attempt to address the perceived problems of bureaucracy through the transfer to the public sector of performance measures and initiatives seen as successful in the private sector, and an emphasis on efficiency, effectiveness and economy.

From the late 1980s the influence of the 'new institutional economics' (Rhodes, 1997) heralded the introduction of more radical changes, including a greater emphasis upon consumer choice and markets. This led to the reduction and removal of functions from local authorities, including through legislation such as the 1988 Education Reform Act, the 1988 Housing Act and the 1988 Local Government Act. Attempts to extend consumer influence over services were also reflected in the introduction of new methods of redress and the introduction of Charters for citizens. However, the use of macro-governance structures, such as quangos, non-departmental government bodies and Next Steps Agencies, to undertake a range of non-essential functions previously undertaken by central and local government, reflected tensions around power and control, which continue to the present day, with the devolution of power and control over non-essential functions such as policy implementation and service delivery, while retaining control over core functions such as policy formulation, described by Rhodes (1997) as indicative of the shift from government to governance.

## Governance under Labour, 1997–2010

When Labour came to power in 1997 they continued the approach of previous Conservative governments in a range of areas, including: stressing the role of local authorities as enablers rather than providers of services; the utilisation of a range of providers from the public, voluntary and private sectors; and the use of mechanisms of audit and inspection to try to improve quality and standards in services. However, at the same time they demonstrated a new and more radical approach in some areas. In particular, following referendums in the autumn of 1997, the Scottish Parliament and the Welsh Assembly came into being on 1 July 1999, while the Northern Ireland Assembly came into existence on 2 December 1999. While there were already significant differences in social policies between the constituent elements of the United Kingdom, the creation of these bodies arguably served to raise awareness of these, as well as enabling the possibility of a greater diversity of approaches, particularly as political control of the UK's various legislative bodies changes. The 1998 Human Rights Act incorporated the European Convention of Human Rights (ECHR) into law, giving individuals who believed that their human rights had been infringed the opportunity to pursue their case in the domestic courts, a cheaper and less time-consuming process than having to appeal to the European Court of Human Rights, which was the process before the Act was passed. In addition Labour sought to 'modernise' local government in England through encouraging, and later requiring, councils to adopt new decision-making structures, mirroring those in Westminster in order to try to improve the transparency and accountability of local government (Department of the Environment, Transport and the Regions, 1998).

As with the Conservatives, in addition to structural change, Labour sought to bring new approaches to policymaking and implementation, including through encouraging 'joined-up government' and 'evidence-based' policymaking. In general, particularly from 1997 to 2005, these changes were associated with a more 'rational' approach to policymaking, with its focus on coordination and cooperation (Bochel and Duncan, 2007). This was also reflected by a somewhat more open and consultative approach, including attempts to engage with pressure groups and the public, and through the use of reviews, commissions and inquiries. However, like the Conservatives, Labour retained a fondness for top-down approaches and for central control, including through the widespread use of performance measures, league tables and mechanisms of audit and inspection. Like the Conservatives they also sought to encourage consumer choice in public services, but while few people would disagree with being given more choice, its presentation as a straightforward uncontested concept is far from the reality of actual choice in public services (Clarke and Newman, 2006).

A preference for a rational approach to policymaking was arguably also visible in other parts of Labour's approach, including through the introduction of the Comprehensive Spending Reviews and Public Service Agreements. Comprehensive Spending Reviews were a tool to enable government to assess its spending priorities. These took a longer-term approach by setting out public spending plans, usually for a period of three years, rather than on the annual basis that had previously been the norm. Linked to this, Labour established Public Service Agreements for government departments, setting out targets for each and how these would be measured (Cabinet Office Strategic Policy Making Team, 1999).

## The Conservatives under Cameron

As noted in Chapter 1 and elsewhere in this book, following their defeat at the 1997 general election the Conservatives found it difficult to respond to the challenge posed by New Labour. Successive Conservative leaders, William Hague, Iain Duncan Smith and Michael Howard, intermittently sought to develop new approaches to social policy, although rarely to the processes of making and implementing social policies, before shifting back towards positions more similar to those held by the party in the 1980s.

However, with David Cameron's defeat of David Davis in the leadership contest of December 2005 came the opportunity for greater change. Cameron almost immediately sought to distance the Conservative Party from its Thatcherite past, including by taking what appeared to be a more liberal stance on some areas of social policy. He also established six policy review groups, including one on 'public services improvement', chaired by Stephen Dorrell and Baroness Perry, and one on 'social justice', chaired by Iain Duncan Smith. While these made a number of recommendations there was relatively little about policymaking or implementation, although there was a clear emphasis on the need for a strong voluntary- or third-sector involvement in the provision of public services, in addition to a sizeable private sector, a desire to increase choice for consumers and a commitment to reduce bureaucracy, but at the same time to retain a significant degree of audit and inspection. However, even following their publication, the leadership remained vague about its commitment to them and firm commitments were rare.

Indeed, while the early years of Cameron's leadership showed a willingness by him to seek to differentiate himself from the party's recent past, including with elements of Thatcher's leadership, it was relatively difficult to discern clear themes in relation to the policy process, and this position arguably continued up to the 2010 general election. Nevertheless, it is perhaps possible to examine the Conservatives' approach on a broad thematic basis, drawing in particular on their general election manifesto, the title of which, *Invitation to Join the Government of Britain* (Conservative Party, 2010e), is itself perhaps of some relevance to the focus of this chapter.

## From big government to 'Big Society'?

The Conservative manifesto, and indeed much of their talk in the run-up to the May 2010 general election, was about the need to mend our broken society and about how a change 'from big government to Big Society' (Conservative Party, 2010e, p vii) could help achieve this. However, this is arguably largely a continuation, albeit in a broader form, of themes – of citizen participation and involvement in decision-making and the shaping of services, and a greater diversity of providers – that were apparent under both previous Labour and Conservative governments, each of which stressed, at various times, the importance of consumer choice, citizen involvement and responsive services, provided by a combination of the public, private and third sectors.

Although the idea of devolving power to the people is not new, the Conservatives produced a range of proposals for doing this, including enabling parents to start new schools (see Chapter 6), giving communities the power to take over local parks and libraries that are under threat, increasing control over the planning system for neighbourhoods (Chapter 7), and holding the police to account through 'neighbourhood beat' meetings with residents (Conservative Party, 2010e, p 38). The 2010 manifesto also proposed a 'community right to buy' scheme to 'give local people the power to protect any community assets that are threatened with closure', as well as a 'right to bid to run any community service instead of the state' (Conservative Party, 2010e, p 75). However, in the Coalition programme the 'community right to buy' scheme was not specifically mentioned, although 'new powers to help communities save local facilities and services threatened with closure' were included (Cabinet Office, 2010, p 12).

While at one level these ideas may be relatively small and incremental in nature, the Coalition's desire to see change through such a devolution of power, not just in the areas highlighted above, but across the public, voluntary and third sectors, does appear to hold out the potential for radical change, particularly when combined with the massive cuts in public expenditure outlined in the budget in June 2010 and the implications of those for public services.

In promoting the 'Big Society' the Conservatives are seeking to encourage increased social action, and there is an expectation that people will take more responsibility for themselves and their communities. However, critics argue that there appears to be a lack of recognition by government that there are limits to people's participation. As is made clear throughout this book, the government is keen that people should work, look after their families, cook healthy meals and bring children up properly, but added to this they want them to participate in the Big Society by setting up free schools, taking over the running of community services and so on. It is perhaps not surprising that a survey by Ipsos MORI for *The Economist* found that 'Most of the public say they do not want to be actively involved in how public services are run' (Ipsos MORI, 2010a; see also Chapter 4, this volume). And, while Ipsos MORI did find significant minorities who said that they did want to get involved 'it is likely that those who are directly affected will be more likely to get involved; for example, parents are far more likely to want to have a say in how Primary Schools work, than people without children' (Ipsos MORI, 2010a). For most people, therefore, the form of 'participation' being referred to here is likely to be 'having a say', rather than a desire to take over and run public services. Clearly 'involvement' means different things to different people, and to government, and there are likely to be significant challenges in putting the Big Society into practice.

Where resources are concerned to support these developments, the Conservatives plan to create 'a Big Society Bank, funded from unclaimed bank assets, to provide new finance for neighbourhood groups, charities, social enterprises and other non-governmental bodies' (Conservative Party, 2010e, p 37). The Co-operative Bank, which will administer the process of reclaiming money from dormant accounts, has estimated that £60m–£100m is likely to be available by April 2011, although the Prime Minister has talked about 'hundreds of millions of pounds' being available in unclaimed assets. The degree of funding provided through the Big Society Bank will be crucial in supporting the charities, voluntary groups and social enterprises that the Coalition want to play a key role in delivering services. Many of these groups have previously received much of their funding from the state, but given the implications of the expenditure cuts for the sector, reliance on alternative sources such as the Big Society Bank may become increasingly necessary.

In addition there are clearly a number of other issues and challenges here, including the extent to which budgets and financial decision-making will be devolved to local communities, the type of support mechanisms put into place to facilitate these arrangements, and how far these participatory approaches to running public services are likely to prove representative of the views of the local community and not just a minority of the local population. They also raise questions about the place, if any, of ideas of fairness and equality, as well as accountability and regulation.

## Reforming the public sector

As with the Thatcher governments, the Conservatives under David Cameron (and the Liberal Democrats under Nick Clegg) have placed significant emphasis on rolling back levels of state intrusion into people's lives, with reforms of the public sector as a key dimension of this. While this is in part about giving people more choice in service provision, as outlined earlier, there is also a clear commitment to reducing public expenditure, cutting waste and giving better value for money. Yet, at the same time, the Conservatives have been clear that they intend to protect popular services, such as the NHS, by ensuring funding increases in real terms each year. In addition, early on in the life of the Coalition government the Prime Minister stressed that 'Freedom, fairness and responsibility ... are the values that will drive our efforts to deal with our debts and to turn this economy around' and that 'this government will not cut this deficit in a way that hurts those we most need to help'. However, in the same speech he signalled a significant reduction of the public sector to 'bring it back in line' with the private sector (Cameron, 2010b). At a time when difficult financial decisions are to be made, it is likely to prove difficult to achieve all of these.

One idea that the Conservatives made much of in the run-up to the general election was efficiency savings in the public sector. Indeed, ever since the publication of the Fulton Committee Report (1968), the use of efficiency measures, performance targets and financial management-type initiatives have been encouraged by governments in pursuit of more economical and more professional approaches. This chimed with the managerialist style of governance favoured by Margaret Thatcher in the 1980s, with the introduction of initiatives such as the Management Information Systems for Ministers, which enabled each component of a department's work to be monitored and assessed individually, enabling areas of weakness to be identified and targeted for improvement, and the Financial Management Initiative, which was aimed at transferring a managerial culture seen as successful in the private sector to central government departments and giving managers at all levels greater responsibility and control. It also fits with a belief that the private sector is a model of good practice that the public sector should mirror, something that is in evidence under the current government. The former BP boss Lord Browne became a 'super-director', charged with transferring private-sector business practices into government, while Sir Philip Green, owner of Topshop and Dorothy Perkins, was appointed to carry out an external audit of government spending over the last three years. These approaches reflect that of Margaret Thatcher, for example when she appointed Derek Rayner (from Marks and Spencer) as an advisor on administrative efficiency, and Roy Griffiths (from Sainsbury's) to report on community care.

The Conservative manifesto provides examples of the type of measures that the government intend to introduce that appear designed to encourage efficiency, and, perhaps, transparency, stating that they would 'introduce and publish a standard set of cost measures that capture the key drivers of departmental spending; help departmental Finance Directors to manage resources more efficiently; implement clear financial performance targets for senior civil servants; and create a focus on delivering strong financial management across government' (Conservative Party, 2010e, p 27).

In addition, plans for the October 2010 Spending Review were explicit in seeking to involve both the private and public sectors. In setting the framework for this, the new Chancellor, George Osborne, announced a consultation with members of the public, voluntary groups, civil servants, think tanks and political parties, arguably in an effort to build consensus on where cuts should fall in the effort to cut the fiscal deficit. In addition, the Chancellor appointed an Independent Challenge Group, of leading civil servants and external experts, to think innovatively about the options for reducing public expenditure and to help minimise the impact on public services.

As discussed in greater detail in Chapter 6, in education, the role and powers of local government appear to be being eroded, with new providers being given the opportunity to enter the education sector. 'Drawing on the experience of the Swedish school reforms and the charter school movement in the United States, we will break down barriers to entry so that any good education provider can set up a new Academy school' (Conservative Party, 2010e, p 53). In addition, 'We will give parents the power to save local schools threatened by closure, allowing communities the chance to take over and run small good schools' (Conservative Party, 2010e, p 53). The way in which some local authorities are run looks set to change, with a number of local councils putting forward radical proposals that would alter the role and powers of their authorities. Barnet's plan for an 'easyCouncil' modelled on budget airline services, and Suffolk's to outsource all but a handful of services, were among the first to be aired.

While widening the diversity of provision, not just in the education sector, but across the public sector, may increase choice for the consumer, at the same time it can create problems in terms of: the fragmentation of services; diseconomies of scale, because of the wide variety of providers; implementation problems arising from the different agendas of the implementing agencies, inadequate resources and because no single body has overall control over these agencies; and problems with accountability, since often no one is sure who is accountable to whom and for what (Clarke et al, 2007).

## Regulation and performance measurement

The Conservative manifesto included a set of 'benchmarks for Britain', saying that 'for the first time, the British people will have eight clear and transparent benchmarks against which they can judge the economic success or failure of the next government' (Conservative Party, 2010e, p 5). These benchmarks included: 'Get Britain working again: We will reduce youth unemployment and reduce the number of children in workless households as part of our strategy for tackling poverty and inequality' (Conservative Party, 2010e, p 5); and 'Reform public services to deliver better value for money: We will raise productivity growth in the public sector in order to deliver better schools and a better NHS' (Conservative Party, 2010e, p 5). Yet these appear to be a broadly similar mechanism to the targets set by Labour early in their first term of office. For example, the green paper *New Ambitions for Our Country: A New Contract for Welfare* (Department of Social Security, 1998) included a number of targets such as: 'a reduction in the proportion of working age people living in workless households', and 'an increase in the proportion of lone parents, people with a long-term illness and disabled people of working age in touch with the labour market' (Bochel and Bochel, 1998, p 67). Just like the targets set by Labour, these benchmarks would appear potentially to be a way to judge the success or failure of the Conservatives in these areas. However, like those set by their predecessors, the Conservative targets are vague, do not set out how they will be measured, and do not include any reference to the time period over which these should be judged. Also, interestingly and importantly, such measures had disappeared in the Coalition's 'programme for government'.

However, the use of performance measures looks set to continue in other areas. In schools, Ofsted is expected to adopt 'a more rigorous and targeted inspection regime, reporting on performance only in the core areas related to teaching and learning. And any school that is in special measures for more than one year will be taken over immediately by a successful Academy provider' (Conservative Party, 2010e, p 53). The intention is to 'publish performance data on educational providers ... and reform league tables so that schools are able to focus on, and demonstrate, the progress of children of all abilities' (Cabinet Office,

2010, p 29). But, there is little or no detail on how this will be done, nor the potential shortcomings of such information. Similarly, the Conservative manifesto says:

> We will keep Key Stage 2 tests and league tables. We will reform them to make them more rigorous.... People expect to be able to make choices about the services they use, based on robust information about the quality on offer. So a Conservative government will reform school league tables so that schools can demonstrate they are stretching the most able and raising the attainment of the less able. (Conservative Party, 2010e, p 52)

The discussion on schools in the Coalition programme is in keeping with this, with the use of measures such as these appearing to be underpinned by the dual motivations of maintaining and improving quality and providing information to parents so that they can make informed choices.

The policies of the Conservatives and those of the Coalition government raise a number of questions around equity, fairness and accountability, as well as quality. Yet, in general, the issue of regulation appears to be dealt with in a very piecemeal way. For example, while higher education institutions have been subject to a variety of forms of audit by the Quality Assurance Agency, ranging from in-depth audits to the 'lighter-touch' Institutional Audit introduced in 2003 by Labour, 'Raising the quality of the student experience' is mentioned in the Conservative manifesto (Conservative Party, 2010e, p 17), and the Coalition programme talks about publishing 'more information about the costs, graduate earnings and student satisfaction of different university courses' (Cabinet Office, 2010, p 32). This was reinforced by the Universities Minister, David Willetts, who has said, 'The system doesn't contain strong incentives for universities to focus on teaching and the student experience, as opposed to research' (Shepherd, 2010). Yet there is at present no real clarity about how any of this will be measured, or whether the Quality Assurance Agency will have a role in this. The fact that this information will be published suggests that it may be intended to contribute to the construction of league tables.

While further inspection and audit loom for schools, universities and others, the Conservatives' manifesto promised that 'We will scrap Labour's failed target regime and instead require every department to publish a business plan, with senior management accountable to more rigorous departmental boards for their performance' (Conservative

Party, 2010e, p 67), and to scrap 'the hundreds of process targets Labour have imposed on councils' and end the 'inspection regime that stops councils focusing on residents' main concerns' (Conservative Party, 2010e, p 76). Similarly the Coalition's programme for government says that 'We will cut local government inspection and abolish the Comprehensive Area Assessment' (Cabinet Office, 2010, p 12). Taken at face value this suggests that local authorities will have more freedom over how they do things and that there will be more decentralisation and less of a top-down approach to governance.

By contrast, in respect of the police the programme for government states that 'We will oblige the police to publish detailed local crime data statistics every month, so the public can get proper information about crime in their neighbourhoods and hold the police to account for their performance' (Cabinet Office, 2010, p 13). This suggests more of a top-down approach to governance and more, rather than less, micro-managing, which was a commitment in the Conservatives' manifesto (Conservative Party, 2010e, p vii).

In terms of health, the programme for government also says that 'We will strengthen the role of the Care Quality Commission so it becomes an effective quality Inspectorate' (Cabinet Office, 2010, p 25). Again, this suggests more rather than less regulation, indicates that it is not effective at present and does not say anything about measures to make it more effective. On the NHS the Coalition also promises to make the NHS work better 'by extending best practice on improving discharge from hospital, maximising the number of day care operations, reducing delays prior to operations, and where possible enabling community access to care treatments' (Cabinet Office, 2010, p 25). This begs the questions of how and by whom best practice will be identified, and what criteria will be used to set best practice. There is also an undertaking to 'significantly cut the number of health quangos' (Cabinet Office, 2010, p 24), but which quangos will be cut, what functions they perform and whether they will be replaced with anything else is not stated.

Clearly, from this brief discussion, the Coalition's overall approach to regulation and performance measurement appears, like that of the Conservative manifesto, to be mixed and inconsistent.

## Reforming politics

Following the scandal in the previous parliament over MPs' expenses, and given their traditional commitments to a smaller state and to greater power (and responsibility) for individuals, it was unsurprising that in their manifesto the Conservatives talked about 'a new agenda for a new politics' (Conservative Party, 2010e, p 63), with plans to 'change Britain with a sweeping redistribution of power: from state to citizens; from government to Parliament; from Whitehall to communities; from Brussels to Britain; from bureaucracy to democracy' (Conservative Party, 2010e, p 63).

However, following the hung parliament and the formation of the coalition between the Conservative and Liberal Democrat parties, the new 'programme for government' not only involved compromises on the part of both parties, such as over electoral reform, but only days after the general election, contained promises to introduce measures not seen in either of the parties' manifestos.

Some of the major reforms proposed by the Coalition are around parliament. For example, the two parties agreed to establish five-year fixed-term parliaments, making it much harder for a prime minister to determine the date of a general election and to pick a time when the opinion polls and circumstances seem to favour his or her party to call an election. While this in not uncommon in other European countries, it is a new development in the UK. The fixed-term parliament bill also introduced a referendum on the alternative vote system for general elections, something that the Conservatives had previously been opposed to. In their manifesto the Conservatives stated that 'We support the first-past-the-post system for Westminster elections because it gives voters the chance to kick out a government they are fed up with' (Conservative Party, 2010e, p 67). As the alternative vote system is not, of itself, necessarily much more proportional than first-past-the-post, it would be unlikely to result in the election to parliament of significant numbers of new parties or interests. It is, therefore, difficult to identify any immediate implications for social policy, although the possibility of hung parliaments in the future might in itself make a difference to policy debates.

As part of the bill there is also a measure to equalise constituency boundary sizes, which would automatically result in a reduction in the number of MPs. This was a commitment in the Conservative manifesto and one that was reflected in the Coalition's programme for government. While this would necessitate a boundary review that would impact differently on the political parties depending on how the boundaries are redrawn, the outcome would almost certainly make it harder for Labour to form a government, with obvious implications for social policy, as well as other areas. In addition, while reducing the number of MPs might result in savings through having fewer MPs' salaries to pay, which might fit with the mood of the public in the aftermath of the MPs' expenses scandal, fewer MPs would also be likely to have impacts at the constituency level. There would be more constituents in a smaller number of constituencies and thus the level of constituency business that each MP has to deal with may increase. MPs and their staff would have less time to spend on each constituent who has a problem (often on social policy-related topics, such as benefits, housing or health provision; see Bochel and Defty, 2007b), and constituents might be less well served by such a system. In addition, unless there were to be a significant reduction in the number of frontbenchers on both the government and opposition sides, there will also be fewer MPs to scrutinise legislation. Norton (2005) identifies both of these activities as important parts of the MPs' role, and both have clear implications for social policy, yet both may be significantly diminished by the Coalition's proposals.

However, it is perhaps some of the Coalition's proposals for the way that parliament operates that might have a more immediate significance on the making and scrutiny of social policy. These include implementing in full the proposals of the House of Commons Reform Committee (2009), which would lead to the establishment of a Backbench Business Committee to give the House of Commons more control over its own timetable. Initially this will cover private members' bills, but it will eventually include government bills and debates. In addition the chairs and members of departmental and select committees are now directly elected by a secret ballot of MPs, removing or reducing the influence of the party whips in this area. Supporters of these reforms argue that they will make it easier for parliament to challenge the executive, and thus lead to improvements in the scrutiny of legislation and the actions of government.

There are also proposals for reform of the House of Lords. While the Conservative manifesto said that 'We will work to build a consensus for a mainly-elected second chamber to replace the current House of Lords' (Conservative Party, 2010e, p 67) the Coalition programme said that a committee would be established 'to bring forward proposals for a wholly or mainly elected upper chamber on the basis of proportional representation' (Cabinet Office, 2010, p 27) by December 2010. However, this was likely to be delayed until the spring of 2011. While, at the time of writing, it remained far from clear what such a chamber would look like, or what powers it would possess, elections based upon a more proportional system would be likely to result in governments having to consider more carefully how to get their legislation through the Upper House, and might lead to some reduction in the 'ping-pong' of bills between the two Houses, which was seen under Labour. In addition, more proportional electoral systems tend to lead to higher levels of representation for women and ethnic minority groups, so that a House elected on such lines might provide a greater degree of descriptive, symbolic and perhaps even substantive representation for such groups (Pitkin, 1967).

In common with the other areas discussed in this chapter there is an emphasis on how the public can get involved in this 'new politics'. Petitioning has in recent years become a more popular way for members of the public to express their opinion on issues, with the Number 10 Downing Street system attracting a number of high-profile e-petitions, and a number of petitions signed by more than 50,000 people on aspects of education and health policy. The House of Commons has a long-standing paper petitions facility and a variety of reports have recommended the adoption of an e-petitioning system (indeed, proposals for an e-petitions system were initially accepted by the Labour government, but then later rejected on the grounds that the costs of the proposed system were too high). The Conservatives suggested that 'any petition that secures 100,000 signatures will be eligible for a formal debate in Parliament' (Conservative Party, 2010e, p 66), and that 'the petition with the most signatures will enable members of the public to table a Bill eligible to be voted on in Parliament' (Conservative Party, 2010e, p 66). However, it is not clear whether this would be an e-petitions system, nor how this system would work, including coping with an increased volume of petitions, given that the current paper system has dealt with an average of 322 petitions per parliamentary session from 1989/90 to 2007/08. It is also far from clear how policymakers and legislators would react to such a system, and whether and to what extent it would alter their behaviour. While it might be an additional means of public input, it might also, for example, overemphasise transient interests and concerns, and there is no indication of whether such systems would simply give another voice to those who are already vocal and influential, or, perhaps more valuably, give a voice to the less powerful.

The theme of enabling the public to participate is also reflected in both the Conservative manifesto and Coalition plans 'to introduce a power of recall, allowing voters to force a by-election where an MP is found to have engaged in serious wrongdoing and having had a petition calling for a by-election signed by 10% of his or her constituents' (Cabinet Office, 2010, p 27).

The Conservative manifesto also proposed to introduce a new Public Reading Stage for bills, to give the public an opportunity to comment on proposed legislation online. While this was taken up in the programme for government it does again raise questions about how this would work, who would manage it and what it might cost, as well as what impact it might have. Given that many interest groups are already involved in the scrutiny of legislation, including through links with MPs, and that the media frequently raise issues of concern, it might be questionable whether this new stage in the legislative process will add any significant value.

To make the 'political system better reflect the people it is meant to represent' the Conservatives planned to 'introduce a £1 million fund to help people with disabilities who want to become MPs, councillors or other elected officials with the extra costs they face in running for office' (Conservative Party, 2010e, p 67). In the Coalition's programme for government this has been reduced to 'extra support for people with disabilities who want to become MPs, councillors or other elected officials' (Cabinet Office, 2010, p 27). Interestingly, neither the manifesto nor the programme for government talks about increasing the number of women MPs, MPs from minority ethnic groups or indeed any other group.

In terms of legislative changes that might have a fairly immediate and significant impact upon social policy, there are perhaps two proposals that stand out. One is the Conservatives' commitment to replace the Human Rights Act with a UK Bill of Rights. However, as the Liberal Democrats disagreed strongly with this, the programme for government passed this on to a commission to consider a bill of rights that 'builds on all our obligations under the European Convention on Human Rights, ensures that these rights continue to be enshrined in British law, and protects and extends British liberties' (Cabinet Office, 2010, p 11).

The second is also concerned with civil liberties, and while reflecting some of the ideas from the Conservative manifesto has the potential to go further. The Freedom Bill is part of 'a full programme of measures to reverse the substantial erosion of civil liberties and roll back state intrusion' (Cabinet Office, 2010, p 11). It is intended to restore freedoms, strengthen the accountability of bodies receiving public funding and strike a balance between protecting the public and protecting civil liberties on issues such as anti-terrorism legislation. The Coalition is also proposing to scrap the ID card scheme, the National Identity register, the ContactPoint Database designed to hold information on all children under 18 and second-generation biometric passports, which were all either proposed by the outgoing Labour government in 2010 or in the early stages of implementation, although some of these also appear to have been justified on the grounds that the plans were very costly.

Other aspects of rolling back the state as set out in the Coalition programme are, however, likely to add costs, for example the extension of the Freedom of Information Act in order to provide greater transparency, and further regulation of CCTV, while others appear to be primarily populist, such as not allowing schools to fingerprint children without parental permission (Cabinet Office, 2010, p 11).

At the local level some of the proposed reforms mirror those at the national level. For example, the theme of giving 'individuals more direct control over how they are governed' by giving 'residents the power to instigate local referendums on any local issue if 5 per cent of the local population sign up' (Conservative Party, 2010e, p 75) appears to reflect the Conservative Party's views on citizen participation through petitions at the national level. This is also reiterated in the Coalition programme, which states 'We will give residents the power to instigate local referendums on any local issue' (Cabinet Office, 2010, p 27) and these duly appeared in the Localism Bill. However, there again appears to be significant potential for populist and possibly transient ideas impacting upon local policy. In contrast, giving councils a general power of competence might appear to give local authorities scope to pursue a wider range of activities, although taken together with proposals for the freezing of council tax, the ability of local people to veto 'excessive' council tax rises through referenda and giving 'communities the right to take over local state-run services', this would appear likely to be limited in reality.

## Devolution

Although devolution is covered in greater depth in Chapter 13, it forms an important element of the governance of social policy. It is, therefore, perhaps worth noting that the Conservative manifesto supported the changes 'proposed by the Calman Commission for clarifying the devolution settlement' and stated that the party 'will not stand in the way of a referendum on further legislative powers requested by the Welsh Assembly' (Conservative Party, 2010e, p 83), a position that effectively carried over into the Coalition's programme for government. Should the Calman recommendations be implemented, and if the Welsh Assembly is granted additional powers (although there will not be a referendum in Wales until 2011 at the earliest), there is clearly the potential for the further development of differences in the making and implementation of social policy, particularly with different political control of the devolved administrations.

## Europe

Given the major differences between the Coalition partners on Europe, the programme for government outlines what is very much a holding position, so that the primary social policy implications are essentially that there will be no further transfer of powers to the EU over the course of the parliament. That said, there is a commitment to the government working to limit the application of the Working Time Directive in the UK. In the longer term the introduction of a 'referendum lock' and a United Kingdom Sovereignty Bill might also be likely to reduce the scope for the expansion of EU competency, including in social policy.

## Conclusions

This chapter has suggested that the general direction of the Conservative Party, and of the Coalition government, reflects many of the ideas of the Conservative governments of the 1980s and 1990s, including the relative merits and shortcomings of private- and public-sector provision, the importance of individual choice, and the attempts to engage charities and social enterprises in the delivery of public services. While some of these may have been echoed under Labour, and, like Labour, they illustrate an enthusiasm for 'improving' some of the mechanisms of government and policymaking, they have clearly been given fresh impetus.

Yet there remain major questions about many of these ideas, including around: the degree of public enthusiasm, or even support, for greater involvement, whether it is 'having a say' over policies and legislation, or running public services; how resources will be allocated and managed, particularly in a time of real financial pressure and cuts in public expenditure; and what the implications are for ideas such as equity and accountability.

At an ideological level the approaches taken by the Coalition also fit well with the positions of many Conservatives, and some Liberal Democrats (particularly those associated with the 'Orange Book' tendency), who favour a small state, greater individual responsibility and a broader mix of welfare provision, including more provision by the private and third sectors. Finally, there is, as yet, little in the Coalition's proposal to suggest a real redistribution of power, particularly to those who currently have least.

# FIFTEEN

# The Conservatives, Coalition and social policy

*Hugh Bochel*

The first few months of the Coalition government's term of office proceeded more smoothly than many might have anticipated. Although there were some (relatively) public disagreements around issues such as tuition fees for higher education and the cap on non-EU immigration, in most respects the partners were likely to have been relatively content with the operation of the Coalition.

However, there were a number of reasons to suspect that this initial period would not be typical. These included the fact that, despite the 'emergency budget' of June 2010 and the Spending Review in October that year, the real scale and impact of cuts in public expenditure and the full implications for jobs and public services would be likely to take several months to become clear. So, for example, while by the end of 2010 it was clear that significant job losses were taking place in local authorities, the impact of these on frontline services was not yet apparent. In political terms as well, with the parliamentary recess over the summer and Labour's leadership election at the same time, there was less scope for high profile analysis and criticism of the Coalition's approach than was likely to follow, and the leaders of both of the Coalition parties were able to head into the summer and the party conference season in the autumn of 2010 in the knowledge that they had successfully returned their parties to power. At the same time, it must have been apparent to all that tough challenges were in prospect, not least in implementing the Coalition's social policies in combination with major reductions in public expenditure.

The remainder of this chapter draws upon the contributions to this book to provide an initial assessment of the state of social policy under the Coalition government.

## The impact of the Liberal Democrats

Although the focus throughout this book has been on the Conservative Party, the creation of a Coalition government for the United Kingdom for the first time since the Second World War makes it appropriate to consider the nature and extent of the influence of the Liberal Democrats on their coalition partners. While the decision of the Liberal Democrats to join the Conservatives in government came as a surprise to many, recent years had arguably seen something of a shift away from the social democratic leaning under previous leaders such as Paddy Ashdown, Charles Kennedy and Menzies Campbell. In particular, the publication of *The Orange Book: Reclaiming Liberalism* (Marshall and Laws, 2010) represented for some, a restatement of the 'fundamental principles' (p 19) of liberalism and an argument that the 'strengths' of economic liberalism (such as choice, competition and the private sector) should be utilised by the Liberal Democrats in the social sphere.

In terms of delivering their manifesto promises, around 40% of the pledges in the Coalition's programme for government (Cabinet Office, 2010) had been included in the Liberal Democrats' manifesto, or those of both parties. It would, therefore, appear to be relatively easy for the Liberal Democrats to claim that they were able to exercise considerable influence over the policies of the new government from the start.

However, some of the manifesto promises of the two parties, and even pledges in the Coalition's programme for government, were watered down or ignored very early in the life of the government, such as the promise to end the detention of children in immigration centres, with the Coalition shifting, in September 2010, to the position that it would try to 'minimise' the numbers held in such circumstances. The Liberal Democrats also performed something of a U-turn on higher education funding. Prior to the election many Liberal Democrat MPs, including Nick Clegg and Vince Cable, had signed a National Union of Students pledge to vote against any increase in fees in the next parliament, and the party's manifesto had promised to phase out tuition fees over a six-year period. However, the Coalition agreement only agreed to allow Liberal Democrat MPs to abstain in any vote, although in the event, when the House of Commons voted on an increase in fees to up to £9,000 the Liberal Democrats split three ways, with some MPs voting for the increase, other against it, and yet more abstaining. At the same time, given at least some of David Cameron's rhetoric since becoming Conservative leader, and as pointed out in relation to a number of policy areas in this book, such as aspects of family policy, there were likely to be some areas where he may have been relatively pleased to have had to make 'concessions' to the Liberal Democrats.

However, as several of the preceding chapters have illustrated, across large swathes of social policy it appears to be the Conservatives' approach that has been dominant. For example, Sonia Exley and

Stephen Ball (Chapter 6) argue that the new government's education policies have been dominated by Conservative thinking, including Michael Gove's 'free schools' and the greater freedom for state schools to become Academies, while where employment is concerned, Alan Deacon and Ruth Patrick (Chapter 9) again show that most of the policies on jobs and work in the Coalition agreement are based upon the ideas of the Conservatives. The Coalition agreement also accepted the Conservatives' commitment to increase spending on the NHS in real terms, a policy previously opposed by the Liberal Democrats, and which would inevitably mean larger cuts in other areas of public expenditure.

Perhaps just as significantly, even before the real extent of public expenditure cuts had become apparent, many had criticised the Liberal Democrats for their willingness to accept the Conservatives' approach to cutting the fiscal deficit. Having argued for delays in making cuts in public expenditure during the 2010 general election campaign, on entering government they appeared to rapidly reverse their position. While the emergency budget of June 2010 saw some evidence of Liberal Democrat ideas (an increase in capital gains tax to 28% – although not to the level that they had originally proposed – and an increase in the personal tax allowance to £10,000 during the lifetime of the parliament), the budget was widely perceived as being regressive rather than progressive, with the respected Institute for Fiscal Studies taking issue with the government's claims for the latter. Indeed, following the Spending Review of October 2010 there were further arguments over the impact on the least well off, with the Treasury asserting that tax and welfare changes combined would be broadly progressive, while others, including the Institute for Fiscal Studies, argued that they would be regressive, particularly looking beyond 2013. With a Liberal Democrat, Danny Alexander, as Chief Secretary to the Treasury, at the heart of debates about public expenditure, the party's position on cuts was also likely to come under heavier focus during the life of the government.

Finally, as Richard Parry points out in Chapter 13, the inclusion of the Liberal Democrats in the Coalition also provided the Conservatives with a degree of political cover in relation to Wales, and particularly Scotland, where a government formed only by the Conservative Party might otherwise have been seen to lack legitimacy. The impact of this on the Liberal Democrats and their electoral support in those areas is likely to be tested in elections to the Scottish Parliament and the National Assembly for Wales in May 2011.

## The Conservative Party and social policy in coalition

One of the features of the Conservative Party is the network of pressure groups and think tanks that surround it, and which contribute to debates around policy, including social policies. While this was familiar from the Conservative governments of the 1980s and 1990s, in addition to those from that period, such as the Centre for Policy Studies and the Institute for Economic Affairs, there has been the emergence of new organisations, not least the Centre for Social Justice, founded by the party's former leader, Iain Duncan Smith, and identified in many chapters of this book as having been a significant influence on party thinking and policy in the years before the 2010 general election. There have also been new groups, including ResPublica and Policy Exchange, which have fed into Conservative thinking. These organisations form a network that provides the Conservative Party with ideas, and which perhaps helps to create an intellectual and ideological underpinning for its policies.

However, while many of the chapters in this volume recognise the influence of these groups, they also make clear that there have been significant differences in the levels of preparedness and approaches to policy of the Conservatives across many areas of social policy. In some fields, such as housing, criminal justice and community care, the Conservative Party's policies were perhaps less clear than in others, such as education and welfare-to-work, where their plans had clearly been worked out well in advance of the election. While these differences make it hard to come to clear conclusions about the overall shape of the Conservatives' policies, the remainder of this chapter seeks to draw out some of the key dimensions that have been identified by the contributions to this book.

### Continuity or change?

One aspect that many of the chapters have considered is the extent to which Conservative policies have reflected those of New Labour, or have taken new directions. Almost inevitably, the policies of any incoming government will be shaped and limited by those of their predecessors, and several of the contributions serve to highlight similarities of approach between the Conservatives and their Labour predecessors. Indeed, in Chapter 5 Rob Baggott notes that even following Labour's election in 1997, the legacy of the previous Conservative government persisted. In the same way, he points out that Conservative policies moved closer to those of Labour between

2005 and 2010, in part because the party sought to gain ground in a policy area that has traditionally been a Labour strength, and where the leadership felt it necessary to reassure the public that the NHS, in particular, would be safe in Conservative hands. Similarly, with regard to education, Sonia Exley and Stephen Ball also note, in Chapter 6, significant continuities, although in this case they then contrast Labour's willingness to invest, intervene and regulate to help drive forward their policies, with the Conservatives' emphasis on reducing regulation and giving schools greater freedom, as well as the encouragement of much larger numbers of Academies and, of course, 'free schools'. In their discussion of social security and welfare reform (Chapter 8), Stephen McKay and Karen Rowlingson also point to continuities with the approach of New Labour, particularly around the idea of making work pay, although one strand of Labour's policies, asset-based welfare, has effectively been jettisoned by the Coalition. At the time of writing, while Iain Duncan Smith had secured funding from the Treasury to introduce the Universal Credit, this was in exchange for bigger cuts to the budget of the Department for Work and Pensions in the future, while many questions remained over the proposals in the White Paper (Department for Work and Pensions, 2010g).

One of the areas where there has perhaps been something closest to cross-party agreement in recent years has been welfare-to-work, and Alan Deacon and Ruth Patrick's discussion in Chapter 9 clearly reflects this, with their identification of a 'framing consensus', with agreement over not only the centrality of rights and responsibilities, but also over the use of private and voluntary agencies to deliver welfare-to-work programmes. Mike Hough's consideration of criminal justice policy (Chapter 12) also identifies very similar approaches by the Conservative and Labour parties in recent years, although in this case he suggests that, despite the relatively hard line taken by both the Conservative and Liberal Democrat parties in their general election manifestos, an opportunity has perhaps been created to move away from agreement on an unnecessarily punitive and expensive penal system, due to the concurrence of the appointment of Kenneth Clarke as Justice Secretary with the likely cuts in public expenditure, which could, perhaps, generate pressures for a more decarceral approach to the criminal justice system.

Prior to the 2010 general election David Cameron did seek to differentiate the Conservatives from Labour with regard to the family, and in particular the importance of marriage, with Paul Daniel noting in Chapter 11 that this may have helped him appeal to sections of his party that may have felt less comfortable with some elements of 'compassionate' or 'progressive' Conservatism. However, he also points out that the Conservatives appear to have signed up to Labour's commitment to eliminate child poverty and in their manifesto also undertook to increase the number of Sure Start health visitors.

In some areas, of course, Conservative thinking has been unclear until relatively recently, or indeed is continuing to develop, so that where housing is concerned, while a number of proposals have emerged, such as the community right to build and flexible tenancies, the overall direction of policy has been less clear, as outlined by Peter Somerville in Chapter 7. This is also the case in relation to social care, where the government's pre-election 'silence' on the significant challenges around the future of community care, and in particular its funding, as identified by Jon Glasby in Chapter 10, was perhaps reflected in its decision to establish a Commission on the Funding of Care and Support, which would not report until July 2011.

## Compassionate, modern and progressive?

A second theme that emerges from the preceding chapters is the influence of divergent strands of thinking within the Conservative Party and the extent to which these are reflected in different policy areas. In particular, many chapters examine the extent to which, under David Cameron, the Conservative Party has sought to differentiate itself from the Thatcher era.

As both Robert M. Page and Nick Ellison illustrate in Chapters 2 and 3, respectively, many of these internal differences have been long-standing and have directed Conservative social policy in different directions at different times. In his discussion of 'progressive' Conservatism, while recognising the embracing of social justice by some contemporary Conservatives, Page highlights the emphasis on the 'broken society', and the responsibility of individuals and society (rather than the state) for 'fixing' it. Crucially, in an observation that resonates with views expressed throughout the book, Page questions whether the desire to make rapid and large cuts in public expenditure as a response to the level of government debt may foreshadow a return to the neo-liberal social policy agenda of the 1980s and 1990s, particularly since it continues to reflect the continued dislike of many Conservatives (and a significant element of the Liberal Democrats) of 'big government', while Ellison also indicates that the response to budgetary issues will define the true intent behind Conservative rhetoric on social justice and the reduction of poverty.

These debates are apparent in fields such as education where, in Chapter 6, Sonia Exley and Stephen Ball note the change in the Conservatives' rhetoric following Cameron becoming leader, and the emphasis on poverty, inequality and social justice, although at the same time pointing out that these have gone hand-in-hand with familiar Conservative criticisms of bureaucracy and regulation, as well as proposals to give schools greater autonomy, to increase their 'freedom' by creating many more Academies, and to allow parents and others to establish 'free schools', based (loosely) on the 'Swedish model'. However, here there are long-standing tensions within Conservative thinking, including between freedom for local providers of services and central control over them, and in particular, perhaps, for 'progressive' or 'compassionate Conservatives', between freedom for schools and the ability to reduce educational inequalities.

Peter Somerville's discussion of housing policy (Chapter 7) also highlights the different approaches within Conservative thinking, in this case contrasting the 'traditional Conservatism' of people like Iain Duncan Smith, with the 'progressive Conservatism' of those such as David Willetts. He concludes that in relation to housing the Coalition government appears more traditional than progressive, with many of the proposals emerging from progressive Conservatism having been ignored by the new government.

The rhetoric of both parties in the Coalition government prior to and in the months following the 2010 general election frequently emphasised 'fairness'. During the lifetime of the Coalition government, as a consequence, there seem likely to be considerable arguments over what actually constitutes 'fairness', as foreshadowed at the conferences of both the Conservatives and Liberal Democrats in the autumn of 2010, and attempts to redefine that concept, along with others, such as 'poverty', may reflect a significant shift in the position of the Conservative Party from that apparently espoused by Cameron and his allies from 2005 up to the 2010 general election. In addition, the respective strengths of the different strands of Conservative thinking will be reflected and reinforced by decisions about public expenditure, as highlighted by McKay and Rowlingson's discussion in Chapter 8 of the tensions between those who prioritise spending reductions and those who see the potential for significant longer-term savings from the benefits system if deeper cuts are forgone in the shorter term.

A quite different perspective is presented by Richard Parry in his discussion of the Conservative Party and the devolved administrations in Chapter 13. While he questions whether there has been any distinctive approach by the Conservatives to social policy in Northern Ireland,

Scotland or Wales, he does suggest that the party's behaviour has changed in those parts of the United Kingdom, in particular in and through their participation in post-election negotiations, although he also notes that there appears to be little likelihood of the Conservative Party at Westminster learning from its non-English colleagues, so long as they deliver little in terms of representation in the House of Commons.

## The future of state welfare

One way or another, the policies of the Coalition government promised to transform state welfare. The speed and depth of the proposed cuts in public expenditure alone were likely to have major ramifications for much welfare provision, other than for the supposedly 'protected' areas of schools and the National Health Service. If any gap left by the retrenchment of state provision were to be filled, whether by the private sector, the third sector or by some version of the 'Big Society', the result would likely be very different from the situation at any point since the end of the Second World War. In this regard, in Chapter 7 Peter Somerville highlights the lack of any clear vision within the Coalition government of a strategic role in relation to housing, and in particular the question of what happens if their reforms, including the 'Big Society', fail to deliver improvements for those in housing need. This lack of a strategic vision in some areas, and the apparent dependence upon individuals, communities and society to provide services, also resonates with Jon Glasby's discussion of the Conservatives' approach to community care (Chapter 10), aspects of which are likely to remain unresolved until at least the report of the Commission on the Funding of Care and Support in the summer of 2011, and with the discussion of the future of childcare by Paul Daniel in Chapter 11.

Even where education and health are concerned, Conservative policies, while largely promising to protect spending, imply major changes to the ways in which services are delivered. While the party's commitment to 'free schools' was clear well before the 2010 general election, where the NHS was concerned, despite the earlier promise not to introduce top-down reforms, which were described in the programme for government (Cabinet Office, 2010, p 24) as having 'got in the way of patient care', in the summer of 2010, the Secretary of State for Health, Andrew Lansley, announced a major reorganisation. This would abolish Strategic Health Authorities and Primary Care Trusts, with commissioning to be undertaken by GP consortia, in all likelihood with the support of private-sector organisations. While the complex politics around the NHS, including the level of public support for it, may mean that it is hard to predict the future direction of health policy, as described by Rob Baggott in Chapter 5, Sonia Exley and Stephen Ball (Chapter 6) conclude that both because and despite of the significant degree of continuity of policy between Labour and the new Coalition government, there is an ongoing disarticulation of the state education system in England, while the analyses of welfare-to-work by Alan Deacon and Ruth Patrick (Chapter 9), and social security by Stephen McKay and Karen Rowlingson (Chapter 8), suggest that the government will continue to look for savings from the benefits system and from moving people into paid work.

Catherine Bochel's discussion of the governance of social policy (Chapter 14) brings together a number of themes from the other chapters, including in its focus on proposals to reform the public sector, the idea of the 'Big Society', and the use of tools such as regulation and performance measures that may become increasingly important if the state is to withdraw from significant parts of the provision of public services and is replaced by a plethora of organisations drawn from communities, social enterprises and the private sector. In such a world new methods are likely to be required if quality is to be ensured and notions of 'fairness' are to be delivered.

Finally, the discussion of the Conservatives in the devolved administrations by Richard Parry (Chapter 13) usefully reminds us that in many areas of social policy, including education, health care and housing, it is necessary to consider the policies of the devolved administrations as well as those pursued in Westminster, and we should be aware that the priorities of governments in those administrations may be increasingly at variance from those of the Coalition government at Westminster.

## Conclusion

Chapter 1 outlined the developments that led to the emergence of David Cameron as Conservative leader and then as Prime Minister. It also put forward a number of possible interpretations of Conservatism under Cameron's leadership. While, in common with the authors of the contributions to this book, many will have their own views on that, future judgements may be coloured, perhaps above all else, by the question of how the Conservatives and the Coalition government deal with public expenditure and public services in the face of the budget deficit. The Conservative manifesto made clear the commitment 'to eliminate the bulk of the structural deficit over a Parliament' (Conservative Party, 2010e, p 5), while the Coalition agreement reiterated that the main burden of deficit reduction would be 'borne by reduced spending rather than increased taxes' (Cabinet Office, 2010, p 15). However, the early months of the Coalition government suggested that not only did they see a clear need to cut back on public expenditure, but that some, at least, saw it as a perfect justification for 'rolling back' parts of the welfare state in a way and to an extent that Margaret Thatcher had been unable to do in the 1980s and 1990s. It is very likely that if the Coalition endures into 2014 or 2015, social policy and the welfare state will look significantly different from the position in 2010. The biggest test for 'compassionate', 'modern' or 'progressive' Conservatives may, therefore, be both in the extent to which they allow that to happen, and in their ability to maintain key areas of state provision and/or develop alternative structures and mechanisms to deliver many of the services that the public have come to expect of their governments, and upon which large numbers of people depend.

# References

Abbott, P. and Wallace, C. (1992) *The Family and the New Right*, London: Pluto Press.

Adam, S. and Brewer, M. (2010) *Couple Penalties and Premiums in the UK Tax and Benefit System*, London: Institute for Fiscal Studies.

Adams, J., Clark, M., Ezrow, L. and Glasgow, G. (2004) 'Understanding Change and Stability in Party Ideologies: Do Parties Respond to Public Opinion or Past Election Results', *British Journal of Political Science*, vol 34, no 4, pp 589–610.

Allen, G. and Duncan Smith, I. (2008) *Early Intervention: Good Parents, Great Kids, Better Citizens*, London: Centre for Social Justice.

Allen, R. (2010) *Replicating Swedish 'Free School' Reforms in England*, Bristol: Centre for Market and Public Organisation.

All-Wales Convention (2009) *Report*, Cardiff: All-Wales Convention. Available online at: www.allwalesconvention.org (accessed 22 September 2010).

Ashbee, E. (2003) 'The US Republicans: Lessons for the Conservatives?', in M Garnett and P Lynch (eds) *The Conservatives in Crisis*, Manchester: Manchester University Press.

Bacon, R. and Eltis, W. (1976) *Britain's Economic Problem: Too Few Producers*, Basingstoke: Macmillan.

Baker, D., Gamble, A. and Ludlam, S. (1992) 'More "Classless" and Less "Thatcherite"? Conservative Ministers and the New Conservative MPs after the 1992 election', *Parliamentary Affairs*, vol 45, no 4, pp 656–68.

Bale, T. (2008) '"A Bit Less Bunny-Hugging and a Bit More Bunny Boiling"? Qualifying Conservative Party Change under David Cameron', *British Politics*, vol 3, no 3, pp 270–99.

Bale, T. (2010) *The Conservative Party from Thatcher to Cameron*, Cambridge: Polity.

Ball, S. (1990) *Politics and Policy Making in Education: Explorations in Policy Sociology*, London: Routledge.

Ball, S. (2008) *The Education Debate*, Bristol: The Policy Press.

Ball, S. (2009) 'Academies in Context: Politics, Business and Philanthropy and Heterarchical Governance', *Management in Education*, vol 23, no 3, pp 100–3.

Ball, S. and Exley, S. (2010) 'Making Policy with "Good Ideas": The "Intellectuals" of New Labour', *Journal of Education Policy*, vol 25, no 2, pp 151–69.

Ball, S., Hoskins, K., Maguire, M. and Braun, A. (2009) 'Disciplinary Texts: A Policy Analysis of National and Local Behaviour Policies', paper presented at the British Educational Research Association annual conference, University of Manchester, September 2009.

Bara, J. and Budge, I. (2001) 'Party Policy and Ideology: Still New Labour?', *Parliamentary Affairs*, vol 54, no 4, pp 590–606.

Barber, M. and Mourshed, M. (2007) *How the World's Best Performing Schools Come out on Top*, London: McKinsey and Company.

Barlow, A., Duncan, S. and James, G. (2002) 'New Labour: The Rationality Mistake and Family Policy', in A. Carling, S. Duncan and R. Edwards (eds) *Analysing Families: Morality and Rationality in Policy and Practice*, London: Routledge.

Barlow, J., Burn, J. and Lockhart, G. (2008) *Weighing In*, London: Policy Exchange.

Barnes, C. (1999) *A Working Social Model? Disability and Work in the 21st Century*, Leeds: Disability Archive. Available at: www.leeds.ac.uk/disability-studies/archiveuk/Barnes/a%20working%20social%20model.pdf (accessed 14 November 2007).

Barnes, C. and Roulstone, A. (2005) '"Work" is a Four-Letter Word: Disability, Work and Welfare', in A. Roulstone and C. Barnes (eds) *Working Futures? Disabled People, Policy and Social Inclusion*, Bristol: The Policy Press.

Barnes, M. and Walker, A. (1996) 'Consumerism versus Empowerment: A Principled Approach to the Involvement of Older Service Users', *Policy and Politics*, vol 24, no 4, pp 375–94.

BBC News (2002) 'Tories "must change or face slaughter"'. Available at news.bbc.co.uk/1/hi/uk-politics/2304181.stm (accessed 16 December 2010).

BBC News (2010a) *Transcript of Third Prime Ministerial Debate*, 30 April, London: BBC. Available at: http://news.bbc.co.uk/1/shared/bsp/hi/pdfs/30_04_10_finaldebate.pdf (accessed 21 May 2010).

BBC News (2010b) 'Council Homes for Life Could Go, Says Cameron', *BBC News*, 3 August. Available at: www.bbc.co.uk/news/uk-politics-10855996 (accessed 16 August 2010).

BBC News (2010c) 'Welfare Spending to Be Cut by £4 Billion Says George Osborne'. Available at: www.bbc.co.uk/news/uk-politics-11250639 (accessed 10 September 2010).

BBC News (2010d) 'Cameron Call on NI Public Sector'. Available at: http://news.bbc.co.uk/1/hi/uk_politics/election_2010/northern_ireland/8641358.stm (accessed 22 September 2010).

BBC Scotland (2010) 'Who's Cheating Who? BBC Scotland Investigates', 25 May. See also www.bbc.co.uk/news/10159717 (accessed 22 December 2010).

Ben-Galim, D. and Sachrajda, A. (eds) (2010) *Now its Personal: Learning from Welfare to Work Approaches Around the World*, London: IPPR.

Bennett, J. (2008) 'They Hug Hoodies, Don't They? Responsibility, Irresponsibility and Responsibilisation in Conservative Crime Policy', *The Howard Journal*, vol 47, no 5, pp 451–69.

Blair, T. (1993) 'Why Crime is a Socialist Issue', *New Statesman*, 29 January, pp 27–8.

Blair, T. (1997) 'The 21st Century Welfare State', speech to Social Policy and Economic Performance Conference, Amsterdam, January.

Blake, R. (1998) *The Conservative Party from Peel to Major*, London: Arrow.

Blekesaune, M. (2007) 'Economic Conditions and Public Attitudes to Welfare Policies', *European Sociological Review*, vol 23, no 3, pp 393–403.

Blond, P. (2010) *Red Tory: How Left and Right have Broken Britain and How We Can Fix It*, London: Faber and Faber.

Blunt, C. (2010) 'Churchill Speech', delivered at NACRO, West Norwood, 23 July. Available at: www.justice.gov.uk/news/sp220710a.htm (accessed 11 October 2010).

Bochel, C. and Bochel, H. (1998) 'The Governance of Social Policy', in E. Brunsdon, H. Dean and R. Woods (eds) *Social Policy Review 10*, London: Social Policy Association.

Bochel, H. and Defty, A. (2007a) 'MPs' Attitudes to Welfare: A New Consensus?', *Journal of Social Policy*, vol 36, no 1, pp 1–18.

Bochel, H. and Defty, A. (2007b) *Welfare Policy under New Labour: Views from inside Westminster*, Bristol: The Policy Press.

Bochel, H. and Defty, A. (2010) 'Safe as Houses? Conservative Social Policy, Public Opinion and Parliament', *The Political Quarterly*, vol 81, no 1, pp 74–84.

Bochel, H. and Duncan, S. (eds) (2007) *Making Policy in Theory and Practice*, Bristol: The Policy Press.

Bogdanor, V. (2010) 'John Major, 1990–1997', in V. Bogdanor (ed) *From New Jerusalem to New Labour*, Basingstoke: Palgrave Macmillan.

Bosanquet, N., de Zoete, H. and Haldenby, A. (2007) *NHS Reform: The Empire Strikes Back*, London: Reform.

Bosanquet, N., Haldenby, A. and Rainbow, H. (2009) *Fit for Recovery*, London: Reform.

Boxer, A. (1996) *The Conservative Governments 1951–64*, London: Longman.

Boyle, D., Coote, A., Sherwood, C. and Slay, J. (2010) *Right Here, Right Now: Taking Co-Production into the Mainstream*, London: NESTA/NEF.

Bradshaw, J. (2002) *The Well-Being of Children in the UK*, York: University of York/Save the Children.

Brewer, M. and Greaves, E. (2010) *Families and Children*, London: Institute for Fiscal Studies.

Brewer, M. and Joyce, R. (2010) 'Welfare Reform and the Minimum Wage: 2010 Election Briefing Note No 8', London: Institute for Fiscal Studies.

Brewer, M. and Shephard, A. (2005) *Employment and the Labour Market*, London: Institute for Fiscal Studies.

Bridgen, P. and Lowe, R. (1998) *Welfare Policy under the Conservatives 1951–1964*, Public Record Office Handbooks No 30, London: Public Record Office.

Brooks, E. (2010) 'Budget Undermines Progress on Roma Inclusion', *The Guardian*, 1 July. Available at: www.guardian.co.uk (accessed 13 July 2010).

Brown, A. and Young, M. (2002) *NHS Reform: Towards Consensus?*, London: Adam Smith Institute.

Browne, J. and Levell, P. (2010) 'The Distributional Effect of Tax and Benefit Reforms to Be Introduced Between June 2010 and April 2014: A Revised Assessment', *IFS Briefing Note BN108*, London: Institute for Fiscal Studies.

Bulpitt, J. (1986) 'The Discipline of the New Democracy: Mrs Thatcher's Domestic Statecraft', *Political Studies*, vol 34, no 1, pp 19–39.

Burkard, T. (2009) *School Quangos: A Blueprint for Reform and Abolition*, London: Centre for Policy Studies.

Butler, D. and Kavanagh, D. (1993) *The British General Election of 1992*, London: Macmillan.

Cabinet Office (2006) *The UK Government Approach to Public Sector Reform*, London: The Stationery Office.

Cabinet Office (2010) *The Coalition: Our Programme for Government*, London: The Cabinet Office.

Cabinet Office Strategic Policy Making Team (1999) *Professional Policy Making for the Twenty First Century*, London: Cabinet Office.

Cameron, D. (2006a) Speech to the Centre for Social Justice, 10 July.

Cameron, D. (2006b) Speech to the Conservative Party conference, Bournemouth, 4 October.

Cameron, D. (2006c) 'Tackling Poverty is a Social Responsibility', Scarman Lecture, London, 24 November.

Cameron, D. (2007a) 'A Radical Passion', *The Guardian*, 7 August.

Cameron, D. (2007b) 'What Makes Me Conservative', *The Daily Telegraph*, 8 September.

Cameron, D. (2007c) 'Why I Described the Debate About Bringing Back Grammar Schools as Pointless', *The Mail on Sunday*, 20 May.

Cameron, D. (2008a) 'Stronger Families', Speech at Relate, 20 June.

Cameron, D. (2008b) 'There is Such a Thing as Society ... And We Must Start to Value it', *Yorkshire Post*, 13 May.

Cameron, D. (2008c) 'Yes, We Can Get the Change We Really Want', speech to the Conservative Spring Forum, 13 March. Available at: www.conservatives.com/News/Speeches/2008/03/David_Cameron_Yes_we_can_get_the_change_we_really_want.aspx (accessed 20 September 2010).

Cameron, D. (2009a) 'The Big Society', Hugo Young Lecture, 10 November.

Cameron, D. (2009b) 'Our Health Priorities', speech 2 November. Available at: http://www.conservatives.com/News/Speeches/2009/11/David_Cameron_Our_health_priorities.aspx (accessed 17 September 2010).

Cameron, D. (2010a) 'Prime Minister's Speech on the Economy', 7 June.

Cameron, D. (2010b) 'We Must Tackle Britain's Massive Deficit and Growing Debt', speech, 7 June. Available at: www.number10.gov.uk/news/speeches-and-transcripts/2010/06/prime-ministers-speech-on-the-economy-51435 (accessed 20 September 2010).

Cameron, D. (2010c) 'We Need Urgent Action to Improve Our Schools', speech, 18 January. Available at: www.conservatives.com/News/Speeches/2010/01/David_Cameron_We_need_urgent_action_to_improve_our_schools.aspx (accessed 20 September 2010).

Campbell, J. (2003) *Margaret Thatcher, Volume Two: The Iron Lady*, London: Jonathan Cape.

Carlton, D. (2010) 'Anthony Eden, 1955–1957', in V. Bogdanor (ed) *From New Jerusalem to New Labour*, Basingstoke: Palgrave Macmillan.

Carpenter, J. (2010) 'Analysis: Fears Over Tory Planning Policy', *Regeneration & Renewal*, 8 March.

Centre for Economic and Social Inclusion (2010) *Emergency Budget 2010*, London: CESI. Available at: http://www.cesi.org.uk/NewPolicy/news/emergency_budget_2010 (accessed 12 August 2010).

Centre for Social Justice (2006a) *The State of the Nation Report: Education Failure*, London: Centre for Social Justice.

Centre for Social Justice (2006b) *Denying the Vulnerable a Second Chance: The State of the Nation Report*, London: Centre for Social Justice.

Centre for Social Justice (2008a) *Breakthrough Glasgow*, London: Centre for Social Justice. Available at: www.centreforsocialjustice.org.uk/client/downloads/BreakthroughGlasgow.pdf (accessed 22 September 2010).

Centre for Social Justice (2008b) *Housing Poverty: From Social Breakdown to Social Mobility*, London: Centre for Social Justice.

Centre for Social Justice (2008c) 'Sanity from Scotland on Drug Treatment – Will England and Wales Follow Suit?'. Available at: www.centreforsocialjustice.org.uk/client/downloads/Scotland%20 drugs%20strategy%20press%20release%20-%20May%202008.pdf (accessed 22 September 2010).

Centre for Social Justice (2009) *Dynamic Benefits: Towards Welfare That Works*, London: Centre for Social Justice.

Centre for Social Justice (2010) *Green Paper on the Family*, London: Centre for Social Justice.

Charlson, P., Lees, C. and Sikora, K. (2007) *Free at Point of Delivery – Reality or Political Mirage?*, London: Reform.

Charmley, J. (2008) *A History of Conservative Politics Since 1830*, Basingstoke: Palgrave.

Chubb, J. and Moe, T. (1990) *Politics, Markets and America's Schools*, Washington DC: The Brookings Institution.

CIH (Chartered Institute of Housing) (2008) *Rethinking Housing: Chartered Institute of Housing's Response to Communities and Local Government's Housing Reform Programme*, Coventry: CIH.

Citizens Advice Bureau (2010) *Not Working: CAB Evidence on the ESA Work Capability Assessment*, London: Citizens Advice Bureau.

Clark, G. (2010) 'Three Actions Needed to Help the Big Society Grow'. Available at: www.communities.gov.uk/newsstories/ newsroom/1652536 (accessed 16 August 2010).

Clark, G. and Kelly, S. (2004) 'Echoes of Butler? The Conservative Research Department and the Making of Conservative Policy', *The Political Quarterly*, vol 75, no 4, pp 378–82.

Clarke, J. and Newman, N. (2006) 'The People's Choice? Citizens, Consumers and Public Services', Paper for International Workshop 'Citizenship and Consumption: Agency, Norms, Mediations and Spaces', Kings College Cambridge, 30 March–1 April.

Clarke, J., Newman, J., Smith, N., Vidler, E. and Westmarland, L. (2007) *Creating Citizen-Consumers: Changing Publics and Changing Public Services*, London: Sage.

Clarke, K. (2010) 'The Government's Vision for Criminal Justice Reform', speech to the Centre for Crime and Criminal Justice Studies, King's College, London, 30 June. Available at: www.justice.gov.uk/ news/sp300610a.htm (accessed 11 October 2010).

Coates, S. and Watson, R. (2010) 'Too Soon, Too Deep, Say Voters as Coalition Faces Backlash on Cuts', *The Times*, 14 September, p 3.

Cockett, R. (1995) *Thinking the Unthinkable*, London: Fontana.

Conservative and Unionist Central Office (1947) *The Industrial Charter*, London: Conservative and Unionist Central Office.

Conservative and Unionist Central Office (1949) *The Right Road for Britain. Charter*, London: Conservative and Unionist Central Office.

Conservative Education Society (2008) 'CES News, September/October 2008'. Available at: http://cnes4education.wordpress.com/the-autumn-edition-of-ces-news/ (accessed 20 May 2010).

Conservative Party (1970) *A Better Tomorrow: The Conservative Party General Election Manifesto 1970*, London: Conservative Party.

Conservative Party (1987) *The Next Moves Forward: The Conservative Manifesto 1987*, London: Conservative Party.

Conservative Party (1992) *The Best Future for Britain*, London: Conservative Party.

Conservative Party (1997) *You Can Only Be Sure With the Conservatives: The Conservative Manifesto 1997*, London: Conservative Party.

Conservative Party (2001) *Time for Common Sense: The Conservative Manifesto*, London: Conservative Party.

Conservative Party (2003) *Setting Patients Free: A Conservative Party Consultation*, London: Conservative Party.

Conservative Party (2005) *Are You Thinking What We're Thinking? Conservative Election Manifesto 2005*, London: Conservative Party.

Conservative Party (2006) *Built to Last: The Aims and Values of the Conservative Party*, London: Conservative Party.

Conservative Party (2007a) *NHS Autonomy and Accountability: Proposals for Legislation*, London: Conservative Party.

Conservative Party (2007b) *The Patient Will See You Now Doctor*, London: Conservative Party.

Conservative Party (2008a) *Delivering Some of the Best Health in Europe: Outcomes Not Targets*, Policy Green Paper No 6, London: Conservative Party.

Conservative Party (2008b) *Work for Welfare: REAL Welfare Reform to Help Make British Poverty History*, Policy Green Paper No 3, London: Conservative Party.

Conservative Party (2009a) *An NHS Information Revolution to Save Lives*, London: Conservative Party.

Conservative Party (2009b) *Control Shift: Returning Power to Local Communities*, Policy Green Paper No 9, London: Conservative Party.

Conservative Party (2009c) *Get Britain Working: Conservative Proposals to Tackle Unemployment and Reform Welfare*, London: Conservative Party.

Conservative Party (2009d) *Renewal Plan for a Better NHS: Plan for Change*, London: Conservative Party.

Conservative Party (2009e) *Strong Foundations: Building Homes and Communities*, Policy Green Paper No 10, London: Conservative Party.

Conservative Party (2010a) *A Healthier Nation*, Policy Green Paper No 12, London: Conservative Party.

Conservative Party (2010b) *A New Welfare Contract*, London: Conservative Party.

Conservative Party (2010c) *Big Society, Not Big Government*, London: Conservative Party.

Conservative Party (2010d) *Ending the Free Ride for Those Who Fail to Take Responsibility*, London: Conservative Party. Available at: www.conservatives.com/News/News_stories/2010/04/ Ending_the_free_ride_for_those_who_fail_to_take_responsibility.aspx (accessed 20 April 2010).

Conservative Party (2010e) *Invitation to Join the Government of Britain: The Conservative Manifesto 2010*, London: Conservative Party.

Conservative Party (2010f) *May: One Million People Have Died or Retired While on Incapacity Benefit under Labour*, London: Conservative Party. Available at: www.conservatives.com/ Activist_centre/Press_and_Policy/Press_Releases/2010/01/May_One_million_people_have_died_or_retired_while_on_ Incapacity_Benefit_under_Labour.aspx (accessed 4 January 2010).

Conservative Party (2010g) *Open Source Planning Green Paper*, Policy Green Paper No 14, London: Conservative Party.

Conservative Party and Liberal Democrats (2010) 'Conservative Liberal Democrat Coalition Negotiations, Agreements Reached: 11 May 2010', London: Conservative Party and Liberal Democrats.

Conservative Party and Ulster Unionist Party (2010) *Invitation to join the government of the United Kingdom – Conservative and Unionists manifesto 2010*, Belfast: Conservative Party and Ulster Unionist Party.

Conservative Party Manifesto (1951) Archive of Conservative Party Manifestoes. Available at: www.conservative-party.net/manifestos/1951/1951-conservative-manifesto.shtml (accessed 1 July 2010).

Conservative Party Manifesto (1979) Archive of Conservative Party Manifestoes. Available at: www.conservative-party.net/manifestos/1951/1951-conservative-manifesto.shtml (accessed 2 July 2010).

Conservative Research Department (2007) *Public Health: Our Priority*, London: Conservative Party.

Cooke, G. and Gregg, P. (2010) *Liberation Welfare*, London: Demos.

Cowen, N. (2008) *Swedish Lessons: How Schools With More Freedom Can Deliver Better Education*, London: Civitas.

Crace, J. (2008) 'Is Inequality Worse Than Ever?', *The Guardian*, 26 August. Available at: www.guardian.co.uk/education/2008/aug/26/schools.socialexclusion (accessed 27 March 2010).

Crawford, R., Emmerson, C. and Tetlow, G. (2009) *A Survey of Public Spending in the UK*, London: Institute for Fiscal Studies.

Crisp, R., Macmillan, R., Robinson, D. and Wells, P. (2009) 'Continuity or Change: Considering the Policy Implications of a Conservative Government', *People, Place & Policy Online*, vol 3, no 1, pp 58–74.

Critchlow, D.T. (2007) *The Conservative Ascendancy*, Cambridge, MA: Harvard University Press.

Crosland, T. (1956) *The Future of Socialism*, London: Jonathan Cape.

Crossman, R. (1972) *Inside View: Three Lectures on Prime Ministerial Government*, London: Jonathan Cape.

Curtice, J. (2008), 'Public Attitudes and Elections', in P. Cairney (ed) *Scottish Devolution Monitoring Report January 2008*, London: The Consultation Unit.

Curtice, J. (2009) 'Back in Contention? The Conservatives' Electoral Prospects', *The Political Quarterly*, vol 80, no 2, pp 172–83.

Curtice, J. (2010a) 'Thermostat or Weathervane? Public Reactions to Spending and Redistribution Under New Labour', in A. Park, J. Curtice, K. Thomson, M. Phillips, E. Clery and S. Butt (eds) *British Social Attitudes: The 26th Report*, London: Sage.

Curtice, J. (2010b) 'Debate: Election 2010: A New Mood on Tax and Spend?', *Policy and Politics*, vol 38, no 2, pp 325–9.

Curtice, J. and Fisher, S. (2003) 'The Power to Persuade? A Tale of Two Prime Ministers', in A. Park, J. Curtice, K. Thomson, C. Bromley and M. Phillips (eds) *British Social Attitudes: The 20th Report, Continuity and Change Over Two Decades*, Sage: London.

Curtice, J. and Heath, O. (2009) 'Do People Want Choice and Diversity of Provision in Public Services?', in A. Park, J. Curtice, K. Thomson, M. Phillips and E. Clery (eds) *British Social Attitudes: The 25th Report*, Sage: London.

Dale, I. (ed) (2000) *Conservative Party General Election Manifestos, 1900–1997*, London: Routledge.

Daniel, P. (2010) 'Children and Families', in H. Bochel, C. Bochel, R. Page and R. Sykes, *Social Policy: Themes, Issues and Debates*, Harlow: Pearson.

Deacon, A. (2005) 'An Ethic of Mutual Responsibility?', in C. Beem and L. Mead (eds) *Welfare Reform and Political Theory*, New York: Russell Sage Foundation.

Denham, A. and O'Hara, K. (2007) 'The Three "Mantras": "Modernization" and the Conservative Party', *British Politics*, vol 2, no 2, pp 167–90.

Dennis, N. and Erdos, G. (1992) *Families without Fatherhood*, London: Institute of Economic Affairs.

Department for Children, Schools and Families (2009) *The Impact of Family Breakdown on Children's Well-Being: Evidence Review*, Research Report 113, London: Department for Children, Schools and Families.

Department for Children, Schools and Families (2010) *Support for All: The Families and Relationships Green Paper*, London: The Stationery Office.

Department for Communities and Local Government (2004) *Firm Foundations: The Government's Framework for Community Capacity Building*, London: Department for Communities and Local Government.

Department for Communities and Local Government (2010a) *New Homes Bonus: Consultation*, London: CLG.

Department for Communities and Local Government (2010b) *Local Decisions: A Fairer Future for Social Housing*, London: CLG.

Department for Work and Pensions (2006) *A New Deal for Welfare: Empowering People to Work*, London: The Stationery Office.

Department for Work and Pensions (2007) *Reducing Dependency, Increasing Opportunity: Options for the Future of Welfare to Work, an Independent Report to the DWP by David Freud*, Leeds: Corporate Document Services.

Department for Work and Pensions (2008) *Realising Potential: A Vision for Personalised Conditionality and Support, an Independent Report to the DWP by Professor Paul Gregg*, Leeds: Corporate Document Services.

Department for Work and Pensions (2009) *Explanatory Memorandum to the Social Security (Flexible New Deal) Regulations 2009*, No 480, London: Department for Work and Pensions.

Department for Work and Pensions (2010a) *21st Century Welfare*, London: The Stationery Office.

Department for Work and Pensions (2010b) 'Government Response to Households below Average Income Figures', Press Release, London: Department for Work and Pensions. Available at: www.dwp.gov.uk/newsroom/press-releases/2010/may-2010/dwp067-10-200510.shtml (accessed 21 December 2010)

Department for Work and Pensions (2010c) *The Work Capability Assessment: A Call for Evidence*, London: Department for Work and Pensions.

Department for Work and Pensions (2010d) *Households below Average Income – 1994/95 to 2008/09*, London: Department for Work and Pensions. Available at: http://research.dwp.gov.uk/asd/hbai/hbai_2009/pdf_files/full_hbai10.pdf (accessed 23 May 2010).

Department for Work and Pensions (2010e) *Welfare Reform*, London: Department for Work and Pensions. Available at: www.dwp.gov.uk/policy/welfare-reform (accessed 2 March 2010).

Department for Work and Pensions (2010f) *The Work Programme – Prospectus – November 2010*, London: Department for Work and Pensions. Available at http://www.dwp.gov.uk/docs/work-prog-prospectus-v2.pdf (accessed 8 December 2010).

Department for Work and Pensions (2010g) *Universal Credit: Welfare that works*, Cm 9757, London: The Stationery Office.

Department for Work and Pensions (2010h) *Get Britain Working*, London: DWP. Available at http://www.dwp.gov.uk/policy/welfare-reform/get-britain-working/ (accessed 8 December 2010).

Department for Work and Pensions (2010i) *Government's response to Professor Malcolm Harrington's Independent Review of the Work Capability Assessment*, London: The Stationery Office.

Department of Health (1989) *Working for Patients*, London: HMSO.

Department of Health (1992) *The Health of the Nation: A Strategy for Health in England*, London: HMSO.

Department of Health (1998) *Modernising Social Services: Promoting Independence, Improving Protection, Raising Standards*, London: The Stationery Office.

Department of Health (1999) *Saving Lives: Our Healthier Nation*, London: The Stationery Office.

Department of Health (2000) *NHS Plan: A Plan for Investment, a Plan for Reform*, London: The Stationery Office.

Department of Health (2004) *Choosing Health: Making Healthier Choices Easier*, London: The Stationery Office.

Department of Health (2010a) *Equity and Excellence: Liberating the NHS*, London: The Stationery Office.

Department of Health (2010b) *Healthy Lives, Healthy People: Our Strategy for Public Health in England*, London: The Stationery Office.

Department of Social Security (1998) *New Ambitions for Our Country: A New Contract for Welfare*, London: The Stationery Office.

Department of the Environment (1992) *Rents to Mortgages and the Right to Buy*, London: Department of the Environment.

Department of the Environment, Transport and the Regions (1998) *Modern Local Government: In Touch with the People*, London: The Stationery Office.

Disability Alliance (DA) (2010) 'Incapacity Benefits Migration', London: Disability Alliance. Available at: http://www.disabilityalliance.org/ibmigrate.htm (accessed 16 August 10).

Disability Benefits Consortium (2010a) 'New Benefits Assessment System Needs Thorough Rethink', London: Disability Alliance. Available at: http://www.disabilityalliance.org/dbcpress.htm (accessed 16 August 2010).

Disability Benefits Consortium (DBC) (2010b) *DBC response to the WCA review,* London: Disability Alliance. Available at: http://www. disabilityalliance.org/dbcpress3.htm (accessed 8 December 2010).

Dorey, P. (2007) 'A New Direction or Another False Dawn? David Cameron and the Crisis of British Conservatism', *British Politics*, vol 2, no 2, pp 137–66.

Dorey, P. (2009) '"Sharing the Proceeds of Growth": Conservative Economic Policy under David Cameron', *Political Quarterly*, vol 80, no 2, pp 259–69.

Downs, A. (1957) *An Economic Theory of Democracy*, New York: Harper and Row.

Driver, S. (2009a) '"Fixing our Broken Society": David Cameron's post-Thatcherite Social Policy', in S. Lee and M. Beech (eds) *The Conservatives under David Cameron: Built to Last?*, Basingstoke: Palgrave Macmillan.

Driver, S. (2009b) 'Work to be Done? Welfare Reform from Blair to Brown', *Policy Studies*, vol 30, no 1, pp 69–84.

Driver, S. and Martell, L. (2002) *Blair's Britain*, Cambridge: Polity.

Driver, S. and Martell, L. (eds) (2006) *New Labour*, Cambridge: Polity.

Duncan, S. and Edwards, R. (1999) *Lone Mothers, Paid Work and Gendered Moral Rationalities*, Basingstoke: Palgrave Macmillan.

Duncan Smith, I. (2010) 'Universal Credit: Welfare that Works', Speech by the Secretary of State for Work and Pensions, 11 November London: Department for Work and Pensions. Available at: http:// www.dwp.gov.uk/newsroom/ministers-speeches/2010/11-11-10. shtml (accessed 12 November 2010).

Durham, M. (1991) *Sex and Politics: The Family and Morality in the Thatcher Years*, London: Macmillan.

Durham, M. (2001) 'The Conservative Party, New Labour and the Politics of the Family', *Parliamentary Affairs*, vol 54, no 3, pp 459–74.

Dutton, D. (1991) *British Politics since 1945: The Rise and Fall of Consensus*, Oxford: Blackwell.

Dwelly, T. and Cowans, D. (2006) *Rethinking Social Housing in the UK*, London: The Smith Institute.

Dwyer, P. (2008) 'The Conditional Welfare State', in M. Powell (ed) *Modernising the Welfare State: The Blair Legacy*, Bristol: The Policy Press.

Elliot, F. (2009) 'Short Hard Life of Ivan Cameron, Whose Suffering Could Change Britain', 26 February. Available at: www.timesonline.co.uk/tol/news/politics/article5805180.ece (accessed 17 September 2010).

Ellis, S. (2007) 'Policy and Research: Lessons from the Clackmannanshire Phonics Initiative', *Journal of Early Childhood Literacy*, vol 7, no 3, pp 281–98.

Evans, M. (1998) 'Social Security: Dismantling the Pyramids?', in H. Glennerster and J. Hills (eds) *The State of Welfare: The Economics of Social Spending*, Oxford: Oxford University Press.

Evans, S. (2008) 'Consigning its Past to History? David Cameron and the Conservative Party', *Parliamentary Affairs*, vol 61, no 2, pp 291–314.

Evans, S. and Williams, S. (2002) *The Wrong Prescription: A Critique of Labour's Management of the NHS*, London: Conservative Policy Unit.

Fawcett, B., Featherstone, B. and Goddard, J. (2004) *Contemporary Child Care Policy and Practice*, Basingstoke: Palgrave Macmillan.

Fazackerley, A. and Wolf, R. (2010) *Blocking the Best*, London: Policy Exchange.

Featherstone, H. and Storey, C. (2009) *Hitting the Bottle*, London: Policy Exchange.

Fielding, S. (2009) 'Introduction: Cameron's Conservatives', *The Political Quarterly*, vol 80, no 2, pp 168–71.

Finer, S. E. (1970) *Comparative Government*, London: Allen Lane.

FitzGerald, M., Hough, M., Joseph, I. and Qureshi, T. (2002) *Policing for London*, Cullompton: Willan Publishing.

Fitzpatrick, T. (2005) 'The Fourth Attempt to Construct a Politics of Welfare Obligation', *Policy and Politics*, vol 33, no 1, pp 15–32.

Flatley, J., Kershaw, C., Smith, K., Chaplin, R. and Moon, D. (2010) *Crime in England and Wales 2009/10: Findings from the British Crime Survey and Police Recorded Crime (Second Edition). Statistical Bulletin 12/10*, London: Home Office. Available at: http://rds.homcoffice.gov.uk/rds/pdfs10/hosb1210.pdf (accessed 11 October 2010).

Fox, G. (2009) 'New Not-For-Profit Private School Chain is a Class Apart', *The Daily Telegraph*, 12 November.

Fox Harding, L. (1999) 'Family Values and Conservative Government Policy', in G. Jagger and C. Wright (eds) *Changing Family Values*, London: Routledge.

Francis, M. (1996) '"Set the People Free"? Conservatives and the State, 1920–1960', in M. Francis and I. Zweiniger-Bargielowska (eds) *The Conservatives and British Society 1880–1990*, Cardiff: University of Wales Press.

Francis, M. (1997) *Ideas and Policies Under Labour 1945–1951*, Manchester: Manchester University Press.

Fraser, D. (2009) *The Evolution of the British Welfare State*, Basingstoke: Palgrave Macmillan.

Freud, D. (2009) 'Whither Welfare-to-Work?', speech by David Freud, Shadow Minister for Welfare Reform, 12 November, London: Institute for Employment Studies.

Fulton Committee (1968) *Report of the Committee on the Civil Service 1966–68, vol 1*, London: HMSO.

Furness, D. and Gough, B. (2009) *From Feast to Famine: Reforming the NHS for an Age of Austerity*, London: Social Market Foundation.

Gainsbury, S. (2009) '"Organic" Reduction in PCTs under Tories', *Health Service Journal*, 27 August, p 4.

Gamble, A. (1994) *The Free Economy and the Strong State*, Basingstoke: Macmillan.

Garnett, M. (2010) 'Built on Sand? Ideology and Conservative Modernization under David Cameron', in S. Griffiths and K. Hickson (eds) *British Party Politics and Ideology After New Labour*, Basingstoke: Palgrave Macmillan.

Garnett, M. and Hickson, K. (2009) *Conservative Thinkers*, Manchester: Manchester University Press.

Garnham, A. and Knights, E. (1994) *Putting the Treasury First: The Truth about Child Support*, London: Child Poverty Action Group.

George, V. and Wilding, P. (1976) *Ideology and Social Welfare*, London: Routledge and Kegan Paul.

Gilbert, B. B. (1970) *British Social Policy 1914–1939*, London: Batsford.

Gilmour, I. (1992) *Dancing with Dogma*, London: Simon and Schuster.

Gilmour, I. and Garnett, M. (1998) *Whatever Happened to the Tories? The Conservatives since 1945*, London: Fourth Estate.

Glasby, J. and Henwood, M. (2007) 'Part of the Problem or Part of the Solution? The Role of Care Homes in Tackling Delayed Hospital Discharges', *British Journal of Social Work*, vol 37, no 2, pp 299–312.

Glasby, J. and Littlechild, R. (2009) *Direct Payments and Personal Budgets: Putting Personalisation into Practice*, Bristol: The Policy Press.

Glennerster, H. (1998) 'New Beginnings and Old Continuities', in H. Glennerster and J. Hills (eds) *The State of Welfare: The Economics of Social Spending*, Oxford: Oxford University Press.

Glennerster, H. (2007a) *British Social Policy 1945 to the Present*, Oxford: Blackwell.

Glennerster, H. (2007b) *Understanding the Finance of Welfare*, Bristol: The Policy Press.

Glynn, S. and Booth, A. (1996) *Modern Britain: A Social and Economic History*, London: Routledge.

Gove, M. (2008a) *A Failed Generation: Educational Inequality under Labour*, London: Conservative Party.

Gove, M. (2008b) 'Why Conservative Social Policy Delivers Progressive Ends', speech to the Institute for Public Policy Research, 4 August. Available at: www.conservatives.com/News/Speeches/2008/08/Michael_Gove_Why_Conservative_social_policy_delivers_progressive_ends.aspx (accessed 18 September 2010).

Gove, M. (2008c) 'We Need a Swedish Education System', *The Independent*, 3 December. Available at: www.independent.co.uk/opinion/commentators/michael-gove-we-need-a-swedish-education-system-1048755.html (accessed 19 September 2010).

Gove, M. (2009a) 'A Comprehensive Programme for State Education', speech to the Centre for Policy Studies, 6 November. Available at: www.conservatives.com/News/Speeches/2009/11/Michael_Gove_A_comprehensive_programme_for_state_education.aspx (accessed 18 September 2010).

Gove, M. (2009b) 'Failing Schools Need New Leadership', speech, 7 October 2009. Available at: www.conservatives.com/News/Speeches/2009/10/Michael_Gove_Failing_schools_need_new_leadership.aspx (accessed 19 March 2010).

Gray, J. (2010) 'Bad Night for Cameron. Very Good One for the Party's Bigoted Tendency', *The Guardian*, 7 May.

Green, D. (2009) 'Feeding Wolves: Punitiveness and Cultures', *European Journal of Criminology*, vol 6, no 6, pp 517–36.

Green, E. H. H. (2002) *Ideologies of Conservatism*, Oxford: Oxford University Press.

Green, J. (2007) 'When Voters and Parties Agree: Valence Issues and Party Competition', *Political Studies*, vol 55, no 3, pp 629–55.

Greenhalgh, S. and Moss, J. (2009) *Principles for Social Housing Reform*, London: Localis Research.

Greenleaf, W. (1983) *The British Political Tradition: The Ideological Heritage*, vol 2, London: Routledge.

Green-Pedersen, C. (2007) 'The Growing Importance of Issue Competition: The Changing Nature of Party Competition in Western Europe', *Political Studies*, vol 55, no 3, pp 607–28.

Gregg, P. and Cooke, G. (eds) (2010) *'People are the Principal Agents of Change in Their Lives …' Liberation Welfare*, London: Demos.

Gregory, J. (2009) *In the Mix: Narrowing the Gap between Public and Private Housing*, Policy Report 62, London: Fabian Society.

Guardian Editorial (2010) 'Iain Duncan Smith: Question Time', *The Guardian*, 31 July, p 28.

Guillebaud Committee (1956) *Report of the Committee of Enquiry into the Cost of the National Health Service*, London: HMSO.

Hague, W. (1999) 'The NHS is Safer in Our Hands', *The Times*, 23 April.

Hall, P.A. (1993) 'Policy Paradigms, Social Learning, and the State: The Case of Economic Policymaking in Britain', *Comparative Politics*, vol 25, no 3, pp 275–96.

Halpern, D. and Mikosz, D. (1998) *The Third Way: Summary of the Nexus On-Line Discussion*, London: Nexus.

Ham, C. (2004) *Health Policy in Britain*, Basingstoke: Palgrave Macmillan.

Ham, C. (2009) 'The Conservative Party's Policies on Health', *British Medical Journal*, vol 338, 1 June.

Ham, C. (2010) 'Why the plans to reform the NHS may never be implemented', *British Medical Journal*, vol 34, c 4716.

Hamblin, R. and Ganesh, J. (2007) *Measure for Measure: Using Outcome Measures to Raise Standards in the NHS*, London: Policy Exchange.

*Hansard (Commons)*, 17 March 2009, columns 863-876.

*Hansard (Commons)*, 27 January 2009, columns 196-214.

Harrington, M. (2010) *An Independent Review of the Work Capabiltiy Assessment*, London: The Stationery Office.

Harris, B. (2004) *The Origins of the British Welfare State*, Basingstoke: Palgrave Macmillan.

Hayman, A. (2010) 'Shapps Defends Tory Planning Green Paper', *Regen.net*, 10 March. Available at: www.regen.net/news/ByDiscipline/housing

Helm, T. and Syal, R. (2009) 'Key Tory MPs Backed Call to Dismantle NHS', *The Observer*, 16 August. Available at: www.guardian.co.uk/politics/2009/aug/16/tory-mps-back-nhs-dismantling (accessed 16 September 2010).

Heppell, T. (2002) 'The Ideological Composition of the Parliamentary Conservative Party 1992–97', *British Journal of Politics and International Relations*, vol 4, no 2, pp 299–324.

Hickson, K. (ed) (2005) *The Political Thought of the Conservative Party*, Basingstoke: Palgrave Macmillan.

Hickson, K. (2008) 'Conservatism and the Poor: Conservative Party Attitudes to Poverty and Inequality since the 1970s', *British Politics*, vol 4, no 3, pp 341–62.

Hickson, K. (2010) 'Thatcherism, Poverty and Social Justice', *The Journal of Poverty and Social Justice*, vol 18, no 2, pp 135–45.

Hilditch, M. (2010) 'A Sign of the Times', *Inside Housing*, 13 August, pp 12–13.

HM Government (2007) *Putting People First: A Shared Vision and Commitment to the Transformation of Adult Social Care*, London: HM Government.

HM Government (2009) *Shaping the Future of Care Together*, London: The Stationery Office.

HM Government (2010a) *Building the National Care Service*, London: The Stationery Office.

HM Government (2010b) *Mutual Benefit: Giving People Power Over Public Services*, London: Cabinet Office.

HM Government (2010c) *Warm Homes, Greener Homes: A Strategy for Household Energy Management*, London: Department of Energy and Climate Change.

HM Government (2010d) *State of the Nation Report: Poverty, Worklessness and Welfare Dependency in the UK*, London: Cabinet Office. Available at: www.cabinetoffice.gov.uk/media/410872/web-poverty-report.pdf (accessed 27 May 2010).

HM Treasury (2010) *2010 Budget*, London: The Stationery Office.

Hobolt, S. and Klemmemsen, R. (2005) 'Responsive Government? Public Opinion and Government Policy Preferences in Britain and Denmark', *Political Studies*, vol 53, no 2, pp 379–402.

Hogg, Q. (1947) *The Case for Conservatism*, Harmondsworth: Penguin.

Hoggart, S. (2006) 'Cameron Offers New Tory Thoughts on the Family', *The Guardian*, 21 June.

Home Office (1990) *Crime, Justice and Protecting the Public: The Government's Proposals for Legislation*, London: HMSO.

Home Office (1998) *Supporting Families: A Consultation Document*, London: The Stationery Office.

Horton, T. (2010) *The New Politics of the Family*, London: Fabian Society.

Hough, M. (2003) 'Modernisation and Public Opinion: Some Criminal Justice Paradoxes', *Contemporary Politics*, vol 9, no 2, pp 143–55.

Hough, M. (2007) 'Policing, New Public Management and Legitimacy', in T. Tyler (ed) *Legitimacy and Criminal Justice*, New York: Russell Sage Foundation.

Hough, M. (2010, forthcoming) 'Gold Standard or Fool's Gold: The Pursuit of Certainty in Experimental Criminology', *Criminology and Criminal Justice*, vol 10, no 1, pp 11–22.

Hough, M. (2011, forthcoming) 'Criminology and the Role of Experimental Research', in C. Hoyle and M. Bosworth (eds) *What is Criminology?*, Oxford: Oxford University Press.

Hough, M., Jacobson, J. and Millie, A. (2003) *The Decision to Imprison: Sentencing & The Prison Population*, London: Prison Reform Trust.

Hough, M., Jackson, J., Bradford, B., Myhill, A. and Quinton, P. (2010) 'Procedural Justice, Trust, and Institutional Legitimacy', *Policing*, vol 4, no 2, pp 203–10.

House of Commons Reform Committee (2009) *Rebuilding the House, First Report of Session 2008–09*, London: The Stationery Office.

Houston, D. and Lindsay, C. (2010) 'Introduction: Fit for Work? Health, Employability and Challenges for the UK Welfare Reform Agenda', *Policy Studies*, vol 31, no 2, pp 133–42.

Hughes, G. (1998) 'Picking over the Remains: The Welfare State Settlements of the Post-Second World War UK', in G. Hughes and G. Lewis (eds) *Unsettling Welfare: The Reconstruction of Social Policy*, London: Routledge.

Hultin, A. (2009) 'Profit is the Key to Success in "Swedish Schools"', *The Spectator*, 3 October, p 17.

Independent Healthcare Association and Department of Health (2000) *For the Benefit of Patients: A Concordat with the Private and Voluntary Health Care Providers*, London: DoH.

Institute for Fiscal Studies (2010a) *Financial Statistics*, London: Institute for Fiscal Studies.

Institute for Fiscal Studies (2010b) Press Release, 9 April. Available at: www.ifs.org.uk/pr/marriage_pr.pdf (accessed 21 September 2010).

Ipsos MORI (2008) 'Private Provision of Public Services'. Available at: www.ipsos-mori.com/researchpublications/researcharchive/poll. aspx?oItemId=2428&view=wide (accessed 4 July 2010).

Ipsos MORI (2010a) 'Economist Poll – Is the Coalition Government Bringing the Public with it?'. Available at: www.ipsos-mori.com/ researchpublications/researcharchive/poll.aspx?oItemId=2616 (accessed 10 June 2010).

Ipsos MORI (2010b) 'Do the Public Really Want to Join the Government of Britain?', London: Ipsos MORI Social Research Institute. Available at: www.ipsos-mori.com/Assets/Docs/News/ Do%20the%20public%20want%20to%20join%20government%20 of%20Britain.PDF (accessed 4 July 2010).

Ipsos MORI (2010c) 'March 2010 Political Monitor'. Available at: www.ipsos-mori.com/researchpublications/researcharchive/poll. aspx?oItemId=2566 (accessed 4 July 2010).

Ipsos MORI (2010d) 'April 2010 Political Monitor'. Available at: www.ipsos-mori.com/researchpublications/researcharchive/poll. aspx?oItemId=2594 (accessed 4 July 2010).

Ipsos MORI (2010e) 'Is the Coalition Government Bringing the Public with it?'. Available at: www.ipsos-mori.com/researchpublications/ researcharchive/poll.aspx?oItemId=2616 (accessed 4 July 2010).

Ipsos MORI (2010f) 'June 2010 Political Monitor'. Available at: www.ipsos-mori.com/researchpublications/researcharchive/poll.aspx?oItemId=2628 (accessed 4 July 2010).

Ipsos MORI (2010g) 'Budget Reaction Poll'. Available at: www.ipsos-mori.com/researchpublications/researcharchive/poll.aspx?oItemId=2633 (accessed 4 July 2010).

Jefferys, K. (1997) *Retreat from New Jerusalem: British Politics, 1951–64*, Basingstoke: Macmillan.

Jefferys, K. (2002) *Finest and Darkest Hours*, London: Atlantic.

Jones, H. (1996) 'The Cold War and the Santa Claus Syndrome: Dilemmas in Conservative Social Policy-Making, 1945–1957', in M. Francis and I. Zweiniger-Bargielowska (eds) *The Conservatives and British Society 1880–1990*, Cardiff: University of Wales Press.

Jones, H. (2000) '"This is Magnificent!": 300,000 Houses a Year and the Tory Revival after 1945', *Contemporary British History*, vol 14, no 1, pp 99–121.

Jones, K. (1989) *Right Turn: The Conservative Revolution in Education*, London: Radius.

Jones, K. (2003) *Education in Britain: 1944 to the Present*, Cambridge: Polity Press.

Joseph, K. (1976) *Monetarism is Not Enough*, London: Centre for Policy Studies.

Jowell, R., Curtice, J., Park, A. and Thomson, K. (1999) *British Social Attitudes: The 16th Report*, Aldershot: Ashgate.

Jowell, R., Curtice, J., Park, A., Thomson, K., Jarvis, L., Bromley, C. and Stratford, N. (2000) *British Social Attitudes: The 17th Report – Focusing on Diversity*, London: Sage.

Joyce, R., Muriel, A., Phillips, D. and Sibieta, L. (2010) *Poverty and Inequality in the UK: 2010*, London: Institute for Fiscal Studies.

Katwala, S. (2009) 'In Maggie's Shadow', *Public Policy Research*, vol 16, no 1, pp 3–13.

Kavanagh, D. (1987) *Thatcherism and British Politics*, Oxford: Oxford University Press.

Kenny, M. (2009) 'Taking the Temperature of the UK's Political Elite', *Parliamentary Affairs*, vol 61, no 1, pp 149–61.

Kerr, P. (2007) 'Cameron Chameleon and the Current State of Britain's "Consensus"', *Parliamentary Affairs*, vol 60, no 1, pp 46–65.

Klingemann, H.-D., Hofferbert, R. and Budge, I. (1994) *Parties, Policies and Democracy*, Boulder, CO: Westview Press.

Kirby, I. (2010) 'Tories Paid an Unhealthy Sum', *News of the World*, 24 January, p 18.

Kirby, J. (2006) *The Nationalisation of the Family*, London: Centre for Policy Studies.

Kirby, J. (2009) 'From Broken Families to the Broken Society', *The Political Quarterly*, vol 80, no 2, pp 243–7.

Labour Party (2010) *The Labour Party Manifesto 2010: A Future Fair for All*, London: The Labour Party.

Lanning, T. (2010) 'Forgotten demand? Welfare-to-work and the UK's missing jobs' in D. Ben-Galim and A. Sachrajda (eds) *Now It's Personal: Learning from welfare-to-work approaches around the world*, London: ippr, pp 28–31.

Lansley, A. (2009) 'Our Chance to Make the NHS the Finest in the World', speech to the Conservative Party conference, 5 October. Available at: www.conservatives.com/News/Speeches/2009/10/Andrew_Lansley_Our_chance_to_make_the_NHS_the_finest_in_the_world.aspx (accessed 20 September 2010).

Laver, M. and Budge, I. (1992) *Party Policy and Government Coalitions*, Basingstoke: Macmillan.

Lawson, N. (1992) *The View from No. 11: Memoirs of a Tory Radical*, London: Bantam.

Lawson, N. (2010) 'Foreword', in J. Cruddas and J. Rutherford (eds) *Is the Future Conservative? Soundings*, London: Compass/Renewal and Lawrence and Wishart.

Lawton, K. (2010) *Spending review will weaken work incentives*, London: Left Foot Forward. Available at: www.leftfootforward.org/2010/10/comprehensive-spending-review-will-weaken-work-incentives/ (accessed 25 October 2010).

Layard, R. (1997) 'Preventing Long-Term Unemployment: An Economic Analysis', in D. J. Snower and G. de la Dehesa (eds) *Unemployment Policy: Government Options for the Labour Market*, Cambridge: Cambridge University Press.

Lee, S. (2009) 'David Cameron and the Renewal of Policy', in S. Lee and M. Beech (eds) *The Conservatives under David Cameron: Built to Last?*, Basingstoke: Palgrave Macmillan.

Lee, S. and Beech, M. (2009) *The Conservatives under David Cameron: Built to Last?*, Basingstoke: Palgrave Macmillan.

Lees, D. S. (1961) *Health Through Choice*, London: Institute of Economic Affairs.

Le Grand, J. and Bartlett, W. (1993) *Quasi-Markets and Social Policy*, Basingstoke: Macmillan.

Le Grand, J. and Vizard, P. (1998) 'The National Health Service: Crisis, Change or Continuity?', in H. Glennerster and J. Hills (eds) *The State of Welfare: The Economics of Social Spending*, Oxford: Oxford University Press.

Letwin, O. (2002) 'For Labour There is No Such Thing as Society, Only the State', in G. Streeter (ed) *There is Such a Thing as Society*, London: Politico's.

Letwin, O. (2008) 'From Economic Revolution to Social Revolution', *Soundings*, No 40, Winter, pp 112–22.

Leunig, T. (2009a) *The Right to Move*, London: Policy Exchange.

Leunig, T. (2009b) 'Risky Business', *Inside Housing*, 18 September, p 17.

Lewis, J. and Glennerster, H. (1996) *Implementing the New Community Care*, Buckingham: Open University Press.

Liberal Democrats (2010) *Liberal Democrat Manifesto 2010*, London: The Liberal Democrats.

Lilla, M. (2010) 'The Tea Party Jacobins', *New York Review of Books*, 27 May, p 53.

Lilley, P. (1994) Speech to the Birmingham Diocesan Conference, 20 June.

Lilley, P. (1999) 'Butler Memorial Lecture'. Available at: http://www.peterlilley.co.uk/article.aspx?id=12&ref=859 (accessed 29 May 2009).

Lister, R. (1999) 'Reforming Welfare around the Work Ethic: New Gendered and Ethical Perspectives on Work and Care', *Policy and Politics*, vol 27, no 2, pp 233–46.

Lister, R. and Bennett, F. (2010) 'The New "Champion of Progressive Ideas"? Cameron's Conservative Party: Poverty, Family Policy and Welfare Reform', *Renewal*, vol 18, no 1, pp 84–109.

Loder, J., Mulgan, G., Reeder, N. and Shelupanov, A. (2010) *Financing Social Value: Implementing Social Impact Bonds*, London: Young Foundation. Available at: http://www.youngfoundation.org/files/images/01_10_Socail_Impact_Bonds_FINAL.pdf (accessed 21 December 2010).

Lowe, R. (1989) 'Resignation at the Treasury: The Social Services Committee and the Failure to Reform the Welfare State, 1955–57', *Journal of Social Policy*, vol 18, no 4, pp 505–26.

Lowe, R. (1996) 'The Social Policy of the Heath Government', in A. Ball and A. Seldon (eds) *The Heath Government 1970–1974: A Reappraisal*, London: Longman.

Lowe, R. (2005) *The Welfare State in Britain Since 1945*, Basingstoke: Palgrave Macmillan.

Lupton, R. and Heath, N. (2008) 'A Failed Generation? A Response to Michael Gove'. Available at: http://image.guardian.co.uk/sys-files/Education/documents/2008/08/26/luptongove.pdf (accessed 19 September 2010).

MacInnes, T., Kenway, P. and Parekh, A. (2009) *Measuring Poverty and Social Exclusion 2009*, York: Joseph Rowntree Foundation.

Macleod, I. and Maude, A. (1950) *One Nation: A Tory Approach to Social Problems*, London: Conservative Political Centre.

Macnicol, J. (1998) *The Politics of Retirement in Britain 1878–1948*, Cambridge: Cambridge University Press.

Maginn, B. (2010) *Total Neighbourhood: Placing Power back into the Community*, London: Localis, available online at: www.localis.org.uk

Major, J. (1999) *John Major: The Autobiography*, London: HarperCollins.

Marquand, D. (2008) 'Labour Has Got Cameron Wrong: This is No Crypto-Thatcherite but a Whig', *The Guardian*, 29 August.

Marquand, D. (2010) 'In Search of Electoral El Dorado', *New Statesman*, 1 March, pp 22–4.

Marshall, P. and Laws, D. (eds) (2004) *Orange Book Liberalism: Reclaiming Liberalism*, London: Profile Books.

Martin, I. (2010) 'IDS Secures a Ring-Fenced £3 Billion for Welfare Reform', *Wall Street Journal*. Available at: http://blogs.wsj.com/iainmartin/2010/08/13/ids-secures-a-ring-fenced-3-billion-for-welfare-reform/ (accessed 21 December 2010).

Mason, W. and Maxwell, L. (2008) *Freedom for Public Services*, London: Centre for Policy Studies.

Maude, F. (2010) 'Bigger the Better', *New Statesman*, 4 October, p 48.

May, T. (2010) 'Tackling Unemployment and Worklessness', Speech by Rt Hon Theresa May, 15 March, London: Conservative Party.

McGowan, J. (2007) *American Liberalism*, Chapter Hill, NC: University of North Carolina Press.

McKay, S. (2010) 'Where Do We Stand on Inequality?', *Journal of Poverty and Social Justice*, vol 18, no 1, pp 19–33.

McKay, S. and Rowlingson, K. (2008) 'Social Security and Welfare Reform', in M. Powell (ed) *Modernising the Welfare State: The Blair Legacy*, Bristol: The Policy Press.

McKibbin, R. (2010) *Parties and People: England 1914–1951*, Oxford: Oxford University Press.

McNeil, C. (2009) *Now it's Personal: Personal Advisers and the New Public Service Workforce*, London: IPPR.

McSmith, A. (2006) 'Cameron Vows to Keep Free Health Service in U Turn on Tory Policy', *The Independent*, 5 January, p 14.

Means, R. and Smith, R. (1998) *Community Care: Policy and Practice*, Basingstoke: Macmillan.

Means, R., Smith, R. and Richards, S. (2003) *Community Care: Policy and Practice*, Basingstoke: Palgrave Macmillan.

Melding, D. (2009) *Will Britain Survive Beyond 2020?*, Cardiff: Institute of Welsh Affairs.

Millar, J. (2006) 'Better Off in Work? Work, Security and Welfare for Lone Mothers', in C. Glendinning and P. A. Kemp (eds) *Cash and Care: Policy Challenges in the Welfare State*, Bristol: The Policy Press.

Millie, A., Jacobson, J. and Hough, M. (2003) 'Understanding the Growth in the Prison Population in England and Wales', *Criminal Justice*, vol 3, no 4, pp 369–87.

Milne, S. (2004) *The Enemy Within*, London: Verso.

Mind (2010) 'New Benefit Test Will Fail to Spot Illness and Disability', London: Mind. Available at: http://www.mind.org.uk/news/3166_new_benefit_test_will_fail_to_spot_illness_and_disability (accessed 16 August 10).

Ministry of Justice (2007) *The Governance of Britain*, London: Ministry of Justice.

Ministry of Justice (2008) *A National Framework for Greater Citizen Engagement*, London: Ministry of Justice. Available at: www.justice.gov.uk/index.htm (accessed 21 December 2010).

Ministry of Justice (2010) *Breaking the Cycle: Effective Punishment, Rehabilitation and Sentencing of Offenders*, London: The Stationery Office.

Mitchell, J. (1990) *Conservatives and the Union: A Study of Conservative Party Attitudes to Scotland*, Edinburgh: Edinburgh University Press.

Mitchell, L. (2007) 'Death and Taxes', *BBC*. Available at http://news.bbc.co.uk/1/hi/magazine/7035693.stm (accessed 29 September 2009).

Montero, J. and Gunther, R. (2003) *The Literature on Political Parties: A Critical Reassessment*, Barcelona: Institut de Ciencies Politiques i Socials.

Montgomerie, T. (2004) *Whatever Happened to Compassionate Conservatism?*, London: Centre for Social Justice.

Morgan, D. (2010) 'Budgetary Measures Implemented in 2010/11: Estimated Impact on the Consumer Prices Index (CPI) and Retail Prices Index (RPI)', London: Office for National Statistics. Available at: www.statistics.gov.uk/cci/article.asp?ID=2462 (accessed 21 December 2010).

Morgan, P. (1995) *Farewell to the Family? Public Policy and Family Breakdown in Britain and the USA*, London: Civitas.

Morgan, P. (2000) *Marriage-Lite: The Rise of Cohabitation and its Consequences*, London: Civitas.

Murray, C. (1990) *The Emerging British Underclass*, London: Institute for Economic Affairs.

Newman, J. (2001) *Modernising Governance: New Labour, Policy and Society*, London: Sage Publications.

Niskanen, W. (1971) *Bureaucracy and Representative Government*, Chicago, IL: Chicago University Press.

Niskanen, W. (1973) *Bureaucracy: Servant or Master?*, London: Institute of Economic Affairs.

Norman, J. (2010) *The Big Society: The Anatomy of the New Politics*, Buckingham: University of Buckingham Press.

Norman, J. and Ganesh, J. (2006) *Compassionate Conservatism*, London: Policy Exchange.

Norton, P. (1990) '"The Lady's Not for Turning" But What about the Rest? Margaret Thatcher and the Conservative Party 1979–89', *Parliamentary Affairs*, vol 43, no 1, pp 41–58.

Norton, P. (1996) 'Philosophy: The Principles of Conservatism', in P. Norton (ed) *The Conservative Party*, Hemel Hempstead: Prentice Hall/Harvester Wheatsheaf.

Norton, P. (2005) *Parliament in British Politics*, Basingstoke: Palgrave Macmillan.

Norton, P. (2008) 'The Future of Conservatism', *The Political Quarterly*, vol 79, no 3, pp 324–32.

Norton, P. (2009) 'David Cameron and Tory Success: Architect or By-stander?', in S. Lee and M. Beech (eds) *The Conservatives under David Cameron: Built to Last?*, Basingstoke: Palgrave Macmillan.

Novak, M. (1998) *Is There a Third Way?*, London: Institute of Economic Affairs.

Oakeshott, M. (1975) *On Human Conduct*, Oxford: Oxford University Press.

Office of the Deputy Prime Minister (2004) *Tackling Social Exclusion: Taking Stock and Looking towards the Future*, London: Office of the Deputy Prime Minister.

Olasky, M. (2000) *Compassionate Conservatism*, New York: Free Press.

Oliver, M. (1996) 'Defining Impairment and Disability: Issues at Stake', in C. Barnes and G. Mercer (eds) *Exploring the Divide*, Leeds: The Disability Press.

One Nation Group (1959) *The Responsible Society*, London: Conservative Political Centre.

Osborne, G. (2009) 'It's Ridiculous to Pretend There Won't Be Cuts', *The Times*, 15 June. Available at: www.timesonline.co.uk/tol/comment/columnists/guest_contributors/article6499028.ece (accessed 20 September 2010).

Osborne, G. (2010) 'Our tough but fair approach to welfare', Chancellor's Speech to the Conservative Party Conference, 4 October, London: The Conservatives. Available at: www.conservatives.com/News/Speeches/2010/10/George_Osborne_Our_tough_but_fair_approach_to_welfare.aspx (accessed 4 November 2010).

Osmond, J. (2000) 'A Constitutional Convention by Other Means: The First Year of the National Assembly for Wales', in R. Hazell (ed) *The State and the Nations: The First Year of Devolution in the United Kingdom*, Exeter: Imprint Academic.

Osmond, J. (2003) *Wales is Waiting: Monitoring the National Assembly September to December 2003*, Cardiff: Institute of Welsh Affairs.

Osmond, J. (2004) 'Nation Building and the Assembly: The Emergence of a Welsh Civic Consciousness', in A. Trench (ed) *Has Devolution Made a Difference?: The State of the Nations 2004*, Exeter: Imprint Academic.

Osmond, J. (2005) 'Wales', in A. Trench (ed) *The Dynamics of Devolution*, Exeter: Imprint Academic.

Page, R. M. (2007) 'Without a Song in Their Heart: New Labour, the Welfare State and the Retreat from Democratic Socialism', *Journal of Social Policy*, vol 36, no 1, pp 19–37

Page, R. M. (2009) 'With Love from Me to You: The New Democrats, New Labour and the Politics of Welfare Reform', *Benefits*, vol 17, no 2, pp 149–58.

Page, R. M. (2010) 'David Cameron's Modern Conservative Approach to Poverty and Social Justice: One Nation or Two?', *Journal of Poverty and Social Justice*, vol 18, no 2, pp 147–59.

Park, A. and Smith, L. (1994) *Evaluation of the Pilot Rents to Mortgages Scheme*, London: HMSO.

Park, A., Curtice, J., Thomson, K., Jarvis, L., Bromley, C. and Stratford, N. (2001) *British Social Attitudes: The 18th Report*, London: Sage.

Park, A., Curtice, J., Thomson, K., Jarvis, L. and Bromley, C. (2002) *British Social Attitudes: The 19th Report*, London: Sage.

Park, A., Curtice, J., Thomson, K., Jarvis, L. and Bromley, C. (2003) *British Social Attitudes: The 20th Report*, London: Sage.

Park, A., Curtice, J., Thomson, K., Bromley, C. and Phillips, M. (2004) *British Social Attitudes: The 21st Report*, London: Sage.

Park, A., Curtice, J., Thomson, K., Bromley, C., Phillips, M. and Johnson, M. (2005) *British Social Attitudes: The 22nd Report*, London: Sage.

Park, A., Curtice, J., Thomson, K., Phillips, M. and Johnson, M. (2007) *British Social Attitudes: The 23rd Report*, London: Sage.

Park, A., Curtice, J., Thomson, K., Phillips, M., Johnson, M. and Clery, E. (2008) *British Social Attitudes: The 24th Report*, London: Sage.

Park, A., Curtice, J., Thomson, K., Phillips, M. and Clery, E. (2009) *British Social Attitudes: The 25th Report*, London: Sage.

Park, A., Curtice, J., Thomson, K., Phillips, M., Clery, E. and Butt, S. (2010) *British Social Attitudes: The 26th Report*, London: Sage.

Park, A., Curtice, J., Clery, E. and Bryson, C. (2010b) *British Social Attitudes: The 27th Report*, London: Sage.

Paton, G. (2010) 'Michael Gove: Academies Will Be Norm in England', *The Daily Telegraph*, 27 May. Available at: www.telegraph.co.uk/journalists/graeme-paton/7767664/Michael-Gove-academies-will-be-norm-in-England.html (accessed 19 September 10).

Peacey, V. (2009) *Signing in and Stepping Up? Single Parents' Experience of Welfare Reform*, London: Gingerbread.

Pensions Policy Institute (2010) *What are the Main Parties' Policies on Pensions?*, Briefing Note 55, London: Pensions Policy Institute.

Petch, H. (2010) 'Housing's "Big" Role', *Inside Housing*, 13 August, p 15.

Pickles, C. (2010) 'Repairing the Broken Society: The Way Forward', *Journal of Poverty and Social Justice*, vol 18, no 2, pp 161–6.

Pierce, A. (1999) 'Ballistic Thatcher Zeroes in on Hague', *The Times*, 24 April.

Pierre, J. and Peters, B.G. (2000) *Governance, Politics and the State*, Basingstoke: Palgrave Macmillan.

Pierson, P. (1994) *Dismantling the Welfare State? Reagan, Thatcher and the Politics of Retrenchment*, Cambridge: Cambridge University Press.

Pierson, P. (2004) *Politics in Time*, Princeton: Princeton University Press.

Pitkin, H. (1967) *The Concept of Representation*, Berkeley: University of California Press.

Powell, E. (1969) *Freedom and Reality*, London: Batsford.

Powell, E. and Maude, A. (1954) *Change is Our Ally: A Tory Approach to Industrial Problems*, London: Conservative Political Centre.

Powell, M. (ed) (2008) *Modernising the Welfare State*, Bristol: The Policy Press.

Power, S. and Whitty, G. (1999) 'New Labour's Education Policy: First, Second or Third Way?', *Journal of Education Policy*, vol 14, no 5, pp 535–46.

Prideaux, S. (2010) 'The Welfare Politics of Charles Murray are Alive and Well in Britain', *International Journal of Social Welfare*, vol 19, no 3, pp 293–302.

Public Health Commission (2009) *We're All in This Together*, London: Public Health Commission. Available at: www.publichealthcommission.co.uk/pdfs/AboutPHC/PHCReport+Summary.pdf (accessed 17 September 2010).

Public Services Improvement Policy Group (2006) *The National Health Service – Delivering Our Commitment,* submission to the shadow cabinet, London: Conservative Party.

Public Services Improvement Policy Group (2007) *Restoring Pride in Our Public Services,* submission to the shadow cabinet, London: Conservative Party.

Pugh, M. (2010) *Speak for Britain! A New History of the Labour Party,* London: Bodley Head.

Purnell, J. (2010) 'Labour wanted these reforms too', *The Times,* 9 November.

Puttick, K. (2007) 'Empowering the Incapacitated Worker? The Employment and Support Allowance and Pathways to Work', *Industrial Law Journal,* vol 36, no 3, pp 388–95.

Pym, F. (1984) *The Politics of Consent,* London: Hamish Hamilton.

Raban, J. (2010) 'Cameron's Crank', *London Review of Books,* vol 32, no 8, pp 22–3.

Rafferty, F. (1998a) 'Alienation on the Fringe', *TES,* 9 October.

Rafferty, F. (1998b) 'Hague Urges More Freedom', *TES,* 31 July.

Raison, T. (1990) *Tories and the Welfare State,* Basingstoke: Macmillan.

Ramesh, R. (2010) *Preacher Duncan Smith aims for holy grail of welfare policy,* London: The Guardian. Available at: http://www.guardian.co.uk/politics/2010/nov/11/iain-duncan-smith-welfare-analysis-randeep-ramesh (accessed 11 November 2010).

Ramsay, C. and Butler, E. (2001) *Medical Savings Accounts,* London: Adam Smith Institute.

Randall, V. (2000) *The Politics of Child Day Care in Britain,* Oxford: Oxford University Press.

Rawnsley, A. (2009) 'David Cameron Needs More Than a Clique of Four to Succeed', *The Observer,* 15 March, p 31.

Regnery, A. S. (2008) *Upstream: The Ascendance of American Conservatism,* New York: Threshold.

Rhodes, R. (1997) *Understanding Governance: Policy Networks, Governance, Reflexivity and Accountability,* Buckingham: Open University Press.

Richards, D. and Smith, M. J. (2002) *Governance and Public Policy in the UK,* Oxford: Oxford University Press.

Riker, W. (1996) *The Strategy of Rhetoric: Campaigning for the American Constitution,* New Haven, CT: Yale University Press.

Robertson, D. (1976) *A Theory of Party Competition,* London: Wiley.

Rollings, N. (1996) 'Butskellism, the Postwar Consensus and the Managed Economy', in H. Jones and M. Kandiah (eds) *The Myth of Consensus: New Views on British History, 1945–64,* Basingstoke: Macmillan.

Rose, R. (1984) *Do Parties Make a Difference?,* London: Macmillan.

Rose, R. and Davies, P. (1994) *Inheritance in Public Policy: Change without Choice in Britain*, New Haven, CT: Yale University Press.

Rose, R. and McAllister, I. (1982) *United Kingdom Facts*, London: Macmillan.

Rowling, J.K. (2010) 'The Single Mother's Manifesto', *The Times*, 14 April.

Royal Commission on Long Term Care (2009) *With Respect to Old Age: Long Term Care – Rights and Responsibilities*, London: The Stationery Office.

Royal Town Planning Institute (2010) 'Localism Must Not Miss the Bigger Picture on Planning'. Available at: www.rtpi.org.uk/item/3937/23/5/3 (accessed 16 August 2010).

Rural Coalition (2010) *The Rural Challenge: Achieving Sustainable Rural Communities for the 21st Century*, available online at http://ruralcommunities.gov.uk/wp-content/uploads/2010/08/RuralCoalitionWEB_MH.pdf

Rutherford, J. (2008) 'Fraternity without Equality, and other Conservative Ideals', *Soundings*, Summer.

Ryan, C. (2010) 'Conservative Contradictions'. Available at: http://conorfryan.blogspot.com/2010/03/conservative-contradictions.html (accessed 19 March 2010).

Santry, C. (2010) 'NHS at the Centre of Tories Election', *Health Service Journal*, 7 January, pp 4–5.

Scott, D. and Brien, S. (2007) *Breakthrough Britain: Briefing Paper Two. Economic Dependency and Worklessness*, London: Centre for Social Justice.

Scottish Conservative and Unionist Party (2010) *Invitation to Join the Government of Britain: The Conservative Manifesto for Scotland 2010*, Edinburgh: Scottish Government and Unionist Party.

Scottish Parliament Finance Committee (2008) *First Report – Stage 2 Budget (Scotland) Bill*. Available at: http://www.scottish.parliament.uk/s3/committees/finance/reports-08/fir08-01-vol1-02.htm

Seawright, D. (2005) 'One Nation', in K. Hickson (ed) *The Political Thought of the Conservative Party*, Basingstoke: Palgrave Macmillan.

Sefton, T. (2005) 'Give and Take: Attitudes to Redistribution', in A. Park, J. Curtice, K. Thomson, C. Bromley, M. Phillips and M. Johnson (eds) *British Social Attitudes: The 22nd Report – Two Terms of New Labour: The Public's Reaction*, London: Sage.

Seldon, A. (1957) *Pensions in a Free Society*, London: Institute of Economic Affairs.

Seldon, A. and Snowdon, P. (2005) 'The Conservative Party', in A. Seldon and D. Kavanagh (eds) *The Blair Effect 2001–5*, Cambridge: Cambridge University Press.

Settle, M. (2010) 'It Could Take 25 Years to Revive Scottish Tories', *The Herald*, 30 August.

Shapps, G. (2010) 'We Need Change …', *Inside Housing*, 13 August, p 17.

Sharma, Y. (2010) 'Swedish Smiles Turn Sour as Rift Widens Where Equity Once Ruled', *TES*, 12 March.

Shepherd, J. (2010) 'David Willetts hints that university students will face higher fees', *The Guardian*, 9 June.

Sherman, A. (2005) *Paradoxes of Power*, Exeter: Imprint Academic.

Skidelsky, R. (1996) 'The Fall of Keynesianism', in D. Marquand and A. Seldon (eds) *The Ideas that Shaped Post-War Britain*, London: Fontana.

Skolverket (2009) *Statistik om gymnasieskolan. Personal i gymnasieskolan*, Swedish Official Statistics, Table 4A. Available at: www.skolverket.se/sb/d/1717 (accessed 11 November 2009).

Sky News (2009) 'Tory Party of NHS Claims in Tatters Again', www.skynews.com, 23 August.

Smith, I. (2006) *Building a World Class NHS*, London. Reform.

Smith, N. (2009a) *New Conservative Welfare Plans: An Analysis*, Touchstone blog: a public policy blog from the TUC, London: TUC. Available at: http://www.touchstoneblog.org.uk/2009/10/new-conservative-welfare-plans-an-analysis/ (accessed 20 April 2010).

Smith, N. (2009b) *Government Emphasises Similarities With Conservative Welfare Policy*, London: TUC. Available at: www.touchstoneblog.org.uk/2009/10/government-emphasises-similarities-with-conservative-welfare-policy (accessed 20 April 2010).

Snowden, P. (2010) *Back From the Brink. The Inside Story of the Tory Resurrection*, London: HarperPress.

Social Justice Policy Group (2006) *Breakdown Britain*, London: Social Justice Policy Group.

Social Justice Policy Group (2007) *Breakthrough Britain*, London: Social Justice Policy Group.

Somerville, J. (2000) *Feminism and the Family: Politics and Society in the UK and USA*, Basingstoke: Palgrave Macmillan.

Somerville, P. (2011, forthcoming) *Understanding Community: Theory, Policy and Practice*, Bristol: The Policy Press.

Stanley, K. (2010) 'Iain Duncan Smith's Welfare Reform Deserves Support', *The Guardian*, Comment is Free, 30 July.

Stanley, K. and Lohde, L. (2004) *Sanctions and Sweeteners: Rights and Responsibilities in the Benefit System*, London: Institute for Public Policy Research.

Stephens, H. (2010) 'A Breach in Security', *Inside Housing*, 20 August, p 29.

Stevens, C. (2002) 'Thatcherism, Majorism and the Collapse of Tory Statecraft', *Contemporary British History*, vol 16, no 1, pp 119–50.

Stewart, W. and Vaughan, R. (2010) 'Tories Would Ditch Pupil Deprivation from Tables', *TES*, 26 March. Available at: www.tes.co.uk/article.aspx?storycode=6039788 (accessed 19 September 2010).

Stockdale, L. (2010) 'Home to Roost', *Inside Housing*, 20 August, pp 21–3.

Stoker, G. (1998) 'Governance as Theory: 5 Propositions', *International Social Science Journal*, vol 50, no 155, pp 17–28.

Strom, K. (1990) 'A Behavioural Theory of Competitive Political Parties', *American Journal of Political Science*, vol 34, no 2, pp 565–98.

Summers, D. and Glendinning, L. (2009) 'Cameron Rebukes Tory MEP Who Rubbished NHS in America', *The Guardian*, 14 August. Available at: www.guardian.co.uk/politics/2009/aug/14/health-nhs (accessed 16 June 2010).

Sweeney, M. (2010) '… But Not Like This', *Inside Housing*, 13 August, p 17.

Sylvester, R. and Thomson, A. (2010) 'It's Not about Class, its About the Classroom, Says Gove', *The Times*, 6 March. Available at: www.timesonline.co.uk/tol/news/politics/article7052100.ece (accessed 19 September 2010).

Taylor, A. (2002) 'Speaking to Democracy: The Conservative Party and Mass Opinion from the 1920s to the 1950s', in S. Ball and I. Holliday (eds) *Mass Conservatism: The Conservatives and the Public Since the 1880s*, London: Frank Cass.

Taylor-Gooby, P. (2004) 'The Work-Centred Welfare State', in A. Park, J. Curtice, K. Thomson, C. Bromley and M. Phillips (eds) *British Social Attitudes: The 21st Report*, London: Sage/NATCEN.

Taylor-Gooby, P. and Martin, R. (2008) 'Trends in Sympathy for the Poor', in A. Park, J. Curtice, K. Thomson, M. Phillips, M. Johnson and E. Clery (eds) *British Social Attitudes: The 24th Report*, Sage: London.

Thatcher, M. (1987) interview for *Women's Own*, 31 October.

Thatcher, M. (1993) *The Downing Street Years*, London: HarperCollins.

*The Daily Mail* (2009) 'Now it's War: David Cameron in Savage Attack on Labour's "Pathological" Refusal to Accept Marriage IS Key to Happy Families', 1 December. Available at: www.dailymail.co.uk/news/article-1232091/Marriage-longer-key-happy-family-says-Ed-Balls-advisor-warns-end-nuclear-family.html (accessed 22 September 2010).

*The Daily Telegraph* (2009) 'Gordon Brown Seizes on Tory Andrew Lansley's Budget Cut Pledge', 10 June. Available at www.telegraph.co.uk/news/newstopics/politics/gordon-brown/5495819/Gordon-Brown-seizes-on-Tory-Andrew-Lansleys-budget-cut-pledge.html (accessed 15 June 2009).

The Rural Coalition (2010) *The Rural Challenge: Achieving Sustainable Rural Communities for the 21st Century*, London: The Rural Coalition/ Town and Country Planning Association.

Thomson, A. and Sylvester, R. (2010) 'Gove Unveils Tory Plan for Return to "Traditional" School Lessons', *The Times*, 6 March. Available at: www.timesonline.co.uk/tol/news/politics/article7052010.ece (accessed 19 September 2010).

Thornhill, J. (2010) *Allocating Social Housing: Opportunities and Challenges*, Coventry: Chartered Institute of Housing.

Thorpe, C. (2010) 'To Build or Not to Build?', *Inside Housing*, 18 June, pp 26–30.

Tickle, L. (2010) 'Sole Survivors', *The Guardian*, Society, 11 August, p 1.

Timmins, N. (1996) *The Five Giants: A Biography of the Welfare State*, London: Fontana.

Timmins, N. (2001) *The Five Giants*, London: HarperCollins.

Timmins, N. (2010) 'Advance Payment for Providers of Welfare-to-Work Schemes', *Financial Times*. Available at: http://www.ft.com/cms/s/0/9ac5b206-fbf0-11df-b7e9-00144feab49a.html#axzz17VsoU26x (accessed 8 December 2010).

Tomlinson, J. (1990) *Public Policy and the Economy since 1900*, Oxford: Oxford University Press.

Tomlinson, J. (2007) 'Tale of a Death Exaggerated: How Keynesian Policies Survived the 1970s', *Contemporary British History*, vol 21, no 4, pp 429–48.

Torrance, D. (2006) *The Scottish Secretaries*, Edinburgh: Birlinn.

Torrance, D. (2008) *George Younger: A Life Well Lived*, Edinburgh: Birlinn.

Torrance, D. (2009) *'We in Scotland': Thatcherism in a Cold Climate*, Edinburgh: Birlinn.

Toynbee, P. (2010) 'Family Life is a Viper's Nest Politicians Should Not Poke', *The Guardian*, 18 January.

Tronto, J. (2001) 'Who cares? Public and private caring and the rethinking of citizenship', in N.J. Hirschmann and U. Liebert (eds) *Women and Welfare: Theory and Practice in the United States and Europe*, New Brunswick, NJ: Rutgers University Press.

Turner, J. (1995) 'A Land Fit for Tories to Live in: The Political Ecology of the Conservative Party, 1944–94', *Contemporary European History*, vol 4, no 2, pp 189–208.

Twinch, E. (2010) 'Tory Green Paper Reveals Crackdown on Illegal Traveller Sites', *Inside Housing*, 19 February.

Tyler, T. R. (2003) 'Procedural Justice, Legitimacy, and the Effective Rule of Law', in M. Tonry (ed) *Crime and Justice – A Review of Research*, vol 30, pp 431–505.

Tyler, T. R. (2007) *Legitimacy and Criminal Justice*, New York: Russell Sage Foundation.

Tyler, T. R. and Huo, Y. J. (2002) *Trust in the Law: Encouraging Public Cooperation with the Police and Courts*, New York: Russell Sage Foundation.

UK Polling Report (2010) 'Voting Intention'. Available at: http:// ukpollingreport.co.uk/blog/voting-intention (accessed 20 September 2010).

Vinen, R. (2009) *Thatcher's Britain*, London: Simon and Schuster.

Walsha, R. (2000) 'The One Nation Group: A Tory Approach to Backbench Politics and Organization, 1950–55', *Twentieth Century British History*, vol 11, no 2, pp 183–214.

Walsha, R. (2003) 'The One Nation Group and One Nation Conservatism, 1950–2002', *Contemporary British History*, vol 17, no 2, pp 69–120.

Wanless, D. (2006) *Securing Good Care for Older People: Taking a Long Term View*, London: King's Fund.

Watt, N. (2010) 'Spending review: welfare bears the brunt as extra £7bn of cuts unveiled', *The Guardian*. Available at: http://www.guardian. co.uk/politics/2010/oct/20/spending-review-welfare-cuts (accessed 8 December 2010).

Webb, P. (2000) *The Modern British Party System*, London: Sage.

Webster, C. (2002) *The National Health Service*, Oxford: Oxford University Press.

Welsh Conservative party (2010) *Invitation to Join the Government of Britain: The Welsh Conservative Manifesto 2010*, Cardiff: Welsh Conservative Party.

White, M. (1999) 'Tory Right out for Hague's Blood', *The Guardian*, 29 April.

White, S. (2003) *The Civic Minimum*, Oxford: Oxford University Press.

White, S. (2005) 'Is Conditionality Illiberal?', in C. Beem and L. Mead (eds) *Welfare Reform and Political Theory*, New York: Russell Sage Foundation.

Whiteside, N. (1996) 'The Politics of the "Social" and the "Industrial" Wage, 1945–60', in H. Jones and M. Kandiah (eds) *The Myth of Consensus*, Basingstoke: Macmillan.

Wiborg, S. (2009) *Education and Social Integration: Comprehensive Schooling in Europe*, New York: Palgrave Macmillan.

Willetts, D. (1992) *Modern Conservatism*, Harmondsworth: Penguin.

Willetts, D. (2005a) 'Compassionate Conservatism and the War on Poverty', Speech to the Centre for Social Justice, 6 January. Available at: http://www.davidwilletts.co.uk/2005/01/06/compassionate-conservative/ (accessed 29 May 2009).

Willetts, D. (2005b) 'A New Conservatism for a New Century', Speech to the Social Market Foundation, 2 June. Available at: http://www.davidwilletts.co.uk/2005/06/02/new-conservatism/ (accessed 29 May 2009).

Willetts, D. (2007) 'Better Schools and More Social Mobility', Speech to the CBI Conference on Public Service Reform, 16 May. Available at: www.conservatives.com/News/Speeches/2007/05/Willetts_Better_schools_and_more_social_mobility.aspx (accessed 19 September 2010).

Willetts, D. (2009) 'The Meaning of Margaret', *Prospect*, May, pp 32–6.

Williams, S (2002) *Alternative Prescriptions: A Survey of International Healthcare Systems*, London: Conservative Policy Unit.

Williams, T. (2010) 'Tories Fail the Housing Test', *Regeneration & Renewal*, 8 March.

Wind-Cowie, M. (2009) *Recapitalising the Poor: Why Property is Not Theft*, London: Demos.

Wintour, P. (2010a) 'Coalition Government Sets Out Radical Welfare Reforms', *The Guardian*, 26 May.

Wintour, P. (2010b) 'Iain Duncan Smith Plots Welfare Revolution Despite Treasury Resistance', *The Guardian*, 30 July.

Wintour, P. (2010c) 'Benefit Health Test to Face Urgent Review', *The Guardian*, 27 July.

Wyler, S. and Blond, P. (2010) *To Buy, To Bid, To Build: Community Rights for an Asset-owning Democracy*, London: Respublica, available online at www.respublica.org.uk

Wyse, D. and Styles, M. (2007) 'Synthetic Phonics and the Teaching of Reading: The Debate Surrounding England's "Rose Report"', *Literacy*, vol 47, no 1, pp 35–42.

Zweiniger-Bargielowska, I. (1996) 'Explaining the Gender Gap: The Conservative Party and the Women's Vote, 1945–1964', in M. Francis and I. Zweiniger-Bargielowska (eds) *The Conservatives and British Society 1880–1990*, Cardiff: University of Wales Press.

Zweiniger-Bargielowska, I. (2000) *Austerity in Britain*, Oxford: Oxford University Press.

# Index